Foundations of Comparative Politics

The new edition of this leading overview of comparative politics once again blends theory and evidence across democratic systems to provide unparalleled coverage. The student-friendly structure and clear, concise writing ensure that complex issues are clearly explained and students engage with the key theories. The third edition is updated throughout, with a new chapter, 'Public spending and public policies', increased coverage of defective democracies, and revised coverage of e-democracy and the power of the media. The pedagogy is simplified, with a focus on 'Briefings' and 'Controversies' that feature examples from across the globe, alongside clear key terms, 'What we have learned'and 'Lessons of comparison' sections, and a wealth of online materials to complete a rich teaching and learning package.

KENNETH NEWTON is Emeritus Professor of Comparative Politics at the University of Southampton.

JAN W. VAN DETH is Professor of Political Science and International Comparative Social Research at the University of Mannheim.

CAMBRIDGE TEXTBOOKS IN COMPARATIVE POLITICS

Series Editors

Jan W. van Deth, *Universität Mannheim, Germany*
Kenneth Newton, *University of Southampton, United Kingdom*

Comparative research is central to the study of politics. This series
offers accessible but sophisticated materials for students of comparative politics at the introductory level and beyond. It comprises an
authoritative introductory textbook, *Foundations of Comparative Politics*,
accompanied by volumes devoted to the politics of individual countries, and an introduction to methodology in comparative politics.
The books share a common structure and approach, allowing teachers
to choose combinations of volumes to suit their particular course.
The volumes are also suitable for use independently of one another.
Attractively designed and accessibly written, this series provides an
up-to-date and flexible teaching resource.

Other books in this series
RICHARD GUNTHER & JOSÉ RAMÓN MONTERO
The Politics of Spain

JAMES L. NEWELL
The Politics of Italy

HERMAN LELIEVELDT & SEBASTIAAN PRINCEN
The Politics of the European Union, 2nd edn

Foundations of Comparative Politics

Democracies of the Modern World

THIRD EDITION

KENNETH NEWTON and JAN W. VAN DETH

CAMBRIDGE
UNIVERSITY PRESS

CAMBRIDGE
UNIVERSITY PRESS

University Printing House, Cambridge CB2 8BS, United Kingdom

Cambridge University Press is part of the University of Cambridge.

It furthers the University's mission by disseminating knowledge in the pursuit of education, learning and research at the highest international levels of excellence.

www.cambridge.org
Information on this title: www.cambridge.org/9781107131835

© Kenneth Newton and Jan W. van Deth 2016

First published 2005
Second edition 2010
Third edition 2016
Reprinted 2016

Printed in the United Kingdom by Clays, St Ives plc

A catalogue record for this publication is available from the British Library

Library of Congress Cataloguing in Publication data
Newton, Kenneth, 1940– author. | Deth, Jan W. van, author.
Foundations of comparative politics / Kenneth Newton and Jan W. van Deth.
Third edition. | Cambridge, United Kingdom : Cambridge University Press, 2016. | Series: Cambridge textbooks in comparative politics | Includes bibliographical references and index.
LCCN 2016003479 | ISBN 9781107131835 (hardback)
LCSH: Democracy. | Comparative government. | Representative government and representation.
LCC JC423 .N484 2016 | DDC 320.3–dc23
LC record available at http://lccn.loc.gov/2016003479

ISBN 978-0-521-13183-5 Hardback
ISBN 978-0-521-58285-9 Paperback

Additional resources for this publication at www.cambridge.org/newton3

This book is dedicated to Konstanza and Joke

Contents

Briefings

Controversies

Figures

Tables

Preface and acknowledgements to the third edition

A major revision of our text book was required after the third wave of democracy slowed down in the 2000s and the financial crises hit many countries in the same decade. The result is this third edition, in which the text has been extensively revised and updated, based in large part on the comments and suggestions of anonymous readers contacted by Cambridge University Press. We could not follow all their suggestions but have acted on most of them, resulting in a great many changes to the book, including a new chapter on public policy and a completely revised chapter on the recent development of democratic states in the world. Joshaa Fischer, Sören Götz and Nicolas Toth-Feher at the University of Mannheim checked many of the entries and provided updated information. In particular, we are very grateful to Claire Dekker for carefully copy editing the whole manuscript.

The three editions of this book are the result of our discussions and contacts with many people at various places in the last ten to fifteen years. Ken Newton would also like to thank colleagues at the University of Southampton, who provided friendship and intellectual stimulation. Jan van Deth would like to thank his collaborators at the University of Mannheim and the Mannheim Zentrum für Europäische Sozialforschung (MZES) for similar friendship and intellectual stimulation. Both of us thank a number of colleagues for their willingness to share their knowledge and experience and provide us with many insights: Matthijs Boogaards, Tom Cusack, Jan Delhey, Wolf-Dieter Eberwein, Benjamin Engst, Dieter Fuchs, Rick Hofferbert, Ron Inglehart, Jana Jughard, Max Kaase, Henk van der Kolk, Hans-Dieter Klingemann, Fritz and Mocha Metzeler, Wolfgang Müller, Christiane Neumann, Marion Obermaier and Edeltraud Roller. Sadly, many of our most brilliant theories and insights were shot down in flames in these discussions, by colleagues who based their criticism on no more than acute intelligence, hard information, a thorough knowledge of the subject and a sharp eye for a weak argument.

As political scientists, not politicians, we cannot blame any faults and errors in this third edition on anybody but ourselves, least of all those named above.

Ken Newton and Jan W. van Deth

Abbreviations and acronyms

AfDB	African Development Bank
ASEAN	Association of Southeast Asian Nations
AV	alternative vote
Benelux	Belgium, Netherlands, Luxembourg economic union
BSE	bovine spongiform encephalopathy
CA	Consumers' Association
CBA	Cost–benefit analysis
CEO	Chief executive officer
CIS	Confederation of Independent States
CND	Campaign for Nuclear Disarmament
CoR	Committee of the Regions (EU)
DARS	Democratic Arab Republic of the Sahara
DGB	Deutscher Gewerkschaftsbund (trade union association, Germany)
EAPC	Euro-Atlantic Partnership Council
ECHR	European Court of Human Rights
ECJ	European Court of Justice
ENA	Ecole Nationale d'Administration
EP	European Parliament
ESA	European Space Agency
ETUC	European Trade Union Confederation
EU	European Union
FBI	Federal Bureau of Investigation (USA)
GATT	General Agreement on Tariffs and Trade
GM	genetically modified
IBRD	International Bank for Reconstruction and Development (World Bank)
ICJ	International Court of Justice
IDA	International Development Association
IISS	International Institute for Strategic Studies
ILO	International Labour Organization
IMF	International Monetary Fund
IOC	International Olympic Committee
IOM	International Organization for Migration

IPU	Inter-Parliamentary Union
IT	information technology
JV	joint venture
MCW	minimum connected winning (coalition)
MITI	Ministry of International Trade and Industry (Japan)
MMD	multi-member districts
MMP	mixed-member proportional voting system
MNC	multinational corporation
MWC	minimum winning coalition
NAFTA	North American Free Trade Association
NASA	National Aeronautics and Space Administration (USA)
NATO	North Atlantic Treaty Organization
NGO	non-governmental organisation
OAU	Organization of African Unity
OECD	Organisation for Economic Cooperation and Development
OFCOM	Office of Communications (UK)
OPEC	Organization of the Petroleum Exporting Countries
OSCE	Organization for Security and Co-operation in Europe
PAC	Political Action Committee (USA)
PPP	purchasing-power parity
PR	proportional representation
R&D	Research and Development
SB	second ballot (voting system)
SES	socio-economic status
SMSP	single member, simple plurality voting system
SNTV	single non-transferable vote
STV	single transferable vote
TI	Transparency International
TNC	transnational Corporation
UK	United Kingdom
UN	United Nations
UNHCR	(Office of the) UN High Commissioner for Refugees
UNITAR	UN Institute for Training and Research
USA	United States
USSR	Union of Soviet Socialist Republics (Soviet Union)
WDIs	World Development Indicators
WEU	Western European Union
WHO	World Health Organization
WTO	World Trade Organization

How to use this book

This book has many special features to help you work your way through the chapters efficiently and effectively and to understand them. This section shows you what these features are and how they help you work through the material in each chapter.

- Each chapter contains an introduction with a brief account of the topics it covers, so that you know what to expect.
- The last part of each chapter presents the main theoretical approaches of the topic.
- Each chapter ends with a summary of its main findings and what we have learned from using the comparative approach to government and politics.
- 'Key term' entries. When a new concept is introduced it is picked out in bold letters in the text and defined in brief and simple terms in the margin. All the key terms are then brought together in the 'Glossary of key terms' at the end of the book. This makes it easy to refresh your memory about concepts.
- 'Controversy boxes' provide you with an overview of the most contentious topics in comparative government and politics.

The end material of the chapters also includes:

- Two or three small projects that you can use to test your understanding and consolidate your learning.
- A short list of further reading and details of useful websites.

The Introduction that follows spells out the main themes that run throughout the book. It tells you what to keep in mind and look out for as you work your way through the chapters. Finally, at the end of the book we have added a Postscript on the main methodological questions in comparative politics.

Extensive online resources, including all the material listed above, are available on the book's website. You can search this material for yourself at www.cambridge.org/newton.

For **students** additional material includes an updated reading list, websites and advanced further reading. Multiple-choice questions allow students to test their understanding of each chapter.

For **instructors**, all figures and tables from the book are available along with lecture slides. Additional student questioning includes exam and essay questions.

Introduction

This introduction does three things. First, it explains why we should bother to study comparative politics at all. Why is it important to know how foreign political systems work? Second, it considers the strengths and weaknesses of the comparative approach to political science. It argues that, in spite of its problems, comparative politics adds something of great importance to our ability to understand what goes on in the political world. Moreover, it is of practical importance for policy making in the real world because it helps us reject false explanations of political phenomena and broadens our understanding of what is possible by examining how things are done in other countries. And third, it provides some signposts to guide you through the general themes that re-occur throughout the book to make it easier and more interesting for you to understand and absorb its contents.

■ Why comparative politics?

Why do we bother to study comparative politics and government? There are many good reasons, but three of the most important are: (1) we cannot understand our own country without a knowledge of others; (2) we cannot understand other countries without a knowledge of their background, institutions and history; and (3) we cannot arrive at valid generalisations about government and politics without the comparative method.

Understanding our own country

To understand our own country, we must study other countries as well. This may sound strange, but it has some powerful logic to support it. We often take the political institutions, practices and customs in our own country for granted, assuming that they are somehow natural and inevitable. Only when we start looking around at other countries do we understand that our own ways of doing things are sometimes unique or unusual, even odd or peculiar. It is said that fish will be the last form of life on earth to realise the existence of water: since they spend their whole life in water with no experience of anything else, they have no reason even to imagine that anything else could exist. For this reason, the writer Rudyard Kipling wrote, 'What knows he of England, who only England knows?', making the point that people who have no knowledge of other countries cannot begin to understand their own.

Understanding other countries

It is obvious that we cannot begin to understand the politics of other countries unless we know something about their history, culture and institutions. And this, in turn, is important because what these countries do often affects us directly or indirectly: they impose import duties on our goods, refuse to sign trade agreements, do not contribute to international peacekeeping forces, threaten us with military force, or are unhelpful in trying to solve international economic problems. On the other hand, they may support us in fighting crime, sign international agreements for pollution control, contribute to international projects, or collaborate to improve infrastructures across national borders. Why do they act this way? Knowing their history, culture and institutions helps us to understand and explain their actions and perhaps change the situation for the better. Ignorance is a recipe for complication and failure; knowledge can help us improve matters.

Constructing valid generalisations

The purpose of science is to arrive at valid generalisations about the world. Such generalisations take the form of 'if–then' statements – if A then B, but if X then Y. Aeroplane designers need to know that if their planes exceed the speed of sound, they will break the sound barrier, affecting how the planes handle and the stress on their structures. Doctors need to know that if a certain drug is administered, then a patient's disease is likely to be cured. Chemists need to know that if two substances are mixed then a third substance may be produced that is useful to us.

To arrive at these if–then statements, scientists carry out systematic experiments in their laboratories, comparing what happens under different circumstances. Aeroplane designers have wind tunnels; drug companies and chemists have laboratories where they manipulate the conditions of their experiments in a careful and systematic manner. Political scientists also try to arrive at valid generalisations about the world of government and politics, but, unfortunately, they can rarely experiment so they rely on comparison instead. For example, political scientists are interested in the effect of different voting systems on the fairness of election results, and it would be nice if we could order our government to use a new voting system to see what happens. Obviously this is not possible. An alternative might be to set up a quasi-experiment that tries to measure how people behave using different voting systems, but laboratory experiments can only approximate the conditions of the real political world. They cannot reproduce them exactly. And political scientists have to be exceedingly careful in their experiments not to break any moral rules or to do harm to their experimental subjects. For the most part, controlling variables in an experimental manner and in laboratory conditions is not an approach open to a good deal of political science research, though not impossible in some.

What political scientists can do, however, is compare things that happen 'naturally' in the real world. For example, different countries have different voting systems and we can compare them to estimate their effects. We can note that countries with voting system A have a higher voting turnout than countries using system B. However, we cannot immediately conclude that A causes a higher voting turnout than B until we are sure that this effect is not caused by factors other than voting systems. Perhaps system A countries happen to be smaller, wealthier or better educated than system B countries and it is size, wealth or education that influences voting turnout. We cannot control (hold constant) all other variables, as laboratory scientists do, but we can use methods to simulate the holding constant of variables. In this way we can make statements such as: 'All other things being equal (size, wealth, education), if a country has a type A voting system, then it will tend to have a higher voting turnout than countries with type B voting systems.'

It would be unwise to try to make general 'if–then' generalisations based on a study of only one country, or even a small handful of them, because it is easy to jump to false conclusions. In fact, this frequently happens when people with an inadequate understanding of the subject conclude that something must be true based on their limited experience of what happens in their own country (see briefing). What we need to do is compare a range of countries of different size, wealth and education to estimate the independent effects of these and voting systems on turnout. Studying one or a few countries might not be enough; we need a range of countries with a spread of characteristics that we think might influence voting turnout.

Comparative politics has increasingly turned to the comparison of either a few carefully selected countries or a large number of them. To study a number of countries using both type A and type B electoral systems we can concentrate on a few countries which are very similar in most of their characteristics but organise their elections differently. In this way we can conduct a 'natural experiment' that provides us with a few countries that have different electoral systems but little variation in other respects that might affect voting

Briefing

Is widespread gun ownership in the USA responsible for its high gun crime figures?
It is commonly claimed that the widespread ownership of guns in the United States is
responsible for the country's high gun crime and murder rate. Yet both Switzerland and Israel
have a high proportion of guns, partly because they train all men (in Switzerland) and all men
and women (in Israel) for military service and because, depending on their duties, those in
service routinely carry small arms or keep them at home. Law-abiding citizens in both countries
are entitled to own guns and in Israel a high proportion of people carry concealed weapons in
their everyday life. In Switzerland, shooting is a popular sport. In Israel, gun crime and the murder
rate is low by international standards and in Switzerland it is so low that there is no need to keep
records of gun crime and gun control is not an issue. Comparison shows that widespread gun
ownership is not the only explanation for the USA's high gun crime and murder rate.

Is the very high population density of Manhattan responsible for its high crime rate?
Experiments with rats show that overcrowding causes aggression and compulsive eating.
Does the high population density of New York (especially Manhattan) have the same
effect on its population of increasing aggression and crime? Some other cities (Hong Kong,
Singapore, Tokyo) with similar or higher density ratios have much lower violent crime and
murder rates than New York, and relatively low crime rates. The conclusions seem to be
that: (1) it can be misleading to draw conclusions about human beings based on animal
experiments; and (2) comparison of New York with other crowded cities suggests that
population density is not a powerful cause of New York's high level of aggression and crime.

   The comparison of gun ownership, population density, gun crime and aggression does
not end here, because quite possibly a combination of causes – guns and density and other
factors – account for gun crime and aggression. The point is that the causes and effects can
only be unravelled by comparing, and cross-national comparisons may be particularly helpful
in this respect.

turnout. Alternatively, comparing a large number of countries with different
voting systems and with a wide variety of other characteristics can reduce the
chances of arriving at false conclusions. In this way, we can see if countries
with one particular kind of voting system have a higher turnout than countries with other voting systems, irrespective of other variations.

■ The strengths and weakness of cross-national comparative political science

Political scientists can compare in different ways; they can compare across
time, across countries and across different places or population sub-groups
within a country. For example, if we want to generalise in an if–then manner about the effects of age, gender and religion on voting turnout, we might
compare, within our own country, the voting turnout of old and young people,
males and females, and different religious groups. This would be using the

comparative method but not the cross-national comparative method. As things have developed in political science, however, the term 'comparative politics' has come to mean research on two or more countries. Although all scientists rely on comparisons, when political scientists use the term 'comparative politics', they are most generally referring to the comparison of political patterns in different countries. Sometimes this is referred to as 'cross-national' research.

Cross-national comparative research has some great strengths. Although we can compare within a given country as well as across different countries, we have already noted that one-country studies can run into problems. For example, we might want to know the effect of different electoral systems on turnout, but could not do this in a single country which had only one electoral system. Of course, it might change its system, in which case we could compare turnout before and after the change, but then other things might also have changed – the parties competing, economic circumstances, composition of the electorate – in which case we would still not know what had caused any alteration in voting unless we took account of all the possible causes. The cross-national method is essential, because it allows us to test generalisations about politics in one set of circumstances against those in a wide variety of circumstances. This means we can put greater confidence in the reliability of our generalisations.

Comparing countries with a broad spread of characteristics also opens up horizons that those stuck in their own narrow surroundings do not know exist. If we know little about the wider world it is easy to slip into the mistake of believing that our way of doing things is the natural or only way. When we start looking around we start noticing that others do things differently which may be better, worse or just different in some respects than ours. For this reason governments thinking of introducing a new policy often send abroad little teams of researchers to see how other countries manage and to pick up bright ideas and get wise to the pitfalls of new policies. There are a great many different ways to bake a cake and, thankfully, the modern global world has widened our appreciation of the possibilities.

■ The problems of cross-national comparative research

In spite of these advantages, comparative politics has its fair share of deficiencies. Common criticisms are:

- It cannot answer questions of values.
- It often lacks evidence.
- It deals in probabilities, not certainties or laws.
- It suffers from the flaw that what is important is often difficult to compare and that what can be measured and compared may not be worth studying.
- It neglects that every country in the world is unique, so comparisons are impossible.

We will now look at these in turn.

It cannot answer questions of values

Questions such as 'Is democracy the best form of government?', 'Should we value freedom more than equality?' and 'Which party should we vote for?' are matters of values and subjective judgements. They are not, in the final analysis, a matter for empirical research. Like all sciences, comparative politics can never answer value questions or matters of subjective opinion, although it may provide evidence that helps some people to make up their mind about them.

It lacks evidence

Although comparative politics deals in facts and empirical evidence, it often lacks even an adequate supply of facts and data. Rarely do we have adequate or comparable measures for a large number and variety of countries. By and large we have more evidence about the wealthiest countries in the world because they are better organised and equipped to produce statistics about themselves. For the same reason, we have more evidence about recent years. But even in the most advanced societies we often lack even the minimum quantity and quality of evidence necessary to answer our research questions satisfactorily. This state of affairs is rapidly improving as data becomes more plentiful and easier to access on the internet, but, meanwhile, the data problem remains a severe one as, indeed, it does for many other branches of the social sciences. The same is true of the natural sciences, which lack information about many things, from the small atomic particles to far distant galaxies, and from global warming to the causes and cures of dementia.

It deals in probabilities not certainties or laws

Comparative politics does not provide us with laws about how government and politics work. It can only make if–then statements of a probable or likely kind. We can reach the conclusion that one voting system is likely to encourage a higher voting turnout than another, but cannot say that this will always or inevitably happen in every case. First, there is the unpredictable human factor and, second, there are large numbers of causal factors involved, some of which can interact in a complex way. Rarely are matters so simple that we can say that A produces B. Most usually it is A, interacting with X, Y and Z but only in the absence of C, D, and E that produces B, or something like it. As a result, comparative politics cannot tell us what will happen with a high degree of certainty but only, at best, what is likely to happen under certain circumstances, and the circumstances may not be present in any given case. Therefore comparativists are fond of the caution words – 'tends to', 'often', 'in some cases', 'probably', 'likely', 'may', 'in a percentage of cases'. Comparativists rarely use the word 'never' and rarely use the word 'always'. In the political world there is almost always an exception to the general rule, and usually a number of them.

We should not be put off by the fact that comparative politics is not a laboratory subject and cannot manipulate its variables at will. Quite a few sciences suffer from the same problem. The human body is such a complex thing that doctors can rarely be certain that a given drug will cure a disease in all cases and are often unsure about its side effects. Similarly, the world's climate system is so complicated that climate specialists cannot tell us whether it will rain or not on a given day, so they talk about the probability of rain. Cosmologists can only speculate about some aspects of the big bang that created the universe, and astronomers cannot get close enough to black holes to tell us what is in them and on the other side of them. Civil engineers cannot be sure that their buildings and structures will survive earthquakes, hurricanes and terrorist attacks. Note that in all these cases, as in comparative politics, scientists cannot control their variables in a laboratory, either because of moral limits (experiments on human beings) or the inability to manipulate the world's weather or its earthquakes. Comparative politics struggles to be as scientific as possible, but, like some other sciences, it falls short of the ideal.

It suffers from the flaw that what is important is often difficult to compare and that what can be measured and compared may not be worth studying

Some critics argue that the information used by comparativists is misleading, false or meaningless, especially the statistics about large numbers of nations. The claim is that what can be studied using such information is of little or no value. The strongest criticism states bluntly that empirical social science is limited to 'counting manhole covers' – something that can be done with great precision by people of the meanest intelligence but is of little interest to anybody and little importance for anything.

It is certainly true that comparative politics is limited in what it can study, and that it can say little or nothing about the important value questions of political theory and philosophy. But comparative politics has things to say of interest and importance about many subjects of concern in modern society. To continue with our example of voting turnout, politicians and political commentators are worried that low or declining turnout shows that something is wrong with the democracies, and comparative politics can say something about whether and why this might be true. The critics might respond with the 'lies, damned lies and statistics' argument that voting turnout figures are of little use because they are inaccurate, misleading or (sometimes) fake – they overlook the possibility of corrupt election practices, compulsory voting, totalitarian countries with a 99 per cent turnout, or the fact that turnout can be calculated in different ways to produce different conclusions. The comparativists would reply that this is all the more reason for knowing about the problems of turnout figures, which means understanding how they are produced in different countries, and when the statistics lie and deceive, and when they are reliable and useful for study.

In the end the debate boils down to how one evaluates the different kinds of question that political science can tackle. Critics argue that comparative politics cannot deal with the big issues of truth, beauty, freedom and justice; comparativists know this but claim they can study some factual matters that throw light on important questions. The critics argue that comparative politics deals with trivial matters, especially the large-scale data being collected in some current surveys. Comparativists acknowledge that this is sometimes true, not always, and that, in any case, science does not always advance in giant leaps and bounds but by inching along in tiny steps before making breakthroughs. And sometimes the study of comparative politics comes up with well-founded, hard evidence that is important, surprising and unexpected, as we shall see in the following chapters.

It neglects that every country in the world is unique so comparisons are impossible

One argument against comparative politics is that since every country is unique, all cross-national comparisons are like comparing apples with oranges. We cannot, according to this thinking, ever learn from other countries because everything is different there. We cannot benefit from studying how the Swedes subsidise their political parties, how the Japanese manage their national economy or how the New Zealanders reformed their political system because each country is special and particular. There is some truth in this argument. The practices that work well in some countries do not always travel well to other places. Nevertheless, it is worth noting that we can often borrow from other countries without much modification: the idea of the Ombudsman (see chapter 4) has been adopted successfully in many countries; the basic ideas of proportional voting systems (chapter 12) have spread throughout the world after its first use in Belgium in 1900; the principle of the separation of powers (chapter 4) as discussed by Montesquieu (1689–1755) is now found in every democracy in the world.

It is true that every country is unique, but it is also true that all countries are the same at a general level. At first sight this is a strange statement, so how do we explain it? An analogy is helpful. Every human being is unique with respect to DNA, physical appearance, personality, background and abilities. At another level, human beings are exactly the same: among other things, they are all *homo sapiens*, warm-blooded primates and vertebrate mammals. At a still more general level, human beings are similar to other primates, especially chimpanzees, gorillas and orang-utans and share 96 per cent of their DNA profile with them. At a still more general level, human beings have something in common with pigs, to the extent that pig organs can be transplanted into human beings.

What is unique and what is comparable depends on the level of analysis and what is being compared. A silly-but-serious question asks, 'Is a mouse more like a frog or a whale?' The critic of comparative politics might answer that these creatures are all different and unique and cannot be compared. The answer of the comparativist is that it depends on what you want to compare. The frog and the mouse are of similar size, but the frog and the whale can live in water, and the mouse and the whale give birth to live young. In some ways Costa Rica is more like the USA than Sweden because Costa Rica and the USA have presidential systems of government (chapter 5). In other respects Costa Rica is more like Sweden because both have unitary forms of government, whereas the USA is federal (chapter 6). At one level each political system is unique; at another level some systems are similar in some respects. What countries you select for comparison depends crucially on what you want to study (see the Postscript). This makes comparative politics both more possible and more complicated than its critics assert.

◼ The themes that run through the book – what to watch for

Although each and every system of government is unique, there are broad similarities between different groups of countries. This makes the job of the comparative political scientists easier because instead of listing the many par-ticularities of each system, which would result in a mind-boggling and fruit-less task rather like reading a telephone directory, we can often reduce this great mass of detail and complexity to a few general themes. These themes running through the book are:

- the importance of institutions
- that history matters
- the social and economic basis of politics
- the importance of politics
- the way in which the infinite variety of detail combines with a few general patterns
- that there are many ways of achieving the same democratic goals.

The importance of institutions

Much of comparative politics focuses on the attitudes and behaviour of indi-viduals: how they vote, their political values, the political culture, the ways in which they engage in politics, and so on (see chapters 9–11). At the same time we should not lose sight of the great influence and importance of institutions – the structures of government that distinguish federal and unitary systems, presidential and parliamentary systems, pluralist and corporatist systems, and so on. As you progress through the chapters you can note the ways in which institutions matter, and how and why they do so.

History matters

History throws a long shadow. Major events centuries ago, and the outcomes they produced, can affect us strongly even now. Sometimes, it seems, a political decision or turning point can create what is known as 'path dependency'. By this we mean that decisions taken in the past can narrow the options that are available to us today, and decisions taken today may limit options in the future. For example, it would be exceedingly difficult for a unitary state to convert itself into a federal one (and vice versa – see chapter 6), so difficult in fact that few states have ever contemplated such reform unless it was seen as absolutely essential. Institutions also tend to develop a life of their own and to preserve themselves because of institutional inertia or the excessive costs of change. This means that an institution that has developed strong roots in government in the past may well influence current events. As we move through our chapters we will see how historical events, sometimes a long time ago, have implications for political patterns and practices today.

The social and economic basis of politics

One school of thought in political science explains political patterns in terms of social and economic patterns or prerequisites. It points out that different social groups think and behave in different ways and draws the conclusion that social conditions have a strong influence on politics (see chapter 2). Some writers go further than this and claim that all politics can be explained in terms of economic models. The chapters that follow will explain the social and economic basis of politics, but they will also deal with the limitations of these explanations.

Politics matters

The social and economic explanations of politics are useful but limited, because they tend to ignore or overlook the importance of political institutions, events, ideas and cultures. Social and economic factors may have a powerful influence, but so also do political considerations – how political elites react to events, how political ideals affect the way people think and behave, how political institutions have an impact, how electoral systems influence electoral outcomes. It may seem like trying to have one's cake and eat it when we insist that social *and* economic *and* political factors influence government and politics, but, in fact, this simply acknowledges the fact that the social, economic and political are tightly interwoven aspects of the same thing in the real world.

From a mass of detail to general types

As we have emphasised, every political system is unique in many ways, but fortunately for the student of comparative politics we do not have to keep track of each and every particularity because, at a more general level, political systems tend to cluster around a few general types. Whether we are discussing executive and legislative power, multi-level government, pressure group systems, electoral systems, the mass media, party systems, party ideologies and so on, we will see how a huge variety of detailed and particular differences between countries often break down into a few general types. This is a blessing for comparative political scientists because it turns a job that would be like reading the telephone directory, where every entry is different from every other in some crucial but boring detail, into the more exciting task of constructing general models and theories that apply to a wide variety of democratic nations across the world. Instead of describing each and every political system, we can analyse their contrasts and similarities in terms of a few general characteristics. We can see families of similar political systems among the huge and bewildering variety of detail. The chapters that follow describe these patterns, types and clusters of characteristics when they arise.

There are many ways of achieving the same democratic goals

The point has already been made that there are different ways of achieving the same democratic goals. No country has a monopoly of the best ways. In the first place, different institutional arrangements are suited to different national conditions – large states may be better run along federal lines, but small ones more suited to unitary government, unless they are marked by deep regional divisions, in which case federalism may be the best option (chapter 6). Similarly, democracy requires a division of powers that place checks and balances on each other, but exactly how this is achieved differs between presidential and parliamentary systems, and both can work well or badly (chapter 5).

In some instances, the choice of means to achieve democratic ends depends on what is wanted. Single-party governments may be able to implement bold and innovative policies, but governments that make big mistakes can also be produced. By comparison, coalition governments may be more centralist and cautious, which may be good or bad in different circumstances.

The study of comparative politics shows how often it is wrong to assume that there is a single best way of achieving democratic government. The chapters that follow analyse the merits and deficiencies of the various options and the arguments surrounding them. In this way, the study of comparative government and politics is not an academic exercise of interest to a few ivory tower scholars, but a practical exercise with far reaching implications for the real world. We can learn an awful lot by comparing countries. This can help us discount false explanations based on limited information, shows the strengths and weaknesses of policies applied in other countries and opens up new possibilities and ways of doing things.

PART I

The state: origins and development

It was already late at night on 4 August 1789 when the French National Assembly continued its debates. The situation was disastrous. A new wave of social unrest, upheaval and looting had swept the country and people were near starvation in many cities. The problems seemed insoluble and the three classes – nobility, clergy and bourgeoisie – were fighting each other and the king. If no agreement could be reached soon, the country would collapse into chaos and civil war. Instead of dealing with these burning problems directly, the Assembly argued about a list of principles that should be used as a guideline and benchmark for political activities. On 26 August 1789, the 'Declaration of the Rights of Man and of the Citizen' was proclaimed. It sought to smash the ancient institutions and end privilege. From that moment on, the power of the state was to be based on the consent of its citizens and the protection of individual rights.

Until the National Assembly declared these principles, France was ruled by the king and his royal clique. The heated debates in August 1789 marked the rise of a new type of government and politics. Political power was no longer based on some 'natural order', God's will, or long-established rights of the nobility. As a citizen, every person had basic and equal rights, and the state was the property of its own citizenry. This double recognition indicated a radical break with previous thinking. Power, government, politics, the state – all these had existed long before the Declaration was proclaimed, but in August 1789 the Assembly knocked down many conventional ideas and replaced them by new interpretations consciously focusing on the crucial position of 'the people'. In this way, the much older idea of the state was given a radically new interpretation.

We start our treatment of comparative politics with an overview of the historical development of the 'state concept' as well as the actual establishment of states around the world. Part I consists of three chapters. Chapter 1 examines the emergence of the state, its main characteristics, and its spread and variety in the latter half of the twentieth century. As will become clear, states are the most important agencies for the organisation of political power. In chapter 2, we will take a closer look at democratic states and welfare states as they originated in the last two centuries. The transition of states into democratic states is discussed in chapter 3. Although the number of states has constantly risen in the last few decades, democracy remains a fragile thing in some places, and several states that were initially democratic returned to less democratic arrangements.

The three chapters of the first part of this book deal with states in general and with democratic states in particular:

- The idea of the state and the development of the modern state
- States and democratic states
- Democratic change and non-democratic developments.

1   The development of the modern state

Watch any newsflash or open any newspaper and you will see headlines such as 'Anglo-French row over migrant camps', 'Obama snubs Netanyahu' or 'Germany expels CIA agent'. These phrases are shorthand. They refer to disputes about migrants in Calais shanty towns seeking passage to the UK, disagreements about US and Israeli foreign policy, and German anger at US spying. Matters such as these are the alpha and omega of politics and governmental affairs. And states are always at the centre.

Indeed, as we have just seen in the Introduction, the study of states and their similarities and differences is at the centre of the study not only of international relations but also of comparative politics and government. Even debates about the 'withering away' of the state in an era of globalisation are possible only if we are clear about the concept of the state to start with. Nor can we understand the politics of the European Union, a form of political organisation that is above and beyond individual states, unless we understand what states are and what they do. This does not mean that states are the only things that matter, nor does it mean that 'the state' is a perfectly clear and straightforward concept. But it does mean that the centrality of states in the modern world cannot be neglected, and that the 'state concept' is one of the most important building blocks of comparative politics. The starting point of our account of comparative government and politics is therefore the nature of the modern state, and we take a pragmatic approach to the question: how do we recognise a state when we see one? In spite of the common use of the term, it is not easy to distinguish states from other organisations and institutes.

The six major topics in this chapter are:

- What is a state?
- Territory, people and sovereignty
- The rise of the modern state
- Catalysts: warfare and capitalism
- Growth after 1945
- Failed states.

■ What is a state?

The state is only one of many different ways of organising government. In the eighteenth century, when the French Assembly issued its '**Declaration of the Rights of Man and of the Citizen**' (see brief-

Declaration of the Rights of Man: The seventeen articles, describing the purpose of the state and the rights of individual citizens, proclaimed by the French National Assembly in August 1789. A similar list had been proclaimed in the USA in 1776 and in a very early form in England in 1215.

ing 1.1), states were not widely spread across the globe. Other forms of political organisation, such as city-states, empires, princedoms and tribes, were more widespread. The state is a relatively recent political invention. Today, however, practically the whole world is divided into states, and the concept of the state has triumphed as a form of political organisation. With the exception of the high seas and Antarctica, every place on earth belongs to one (see figure 1.1). Several areas are disputed among states and wars over territory are waged, but in general there is no quarrel about the fact that states are the main actors in these disputes.

Briefing 1.1

First three articles of the Declaration of the Rights of Man and of the Citizen (Paris, 1789)

1. Men are born and remain free and equal in rights. Social distinctions may be founded only upon the general good.
2. The aim of all political association is the preservation of the natural and imprescriptible[1] rights of man. These rights are liberty, property, security, and resistance to oppression.
3. The principle of all sovereignty resides essentially in the nation. No body or individual may exercise any authority which does not proceed directly from the nation.

(www.yale.edu)

[1] 'Imprescriptible' means self-evident and obvious, and not derived from or dependent upon any external authority.

Figure 1.1: States of the world

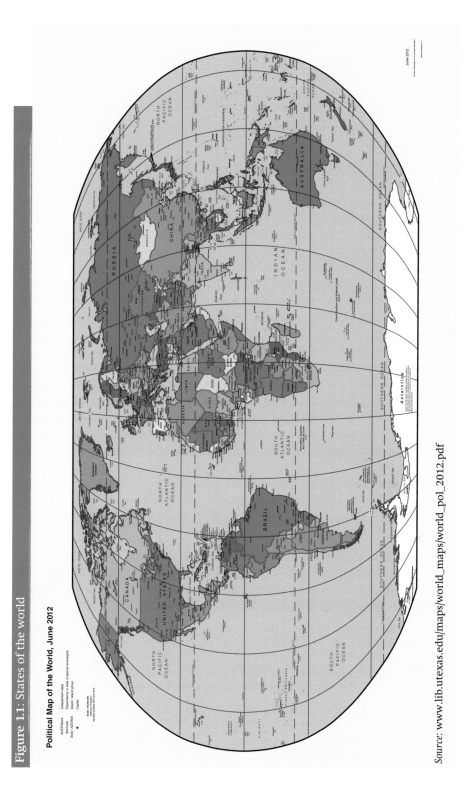

Political Map of the World, June 2012

Source: www.lib.utexas.edu/maps/world_maps/world_pol_2012.pdf

Though states are universal, they still present a puzzle. Philosophers, politicians, jurists and political scientists have argued about them for centuries. It goes without saying that France, Denmark, Uruguay and South Africa are states: all are independent political entities and each of them is recognised by the others as a state. You can find them on maps, their representatives meet in New York or Paris and you hear their national anthems on various occasions. Still, five key difficulties can arise when we try to characterise states in general terms.

- States vary hugely, ranging from France under Louis XIV to South Sudan, recognised in 2011 as one of about 193 independent states in the world. Modern states range from India and Canada to Mauritius and Trinidad and Tobago, and from Stalin's Soviet Union to Germany under Hitler. How can we put such a diverse collection of political phenomena into the same box labelled 'states'?
- Some forms of government look like states in some respects, but they are not. The European Union performs many state-like functions, but is not the same as Argentina or Latvia. Similarly, the Vatican, Luxembourg, Monaco and San Marino are not comparable with their neighbours, France and Italy.
- Some states have been recognised for centuries, but others, such as Israel and Palestine, are disputed. Is the latter a state simply because it calls itself one?
- Even for undisputed states such as France it is not easy to reach agreement about the exact date of its beginning. Was it in 1789? Or should we go back to the Treaty of Verdun in 843? Did states exist in Africa or Asia before European colonisers drew borders, almost haphazardly, through these continents? Were Babylon or Ancient Rome states as we understand them today?
- The term 'state' is quite close to other but different terms, such as 'country', 'nation', 'political system', 'nation-state' and 'empire'. To make things even more complicated, these terms are often confused or loosely used as synonyms.

We can get a clearer picture of what a state is by following in the footsteps of the Greek philosopher Aristotle (384–322 BC). He began with the question: What distinguishes a state from other forms of social life? In the opening sentences of book I of his *Politics*, Aristotle remarks:

> Every state is a community of some kind, and every community is established with a view to some good … But, if all communities aim at some good, the state or political community, which is the highest of all, and which embraces all the rest, aims, and in greater degree than any other, at the highest good. (Aristotle, *On Man in the Universe*, ed. Louise R. Loomis. Roslyn, NY: Black, 1943: 249)

This characterisation contains a number of important assertions. First of all, a state is not some abstract construct, but a variant of human social life (a 'community'). It is, furthermore, not just any variant of social life, but the most important one ('the highest of all') and it can also be called a 'political community'. Finally, all other communities are included in the state because it 'embraces all the rest'. Modern states still claim to be the dominant force, just as Aristotle noted. In order to obtain and keep its place as the highest and most encompassing 'community', a state must be more powerful than any of the 'communities' it incorporates. This characterisation immediately suggests that **power** is vital for any discussion of states and politics. And yet even this focus on power, important though it is in defining the state, is not sufficient. States also have other characteristics to do with territory, people and sovereignty (controversy 1.1).

> **Power:** The ability to make other people do what they do not want to do. Power is the ability to apply force.

CONTROVERSY 1.1

What is a state?

1. Do we have a clear idea about the state?

   What is a (or the) nation? No satisfactory criterion can be discovered for deciding which of the many human collectivities should be labelled in this way.

   (Eric Hobsbawm, *Nations and Nationalism since 1780,* Cambridge: Cambridge University Press, 1990: 5)

   As a concept the state has been somewhat overlooked in the political theory and research of the last century, especially in the Anglo-Saxon world, and still creates a good deal of confusion and uncertainty.

   (David Robertson, ed., *The Penguin Dictionary of Politics,* Harmondsworth: Penguin, 1985: 308)

2. Is the rise of states self-evident?

   Of the many theories addressing the problem of state origins, the simplest denies that there is any problem to solve. Aristotle considered states the natural condition of human society, requiring no explanation. His error was understandable, because all societies with which he would have been acquainted – Greek societies of the fourth century BC – were states. However, we now know that, as of AD 1492, much of the world was instead organised into chiefdoms, tribes, or bands. State formation does demand an explanation.

   (Jared Diamond, *Guns, Germs, and Steel,* New York: Norton, 1999: 283)

3. Where do states come from?

   If we now ask, where the state comes from, the answer is that it is the product of a long and arduous struggle in which the class which occupies what is for the time the key positions in the process of production gets the upper hand over its rivals and fashions a state which will enforce that set of property relations which is in its own interest. In other words any particular state is the child of the class or classes in society which benefit from the particular set of property relations which it is the state's obligation to enforce... the state power must be monopolized by the class or classes which are the chief beneficiaries.

   (Paul M. Sweezy, *The Theory of Capitalist Development,* New York: Monthly Review Press, 1942: 242–3)

■ Territory, people, sovereignty

States collect taxes, provide schools and highways, wage wars, control the opening hours of shops, regulate the sale of alcohol and cigarettes, and promote economic growth. They erect police stations and tax offices, municipal swimming pools and embassies abroad, mints and hospitals and they employ fire fighters and soldiers. Some states improve the living conditions of their citizens and provide services for the young and old, the sick and disabled, and the poor and unemployed. But it is not difficult to find examples of states that behave quite differently – ranging from the protection of illegal money deposited in Swiss banks to war and the genocidal killing of innocent millions for 'reason of state'. How, then, do we recognise a state if virtually anything can and has been done in their name?

State: The organisation that issues and enforces binding rules for the people within a territory.

In spite of confusion and continuing debate, it seems to be rather easy to recognise a **state**. Almost every state calls itself a 'state' and emphasises its uniqueness by having a national anthem, a flag, a coat of arms, a national currency, a national capital and a head of state. States are acknowledged by other states as 'states', and they exchange ambassadors. These are, however, the symbols of statehood. At the heart of the matter lie a minimum of three core features:

- A state entails a **territory** that it considers to be its own. This area can be as huge as Canada or India, or as tiny as Slovenia or Tuvalu. It can be an island or a continent (or both, in the case of Australia), and its borders may have been undisputed and secure for centuries or constantly challenged. To the territory of a state belongs the air space above it as well as its coastal waters. The only restraint on the territorial aspect of the state is that it has to be more or less enduring; an ice floe – even one as large as France or Uruguay – does not count. Sometimes the label 'territorial state' is used to underline the importance of this geographical feature. Less precisely, we commonly use the term '**country**'.

Territory: Terrain or geographical area.

Country: An imprecise synonym or short-hand term for state or nation-state.

- A state entails a **people**, that is, *persons living together*. Here, too, numbers are irrelevant (think of China, India, the Palau Islands and Iceland). To be a people, the individuals concerned must have something in common, but exactly what they must share to be called 'a people' – language, religion, a common history, a culture – is a highly contested matter. But at a minimum the people of a state are called **citizens** and have the rights and duties that this entails. In this respect they are different from those who live in a state but are not citizens of it – immigrants and visitors who are known as denizens. As the number of exiles, international migrants, and asylum

People: A group of people whose common consciousness and identity makes them a collective entity.

Citizen: A legally recognised member or subject of a state (or commonwealth) with all the individual rights and duties of that state.

Briefing 1.2

Not every human being is a citizen…
Those of us lucky enough to be secure in our citizenship are likely to take it for granted, but its great importance in our lives can be seen in the plight of those who are deprived of citizen rights – no residency rights, no working rights, no passport, no welfare services, no driving licence and perhaps no bank account. More and more people are in this situation as the number of migrants, exiles and asylum seekers grows. Which state should provide a stateless person with a passport, work rights, or unemployment support? Many are very reluctant to take in citizens of other states and offer them the same rights as their own citizens.

In 1950, the UN created the post of High Commissioner for Refugees (UNHCR), whose responsibility was to deal with exiles and refugees, and whose main aim was to find new places to live for about 400,000 people who had been forced to leave the place where they lived in Europe after the Second World War. Initially, UNHCR was founded for three years, but in 2014 it was working harder than ever, faced with the problems of more than 51 million refugees, displaced persons and asylum seekers, up 6 million on the year before. Its organisation now has 7,600 employees in over 125 countries worldwide (www.unhcr.org).

seekers increases, so the numbers of denizens and stateless people rises, sometimes creating acute problems (see briefing 1.2).

- A state is sovereign, that is, it holds the highest power and, in principle, can act with complete freedom and independence: it has **sovereignty**. Aristotle had something like this in mind with his remark that the state is a community 'which is the highest of all, and which embraces all the rest'. Sovereignty is a claim to ultimate authority and power. Usually, two types are distinguished: (i) internal sovereignty, meaning that within its own territory every state can act as it wishes and is independent of other powers; and (ii) external sovereignty, referring to the fact that the state is recognised as a state by other states. Sovereignty means that a state is independent and not under the authority of another state or 'community'. Here we must distinguish between power and sovereignty: the USA and Mauretania are equal as sovereign states, though the USA is vastly more powerful. States are also sovereign in principle, as we noted above. This does not necessarily mean that they are free to do whatever they want, because all sorts of factors may limit their powers – other states, the global economy, even the weather. Moreover, states may voluntarily limit their power by signing international agreements, although if they are sovereign states they may also decide to revoke these agreements if circumstances change. After the genocides in Bosnia and Herzegovina (1992) and Rwanda (1994), states increasingly accept the idea that sovereignty cannot be invoked when genocide, ethnic cleansing and crimes against humanity occur. Nor can states ignore those events beyond their borders simply because action does not suit their national interests (see briefing 1.3).

> **Sovereignty:** The highest power that gives the state freedom of action within its own territory.

Briefing 1.3

R2P: sovereignty entails responsibility

Each individual State has the responsibility to protect its populations from genocide, war crimes, ethnic cleansing and crimes against humanity. This responsibility entails the prevention of such crimes, including their incitement, through appropriate and necessary means. We accept that responsibility and will act in accordance with it. (Resolution adopted by the UN General Assembly: 60/1. 2005 World Summit Outcome)

… recognising that this responsibility lies first and foremost with each individual state, but also that, if national authorities are unable or unwilling to protect their citizens, the responsibility then shifts to the international community; and that, in the last resort, the United Nations Security Council may take enforcement action according to the Charter. (Statement by Kofi Anan, UN Secretary-General, to the General Assembly, 21 March 2005 (www.un.org/largerfreedom/sg-statement.html))

The *Responsibility to Protect* means that no state can hide behind the concept of sovereignty while it conducts – or permits – widespread harm to its population. Nor can states turn a blind eye when these events extend beyond their borders, nor because action does not suit their narrowly-defined national interests. (www.responsibilitytoprotect.org/index.php/pages/2)

Each state is characterised by these three features of territory, people and sovereignty; each claims sovereign power over its people and its territory. More specifically, we can speak of a state as an organisation that issues and enforces rules for a territorially defined area that are binding for people in that area. Sovereignty does not mean that the state is above the law and that those in charge of the state can do whatever they like. Indeed, most states try to constrain their sovereign powers by subjecting them to the exacting and precise rules of a constitution (see briefing 1.3 and chapter 4).

Straightforward as this definition of a state may seem to be, there are still complications. Some regions in the south of Italy used to be controlled by the Mafia in a state-like manner. Multinational companies (MNCs) such as Google, Nike and Shell, and organisations such as the IMF, are also hugely powerful. Did the states of the Netherlands and Belgium disappear when they were occupied by Germany in the 1940s?

In order to deal with those complications, the notion of the state is further specified by looking more closely at the concept of sovereignty. The German social scientist Max Weber (1864–1920) did this by stressing that the abstract term 'sovereignty' means that the state possesses the monopoly of the use of physical force. Only if the state controls the use of physical force can it impose its rules and realise its claims as the most important 'community'. Weber moved one crucial step further. In his view, the control of naked physical force

Legitimacy: The condition of being in accordance with the norms and values of the people. 'Legitimate power' is accepted because it is seen as right.

is not sufficient for statehood; it also requires a 'monopoly' that is accepted as right – a monopoly that is not only legal, but also has **legitimacy**. The Weberian definition of the state, then, consists of four elements.

- Weber accepts the three conventional characteristics of a state – territory, people, sovereignty.
- He specifies the meaning of 'sovereignty' by referring to the distinction between 'legal' and 'legitimate'. It is not sufficient to base physical force upon the law (legality). The use of physical force must also be accepted as right, and morally legitimate by citizens.
- The use of physical force alone, therefore, does not distinguish between states and other organisations. Organisations such as Microsoft, the World Bank, the IMF, the Mafia and the European Union are powerful, and may be more important for many people than, say, the state of Latvia or Iceland. Some of these organisations use physical force, but none of them claims the monopoly of the legitimate use of this force over its people as states do.
- Finally, Weber points out that one actor or institution must monopolise the legitimate use of physical force if the state is to avoid the danger of anarchy and lawlessness. Usually, we call this actor or institution the **government** of a state.

> **Government:** A government has a monopoly of the legitimate use of physical force within a state. Securing internal and external sovereignty of the state are major tasks of any government.

We can see these elements in Max Weber's definition of the state:

> A compulsory political organisation with continuous operations will be called a 'state' insofar as its administrative staff successfully uphold the claim to the *monopoly* of the *legitimate* use of physical force in the enforcement of its order. (Max Weber, *Economy and Society: An Outline of Interpretative Sociology*, ed. Guenther Roth and Claus Wittich, New York: Bedminster Press 1968: 54; emphasis in the original)

Can we recognise a state if we see one with the help of Weber's characterisation? Most of the time it will not be too difficult to grasp that a trade agreement between Chile and Argentina will involve two states, or that Croatia's application for EU membership is an act of state. Similarly, building regulations are enforced by the state as are traffic regulations enforced by the police in the name of the state. All these are based on the claim of a monopoly of the legitimate use of physical force over people living in a specific area – and so all are acts of state.

We mentioned earlier that other terms are sometimes used in place of 'state'. States are often referred to as 'countries' or 'nations' or as '**nation-states**', so we now examine what makes a country a state and a state a nation-state, by looking at the development of the modern state and the processes of state and nation building.

> **Nation-state:** A state based on the acceptance of a common culture, a common history and a common fate, irrespective of whatever political, social and economic differences may exist between the members of the nation-state.

■ The rise of the modern state

The state emerged in medieval Europe, between about 1100 and the sixteenth century. In that period, territorially based rulers claimed independence and created their own administrations and armies. At the same time, the idea of sovereign power was developed. However, each state has its own unique historical patterns in its progress towards modern statehood, and none follows quite the same path. Any discussion of state formation and the development of states must therefore start from a two-fold assertion: (i) the state concept is inextricably bound up with European history and Western political theory; and (ii) there is no uniform or general law that governs the appearance, or disappearance, of states.

Historical origins and development

States originate in many different ways and their development follows no single pathway. There are three general patterns, however:

- *Transformation* First, states arose on the basis of the gradual transformation of existing independent political units – mostly medieval monarchies. Major examples were Britain and France, whose independence goes back to the Middle Ages and whose development as states took several centuries. In Europe the Treaty of Westphalia signalled the final triumph of the state as a form of political organisation, as well as settling the borders of many states (see briefing 1.4).
- *Unification* Second, some states arose by the unification of independent but dispersed political units. This process was mainly concentrated in the nineteenth century and major examples were Germany and Italy.
- *Secession* Finally, states arose from the secession or break-up of independent political units – mostly empires or large heterogeneous states – into one or more states. The break-up of the Austro-Hungarian Empire and the

Briefing 1.4

The Treaty of Westphalia (1648)
The first decades of the seventeenth century were characterised by a series of wars between Spain, France, Sweden, Bavaria, the Netherlands, Denmark and countries in central Europe, known as the *Thirty Years War* (1618–48). It destroyed about 2,000 castles, 1,600 cities and more than 18,000 villages across Europe. The population of the war-torn area declined by about 50 per cent in rural areas and up to 30 per cent in urban regions. This changed the economic, demographic and political landscape in Europe profoundly and eventually led to a settlement that, in effect, created the state system of the modern world.

In a situation of continual wars and conflicts, it slowly became clear that a solution could be based on a 'package deal' between different sides. In 1648, delegates from the warring factions met in the cities of Osnabrück and Münster in Westphalia to negotiate an all-encompassing peace treaty. The final set of agreements, the *Treaty of Westphalia* or the *Peace of Westphalia*, had very important consequences for the development of states in Europe. They recognised the rights of states and their sovereignty, settled religious disputes and resolved territorial claims. Most important, the Treaty established a system of states and diplomatic relations between them that has lasted more or less intact until the present day.

Ottoman Empire after the First World War are examples. In Africa and Asia decolonisation after the Second World War resulted in many new states after former occupied territories gained independence. More recently, Czechoslovakia split into two independent states: the Czech Republic and Slovakia.

Most new states today, such as those born out of the collapse of the Soviet Union and Yugoslavia, are the product of secession.

State formation and nation building

One of the best-known accounts of the different historical paths taken by the modern states of Europe is presented by the Norwegian political scientist Stein Rokkan (1921–79). In his view, the formation of modern states proceeded in several phases, which are closely linked to basic societal conflicts ('**cleavages**'). Rokkan also distinguished between state formation and nation building. The first concerns the creation of state institutions, especially an army, a bureaucracy and a system of government. The second involves welding the population of the state into a single 'people' with a shared sense of belonging that often comes from a common language, religion, education, historical heritage and culture.

> **Class:** A group of people sharing certain attributes determined by economic factors, notably occupational hierarchy, income and wealth.

> **Cleavages:** Cleavages are deep and persistent differences in society where (1) objective social differences (class, religion, race, language, or region) are aligned with (2) subjective awareness of these differences (different cultures, ideologies and orientations).

Rokkan discerned four stages of development. The first two are generated by powerful elites who attempt to consolidate their power and territorial independence. The second two are of a quite different nature and concern the internal restructuring of established states.

The four stages are:

- State formation
- Nation building
- Mass democracies
- Welfare states.

State formation: penetration

In the first phase, elites took the initiative for the *unification* and *centralisation of a given territory*, usually the elites of major urban centres who consolidated their control over peripheral and rural areas. Local elites usually opposed these attempts because they meant loss of their own power and usually resulted in taxation and other duties. Consequently territorial consolidation was achieved mainly by economic and military force. The invention of the cannon was important because it meant that the centralisers could knock down the stone walls and fortifications that had protected the towns and castles of local interests. Thus we see how technology and politics combined to bring about fundemental change in society. But this was not enough to consolidate power over newly won territories. In order to secure their compliance, institutions were built to provide internal order and deal with disputes (police and courts), to provide external security (armed forces and diplomatic services), to extract resources (taxes and tolls) and to improve communications (roads and bridges), often so that soldiers could reach outlying areas quickly in order to put down local resistance to centralisation and unification. Clear demarcation of territory was crucially important, and this, in turn, required agreement between kings, princes and dukes about who owned what, although this often involved centuries of warfare. Broadly speaking, the period of state formation in Europe started in the high Middle Ages and lasted until the foundations of the western European state system, enshrined in the Treaty of Westphalia (see briefing 1.4).

Nation building: standardisation

During the second phase of nation building the main concerns were cultural issues of a common language, religious differences and compulsory education. The aim was to create feelings of a common identity and a sense of allegiance to the political system among the often disparate populations of the new states. A common, standardised language was spread alongside a common currency and a system of weights and measures. Military conscription for young men strengthened feelings of identity with the nation. The central idea of the nation-state is the acceptance of a common culture, a common history and a common fate, no matter what social and economic differences there were between individuals. If the historical roots of this common fate were not self-evident – and usually they were not – national myths about shared experiences and historical destinies were often created and spread. In order to heighten national identity, 'system symbols' – such as a national hymn, national flag and national emblems – were emphasised. Each country created its own folk-tales about brave and glorious national heroes who, against all the odds, had triumphed over adversity and the nation's enemies.

This period of nation building took place over many centuries after the initial conquests of territories and, indeed, it could be argued that it is being for ever renewed among modern democratic states which are constantly building and rebuilding their national pride and sense of national identity. Among the new democracies of the world, this is an important function of the media, the arts, the education system and the churches.

Mass democracies: equalisation

Although the nation-state was made the 'property' of all its citizens in the second phase, it was elites who originally created and ruled it. In the third phase of state building the masses conquered the right to participate in governmental decision making. In other words, democratic states (or democracies) were created. Political parties were founded to link citizens with elites in assemblies and parliaments. Less visible – but certainly not less significant – was the recognition that opposition parties and interests were allowed to exist and voice their opinions: gradually these political systems accepted the idea that peaceful opposition to the government was legitimate, and even the idea of peaceful change of groups or parties in government. The idea of the alternation of parties in government was associated with the belief in the principle of the legitimacy of popularly elected government. In this period the right to vote in national elections was broadened to include larger sections of the population, although women usually had to wait much longer to vote. In mass democracies, political power is legitimated by mass participation and elections. The earliest mass democracies arose in Europe towards the end of the nineteenth century. This, in turn, required educating the masses ('we must educate our masters') so that they could play their role in the economic system and learn about their national history and its heroes.

Welfare states: redistribution

The last phase in the development of the territorial state was the strengthening of economic solidarity between different parts of the population. Public welfare services were created and funded by progressive taxes and state contributions. **Welfare states**, characterised by redistribution and equality of opportunity, were created particularly in north-western Europe after the Second World War.

> **Welfare states:** Democracies that accept responsibility for the well-being of their citizens, particularly by redistributing resources and providing services for the young, old, sick, disabled and unemployed.

Few states went through these four stages from the medieval period to the third millennium in a regular and ordered way (France and Britain are exceptional). In many cases, the order of the four stages was interrupted by revolution, war or foreign occupation (as for Germany) and it is not easy to say when some phases started or how long they lasted. When, for example, did Italy become a welfare state? In some instances, phases overlapped or coincided. Spain combined the last two phases after its transition to democracy in the 1970s. Some phases are very long in some states, but hardly discernible for others. In other words, the history of each state is too complex and diverse to be covered by a simple, uniform scheme. Rokkan's four phases help us understand the process of state and nation building not because each state follows exactly the same pattern but because we can compare and understand how they developed by describing how each deviates or conforms to the general pattern. In spite of their differences, however, the developments of almost all states were in the early stages driven by two fundamental and enormously powerful forces: war and capitalism.

Catalysts: war and capitalism

The initial phase of the state building process in Europe, as we have seen, is focused on securing the compliance of territories with the wishes of centralising elites. Military might was important in this process. Military technology changed in the late medieval period, replacing the heavy cavalry with massed infantry and, later, with artillery and guns. The small private armies of feudal lords were replaced by large standing armies serving the state. The rights and powers of local landowners and of the nobility were replaced by centralised state power and resources. At the same time, the need to wage war against internal and external enemies functioned as catalysts for state formation, because only states were able to organise and pay for the large armies and the wars they fought. War was a normal state of affairs for the emerging states of the sixteenth and seventeenth centuries: great powers such as Spain, France, England, and the Netherlands were frequently embattled during this period. Persistent involvement in wars and the long-term struggle for domination of European territories can thus be seen as the primary factor behind the emergence of the modern state and all its powers and capacities.

The rise of capitalism in the eighteenth and nineteenth century also facilitated the emergence of the modern state. The capitalist mode of production brings together two important factors – labour and capital – for the creation of goods that can be sold at a profit. But this production process depends on the availability of a secure infrastructure; investment and profit depend on social and physical security and stability. The infrastructure necessary for capitalism and profit includes not just roads, bridges, harbours, canals and railways but also educational and health facilities, as well as police to protect property and a legal system regulating contracts and commercial disputes. Capitalism is also impossible without a common and guaranteed currency, a common set of weights and measures, and a minimal level of trust between those engaged in business transactions. Some of these can be produced only by a central power, others require central regulation and control.

Capitalism, then, requires an agency capable of the following four tasks:

- To secure investments
- To provide social and physical infrastructure
- To control and regulate conflicts between capitalists and other classes
- To protect the interests of capitalists and other classes against foreign competition and, in the extreme cases, foreign invasion.

The obvious institution to perform these functions is the state, with its territorial boundary, its monopoly of the legitimate use of physical force, and its power to tax and provide collective facilities and services. No other institution can perform these functions as effectively, and without the state there could be no sustained and organised capitalism.

Was the state created to wage war and promote capitalism? In large part, yes, but this interpretation is too simple for the complex, difficult and varied process of state formation. War and capitalism are certainly very important in the formation of states but they do not account for the initial rise of independent territorial units and the idea of sovereignty. They were important catalysts rather than direct causes of state formation.

Growth after 1945

From Europe, the idea of the state rapidly spread over the world, but it was not until the second half of the twentieth century that the number of states suddenly increased. After the First and Second World Wars, states founded special organisations to deal with relations among themselves, especially with regard to international conflicts. Some observers even looked forward to the creation of a single 'world state'. The League of Nations was created in 1919, but not all those eligible applied for membership and the organisation remained rather weak. After the Second World War a new organisation was created: the United Nations (UN). UN membership is an unambiguous sign of internationally recognised statehood, and virtually all states have joined. Only the Vatican, DAR Sahara, Kosovo and Taiwan are not members of the UN, although they can be considered states. For a long time Switzerland declined membership to underline its international neutrality, but it joined in 2002. Palestine was recognised as a 'non-member state' by the UN General Assembly in late 2012.

The spread of states over the world is illustrated by the steady growth of UN membership. Figure 1.2 shows the increase from about fifty states in 1945 to 193 in 2014. Three stages of growth are evident.

- A first wave of decolonisation (e.g. Ghana, Morocco, Tunisia, Libya, Laos) took place in the second half of the 1950s. The recognition of 'spheres of influence' for the USA and the Soviet Union (USSR) allowed a number of states (e.g. Albania, Austria, Finland, Japan, Romania) to become UN members.

Figure 1.2: UN member states, 1945–2014

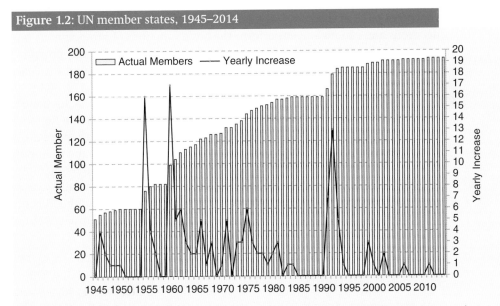

Based on: United Nations: Growth in the United Nations Membership, 1945–2014 (www.un.org/en/members/growth.shtml#1940)

- Decolonisation also marks the second wave of the spread of states, which started in the early 1960s (including Algeria, Gabon, Senegal, Chad) and lasted until well into the 1970s (Surinam, Mozambique, Vietnam). By 1980, more than 155 states were UN members.
- The last rapid increase took place after 1989, when the collapse of the Soviet Union and the end of communist rule in central and eastern Europe caused a fresh wave of nation-state creation in places such as Hungary, Latvia, Lithuania and Poland. The spread of states, however, continued because of the foundation of new ones (including Bosnia-Herzegovina, the Czech Republic and Slovakia in the 1990s, Kosovo in 2008 and South Sudan in 2011), and because of the recognition of existing countries such as Kiribati and Tonga.

Occasionally states disappear. This was the case with the unification of East and West Germany in 1990 and North and South Yemen in the same year. Attempts to obtain independence by regional, ethnic or religious separatist movements in some parts of the world probably mean that states will continue to increase in number in the coming decades.

Failed states

Although there are many pathways towards statehood, and although the UN has 193 member states, it does not follow that all countries and territories that set out along the path inevitably reach their goal. There are quite a few **failed states** in the world – that is, countries whose governments have lost control of parts of their territory, no longer have authority to make collective decisions and can no longer perform the basic functions of protecting its border, keeping its population safe and providing basic services. Early in 2015 the Fund for Peace (www.ffp.statesindex.org/), listed 178 states in the world of which four are on 'very high alert' (South Sudan, Somalia, Central African Republic and Sudan) and another twelve on 'high alert', meaning that they are all in danger of failing. The problem here is not just for the countries and their populations but also for the international system, because failed and fragile states are prey to violence, corruption, transnational crime, terrorism and waves of refugees that become an international problem. But just as statehood is not automatic, neither is failure, and countries can and do pull themselves out of the 'alert' category to put themselves on a firmer footing.

> **Failed state:** A country that has lost control of some of its territory and government authority and is unable to fulfil the basic functions of a sovereign state.

■ State theories

The state has fascinated political theorists since the rise of the Greek city-state and the writings of Aristotle and Plato more than 2,400 years ago. Modern theories fall into two very broad categories. First, there are **normative**

political theories. These are based on values and judgements about how the world should be, and what governments ought to do. Normative theories of the state are discussed in some detail in chapter 14. Second, there are **empirical political theories**, completely different from normative theories, about how the state actually operates and why it operates that way.

> **Normative political theories:** Theories about how the world should be.
>
> **Empirical political theories:** Theories that try to understand, by examining the evidence, how the political world actually works and why it works that way.

We present an overview of empirical theories of the state based on the relations between states and societies at the end of chapter 2. For the moment, it is enough to note that political scientists, historians and philosophers have presented a very large and diverse array of theoretical approaches to the state and its origins, which is surpassed only by their actual number. However, the four most common approaches are:

- constitutional
- ethical and moral
- conflict
- pluralist.

Constitutional approaches

According to these theories, the state is established by some agreement or social contract between citizens and rulers that defines the major functions and tasks of the state and the powers of its rulers. Social contract theorists know very well that there never was an actual 'contract' of this kind, but they conduct a sort of mental experiment in order to understand what sorts of agreement between citizens and rulers are necessary to establish an ordered and stable state. The main concern of these theories is the question of how the *legitimacy* of the state is established.

Ethical and moral approaches

The starting point of these theories is how we can organise society so that individuals can live together in peace and harmony. Some take the view that society consists of individuals who should be as free as possible to do what they wish, so the functions of the state should be as minimal as possible. Others view society as a collective entity that should ensure the collective well-being and welfare of its individual citizens, which means a proactive state with many functions and powers. Others believe that the state should establish the rule of God on earth, or ensure that it conducts its affairs according to God's intentions and rules. Some hold to the anarchist view that there is actually no need for states at all, and that people can live better with free and non-hierarchical associations.

Conflict approaches

These theories stress the conflicting nature of interests and values in society and see the state as a device to exercise the power necessary to regulate these conflicts. Marxist theories are one version of this approach. They emphasise the struggle between different classes and their incompatible economic interests, and claim that the state is nothing other than an instrument by which property owners maintain their power over the great mass of the working class. As we have already seen, capitalism and state building were closely connected, and from this it might be argued that the state is the means by which capitalists control other classes in society in order to secure their own interests. Feminist theories of the state are similar in some respects to class theories, but see the world as divided between male and female interests. Feminists argue that the state has been used by men to control women, and that it should now become the battle ground for women's liberation and the creation of non-sexist forms of government and politics.

Pluralist approaches

Like conflict approaches, pluralist theories see the state as the main instrument for the regulation of conflict and the reconciliation of competing interests. But rather than arguing that the state is the instrument of oppression, enforced order or of the ruling class, pluralists see it as a kind of referee that uses its legitimate authority (force if necessary) to make sure that competing interests are resolved without violence or socially disruptive consequences. Pluralists view the state as a battle ground for competing groups, but the battles are fought according to state-enforced rules that encourage peaceful resolutions. If this cannot be achieved then the state has the final decision and the power to enforce it.

Other theories

This does not exhaust the main theories of the state, nor the many variations on each of the main approaches, and you will inevitably encounter other theories and other variations. It will be helpful to ask four questions about any new theory in order to get an idea of its main content and concerns.

1. Is the theory a normative one that deals with the ideals and goals of the state, or is it an empirical theory that tries to describe and understand the way the state actually operates as opposed to how it should operate?
2. Does the theory start from individual rights and duties and the importance of preserving them (in which case it is probably an individualist one)? Or does it start from the mutual obligations and interdependence of citizens (in which case it is probably a collectivist one)?
3. Does the theory emphasise the laws and the formal structure of institutions of the state (in which case it is likely to be a constitutional approach) or does

it start from an account of the history and culture of a people (in which case it is more societal)?

4. Does the theory concentrate on the competing interests of classes, ethnic groups, or men and women (in which case it is likely to be a conflict theory), or does it emphasise the capacity of the state to reconcile and integrate the interests of different social groups (in which case it is likely to belong to the pluralist family)?

◼ What have we learned?

This chapter has dealt with the difficulties of characterising and defining states, and with their historical development.

- Although globalisation is widely said to be reducing the power and importance of the state, or even causing its death, the number of states in the world has been rising. With the exception of Antarctica and the high seas, almost every part of the landmass on earth belongs to one of the 193 member states of the United Nations.
- States are characterised by three main features: territory, people and sovereignty.
- Ultimately, states are based on the power of their armies, police and the law, but to be stable and democratic the use of state force must be regarded as legitimate by its citizens. That is, the use of power should be in accordance with the norms and values of its citizens. The term 'legitimacy' is especially used by Max Weber in his definition of the state.
- Globalisation is widely claimed to cause the declining power of the state, even its death, but states retain a huge amount of power over their citizens and as actors in the international system.

◼ Lessons of comparison

- States are only one of many forms of political organisation. They developed in Europe in the late medieval period and their rights and sovereignty were recognised by the Treaty of Westphalia (1648). From Europe they gradually spread over the rest of the world.
- States arise out of the transformation of existing political units, from the unification of different political units and as a result of the secession of political units that become independent.
- Historically, the creation of each state has followed a unique path, but in general, four main stages of development can be discerned: state formation, nation building, mass democratisation and welfare development. However, the presence of failed or fragile states shows that progression to statehood is not inevitable.
- War and capitalism have played a major role in most cases.

Projects

1. Would you call the place you live in a 'country', a 'nation' or a 'nation-state'? What makes it a country, state or nation-state, and when and how did it achieve this status?
2. Identify three ways in which your state fits the conflict theory and three ways in which it fits the pluralist theory. Which theory do you prefer?
3. Why has the number of states in the world increased? And why has the number become more or less stable for the last decade?

Further reading

P. Collins, *The Birth of the West: Rome, Germany, France, and the Creation of Europe in the Tenth Century*. New York: Public Affairs, 2013. A detailed historical account of early political developments resulting in different state building processes across Europe.

J. Dryzek and P. Dunleavy, *Theories of the Democratic State*. Basingstoke: Palgrave Macmillan, 2009. A recent discussion of four theories of the democratic state – pluralist, elitist, Marxist and market liberal – with an account of how states have changed and of four critiques of them – democratic renewal, feminist, environmental and the conservative reaction.

T. Ertman, 'State formation and state building in Europe', in T. Janoski et al., *The Handbook of Political Sociology*. Cambridge University Press, 2005: 367–83. A review of work on the origins and development of the concept of the state and the major theoretical approaches to it.

D. Held, *Political Theory and the Modern State*. Chichester: John Wiley, 2013. A set of advanced essays on the concept of the state, power, sovereignty, stability and crisis, and the future of democracy.

C. Pierson, *The Modern State*, 3rd edn. London: Routledge, 2011. An excellent, up-to-date introduction to the theory and practice of modern states with an account of their place in the international order of the twenty-first century.

H. Spruyt, 'The origins, development, and possible decline of the modern state', *Annual Review of Political Science*, 5, 2002: 127–49. An excellent review of the main streams of thought analysing the rise and possible decline of the state.

Websites

www.countrystudies.us.
Detailed but slightly dated accounts of the political history of states and of many of their political institutions.

www.state.uni-bremen.de.

Up-to-date studies of how pressure from globalisation and liberalisation over the past thirty years have changed the core institutions and functions of the classic nation state.

www.nationmaster.com.

Presents statistics for almost every country in the world on a wide variety of matters, including government, and enables you to pick your countries and organise the data as maps, graphs and tables. It also contains more detailed information about the administrative, political and constitutional organisations of countries. A mine of information of many kinds about the government of modern states.

www.qog.pol.gu.se/data.

Extensive data bank providing information about a large number of characteristics of countries around the world. the time series especially are very useful for comparative analyses.

2   States and democracy

In an increasingly global world there are organisation that are not states that have a big impact on politics and on daily existence in general. The European Union, Microsoft, Toyota and al-Qa'ida are more significant in their ways than many states. They affect the lives of millions of people. If it is true that the power of states is in decline, then why should we try to understand the state and its actions when newer political actors appear to be so important? This chapter starts with the question of why we continue to regard states as the most important building blocks of comparative analysis, when some writers claim that they are being replaced in importance in an increasingly global society.

The second problem is that, even if we concentrate attention on states as a form of political organisation, there are a great many of them in the world and they come in a huge variety of shapes and sizes. Some are as old as France or as new as Kosovo and South Sudan; some are large like Canada and India or small like Tuvalu and Nauru in the South Pacific; some are as rich as Luxembourg or as poor as Zimbabwe. To cover all of them in a satisfactory manner is not possible in a single book, so in this one we concentrate on the sixty or so democracies in the world. This, of course, simply raises the question of how we recognise a democratic state when we see one. What are the most important defining characteristics of democracies and how do they function in relation to the societies they govern?

Major topics covered in this chapter, therefore, are:

- Why study states in a globalised world?
- The modern state and democracy
- The rise of democratic states
- Measuring and comparing democracies
- Redistribution and the active state
- Theories of state and society.

■ Why study states in a globalised world?

It is a paradox that the power and importance of states seems to be in decline at the very time that states have captured almost every corner of the world's surface and when the number of states is at an all-time high. New technologies have made it possible to locate the production of goods and services almost anywhere on the globe. Transport and communications, and especially information technology (IT) are said to have created a 'global village'. Even wars are no longer restricted to conflicts between neighbouring states, but involve terrorist groups and special forces all over the world. As a result, the powers of states are increasingly limited by growing international interdependencies and interconnections, and by thousands of collective international arrangements and agreements that limit the freedom of any one state to control its own affairs. The world, it is argued, is increasingly forming a single system, a trend described as **globalisation**.

Globalisation: The growing interdependencies and interconnectedness of the world that reduces the autonomy of individual states and the importance of boundaries between them.

Part of the globalisation process involves the emergence of international organisations that challenge the pre-eminence of states. The United Nations (UN) and the European Union (EU) are perhaps the most conspicuous, but they are not alone, for there are other transnational organisations such as the North American Free Trade Association (NAFTA) and the Association of Southeast Asian Nations (ASEAN), as well as bodies such as the World Bank (IBRD – International Bank for Reconstruction and Development), and the International Monetary Fund (IMF). In recent decades a wave of new organisations known as non-governmental organisations (**NGOs**) such as Greenpeace, Transparency International, and Médecins Sans Frontières have joined the long list of older organisations that include the Catholic Church, the International Labour Organization (ILO) and the Red Cross. All operate on a world-wide scale and wield considerable power within their own spheres of influence.

NGOs: Non-profit, private and non-violent organisations that are independent of government but seek to influence or control public policy without actually seeking government office.

Nor should we forget the growth of huge and powerful multinational business corporations (MNCs). ExxonMobil, Walmart, Toyota and Apple are wealthier and more powerful than quite a few member states of the UN. If multinational companies, non-governmental organisations and international bodies are now beyond full state control and regulation, then should we perhaps pay less attention to states and concentrate on the really important and powerful actors on the world stage (see controversy 2.1)?

CONTROVERSY 2.1

Focusing on the state is...

Area of debate	... right, because	... wrong, because
Euro-centrism	The idea of the state was originally European, but every corner of the world is now claimed by states.	The idea of the European state should now take account of political arrangements in other cultures.
National sovereignty and globalisation	States still claim sovereignty and only a very small part of the world (covered by the EU in Europe) has established transnational forms of government that may render the state obsolete.	The rise of regional and transnational forms of government (EU, NAFTA and UN), of international government agencies (IMF, World Bank), of international NGOs (Greenpeace, ILO) and MNCs (Microsoft, Ford) shows that national sovereignty is losing its relevance.
Legacy and impact	States continue to exercise a powerful influence on social, political and economic life.	States are based on old ideas and practices and should be replaced by concepts more appropriate for the 21st century.
Number	The number of states has increased continuously.	The number of powerful states does not change; the newest states are small and unimportant.
Power	States are the most important actors in politics and they are in charge of military and economic power.	Only a few large states are important. Organisations such as the EU, Microsoft and the World Bank have more power than many states.
Financial liability and security	Only states can regulate markets and are able to accept liabilities when private actors and NGOs fail.	Market failures and crises show the lack of power of states to protect their citizens. Only international action can deal with these problems.
Regional separatism	Many serious conflicts in the world – the Middle East, Caucasus, etc. – are a direct consequence of the struggle for independence and recognition as a state.	Restricting political independence to the founding of states is the cause of these conflicts and hampers more innovative approaches.

Area of debate	... right, because	... wrong, because
Terrorism and crime	States are the most important objects of international terrorism.	International terrorism and crime is not primarily state organised and is a threat to state power.
Genocide, war crimes, ethnic cleansing, crimes against humanity	Conflicts about state power cause these problems and states are responsible for the protection of their citizens.	The spread of these problems shows the lack of power of states to protect their citizens. International action is the only solution.
Waning importance	Growing interdependency between states confirm their crucial role. Interdependencies best understood in terms of changing relations between states, rather than their decline.	Growing interdependence shows that states are losing their central position. It is more appropriate to focus on interdependencies and contacts and accept the decline of the state.
War	Wars are waged between states.	International terrorism means that the most important acts of violence are no longer restricted to states.

Could it be that the European state, first given its seal of approval in the Treaty of Westphalia (see briefing 1.4), is now as outdated as the horse and carriage? Some writers have confidently predicted the 'twilight of the state' and although this idea may seem realistic and up-to-date, it fails to take account of the fact that states are still the most important single group of actors in politics. They continue to be sovereign within their own territory, even if this sovereignty (see chapter 1) is now more circumscribed by international forces than it used to be. Even international terrorism is directed towards states and their representatives. Moreover, genocide, war crimes, ethnic cleansing and crimes against humanity all are directly linked to states and struggles for state power and independence. States have the main responsibility to protect their populations against those crimes. States have governments with supreme power within their borders and international relations continue to be conducted on this basis. Only states have the funds to bail out private financial institutions in times of huge financial crisis, and only states have the necessary credibility to offer their populations security in such times of crisis (see briefing 2.1). In short, states remain pre-eminently important, and they remain, therefore, the main focus and point of departure for the comparative approach to politics and government.

The emerging pattern seems to be one in which states and international agencies have combined to increase their joint capacities. The result has been the reduction of state powers in some respects but an enhanced ability

Briefing 2.1

State power in transition

■ ## Only the state can bail out private actors and guarantee financial security

With the collapse of the housing and finance markets in the USA in September 2008 many of these credits and debts appeared to be virtually worthless, and even the largest and wealthiest banks could not avoid the threat of bankruptcy. The result was not only massive loss of money and capital value but also loss of confidence in the whole system. The whole American finance system was instantly endangered – and with it almost every other financial system in the world. Only states had enough resources and credibility to bail out private actors and restore confidence in the financial system, and in these extraordinary circumstances governments and central banks injected huge amounts of money in order to stabilise the financial system. This underlines and reaffirms the uniqueness of states among the large organisations of the world.

Source: International Herald Tribune, October 14, 2008

■ ## Globalisation and state power

A more fruitful conceptualisation allows for the possibility that globalisation may actually complement and co-exist – as opposed to undermine or compete – with national socio-spatial networks of interaction. This in turn paves the way for a more nuanced appraisal of the differential impact of economic openness on the capacity for national governance. Specifying the conditions under which state capacities may be either enhanced or diminished, sidelined or strengthened, remains the key task for students of the politics of international economic relations.

Source: Linda Weiss (www.isdpr.org/isdpr/publication/journal/29–1/1Linda%20Weiss.pdf)

■ ## The transformation of the state

[T]he state still has formidable discretionary competences and organisational power. Furthermore, ultimate responsibility for the provision of normative goods is still ascribed to the state: In case of critical situations – such as the international financial system threatens to collapse, the Euro starts to become weak, or rivers burst their banks due to global climate change – the state is the first addressee for help and accusations. The state is expected to help and take remedial action – no matter whether the state was causatively involved in the deficiencies and crisis. Thus, the diffusion of state does not signal the end of statehood. It rather indicates that the state is better characterised as a governance manager than as a governance monopolist.

Source: www.state.uni-bremen.de/pages/forKonzept.php?SPRACHE=en

to tackle problems in others. Indeed, it is states that have promoted international and supra-national organisations such as the European Union (EU), the North American Free Trade Association (NAFTA) and APEC (Asia-Pacific Economic Cooperation), and it may be that such organisations thrive best when they are linked to strong and stable states.

States exist in such a huge variety of forms that we cannot deal satisfactorily with all of them between the covers of a single volume. Therefore, we concentrate on that especially important and increasingly widespread group of states that are democracies. Concentrating in this way on democracies enables us to compare and contrast a group of similar states: we are able to compare apples with apples, and not apples with oranges. At the same time, many of the democracies are found in European, Anglo-Saxon and North American countries and, therefore, these are inevitably over-represented in our analyses. We will return to this difficulty in the Postscript.

■ The modern state and democracy

Mass political involvement transformed states into 'mass democracies' when the rights of opposition were recognised and general suffrage granted. Stein Rokkan emphasised the fact that the internal restructuring of the state converts subjects of the state into citizens, collectively known as the 'masses' or 'the people' (see chapter 1). But how do we distinguish between democratic and non-democratic states in the first place? Usually, this question is answered by referring to three things – citizens' rights, elections and parliamentary accountability.

Citizens' rights

Discussions about political power and the rights of citizens have always been at the centre of debates about democracy. As the members of the French National Assembly confirmed in August 1789, the struggle for political power should not be an aim in itself. It is what can be done with that power that matters. After all, Article 2 of the Declaration of the Rights of Man and of the Citizen published in Paris (briefing 1.1) talks about the goal of all political institutions being 'the natural and inalienable rights of man'. In a similar way, the Virginia Bill of Rights – published in the USA in 1776, thirteen years earlier than the French document – stressed the universal nature of these rights. The Virginia Bill of Rights borrowed, in its turn, from the English Magna Carta, dating back to 1215. A first characteristic of democracies, then, is the acknowledgement that it is not power but the protection of rights ('**human rights**') that is of prime concern.

> **Human rights:** The innate, inalienable and inviolable right of humans to life, liberty and security of person, as the UN Charter puts it. Such rights cannot be bestowed, granted, limited, bartered or sold away. Inalienable rights can only be secured or violated.

The constitutions of many states start with an enumeration of human rights before political institutions and powers are defined (see chapter 4). Some constitutions even borrow heavily from the documents published in Paris and Virginia in the late eighteenth century.

The most common rights include:

- freedom of speech and the press
- freedom of religion and conscience

- freedom of assembly and association
- right to equal protection of the law
- right to due process of law and to fair trial
- property rights to land, goods and money.

Protecting these rights is the first aim of democratic political systems. Apart from anything else, they have a special political importance for both ordinary citizens and political leaders. If human rights are protected, citizens and leaders can engage in peaceful political conflict without fear of reprisals so that free competition for political power should result on election day in a government formed by those winning most popular support. Competition alone is not sufficient to guarantee this, however; challengers must be allowed to join the struggle and losers should not be victimised because they were on the losing side. In this way, democracy can gain the consent of losers and winners alike and so it can also be 'government of the people, by the people, for the people', as the American president Abraham Lincoln (1809–65) stated in his famous Gettysburg Address.

Elections and parliamentary accountability

Mass democracy began in a few countries in the nineteenth century. The basic idea at the time was not that citizens should be directly involved in politics or have any direct power over public affairs, but that they should rely on representative elected political leaders. The main political task of citizens was to elect representatives (see chapter 12) who would govern on their behalf (**representative democracy**). Although this was an important step towards democracy, it was not 'democracy' as we would define it today. Only much later, and then only after long struggles, was it recognised that a more advanced form of democracy involved the direct participation and influence of ordinary citizens in public affairs, something that came to be called **participatory democracy**. Meanwhile in the earlier form of democracy, citizens were largely restricted to the role of choosing their leaders and little else, an important step because it meant that the principle of parliamentary accountability to citizens came to be incorporated into the democratic ideal. This was accepted in France in 1870 and in Germany in 1918, but not until 1976 in Spain (see table 2.1). In several countries it took a long time before the new constitutional rules were realised in practice, often because autocrats and elites had to surrender their privileges first. The Dutch constitution of 1848 formulated the principle of accountability, but it was not actually put into practice until 1866.

Similarly, voting rights were extended only slowly and in stages. Several democracies completed universal male suffrage in the nineteenth century

Representative democracy: That form of democracy in which citizens elect leaders who govern in their name.

Participatory democracy: That form of democracy in which citizens actively and directly participate in government.

Table 2.1 Parliamentary accountability and universal suffrage, selected countries

	Parliamentary accountability		Universal adult suffrage	
	Accepted	Constitutionalised	Male	Female
Austria[a]	1918	1920	1907	1918
Belgium[b]	1831	1831	1893	1948
Denmark[c]	1901	1953	1901	1918
Finland[d]	1919	1919	1906	1906
France[e]	1958 (1870)	1958	1848	1944
Germany	1918	1919	1869	1919
Greece	1974	1975	1877	1952
Iceland[f]	1904	1944	1915	1915
Ireland[g]	1922	1937	1918	1918
Italy	1948	1948	1912	1945
Luxembourg	1868	1868	1919	1919
Netherlands	1848 (1866)	1983	1917	1919
Norway[h]	1905 (1814)	1905	1897	1913
Portugal[i]	1910	1976	1911	1931
Spain	1976	1976	1869	1931
Sweden[j]	1809	1975 (1809)	1909	1921
Switzerland	1848	1848	1919	1971
UK	1689 (Bill of Rights)	–	1918	1918

Notes:
[a]Austria: The constitution of 1918 was considered 'provisional' until 1920. The rights of parliament to elect the cabinet were modified in 1929.
[b]Belgium: Constitutional monarchy in 1831 with a potential for further parliamentarisation.
[c]Denmark: Parliamentary accountability from 1901 onwards, constitutionalisation in 1953.
[d]Finland: An autonomous Russian district until 1919.
[e]France: Only for Fifth Republic. Parliamentary accountability for the Third Republic from 1870–5 to 1940 and for the Fourth Republic from 1946 to 1958. In the Third and Fourth Republic, the parliament had more control than during the other periods.
[f]Iceland: Independent of Denmark since 1944.
[g]Ireland: Independent of Great Britain since 1937.
[h]Norway: Enforced political union with Sweden, 1814–1905.
[i]Portugal: An unstable, semi-presidential, parliamentary republic, 1910–17.
[j]Sweden: The 1809 constitution was formally effective until 1975.
Sources: Parliamentary accountability: Jan-Erik Lane and Svante Ersson, *Politics and Society in Western Europe* (London, Sage, 1998). Suffrage: Jan-Erik Lane, David McKay and Kenneth Newton, *Political Data Handbook* (Oxford University Press, 1997: 118).

and many followed in 1918 directly after the First World War. But only in a few countries were men and women given voting rights in the same year. Universal female suffrage was enacted in New Zealand in 1893 and a year later in Australia, but in France women had to wait almost a hundred years (until 1944) before they had the same voting rights as men.

There is certainly no inevitability about a state becoming democratic, and many reasons why non-democratic elites resist giving up or sharing power, but, nevertheless, the number of democracies rose rapidly in the twentieth century. In 1900 not one of the fifty-five states in existence at the time could be called democratic, if by that we mean the presence of free political competition, universal suffrage and the peaceful transition of power between parties, brought about by democratic election. Even the most democratic, such as the USA or Britain, restricted the voting rights of women or black Americans. Monarchies and empires were the dominant state forms. The picture changed dramatically in the second half of the twentieth century. By 1950, the total number of states had risen to eighty, and twenty-two of them could be characterised as 'democracies', which meant that about 31 per cent of the world population was living under democratic rule.

The second half of the twentieth century saw a decline in colonial rule in Africa and Asia, changes in Latin America, and the collapse of communist rule in eastern and central Europe. As a result the number of democracies more than trebled the 1950 figure, covering almost half the total number of countries and almost half the world population. The growth of democracy was not always sustained, however, and some countries slipped into a 'democratic recession'. In 2015 nearly twice as many countries (61) suffered democratic decline as registered improvement (33).

It must be carefully noted, however, that these figures depend heavily on how democracy is defined and measured, and there is not complete agreement among political scientists about this. There is not even agreement about how we should label democracy and its different types. Some use the term 'political democracy' or 'liberal democracy' as synonyms for what are here called 'democracies' or 'democratic states'. The political scientist Seymour Martin Lipset (1922–2006) provided one of the clearest definitions, explicitly spelling out the main features of a democracy as a system of government:

> First, competition exists for government positions, and fair elections for public office occur at regular intervals without the use of force and without excluding any social group. Second, citizens participate in selecting their leaders and forming policies. And, third, civil and political liberties exist to ensure the integrity of political competition and participation. (Seymour M. Lipset, ed., *The Encyclopedia of Democracy*, London, Routledge, 1995: iv)

This is a useful and succinct statement, but the problem of how exactly to measure and compare democracy in the modern state is a more complicated matter, as we will see now.

■ Measuring and comparing democracies

There are many different attempts to define, measure and compare democracies in the world, as briefing 2.2 shows. Here we will discuss two of them to illustrate their differences and similarities in methods and results – the Freedom House and the Economist Intelligence Unit ratings.

Briefing 2.2

Comparing democracy and democratic development: major indicators

Name	Description	Scope	Source
Freedom House Index	Political rights and civil liberties.	Detailed country reports. Trends are pointed out. 213 countries and territories.	www.freedomhouse.org
Economist Intelligence Unit, Democracy Index	Electoral process and pluralism; civil liberties; the functioning of government; political participation; and political culture.	165 states since 2006 with in-depth country reports, analysis of global regions and trend analysis.	www.eiu.com/Handlers/ WhitepaperHandler .ashx?fi=Democracy- index-2014.pdf&mode=w p&campaignid=Democra cy0115 (it is necessary to register for this web site.)
Democracy Barometer	Encompassing measure of the quality of democracy based on liberal as well as participatory concepts.	Scores for 100 indicators of democracy; 70 countries; per year since 1990.	www.democracybarometer .org
Bertelsmann Transformation Index (BTI)	Democratic and economic development and capabilities of the executive.	Detailed country reports. Trends are pointed out. 129 countries.	www.bti-project.de/ bti-home/
Polity-Index	Monitors regime changes/political stability, authority, quality of executive.	Country reports point out specific developments. 167 countries.	www.systemicpeace.org/ polity/polity4.htm
Polyarchy and Contestation Scales	Fairness of elections, freedom of organisation, freedom of expression, media pluralism, extent of suffrage.	Detailed country reports. 196 countries.	www.nd.edu/~mcoppedg/ crd/datacrd.htm

Name	Description	Scope	Source
Democracy and Development	Focus on political features and pure regime type determination.	Detailed country reports. 135 countries.	politics.as.nyu.edu/object/ przeworskilinks.html
Unified Democracy Scores (UDS)	Synthesised indicator of democracy based on the ten commonly used indicators of democracy.	Worldwide democracy scores for the 1946–2000 period.	www.unified-democracy- scores.org/
Perceptions of Electoral Integrity Project (PEI)	Survey of expert perceptions of the quality of elections.	107 countries; 127 elections; starting July 2012.	https://sites.google.com/site/ electoralintegrityproject4/ projects/expert-survey-2

The **Freedom House study Freedom in the World 2015** evaluates 195 countries and 15 territories. Each country and territory is assigned a score on the two measures of political rights and civil rights. Scores range from 1 to 7 with 1 representing the most free and 7 the least free. The scores are based, in turn, on 25 detailed indicators that were estimated for each country and then averaged to produce two general scores for political and civil rights. Freedom House reports country scores and also groups them into three categories which they name 'Free', 'Partly Free', and 'Not Free'.

Freedom in the World 2015 assesses the real-world rights and freedoms enjoyed by individuals, rather than governments or government performance. Political rights and civil liberties can be affected by both state and non-state actors, including insurgents and other armed groups. Freedom House uses its own staff and a panel of outside experts to reach agreement about country scores which are intended to be consistent across time and place, making it possible to compare countries and trends over time.

Freedom in the World, as its title states, concentrates on political and civil freedom. It gives eighty-nine countries in the world the highest ranking of 'Free', representing 46 per cent of all countries in the study, and 40 per cent of the world population. Another fifty-five countries are graded 'Partly Free', covering 24 per cent of the world population.

The **Economist Intelligence Unit's Democracy Index** takes a different approach to democracy, what it calls a 'thick' approach to conceptualising and measuring democracy, rather than the 'thin' approach of Freedom House that concentrates on political and civil rights. It argues that freedom and democracy are not the same thing and that democracy is a set of practices and principles that institutionalise freedom and thereby protect it. In other words, democracy forms the basis on which freedom is built and preserved and is, therefore, fundamental to, but not synonymous, with freedom. It goes on to say that while few agree on the precise definition of democracy, most would agree that its fundamental features are (1) government based on majority rule and the consent of the governed; (2) the existence of free and fair elections; (3) the protection of minority rights and respect for basic human rights; (4) equality before the law; (5) due legal process; and (6) political pluralism.

In line with this reasoning, the Index is based on five categories: electoral process and pluralism; civil liberties; the functioning of government; political participation; and political culture. These categories are measured using sixty indicators and the scores averaged to produce a single overall figure ranging from 1 to 10. The result is a continuous scale ranging from the highest, of 9.93 (Norway), to the lowest, of 1.08 (North Korea). The Index then groups these into four categories, as follows.

1. Full democracies – scores of 8 to 10
2. Flawed democracies – scores of 6 to 7.9
3. Hybrid regimes – scores of 4 to 5.9
4. Authoritarian regimes – scores below 4

The Democracy Index ranks twenty-four countries as 'full democracies', which constitutes 14.4 per cent of all countries and 12.5 per cent of the global population. It is clear that the 'thick' approach of the Intelligence Unit is the tougher of the two measures.

The results of the two sets of democracy measures are shown in table 2.2.

Nevertheless, the two democracy measures overlap a lot in the sense that all the 'full democracies' appear in the 'Free' list of Freedom House with the best score of 1. Insofar as they agree on the most advanced democracies, there is no difference between them. What is notable, however, is that the UK and USA rank sixteenth and nineteenth in the list of twenty-four full democracies picked out by the Economist Democracy Index. France barely makes it into the list of full democracies at all, being ranked twenty-third out of twenty-four.

It is only when less advanced cases are considered that differences between the two ratings emerge. Belgium, Spain, Italy, Portugal, Israel and Greece qualify only as 'flawed democracies'. This is not a problem. If the feeling is that the club of twenty-four 'full democracies' is too exclusive, then there is always Freedom House's larger one of forty-seven countries with the highest possible score on both political and civil rights. Alternatively, one might simply use a different cut-off point from the Intelligence Unit's and draw it at number forty-seven, which is Panama with a score of 7.08. Cut-off points are arbitrary, and different ones are perfectly admissible.

Debates and differences of the kind between Freedom House and the Economist Intelligence Unit remind us of the difficult problems of applying the abstract concept of 'democracy' to actual political systems. Different measures and definitions give us different results when we try to classify states as

Table 2.2 Free and independent states, 2014 (selected states with more than 1 million inhabitants are listed)

State	Freedom House Index	EIU Democracy Index	Population (million, 2014)	Area – total (000 km²)	GDP[b] (US$, 2013 est.)
Argentina	2.0	52 DD[a]	43.024	2,780	18,600
Australia	1.0	9	22.508	7,741	43,000
Austria	1.0	14	8.223	84	42,600
Belgium	1.0	26	10.449	31	37,800
Benin	2.0	90	10.161	113	1,600
Botswana	2.5	28	2.156	582	16,400
Brazil	2.0	44 DD	202.657	8,514	12,100
Bulgaria	2.0	55 DD	6.925	111	14,400
Canada	1.0	7	34.835	9,984	43,100
Chile	1.0	32 DD	17.364	756	19,100
Costa Rica	1.0	24	4.755	51	12,900
Croatia	1.5	50 DD	4.471	57	17,800
Czech Rep.	1.0	25	10.627	79	26,300
Denmark	1.0	5	5.569	43	37,800
Dominican Rep.	2.5	59	10.350	49	9,700
El Salvador	2.5	64 DD	6.126	21	7,500
Estonia	1.0	34	1.258	45	22,400
Finland	1.0	8	5.269	338	35,900
France	1.0	23	66.259	643	35,700
Germany	1.0	13	80.997	357	39,500
Ghana	1.5	68	25.758	239	3,500
Greece	2.0	41	10.776	132	23,600
Hungary	1.5	51	9.919	93	19,800
India	2.5	27	1.236.345	3,287	4,000
Indonesia	3.0	49 DD	253.610	1,905	5,200
Ireland	1.0	12	4.833	70	41,300
Israel	1.5	36	7.822	21	36,200
Italy	1.0	29	61.680	301	29,600
Jamaica	2.5	43	2.930	11	9,000
Japan	1.0	20	127.103	378	37,100
Korea, South	2.0	21	49.040	100	33,200
Latvia	2.0	39	2.165	65	19,100
Lesotho	2.5	60	1.942	30	2,200
Lithuania	1.0	38	3.506	65	22,600
Mali	4.5	83	16.456	1,240	1,100
Mauritius	1.5	17	1.331	2	16,100
Mexico	3.0	57 DD	120.287	1,964	15,600
Mongolia	1.5	61	2.953	1,564	5,900
Namibia	2.0	73	2.198	824	8,200

State	Freedom House Index	EIU Democracy Index	Population (million, 2014)	Area – total (000 km²)	GDP[b] (US$, 2013 est.)
Netherlands	1.0	10	16.877	42	43,300
New Zealand	1.0	4	4.402	268	30,400
Norway	1.0	1	5.148	324	55,400
Panama	2.0	47 DD	3.608	75	16,500
Peru	2.5	63 DD	30.148	1,285	11,100
Poland	1.0	40	38.346	313	21,100
Portugal	1.0	33	10.814	92	22,900
Romania	2.0	57 DD	21.730	238	14,400
Senegal	2.0	74	13.636	197	2,100
Serbia	2.0	56	7.210	77	11,100
Slovakia	1.0	45	5.444	49	24,700
Slovenia	1.0	37	1.988	20	27,400
South Africa	2.0	30	48.376	1,219	11,500
Spain	1.0	22	47.738	505	30,100
Sweden	1.0	2	9.724	450	40,900
Switzerland	1.0	6	8.062	41	54,800
Taiwan	1.5	35	23.360	36	39,600
Trinidad & Tobago	2.0	48	1.224	5	20,300
UK	1.0	16	63.743	244	37,300
USA	1.0	19	318.892	9,827	52,800
Uruguay	1.0	17	3.333	176	16,600

Notes:
[a]DD = Defective democracy according to some research.
[b]PPP per capita (PPP: Purchasing power parity).
Sources: Freedom House (2014), **Freedom in the World. Combined Average Ratings –** Independent Countries (https://freedomhouse.org/report/freedom-world/freedom-world-2014# .VRLUd2Z94nS); Central Intelligence Agency (2014), **The World Factbook. Rank Order** (https:// www.cia.gov/library/publications/the-world-factbook/rankorder/2119rank.html; https://www.cia .gov/library/publications/the-world-factbook/rankorder/2147rank.html; https://www.cia.gov/library/ publications/the-world-factbook/fields/2004.html#85edirect.html)

'democratic' or not, or if we try to grade them on a continuum. Nevertheless, when we set the result of different measures of democracy side by side (all the main ones, not just the two discussed here) three conclusions are clear.

1. The number of democratic states in the world has expanded since the mid-1970s, so the idea that democracy is the best form of government is now widely accepted (see briefing 2.3).
2. The results of most of the different measures of democracy differ, but in general there is a high degree of agreement between them.
3. We can group democracies into categories (full, partial, imperfect, flawed, etc.) or give them individual scores and rank them, but we should remember that

Briefing 2.3

Democracy: universal principles and limitations

We reaffirm that democracy is a universal value based on the freely expressed will of people to determine their own political, economic, social and cultural systems and their full participation in all aspects of their lives. We also reaffirm that while democracies share common features, there is no single model of democracy, that it does not belong to any country or region, and reaffirm the necessity of due respect for sovereignty and the right of self-determination. We stress that democracy, development and respect for all human rights and fundamental freedoms are interdependent and mutually reinforcing.

Resolution adopted by the UN General Assembly: 60/1. 2005 World Summit Outcome (http://unpan1.un.org/intradoc/groups/public/documents/UN/UNPAN021752.pdf).

the cut-off points for assigning countries to categories is arbitrary, and that individual scores are sometimes so close as to make virtually no difference. For example, the Freedom House Index groups countries into scores of 1.0, 1.5, 2.0 and 2.5 … 7.0, but if it had chosen, instead, to group them according to scores of 1, 2, 3 … 7, its picture would have been slightly different. Similarly, the differences between some countries' scores in the Economist Index are so small that they are within the measurement error, and so the gap between some countries is, to all intents and purposes, negligible.

■ Redistribution and the active state

As states move gradually towards political freedom and democracy, so they will be confronted, as Rokkan points out, with growing citizen demands and a need to strengthen national identity. The minimal states of the eighteenth and nineteenth centuries limited themselves to what is often called the 'night watchmen' functions of protecting national boundaries and its citizens from crime and breach of contract. As more citizens gained the right to vote, plus a variety of social and economic rights, so the role of the state expanded to include a wider variety of provisions. They began to provide street lighting, public libraries, museums and parks, and they improved police, fire and health services. Most important, they introduced compulsory education, pensions and welfare measures. All helped to convert subjects of the state into citizens with a sense of national identity, and to improve the productivity of the labour force. Night-watchmen states gradually became active agents for economic growth, nationhood and welfare, but they did so in different ways and at their own speed.

As can be seen in the right-hand column of table 2.2, democratic states vary enormously in their level of economic development. A widely used indicator for economic development – the **gross domestic product** (GDP) per citizen – ranged in 2014 from US\$1,100 in Mali to US\$55,400 in Norway. Most democratic

GDP: The value of all final goods and services produced within a state in a given year. In order to compare the wealth of states the measure used is normally GDP per capita.

states are wealthy, though not all of them are, but what most of them have in common is a rapid expansion of state activities since the Second World War. Even a cursory look at economic trends in democracies over past decades shows a remarkable growth of state spending and public employment. Many of them abandoned traditional laissez-faire policies and free-market economics after the traumatic experiences of the Great Depression of the 1930s and the war and post-war economic problems of the 1940s. As they increasingly accepted responsibility for the young and old, the sick and disabled, the unemployed and poor, and for education, housing and pensions, these states developed into welfare states (chapter 1).

The expansion of state activities can be illustrated with a few basic figures. For example, average tax revenues in OECD countries rose from 25 per cent of GDP in 1965 to 34 per cent in 2013. On average, total spending of the twenty-seven member states of the European Union reached almost 49 per cent of their GDP in 2011. Even more striking, the growth of public expenditure and public services are directly linked to the consolidation of democracy in many states. State spending varies very considerably from one country to another, but the longer a state is a democracy, the higher its public spending is likely to be. Once a high level of spending is reached, it becomes difficult to reduce the state's spending: large parts of the population benefit from these measures and it is hard to find a majority favouring cuts and reforms.

Although the upward climb in state spending levelled off in many countries after the early 1990s, state services of one kind or another continue to play a major role in the life of the average citizen. The reverse side of this coin is, of course, that welfare states are also tax states, with state revenues growing almost as fast as public spending. As a result, modern states function as huge redistribution agencies collecting taxes and supporting parts of the population in complicated ways (see chapter 15). In this sense there is no escaping the state, its taxes and its services in modern society. As the saying goes: in this life, only death and taxes are certain.

■ Theories of state and society

As we saw in chapter 1, modern political theories about the state fall into two very broad categories: normative theories about what the state ought to do and empirical theories about how the state actually operates and why it operates that way. We shall discuss empirical theories now. As the relationship between democracy and state spending shows, the nature and functioning of the state is closely related to the society it governs. In fact, one way of distinguishing between different theories of the state is to look at how they conceptualise the relationship between state and society. Broadly speaking, there are four major approaches to the relationship between 'state' and 'society':

- state supremacy
- state dependency

- interdependency
- separation and autonomy.

State supremacy

Some theories presume the supremacy or dominance of the state over society. According to these theories, the state does not so much reflect the characteristics of broader society, but is independent of them and above them. This idea is found in legal theories that stress the formal sovereignty of the state. Aristotle, for example, saw the state as a political community 'which is the highest of all, and which embraces all the rest'. According to this view the state is a self-regulating and supreme power. It is not the product of society or the social and economic groups within it; on the contrary, they are part of the state from which they arise. Such theories are summarised under the label '**Etatism**'. Although some writers regard state supremacy as a threat to individual rights and liberty, others reach very different conclusions, regarding the state's main role as the preservation of law and order (the 'night watchman' role) and the defence of the full independence of the private sector, whether individual or collective.

Etatism: A very strong emphasis on state power and an accompanying reduction of social and individual rights.

The view that the state is an independent and dominant power has become more and more problematic as we have gained a better understanding of government. At first sight, the huge increase in the activity and powers of the modern state may, indeed, suggest that it invades society as a conqueror that gains greater and greater control over the lives of citizens. But a closer look reveals a more complicated development in which the relationship between state and society is mutually interdependent: the state influences society and helps to mould it, but society also creates the state, giving it powers, but also setting limits on these powers. Besides, states are not single or monolithic entities that control societies, as a field marshal might control his troops on a battlefield. They are highly complex 'communities' made up of different institutions and organisations, with their own histories and interests, and expressing the outcomes of all sorts of past and present political battles between competing social and economic groups. Most political scientists today, therefore, do not see the state as something 'above' or controlling society, which leads us away from the notion of a dominant state and towards the idea of an interdependent one.

State dependency

Some theories see the state not as a supreme agency that dominates society, but, quite the opposite, as dependent on society, especially in its economic relations. Disputes about this view of the state and its relationship with social and economic forces have a long and complicated tradition in political analysis. The work of the German theorist Karl Marx (1818–83) inspired the idea that the state is only and always the expression of the struggle between classes in society – or, more specifically, that the power of the state is always an instrument of the dominant class. According to Marx, the state is nothing more or less than 'a committee for managing the common affairs' of the dominant class. In modern society, this is the capitalist class, who own and control the means of production. According to this theory, the state is not a neutral referee that adjudicates between the competing interests of different classes or social groups, nor is it an agency that is above and independent of society. It is, and can only be, an instrument to strengthen the dominant position of specific groups in society – in a capitalist society, this means the interests of the capitalist class.

Marxists argue about whether and to what extent the state can be independent of economic forces and the interests of the capitalist class. The earlier writings of Marx argued that the state is merely a 'superstructure' whose shape and power is the inevitable product of the economic substructure. Later, Marx seems to have allowed for a degree of independence of the state, and twentieth-century Marxists have picked up this idea. Usually, they emphasise particular 'structural tensions' in capitalist societies arising from the fact that modern states have conflicting, and even contradictory, tasks. On the one hand, they are expected to protect the free market necessary for making profits, but at the same time, they are also expected to maintain social order and ensure that the population is educated and healthy enough to provide an efficient workforce. This means taxing business, which reduces profits. Another tension results from the great increase in state activities, which overstretches and overloads the state apparatus, and leads it into all sorts of activities that it cannot afford or perform well. As a result, the state becomes increasingly intertwined with social and economic forces and becomes increasingly dependent upon them. This leads us away from the notion of a dependent state towards an interdependent one.

Interdependency

A third set of theories stresses the interdependence of state and society, or the relationships of exchange between them. In these approaches, the modern state has become ever more deeply involved in social and economic regulation. At the same time, as society has become increasingly complex and differentiated, it requires more state co-ordination, regulation and arbitration. These developments are different sides of the same coin, and it is not possible to say that one causes the other or that one dominates the other. They are mutually interdependent.

Neo-corporatist theories stress the close mutual dependency of state agencies, on the one hand, and major economic interest groups on the other. In traditional variants of this approach, trade unions and employer associations negotiate directly with state agencies about economic policies. More recent theories of governance stress the participation of a wide range and variety of organised social groups in making and implementing public policy of all kinds. We shall say more about the interdependency of state and society in our later discussions of governance and neo-corporatism (especially chapters 4, 10 and 15).

Separation and autonomy

Finally, some theories depict state and society as distinct and autonomous areas, each with its own rules and development, and each with its own imperatives and 'logic'. Deep social forces produce social groups, interests and organisations that neither can nor should be controlled or regulated by the state. Equally, the state cannot and should not be captured by any particular interests or class (as the Marxists claim), because the state is a battlefield occupied by many conflicting groups and interests. State activities have their limits, just as social interests and organisations do, and to try to exceed these limits is to undermine the democratic principles of a proper balance between the state and private interests. Pluralist and civil society theories stress the need for an area of social life and organisation outside the power of the state (see chapter 10).

The four approaches are only a brief beginning to our analysis of state and society. We will have much more to say about each as we progress through the chapters that follow and add greater breadth and depth to our understanding. Meanwhile, we can certainly conclude that modern states are characterised by complex connections with their society, and that it is difficult to say which of the four approaches is best. Each seems to explain some aspect of the affairs of states better than the others. For instance, neo-corporatist and pluralist approaches explain the rise of welfare states in the 1960s in those states where welfare programmes and economic policies and practices were the result of close collaboration between the state and powerful economic interest groups. However, the spread of political dissatisfaction and frustration among large sections of society in some countries after the 1960s seems to be better explained in terms of 'structural tensions' between an increasingly active state that is also increasingly weaker in some respects. Only after looking more closely at the multifarious institutions, structures and activities of the modern state can we come to a more sensible judgement about the strengths and weakness of the various theories.

■ What have we learned?

This chapter has dealt with the difficulties of characterising and defining states, and with the historical development of modern states, especially democratic ones.

- Democracy is a variable, not a constant. Accepted ideas about what democracy is, and how it operates, are changing as standards rise.
- Democracy is a contested concept, but most definitions stress the importance of universal citizenship with its accompanying political and civil

rights and duties, political competition for support in regular and free elections, and parliamentary accountability with a mixture of representative and direct participatory democracy.

- Most democratic states are among the wealthiest in the world, and hence they include a disproportionate number in Europe, North America and the English-speaking world.
- Growing political demands among citizens lead to redistribution and to welfare states that accept responsibility for the young and old, the sick and disabled, and the unemployed and poor. Not all democracies have developed their welfare provisions to the same extent, however.
- The number of democracies has risen, and currently almost half the world's states and population can be labelled 'free'. There has been a 'democratic recession' in recent years in some countries.

■ Lessons of comparison

- Although states across the globe, from the strongest to the weakest, are increasingly confronted with other powerful organisations, especially international business (MNCs), non-governmental organisations (NGOs) and international agencies, they are still the most important political actors in the world.
- States and societies are intimately bound together in a wide variety of different ways.
- Comparative theories of the state can be distinguished according to how they conceptualise the relationship between state and society. Broadly speaking, there are four main theories of state and society: state supremacy, state dependency, interdependency, and separation and autonomy.
- Comparison across time and across states shows that democracies have evolved from 'night-watchmen' to 'active states', but each has done so in its own way and at its own speed.

Projects

1. Comparing any two countries in table 2.2 with ExxonMobil, the IMF and Greenpeace, list the features that distinguish them as states, multinational corporations, NGOs or intergovernmental agencies.
2. Do you live in a democracy? Present a brief overview of the features that define your country as a – more or less – democratic state.
3. Explain why most welfare states are democracies, but not all of them.
4. Explain why states were the only organisations that could bail out private organisations and restore economic confidence after the financial crisis starting in 2008. Why, given the magnitude of the crisis and the experience of the Great Depression in the 1930s, did not states take measures to prevent it in the first place?

Further reading

J. Baylis, S. Smith and P. Owens (eds.), *The Globalisation of World Politics: An Introduction to International Relations*. Oxford University Press, 2013. Ch. 25 deals with globalisation, nationalism and the state.

B. Eichengreen and D. Leblang, 'Democracy and globalisation', *Economics & Politics*, 20 (3), 2008: 289–334. (www.nber.org/papers/w12450.pdf). A research article on how globalisation and democracy can act as both cause and effect on each other.

R. King and G. Kendall, *The State, Democracy and Globalisation*. Basingstoke: Palgrave Macmillan, 2003. Presents a concise overview of the development of modern states and democracies.

M. Levi, 'The state of the study of the state', in Ira Katznelson and Helen Milner (eds.), *Political Science: The State of the Discipline*. New York: Norton, 2002: 33–55. A critical evaluation of debates about the notion of the state in contemporary political science.

M. L. van Creveld, *The Rise and Decline of the State*. Cambridge University Press, 1999. Examines how the state came to replace rival forms of political organisation and is now in decline.

L. Weiss, 'The state-augmenting effects of globalisation', *New Political Economy*, 10 (3), 2005: 345–53 (also available on researchgate.net and Google scholar). Presents the argument that globalisation reinforces and augments the state's importance for social life.

Websites

www.freedomhouse.org.
Provides information about democracy and human rights for states of the world.

www.freedom.indiemaps.com.
An interactive website covering large numbers of political indicators and countries.

www.oecd.org.
Official Website of the Organisation for Economic Co-operation and Development (OECD). It provides information about the OECD and the economic development of its member states.

www.developmentgateway.org.
Provides information about sustainable development and poverty reduction in many developing countries.

www.worldbank.org.
Statistical information about economic, social, political and demographic developments in many states. Provides information about reduction in poverty, etc. and the World Development Indicators (WDIs).

3 Democratic change and persistence

Democratic states appear in many different forms and stages of development, but when we look at the historical growth of **democratisation** we can distinguish three distinct waves. The first, from the mid-nineteenth century to the 1920s, coincided with the rise of the nation-state. The second wave, starting after the Second World War and continuing to the early 1960s, was mainly the result of decolonisation. The

Democratisation: The sustained process of transforming a political system towards more democratic arrangements.

third wave, from about 1975 to the end of the twentieth century, followed the spread of democracy in Latin America and Asia, and the disintegration of the Soviet Union. Although the third wave was expected by some to flow on irresistibly into the twenty-first century, it had died by then because transition to democracy is by no means inevitable or permanent. Some countries have retained their authoritarian or totalitarian regimes, others have created partial, limited or illiberal forms of democracy, and a third group has slipped back from democratic reforms that did not take root. Neither North Korea nor Syria, Saudi Arabia or Sudan seem to be on the way to democracy at all. China and Cuba have frustrated some steps in this direction, and Zimbabwe and Russia have deliberately abolished some democratic institutions and practices. At the end of the twentieth century the third wave of the democratic tide had lost its momentum and, if anything, had reversed itself in some places.

The end of the third wave and the appearance of partial democracies have prompted a change in how political scientists approach democracy and democratisation. The earlier interest was in the way new democracies put down firm roots to become stable, but research has broadened to include states that are partial or failed democracies and those that remain firmly short of full democratic status. The terms 'failed democracy', 'partial democracy' and 'illiberal democracy' have been introduced to deal with the fact that democratisation can be reversed or remain stuck at an incomplete stage.

This chapter discusses democratic change and consolidation, first from the perspective of sustained democratisation: what factors account for the success of the three waves of democratisation? Second, it focuses on the stability of democracy: what makes democracy endure and why do some states fail to achieve full democratic status? Next, the rise of defective democracies and the return of undemocratic rule are considered: are defective democracies really democratic, or do they simply try to cover their failings with false claims and democratic pretensions? But, first, the chapter considers how to measure and compare democracies, a controversial matter in itself.

The major topics in this chapter are:

- transitions to democracy
- the limits of democratisation
- embedded, partial and defective democracies
- theories of democratic change and persistence.

■ Transitions to democracy

As democracy spread across the world in the twentieth century, so it seemed to be the final, natural and inevitable point of political development – history was the story of progress from **authoritarian rule** to democracy. Stein Rokkan (1921–79) examined the transition from authoritarian rule to democracy in very broad terms, in some cases tracing it back centuries to the early formation of states and nations in western Europe (see chapter 1). He stressed the long-drawn-out and changing circumstances of citizens and groups that followed the growth of industrial and urban society. He also included the importance of revolutions, wars and foreign intervention which often brought about rapid change. Each country followed its own path, and just as the rise of the state was a complex historical process with a unique constellation of circumstances in each case, so also was the development of democracy. Once it had been established in some parts of the world, it was easier to copy and then the process could be much quicker, although still difficult and uncertain, and by no means guaranteed. In the 1980s and 1990s there was talk of the 'end of ideology' and 'the end of history', in which it was assumed that

Authoritarian rule: Obedience and submission to authority – that is, the concentration of power in the hands of a leader or elite that is not responsible to parliament. No overt opposition is allowed to compete for power.

democracy was the final, natural and inevitable point of political development, but history now shows that this is not the case.

In spite of these particularities, there are some patterns of democratic transition. One of the most obvious is that democracy is best established in economically developed and industrialised countries. In fact, until recently it was difficult to find a democracy outside the select group of wealthy nations of western Europe, North America, Australia and New Zealand – with the single exception of India. As a result, many authors conclude that economic development and the emergence of a property-owning middle class were essential for democracy. A middle class is thought to be crucial because:

1. This group forms a middle level between the traditional elites (landowners, the military and nobility) and the majority of working people (peasants, artisans, labourers, farm workers).
2. In the struggle to secure their economic position and political power, the rising middle class demands personal freedom and the right to participate in government affairs.
3. Employers also press for education, health care, improved housing and geographical mobility to improve the quality of their workforce. Military leaders pointed out that they could not win wars with illiterate and unhealthy soldiers.
4. The middle class forms its associations and voluntary organisations which form the backbone of civil society that further stimulates democratisation and puts organised pressure on the old ruling class and landed aristocracy.
5. Finally, the middle class, with its demands for stability and predictability in economic and social affairs, had a moderating impact on social conflicts, preferring moderate solutions and rejecting extreme positions.

The shortest summary of this interpretation is: 'no bourgeoisie, no democracy'. This claim does not presume that the middle class is necessarily altruistic or concerned with the fate of others – it shows only that this class favoured democracy for reasons that were not necessarily self-interested.

Convincing as economic explanations of democratisation might be at first sight, a number of complications are obvious:

- Deviating cases are easy to find and cast doubts on the general validity of the relationship. Germany was economically highly developed, but succumbed to Nazi dictatorship in 1933. India is a deviant case of a poor, but democratic country. It seems that economic development is conducive to democracy, but that is not the whole story.
- A close correspondence of economic development and democracy does not mean that the former causes the latter. There might be a common background variable such as a religion, the absence of a peasant class or a set of historical events that cause both democracy and economic development. Protestantism has been picked out for its special role in promoting both economic development and democracy, because early Protestants

saw wealth as a sign of God's favour and believed that every individual was equal in the sight of God.

- Economic development is a broad concept which covers a large number of complex processes (such as industrialisation, urbanisation, stratification, bureaucratisation and rising levels of wealth, literacy and education). It is unclear how each of these contributes exactly to democracy.
- Even if economic development is conducive to the early stages of transition to democracy, it does not follow that economic factors count for its consolidation.

Explanations of political phenomena relying on economic forces always run the risk of being one-sided. So, too, do explanations relying entirely on the power of political structures and institutions. States with perfectly good constitutions, and even those with an array of democratic institutions, have failed to sustain democratic practices. Democracy cannot be reduced to the material conditions of economic development, or to the institutional apparatus of the state, because the wishes, demands and expectations of people also have to be taken into account. In a seminal article on the 'social requisites of democracy' published in 1959, Seymour Martin Lipset (1922–2006) stressed the importance of economic factors for democracy, but he also pointed out that the ideas and values of citizens on the one hand, and the ability of the political system to satisfy citizen needs and demands on the other, are also important.

In other words, the ideal as well as the material interests of citizens matter for democracy, and this means investigating the importance of ideas in human affairs – ideas about liberty, equality, justice and the good life. The simple approach of explaining structures in terms of ideas and, vice versa, of explaining ideas in terms of structures or economics, is unsatisfactory. For these reasons, an explanation of democratisation must take a more inclusive approach. This can be done by looking more closely at the three waves of democratisation.

If combinations of economic, social and cultural factors are important for the spread of democracy, it is unclear which combinations are sufficient, and different combinations may work best in different times and places. This idea is implicit in the book *The Third Wave: Democratization in the Late Twentieth Century* by the American political scientist Samuel P. Huntington (1927–2008), published in 1991. He shows that democratisation proceeds not as a continuous process, but in surges and reversals – a kind of ebb and flow or two-steps-forwards, one-step-back process. In each 'wave' a relatively large number of non-democratic states make their first moves towards democracy:

- The first wave is very long and covers the second half of the nineteenth and the first part of the twentieth century. It was long because inventing something takes time; copying it is quicker. In this period, some Western nation-states were transformed into mass democracies, but apart from the common processes of economic development and nation building, many peculiar historical factors are needed to explain the differences between democratisation in, say, Britain, Germany and Sweden. In this period around thirty democracies, depending on how they are defined and measured, were established but not all made the transition permanent, and the first wave ends with the fascist reversals of Italy in the 1920s, and later in Spain, Portugal and Germany.

- The second wave is much shorter and starts with the end of the Second World War. In the direct aftermath of the war, many states were newly founded (for instance, Yugoslavia, and West and East Germany), a large number gaining independence with decolonisation, sometimes bitterly fought for, sometimes less violent (for instance Indonesia, India and Algeria). Quite a number of these newly founded states tried to implement democratic rule, but not all managed it, and the second wave depended on political and economic opportunities as well as on colonial legacies and local cultures. Sometimes ethnic and religious divisions were too deep to overcome, and sometimes foreign support was crucial, West Germany and Japan being notable examples. The second wave ebbed away when some countries reverted to authoritarian rule in the 1960s (for example, Greece, Brazil, Argentina, Nigeria).

- The third wave started in the mid-1970s and faded away at the end of the twentieth century. In this period, some of the non-democratic countries of Latin America and Asia were democratised, frequently on the basis of mass movements opposing ruling cliques and autocrats (for example, in South Korea and the Philippines). The disintegration of the Soviet Union resulted in an additional growth of democratic states in central and eastern Europe. Here, too, mass pressure and the unity of opposition groups played a decisive role (for instance, in Poland, Ukraine and Hungary). The European Union has played a similar role to the post-1945 allies in supporting democratisation in central and eastern Europe.

Whereas democracy was a minority phenomenon until recently and mainly limited to north-western Europe and North America, the third wave changed this situation. By the end of the twentieth century democracy had reached every part of the world, South America, all of western and central Europe, and considerable parts of Asia included. Yet, since 2006, no increase in the number of democratic states can be observed. Even if we include the countries that are not full democracies, but limited to the much more restricted form of 'electoral democracy', a ceiling seems to have been reached of about 60 per cent of the total in the world. The Arab Spring of 2010 did little to increase the 60 per cent figure. In that year a wave of revolutionary movements across north Africa and the Middle East promised to bring an end to military and authoritarian government. Some were initially successful in removing leaders from power, but not in establishing and sustaining democracy. Others were crushed by military force and in the end, spring turned to a long winter of civil disturbance, civil wars, economic decline and massive movements of refugees – all testifying to the difficulties of successful transition.

Two conclusions seem to be in order. First, the three waves of expansion are characterised by different processes, and the same explanations do not work for all of them. Second, just as there is no general explanation for the three waves, so also there is no general explanation for the periods of decline and stagnation that have followed them. Democracy can be reached along many paths, and it can falter or fail in different ways as well. One classic example is described in briefing 3.1.

Briefing 3.1

Uruguay: (eventually) a success story

For much of its history, the territory now known as Uruguay was fought over by Portugal, Spain, Britain, Argentina and Brazil, becoming an independent state with a population of around 75,000 in 1828. There followed 157 years of war, military coups, civil wars, invasions, naval blockages, a siege of Montevideo lasting nine years and military dictatorships with liberal periods in between them. Nevertheless, in this period, the population grew (with many Italian and Spanish immigrants), as did the economy and a stratum of middle-class business people who organised a network of voluntary associations to form the beginnings of a civil society. Such organisations are believed to be an important platform for the development of democracy, and with them the Uruguayan middle class succeeded in gaining a modest degree of political influence and inclusion. In spite of more civil wars in the early twentieth century, the country developed economically and politically, even introducing some welfare schemes and governments representing a variety of interests. This was reversed once again by a new dictatorship and a period of instability and economic hardship following the great depression of 1933. The country then swung between dictatorship, civilian–military government and limited democracy until, in the 1960s, the country suffered acute economic problems caused by a downturn in world trade in foodstuffs and by the urban guerrilla movement known as the Tupamaros. A new military president used the army to defeat the Tupamaros and seized political power in 1973. The regime remained in control for the next twelve years, using torture, imprisonment and murder to maintain its control.

In 1984 more economic problems, widespread protests and a failed referendum for a new constitution (signalling popular refusal to accept an authoritarian system) led to the regime proposing civilian government. This was elected in 1985 and it managed to consolidate democracy, introduce economic and social reforms and weathered more economic problems. In the next years, the country managed to pass a series of crucial tests of changing government peacefully by democratic election, and this became standard procedure by the end of the century. In 2009, a new president was elected who had spent fifteen years in prison during the dictatorship. His government passed reforms including gay marriage, the legalisation of abortion and decriminalisation of marijuana.

The explanation of Uruguay's transition to democracy is a subject of controversy, but it helps that the country had a high rate of literacy and was comparatively wealthy, in spite of periodic economic problems. It also helps that it had a substantial and organised middle class, and that 1985 was not so much democratisation as a re-democratisation after periods of limited democracy in the twentieth century. Uruguay was one of the first Latin American countries to enfranchise males, in 1918.

The circumstances of the transition in 1985 were also special. A large civilian coalition negotiated a phased introduction of elections and of civilian government with the military, after which the soldiers were able to retire to their parade grounds with a sense of security provided by an amnesty from prosecution for their crimes while in power. The victims of military rule were also awarded reparations. Some analysts argue that democracy brings risks and uncertainty to groups that are protected by dictatorship and that, somehow, their fears must be settled. The new civilian government managed this problem with great success. It also helped the transition that the first elected government did not have an absolute majority and the outcome was a coalition government of national unity. Finally, unlike many new democracies which tend to suffer from economic decline immediately after reform, Uruguay managed to maintain and improve its economy.

This complex mixture of factors contributing to democratic transition is particular to Uruguay, but elements of it are common to other examples of democratic success – a literate and comparatively prosperous middle class, an amnesty for the military and compensation for its victims, national wealth, experience of partial democracy in previous eras, a common and unified civilian front and a government of national unity.

In 2014, Uruguay ranked seventeenth in the Democracy Index, marginally behind the UK and marginally ahead of the USA, Japan, Spain and France. In the Freedom House study, Uruguay scores the highest marks for political and civil rights (see table 2.2).

■ The limits of democratisation

What are the chances that new democracies survive their initial transformation? What makes them endure? Democratisation is a process that takes some time. It is not achieved by a single leap into a new form of government. Several phases can be discerned between the breakdown of an old system and the **consolidation** of the new one:

> **Consolidation:** Process of maturing and stabilising a new political system by strengthening and institutionalising its basic arrangements.

- *Initial phase* Opposition towards the ruling elite and undemocratic arrangements are mobilised; demands for more liberty are broadly accepted and generally seen as the main goal of political reform. Mass peaceful opposition is sometimes more effective than violence, which often provokes repression, although peaceful protest is sometimes met with force and bloodshed.
- *Emerging phase* The old, undemocratic arrangements no longer function and new ones are set up; liberty is still the main common concern; a new constitution is declared and general elections are introduced for the first time; return to the old system is possible, but no longer easy.
- *Advanced phase* Liberty is now taken for granted and attention shifts towards the achievements of the new democracy; providing liberty is no longer sufficient; group interests have to be satisfied; economic and public service performance become important; there is increasing stress on equality of rights and opportunities.
- *Phase of consolidation* The new arrangements are institutionalised and the system is able to meet the demands and expectations of large parts of the population. A balance of liberty and equality is reached and broadly accepted.

It is clear from this that successful democratisation depends on many factors and that progress can be slowed, halted or reversed at any stage. Moreover, the important factors prompting development can change at each stage. Whereas formal rights, especially voting rights, are decisive in the early phases, the satisfaction of material demands is more important later. For the endurance of democracy, then, economic stability turns out to be important once again. New democracies can be jeopardised by large or growing inequalities: if the rich get richer and the poorer suffer, democratic arrangements are less likely to survive the third phase. This is not to say that people forget about political principles in favour of economic performance. On the contrary, even if material and economic conditions worsen, citizens may defer gratification and maintain their support for democracy, as they did in some post-communist countries of central Europe.

Even if the starting point of democratisation can be easily identified – the end of a war, the expulsion of a dictator, a popular uprising, the first democratic constitution – consolidation can be slow and nothing can be taken for granted until democratic principles are widely supported and entrenched in daily political life. Many aspects of the old non-democratic practices may live on during transition: senior people in the old elite remain in office, and social and economic problems and inequalities may persist in new democracies. Corruption is deeply rooted in some countries and international organisations, and it is a corrosive condition that is difficult to remove. Citizens may evaluate their political system in terms of its performance, and if it fails over the long run, they may turn into 'unsatisfied democrats' who retain a strong belief in democracy, but believe that their own system of government fails to meet their expectations. In the long run, no system can survive if many people are seriously dissatisfied.

Dividing the process of democratisation into different phases, and then identifying the different factors that operate in each phase, helps us deal with the many different routes to democratic consolidation. Yet concentrating on how countries eventually reach a state of advanced and stable democracy runs the risk of assuming that this is an inevitable and preordained development that all countries will naturally follow. It should not be assumed that undemocratic and unconsolidated systems are like small children that inevitably grow up and mature. Theories of 'the end of ideology' and 'the end of history' in the 1980s and 1990s seem to assume this, but history shows it to be wrong. There are many twists and turns on the roads to democracy and some paths lead back to autocracy or to a dead end of defective democracy before the destination is reached.

■ Embedded, partial and defective democracies

When a country has the full array of characteristics of a democracy and when these are sustained for a period of time, say three successive national elections, it is known as '**embedded democracy**'. But not all democracies are like this. No democracy is perfect and all have defects of one kind or another, but some are missing one or more of the necessary features of embedded democracy (see figure 3.1). They have been variously described as illiberal democracies, pseudo-democracies, limited democracies, electoral democracies, defective democracies and diminished democracies. These terms point to something missing, but how they are labelled depends on what it is. The main examples are as follows.

> **Embedded democracy:** A consolidated and stable system that is founded on a well-developed civil society, secure civil and political rights, a set of autonomous institutions of government that act within the rule of law, a system of free and fair elections, and a government with effective power to perform its duties.

1. *Incomplete suffrage* Where some groups are excluded from voting rights (e.g. Switzerland until 1971, when women were given voting rights, and the USA and Northern Ireland until recently, when all ethnic and religious groups were given full voting rights). Where suffrage is limited, it is sometimes called limited, male or oligarchic democracy.
2. *Free electoral competition* Where one or more political groups is excluded from elections. These have been called limited, controlled or one-party democracies.
3. *Civil liberties* Where political liberties such as freedom of speech or association are limited or where the rule of law is not observed for all cases. These have been called electoral, hard or illiberal democracies.
4. *Ineffective government* Where government is unable to perform its proper role because anti-democratic forces are powerful. Sometimes this is the army, sometimes it is a church or religious group, and sometimes it is a traditional group of aristocrats, business interests or landowners. The terms 'guarded', 'tutelary' and 'protected' democracy have been used to describe such cases.

Figure 3.1: Partial democracies: examples of diminished sub-types

1. Diminished from procedural minimum definition

(1a)	(1b)	(1c)
Missing attribute:	Missing attribute:	Missing attribute:
Full suffrage	Full contestation	Civil liberties
– Limited Democracy	– Controlled Democracy	– Electoral Democracy
– Male Democracy	– De facto One-Party Democracy	– Hard Democracy
– Oligarchical Democracy		– Illiberal Democracy
	– Restrictive Democracy	

2. Diminished from expanded procedural minimum definition

Missing attribute: Elected government has effective power to govern

– Guarded Democracy

– Protected Democracy

– Tutelary Democracy

In other cases, democracies are flawed because while they take seriously the procedural rules for elections, the rule of law, civil rights, and so on, the government is unable to perform its proper role, because anti-democratic forces are powerful. Sometimes this is the army, sometimes it is a church or religious group, and sometimes it is a traditional group of aristocrats, business interests or landowners. Democratic failures of these kinds do not always occur in the early 'nursery school' stages of democratisation. They may emerge later when old elites reverse the process or, indeed, when new elites protect their privileges by cancelling elections or suppressing oppositions (see briefing 3.2).

It might seem that flawed democracies suffer from relatively minor problems that can be cured by reform, but the argument is that democracy consists, at a minimum, of a complete set of necessary characteristics, not a few of them. One flaw cannot be regarded as a slight blemish in the complete thing. It is like a bucket with a hole in it or a car that is in perfect working order apart from a flat tyre. One failing undermines the whole arrangement and therefore these countries form a separate sub-type of **defective democracies**. Nor is defective democracy necessarily a phase on the road to embedded democracy. Some countries stay stuck in the phase and show no sign of maturing into the full state.

Defective democracies: Systems of government that are neither democratic nor undemocratic, but maintain some democratic characteristics as well as some undemocratic ones that damage and disrupt the institutional logic of embedded democracy.

There are many reasons why a given country might stumble along the way to democracy, regressing a little or failing seriously. The phase model of democratic consolidation suggests some of the causes. In the first phases, agreement has to be reached about how new liberties and rights are organised and how decision making is carried out. Large or strong minority groups that are not satisfied with their treatment may have the power to veto or limit such reforms. In the later phases of transition, the economic achievements of the new democracy and confidence in its future performance can be crucial, and

Briefing 3.2

Expediency takes the place of democracy
After general elections in Zimbabwe and in Kenya in 2008, the ruling presidents refused to step down. In both countries a period of severe violence with many deaths ended as negotiations between the ruling party and the opposition started.

In Zimbabwe, as was the case in Kenya earlier this year, a government of unity is being pushed as an emergency measure to stop violence and a spiral down toward civil war. After peace is restored, the thinking

goes, truth and reconciliation commissions, constitutional reforms, and finally democracy, will follow. But this is a pipe dream. A government that does not respect the people's vote will not concede power down the line. And an opposition that does not stand for the people, and for democracy when it matters most, is easily appeased with a nice chunk of the national cake.

MukomaWaNgugi, 'Zimbabwe's misguided talks', International Herald Tribune, 25 July 2008.

since it is not unusual for new democracies to fail expectations, it is not unusual for hopes to turn sour.

Although half the global population lived in a democracy of sorts in 2015, recent years have seen a failure of popular movements or a weakening or reversal of reforms. Table 3.1 shows that the list of such cases is a long one. There is no sign of a fourth wave of democratisation on the horizon at present. On the contrary, in many cases there is, if anything, a decline of confidence in democratic institutions and trust in political leaders. The financial crash of 2008 has not helped matters. Even in the full and embedded democracies,

Table 3.1 Breakdowns of democracies, 2000–2014

Year of breakdown	Country	Year of return	Type of breakdown
2000	Fiji	–	Military coup
2000	Russia	–	Executive degradation, violation of opposition rights
2001	Cent. Af. Rep.	–	Military rebellion, violence, human rights abuses
2002	Guinea-Bissau	2005	Executive degradation, violation of opposition rights (military coup the following year)
2002	Nepal	2013	Rising political instability, monarchical coup
2004	Venezuela	–	Executive degradation, violation of opposition rights
2005	Thailand	2011	Military coup, then military constraint
2006	Solomon Islands	–	Decline of democratic process
2007	Bangladesh	2008	Military 'soft coup'
2007	Philippines	2010	Executive degradation
2007	Kenya	–	Electoral fraud and executive abuse
2008	Georgia	2012	Electoral fraud and executive abuse
2009	Honduras	2013	Military intervention
2009	Madagascar	–	Unconstitutional assumption of power by opposition; suspension of elected parliament
2009	Niger	2011	Presidential dissolution of Constitutional Court and National Assembly to extend presidential rule
2010	Burundi	–	Electoral fraud, opposition boycott, political closure
2010	Sri Lanka	–	Executive degradation
2010	Guinea-Bissau	–	Military intervention, weakening civilian control, deteriorating rule of law
2012	Maldives	–	Forcible removal of democratically elected president
2012	Mali	2014	Military coup
2011	Nicaragua	–	Executive degradation
2012	Ukraine	2014	Electoral fraud (parliamentary elections), executive abuse
2014	Turkey	–	Executive degradation, violation of opposition rights
2014	Bangladesh	–	Breakdown of electoral process
2014	Thailand	–	Military coup

Larry Diamond, 'Facing Up to the Democratic Recession', *Journal of Democracy*, 26(1), 2015: 145.

there has been a notable decline of political confidence and trust in some countries, though there is no evidence of loss of faith in democracy as the best form of government. The danger for transitional states is the belief that democracy has failed to deliver its promised benefits.

The good news is that democracies are able to rely on their initial consolidation as a significant factor for further development: democracies are clearly more likely to survive if they have already lasted a while. In spite of all the difficulties and dangers that can threaten a new democracy, the fact remains that democracy has spread and become firmly rooted in many parts of the globe.

■ Theories of democratic change

Democratic transformation and consolidation are complex processes that are not easily explained and are difficult to generalise about. The starting point for many approaches is the observation that – so far –democracy can only be found in countries with a capitalist market economy. For a long time, the seminal work of Seymour Martin Lipset focused the debates on the importance of economic development as a necessary precondition for democracy. The more recent focus on **modernisation** theory takes a broader approach. This argues that economic and technological developments are closely linked and result in fundamental

> **Modernisation:** The dual processes of technological and economic development and the societal responses to these changes.

changes in every area of society (for example, industrialisation, urbanisation, social and geographical mobility, and education), including the ways that people think about themselves and the social, economic and political world around them. Modernisation theory stresses the interactions between social, economic and political factors, rather than the primacy of economic development. In this sense, democracy may be both a cause and consequence of economic development. Usually, the rise of the middle class is seen as crucial for democracy – and a large and strong middle class is the result of the manifold processes called modernisation.

Although modernisation theory is a good starting point for explanations of democratic transformation and consolidation, it is clear that the theory relies heavily on European experience and is too broad and general to provide us with exact explanations for democratisation. Many aspects of modernisation (changing class structure, growing literacy and skills, spread of wealth and so on) are clearly important for democratisation. But why would we refer to a rather vague theory of modernisation when transformations towards democracy might be explained in more concrete and specific ways such as, say, changing class structures, GDP growth or growing literacy? Apparently, the highly generalised nature of modernisation theory comes with a cutting edge that is too blunt to dissect particular cases.

Broadly speaking, two alternative approaches are available. Both accept the basic idea of modernisation theory that technological and economic developments are highly relevant for democratisation. Both attempt to avoid a European bias and try to specify the exact mechanisms that lead to democratic transformations and consolidation. Cultural theories stress the fact that the expectations and demands of citizens are crucial for democracy. The basis for this approach has been laid out by Gabriel Almond (1911–2002) and Sidney Verba (1932–) in *The Civic Culture*, published in 1963. In their view, democracy can only survive when political institutions are matched with citizens with a mixture of political and social values. These include pride in one's government and the expectation of being treated correctly by it, social and political trust, and a culture of political participation and interest. A democracy will survive with a mixture of pragmatism and commitment – not with the requirement that average citizens are expected to be intensely involved in politics all the time, but with the idea that citizens can always participate if they wish and that their opinions will be heard by government. Since Almond and Verba's publication, many different cultural theories have been presented, all characterised by the idea that the social and political orientations of citizens are crucial for democracy (see chapter 9).

Cultural theories have been criticised for neglecting the institutions of society. Institutional theory argues that citizens do not develop their attitudes and behaviour in a vacuum or by sitting down and working them out for themselves. They respond to the possibilities, opportunities and restrictions created by the institutional framework of government and politics. If the civil rights of freedom of assembly and association are protected, then citizens can form groups and political parties. If courts are independent of government, citizens will be more likely to form peaceful opposition parties and to develop a sense of allegiance to the state. If the rule of law is applied to all, individuals are more likely to trust and cooperate with each other and their government for mutual benefit. If government and its institutions are free of corruption, then citizens are more likely to engage with civic affairs, to participate in political life and pay their taxes. Institutional theories emphasise the relevance of these institutional arrangements for democracy, and especially for democratic transformation and consolidation. Institutional theories are based on the idea that people make certain choices and develop certain attitudes and values because alternatives are made available by democratic institutions of government and politics. We will revisit this argument in the next chapter.

■ What have we learned?

This chapter has dealt with democratic transition and consolidation. It has also examined democratic failure and defective democracy. The chapter shows that:

- Democracy is difficult to define and measure and, therefore, difficult to compare. Hence there are various empirical scales and indices, and although these differ in detail, their results generally coincide a good deal.

- There have been three major waves of democratisation. The first was from the mid nineteenth century to the 1920s and occurred mainly in western Europe, North America, and Australia and New Zealand. The second started after the Second World War, with the redrawing of state boundaries and then a period of decolonisation, mainly in Africa and Asia. The third, lasting from about 1975 to the end of the twentieth century, involved the spread of democracy in parts of Latin America and Asia, and the collapse of the Soviet Empire in central and eastern Europe.
- Democratisation is not historically inevitable and its progress cannot be taken for granted. Some countries have never created democratic forms of government, some have partially succeeded, and some have failed and slipped back into dictatorship and autocracy. Some have successfully made the full transition to democracy, others are stuck in a form of defective democracy.
- In spite of all the obstacles in the path of successful transition to full democracy, almost half the world now lives in a country with a form of one kind or another of it.
- Some theories of democratisation stress the importance of political culture and of citizens' attitudes and behaviour; others stress the importance of institutions and structures that encourage certain ways of thinking and behaving. Among the more specific factors said to be associated with the development of democracy are economic development and literacy, a middle class with its own voluntary associations, an emerging civil society that is independent of government control, and a democratic political culture that matches and sustains democratic institutions.
- Other theories emphasise particular historical events such as the redrawing of state boundaries at the end of war, economic depression, and decolonisation.

■ Lessons of comparison

- Just as there are different routes to state formation, so there are also different pathways to democracy. No two countries follow exactly the same path, but there are some general patterns.
- Economic development is an important factor, though not the whole story. Not all economically developed countries are democratic and some democracies are poor.
- The process of democratic consolidation can be divided into phases. In the early phases, the creation of institutions that guarantee freedom, civil rights and the rule of law are important. Later, these are taken for granted and economic performance and social and economic equality become more important.
- Economic and social inequalities have threatened democratic consolidation in some countries.

- Comparison across space and time show that defective democracy is not a temporary state but can last a long time and can take different forms – hence the many different words to describe them.

Projects

1. Do democracies that have lasted for a while survive thereafter?
2. Discuss the statement, 'Every democracy is a deficient democracy but not every democracy is a flawed democracy.'
3. Comment on the statement, 'No bourgeoisie, no democracy?' Is it possible to have a bourgeoisie and no democracy?
4. Where does your country rank in the Freedom House and Democracy Index measures and do you agree with this ranking and measurement? How would you improve on it?

Further reading

D. Berg-Schlosser (ed.), *Democratization. The State of the Art*. Wiesbaden: VS Verlag, 2004. Summarises the academic debates about democratisation from different points of view.

L. Diamond, *The Spirit of Democracy: The Struggle to Build Free Societies throughout the World*. New York: Holt, 2008. A comprehensive, excellent and accessible overview of the many aspects of democratisation around the world.

'Is Democracy in Decline?' Twenty-fifth anniversary issue of *Journal of Democracy*, 26 (1), January 2015.

J. Markoff, 'Transitions to Democracy', in T. Janoski, R. R. Alford, A. M. Hicks and M. A. Schwartz (eds.), *The Handbook of Political Sociology*. Cambridge University Press, 2005. A good general discussion of the transition to democracy.

W. Merkel, 'Embedded and defective democracies', *Democratization*, 11 (5), 2004: 33–58. Elaborates on the distinction between embedded and defective democracies, and the failings and persistence of the latter.

NCCR Democracy, H.-P. Kriesi and L. Müller (eds.), *Democracy: An Ongoing Challenge*. Zurich: Lars Müller Publishers, 2014. An illustrated collection of essays on the many images of democracy and their historical changes.

C. Welzel, *Freedom Rising: Human Empowerment and the Quest for Emancipation*. Cambridge University Press, 2013. The most extensive empirical analysis available of cultural and political changes and a detailed explanation of the spread of democracy around the world.

Websites

www.freedomhouse.org.
Provides information about democracy and human rights for each state of
the world.
www.ned.org/research.
Website of the International Forum for Democratic Studies, providing information for anyone interested in democracy and democratisation.
www.participedia.net/en.
Website of the global community of democracy researchers focusing on
crowd-source data on democratic innovations from around the world.
See briefing 2.2 for further websites with information about democratic
developments and the extensive list of links to websites on democracy:
www.democracybarometer.org/links_en.html.

PART II

The polity: structures and institutions

Part I of this book considered the nature and development of the modern democratic state in general terms. Part II looks more closely at internal structures and institutions – sometimes referred to as the 'machinery of state' or the 'nuts and bolts of government', because they are the permanent structures of the political system. They are important because they set the framework within which individuals and organisations behave in everyday political life. In this sense we can distinguish between government, with its formal structures and institutions, on the one hand, and politics, with its political behaviour and processes, on the other. Following this distinction, Part II concentrates on structures and institutions of government, while Part III focuses on the political behaviour of individuals, groups and organisations. Although this is a convenient and useful way of dividing up the book, we should not forget that structures influence and mould behaviour, just as much as behaviour helps to create structures – the two are simply different sides of the same coin.

Chapter 4 deals with the constitutional framework of modern democracies. Constitutions are sometimes overlooked in modern comparative politics, but the fact is that they are enormously important. They try to grapple with the basic problem of all democracies – how to balance the necessary powers of the state against the individual rights of citizens, and how to ensure that government does not become too powerful and remains responsible and accountable to its citizens. Constitutions are the blueprints of power in democracies.

Chapter 5 turns to the three main branches of most democratic governments – the executive, legislative and judicial branches. It shows how, in spite of the bewildering variety of constitutional arrangements, most states fall into one of two general types, either presidential or parliamentary systems, and how these work in practice.

Chapter 6, on multi-level government, looks at how government is divided in a different way. Few states are so small that they can be ruled by a single centre of national government. Most democracies are divided geographically with national government sitting on top of layers of regional, local and community government. Similarly, no democratic state can run its own affairs as if it were an island on its own. All have arrangements, agreements and treaties with other sovereign states. Chapter 6, therefore, examines multi-level government from the global and the international down to the local community.

Chapter 7 considers the two most important functions of government – the executive and the legislative. These two overlap to a considerable extent, but the executive is primarily responsible for executing (that is, carrying out) the affairs of state and the policies of the government, while the legislative is mainly concerned with representing the views of citizens, turning them into laws and keeping a watching brief on the executive.

Finally, Chapter 8 examines the administrative backbone of the state – the public bureaucracy. Bureaucrats are important, and potentially enormously powerful, because politicians rely heavily on the people who staff the government ministries to run the daily business of government.

The five chapters of Part II of the book, therefore, examine the main structures and institutions of government:

- constitutions
- presidential and parliamentary government
- multi-level government
- policy making and legislating
- implementation.

4   Constitutions

Although the citizens of a given state may feel that theirs is the only or the best way of doing things, there is nothing natural or God-given about having a president rather than a prime minister, a unitary rather than a federal system, or two legislative assemblies rather than one. In fact, it is probably true to say that every modern democracy (chapter 2) has a unique set of government institutions. It is certainly true that there is no agreed formula or set of institutions that will produce a democracy; each country follows its own special path and makes its own particular arrangements.

The particular configuration of institutions in any given state is defined by its **constitution**. This is the most basic set of laws, establishing the shape and form of the political structure. We start this chapter, therefore, by considering the nature and purpose of constitutions – what they are and why we have them. Constitutions try to create a complex set of checks and balances – checks on the power of any one part of the system, and a balance of power between all of them. The basic idea is that power should be limited and therefore spread. We then introduce the three main branches of government – the executive, the legislature and the judiciary – and outline their basic purpose and design. Constitutions, however, are only the beginning, not the end, of the story of comparative politics, so we also discuss the limits of constitutionalism and why it is necessary to go beyond formal laws to understand how democracies work in practice. Finally,

> **Constitution:** A set of fundamental laws that determines the central institutions and offices, and powers and duties of the state.

we consider various theories of political institutions and how they help us to understand the structure and operations of the modern state.

The major topics in this chapter are:

- what a constitution is, and why we have them
- the division of powers
- the limits of constitutionalism
- constitutional and institutional theories.

■ What a constitution is, and why we have them

In some respects government is like a game: before the players can even take to the field to compete, they need to agree on a set of rules that decide how the game is to be played. Constitutions are the rules of the political game – who can vote, who can stand for office, what powers they are to have, the rights and duties of citizens and so on. Without these basic rules politics would degenerate into arbitrariness, brute force or anarchy. If the rules work well, we tend to take them for granted and concentrate on the day-to-day game of politics, just as we take the rules of our favourite sport for granted and concentrate on today's match. Nonetheless, constitutions are important because they have a profound influence over how the game of politics is played, and therefore over the outcome of the game – who gets what, and when? For this reason, some theories of politics place great importance on constitutions, and on the political institutions that they create and shape.

Constitutions are sets of laws, but they are very special ones that lay out the most important institutions and offices of the state and define their formal powers (see briefings 4.1 and 4.2). Consequently, they have four main features:

1. *Fundamental laws* Constitutions are laws about the political procedures to be followed in making laws. They are supreme laws, taking precedence over all others and defining how all the others should be made. Some analysts call them 'meta-rules' (rules about how to make rules), but the German constitution calls them 'the Basic Law'.
2. *Entrenched status* Constitutions have a special legal status. Unlike other laws, constitutions usually state the conditions under which the constitution can itself be changed. These conditions are often very demanding in ways that are intended to make sure that the change is not hasty or undemocratic, and that it has widespread support.
3. *Codified document* Constitutions are written down, often in a single document that presents the constitution in a systematic manner.
4. *Allocation of powers* Constitutions outline the proper relations between institutions and offices of the state, and between government and citizens. This is probably the most crucial part, because it allocates powers and functions to government and specifies the *rights and duties* of governments and citizens – who can do what, to whom, and under what circumstances.

Briefing 4.1

Constitutions

Constitutions vary so much that no two are likely to be the same in any particular respect. Some are long and detailed (India's has 444 articles in 22 parts, 12 schedules and 118 amendments, and in English translation totals 117,369 words), some short (the USA's has seven articles and twenty-seven amendments). Many are general, but others try to specify the kind of society and political system to which they aspire – Sweden's sets out specific regulations for social security and labour laws, Japan's renounces war and Croatia's states that some rights can be restricted in case of war. Some are contained in a single document, some refer to other documents or to international agreements such as the UN Declaration of Human Rights (1948). Some have been changed comparatively frequently, others rarely. Some are old, some new. In a few cases, the constitution is said to be unwritten (Britain and Israel), but, in fact, it is better to refer to them as 'uncodified', because while much is written down, it is not consolidated in one main document.

It is easy to obtain the constitution of every nation in the world from websites (see the end of this chapter), so no examples are provided here. In spite of their huge variety, most constitutions fall into four main parts:

- *Preamble* The preamble tends to be a declaration about nationhood and history, with references to important national events, symbols and aspirations. The preamble tends to be inspirational rather than legal or rational.
- *Fundamental rights (Bill of Rights)* A list of civil and political rights and statements about the limits of government powers. Some constitutions refer also to economic, social and cultural rights. Many of the newer constitutions simply adopt the 1948 UN Universal Declaration of Human Rights.
- *Institutions and offices of government* The main structures or institutions of government are described, together with their powers and duties. Usually this means the executive, legislative and judicial branches of national government, and sometimes lower levels of government as well.
- *Amendment* The procedures to be followed in amending the constitution.

Because constitutions are so important, they are often the focus of fierce political battles between different groups who want to frame the rules according to their own interests or beliefs. Democratic constitutions therefore try to impose rules that are fair and impartial to all groups and interests in society, so that all can compete on a 'level playing field'. They try to do this by incorporating a set of seven basic principles:

1. *Rule of law* According to Albert V. Dicey (1835–1922), the nineteenth-century British constitutional theorist, the rule of law underlies the idea of constitutionalism. The rule of law, not the arbitrary rule of powerful individuals, is the hallmark of democracy.
2. *Transfer of power* Democracies are marked by a peaceful transfer of power from one set of leaders or parties to another. Democratic constitutions typically state the conditions for this – how and when government is to be elected, by whom and for how long. The peaceful transfer

Briefing 4.2

The constitutions of Argentina, France and Japan

Argentina

Type of government	Presidential republic: federal state.
Date of constitution	1853, revised 1994
Head of state	President
Executive	Cabinet appointed by President
Legislature	Bicameral National Congress
	Senate: 72 directly elected, six-year term, half every three years. Chamber of Deputies: 275 directly elected, four-year term, half every two years
Judiciary	Judicial review by Supreme Court
Sub-national government	23 provinces and one autonomous city (the Federal Capital of Buenos Aires)

France

Type of government	Republic: unitary state
Date of constitution	1958, amended in 1962, and in 1992, 1996 and 2000 to comply with EU requirements, and in 2000 to reduce presidential term of office from seven to five years
Executive	Head of State: President, directly elected. Head of Government: Prime Minister nominated by National Assembly majority and appointed by President. Cabinet appointed by President at suggestion of Prime Minister
Legislature	Bicameral
	Senate: 321 seats, indirectly elected for nine years, one-third every three years
	National Assembly: 577 seats, directly elected for five years
Judiciary	Supreme Court of Appeal plus Constitutional Council for constitutional matters
Sub-national government	22 regions, 96 departments

Japan

Type of government	Unitary state with constitutional monarch and parliamentary government
Date of constitution	1947

Head of state	Emperor
Executive	Prime Minister. Cabinet appointed by Prime Minister
Legislature	Bicameral
	House of Councillors: 247 seats, six-year term, half every three years
	House of Representatives: 480 seats, elected for four years
Judiciary	Judicial review of legislation by Supreme Court
Sub-national government	47 prefectures

Source: http://confinder.richmond.edu/

of power is so important that some political scientists define democracy in these terms.

3. ***Separation of powers*** *and checks and balances* According to classical political theory, democracy is best protected by creating separate branches of government with different functions and powers, each checking and balancing the power of the others.

> **Separation of powers:** The doctrine that political power should be divided among several bodies or officers of the state as a precaution against too much concentration of power.

4. *Relations between government and citizens* At the heart of any democracy is the relationship between citizens and their government, so constitutions often include (or refer to) a Bill of Rights that enumerates the rights and responsibilities of citizens and the limits of government power over them. Constitutions set clear limits on the power of government in order to guarantee the rights of citizens.

5. *Locus of sovereignty* Since there must be a governing body or office capable of making authoritative decisions (see chapter 1), constitutions usually specify who or what is to be the ultimate authority to make and enforce law.

6. *Government accountability* Democratic governments are accountable to their citizens, and constitutions normally try to pin down the mechanisms of this accountability – who is answerable to whom, and under what circumstances.

7. *Final arbiter* Constitutions are sometimes disputed because none is fully clear, consistent, unambiguous, or comprehensive. The last job of a constitution is to say who is to be the final arbiter of its meaning and how it may be changed.

■ The separation of powers

Democratic constitutions attempt to create limited (not autocratic or totalitarian) government that is accountable to, and responsive to the will of, its citizens. According to classical political theory – John Locke (1632–1704),

Montesquieu (1689–1755) and the *Federalist Papers* (1777–8) in the USA – this is best achieved by dividing power between the executive, legislative and judicial branches of government, and by creating checks and balances between them so that no one branch can become too powerful.

Executives

Most large organisations have a person, or small group, to take final decisions, decide policies and take ultimate responsibility. Businesses have company chairmen and chief executive officers (CEOs). Governments have

Executive: The branch of government mainly responsible for initiating government action, making and implementing public policy, and coordinating the activities of the state.

political executives (from the Latin term 'to carry out') who do the same job, and who are usually known as presidents or prime ministers. The **executive** branch of government, being at the top of the political pyramid, performs three main functions:

1. *Decision making* – initiating government action and formulating public policy
2. *Implementation* – executives implement (apply) their policies, which means they must also run the main departments and bureaucracies of state
3. *Coordination* – coordination and integration of the complex affairs of state.

In most modern democracies the executive officer is called a president or prime minister. But, to complicate matters, presidents are not always political executives. For example, both the USA and Germany have presidents, but they do entirely different jobs. In the USA, the elected president is the executive head of government and the head of state, which is an enormously powerful and important position. The German president is a non-executive head of state, but not head of government, and is a largely ceremonial figure who is, in some respects, rather like a constitutional monarch (see briefing 4.3).

Presidential heads of state and government are normally directly elected by popular vote in a national election. In most states the executive presidency is normally held by a single person, but a few countries (Bosnia and Herzegovina, Cyprus and Uruguay) have experimented with joint presidencies, usually unsuccessfully.

Non–executive presidents may be elected or appointed and some are elected directly by popular vote or indirectly by a body that is itself directly elected by popular vote. Surprisingly, quite a few heads of state in established democracies are monarchs – Belgium, Denmark, Japan, the Netherlands, Norway, Spain, Sweden and the UK. This is because these countries have often avoided revolution and adapted slowly to democratic pressures, leaving their kings and queens in place while adapting institutions around them. Apart from the monarchies, non-executive presidential heads of state, performing a largely ceremonial role, are found in Austria, Germany, Greece, Ireland, India, Israel, Japan and Italy.

Briefing 4.3

Heads of state and heads of government

■ Presidential heads of state

- In presidential systems, the directly elected president is both head of state and head of government.
- In parliamentary systems, the head of state is a largely ceremonial function carried out either by a monarch or a president, while the head of government, a position of real power, is normally filled by a prime minister or chancellor.
- Presidential heads of state may be elected or appointed, but presidential heads of government in democracies are always directly elected.
- Surprisingly, quite a few heads of state in established democracies are monarchs – Belgium, Denmark, Japan, Netherlands, Norway, Spain, Sweden and the UK. This is because these countries have often avoided revolution and adapted slowly to democratic pressures, leaving their kings and queens in place while adapting institutions around them.
- Apart from the monarchies, non-executive presidential heads of state, performing a largely ceremonial role, are found in Austria, Germany, Greece, Ireland, India, Israel, Japan and Italy.

■ Presidential heads of government

- Usually the president is a single person, but a few countries (Bosnia-Herzegovina, Cyprus and Uruguay) have experimented with joint presidencies, usually unsuccessfully.
- There are now more than 90 presidential systems of different kinds, making them the most common in the world. Many of them have been formed since 1990, especially in Latin America, where the influence of the USA is felt, and it remains to be seen how many of these will remain presidential if these systems change.
- Presidential systems are found mainly in Latin America, which has been influenced by the USA, and in the new democracies of central and eastern Europe.

Legislatures

Executives are the decision-making branch of government, and **legislatures** are the law-making branch. The term derives from the Latin words 'legis' (law) and 'latio' (bringing). Historically the precursor of modern parliamentary legislatures is probably the Althingi,

> **Legislature:** The branch of government mainly responsible for discussing and passing legislation, and keeping watch on the executive.

the assembly established by Viking settlers in Iceland about a thousand years ago, but they also evolved from the assemblies that medieval monarchs called to agree to some royal action – to levy taxes or wage war. These assemblies started meeting regularly, and eventually came to be elected by all citizens of the state and so they acquired legitimacy as representative parliaments or assemblies. Technically, a legislature is any law-making body, however constituted, but in a democracy the legislature gets its legitimacy from the fact that it is directly and popularly elected by citizens.

Legislatures are known by a variety of names – assemblies, parliaments, houses and chambers – but all amount to much the same thing: they are bodies of elected representatives who meet to discuss public affairs. Basically, parliaments (from the French word 'parler', 'to talk') are 'talking shops'; houses and chambers are the places where assemblies and parliaments meet – the House of Commons, the House of Representatives, the Chamber of Deputies.

Legislatures may be formed by one (unicameral) or two (bicameral) houses. Two houses are usually preferred if specific interests among the population have to be represented explicitly. If we remember that democratic government is already divided between three main branches, one might well ask why the legislative body should be further divided into two chambers, when two may only complicate matters:

- Which of the two is to be the stronger and have the last word if they disagree?
- If the first is elected in a democratic fashion, how is the second to be constituted, and if it is also elected won't it inevitably clash with the first?

For these reasons, there is a great debate about whether unicameralism is better than bicameralism (see controversy 4.1), but it turns out that most democracies are bicameral. This is because it is usually not too difficult to sort out a system that enables two houses to work together effectively. Whatever the abstract and theoretical problems may be, it is generally possible to solve them in a practical way. At the same time, it is also evident that bicameralism is well suited to large countries and those with diverse populations. The larger the country, in terms of population or area or both, the more likely it is to be bicameral. On average, unicameral democracies have populations that are less than half that of bicameral systems.

Strong and weak bicameralism

Bicameral legislatures come in two forms: *weak* and *strong*. In the strong systems, both assemblies are of equal strength, but since this is a recipe for conflict – even deadlock – there are rather few cases of successful strong bicameralism. Many of them are found in federal systems (see chapter 6), including Australia, Belgium, Germany, Switzerland and the USA. Most bicameral systems are 'weak', which means that one assembly is more powerful than the other. To complicate matters the stronger (first chamber) is usually known as the 'lower house', while the weaker (second chamber) is the 'upper house', usually called the Senate. Weak bicameralism is also known as 'asymmetric bicameralism' – that is, the two houses are of unequal power. Typically in weak bicameral systems, the lower house initiates legislation and controls financial matters and the upper house has limited powers to delay and recommend amendments.

Membership of the second house

Since democratic lower chambers are directly elected by the popular vote, many upper chambers are constituted on a different basis. Most are not

CONTROVERSY 4.1

One chamber or two?

Pro-unicameralism	Pro-bicameralism
• Power is mainly located in one assembly. No confusion of roles, responsibilities, or accountability.	• Two chambers provide another set of checks and balances, with powers to delay, criticise, amend, or veto – a constitutional backstop.
• No overlap or duplication between assemblies. Two assemblies can result in rivalry and even deadlock between the two.	• Two forms of representation, usually direct election to the lower chamber, and another form of election (indirect) or appointment to the higher.
• There is room for only one elected, representative body. 'If the second chamber agrees with the first, it is useless; if it disagrees it is dangerous' (Abbé Sieyès).	• A second chamber can reduce the workload of the first by considering legislation in detail, leaving the first chamber to deal with broad issues.
• Most legislatures are unicameral, and the number is increasing. Many new states have adopted unicameralism with apparent success, especially in Africa and the Middle East.	• A majority of democracies have bicameral legislatures – e.g. Australia, Britain, Canada, France, India, Italy, Japan, Mexico, Brazil, the USA, South Africa and Switzerland.
• Unicameralism is particularly suitable for unitary states (three-quarters are unicameral).	• Bicameralism is suited to federal systems, where territorial units of government within the state can be represented at the national level: 80 per cent of bicameral systems are in federal states.
• Costa Rica, Denmark, New Zealand and Sweden have abolished their second chambers, without apparent adverse effects.	• Some claim that the main defence of bicameralism is political – upper chambers are conservative bodies with the job of tempering the actions of the lower house.
• Unicameralism seems to work best in small countries.	• Bicameralism seems to work best in countries that are large or socially and ethnically diverse – it helps to resolve regional conflict.
• Second chambers with appointed members are often criticised as being places where 'has-been politicians' go to die.	• A second chamber offers the opportunity for experienced politicians or non-politicians to be involved in political decision making at some distance.

directly elected by the population as a whole, but are either indirectly elected or appointed, or some combination of both. Some upper chambers, however, are directly elected, usually in federal systems (see chapter 6) but on a different basis from the lower house. Directly elected upper houses are often based on different geographical constituencies.

Tenure and size

The terms of tenure of upper houses are usually different. They are often elected for a longer term of office (five to nine years, rather than the three to five years of lower chambers). Upper chambers sometimes have an older qualifying age, and they are usually much smaller than lower ones.

Judiciaries

The third major branch of government is the judiciary, whose job it is to overlook the implemention of the laws passed by the executive and legislative branches but also to interpret the laws and to decide what is constitutional and what is not. Why should lawyers be mixed up with government and politics? Shouldn't politicians be the final judge of how the constitution should be interpreted? The danger is that the government of the day will try to manipulate matters in its own interests. Therefore, constitutions are, in the words of David Hume (1711–76), a set of 'institutions designed for knaves'. This does not presume that all politicians actually are knaves, but takes full account of the possibility that they might be, and that a constitution needs a safeguard against the possible dangers of politicians regulating themselves.

Judiciary: The branch of government mainly responsible for the authoritative interpretation and application of law.

Since a constitution is primarily a legal document, it is argued that lawyers should be the final arbiter of it. Besides, judges (the **judiciary**) are often thought to be the best independent and incorruptible source of experience and wisdom on constitutional matters. This, in turn, requires judicial independence to protect judges from political interference and from the temptations of corruption. For this reason, judges are often appointed for life and paid well. Some countries have created special constitutional courts, but most use their regular courts.

Judicial review: The binding power of the courts to provide an authoritative interpretation of laws, including constitutional law, and to overturn executive or legislative actions they hold to be illegal or unconstitutional.

In several democracies the interpretation and enforcement of laws is placed in the hand of elected officials, not of judges appointed for life; that is, not all democratic countries accept the principle of **judicial review** of the constitution (e.g. Belgium, Finland, Netherlands, Switzerland). It may be rejected for two main reasons:

1. It is difficult to guarantee the political independence of the judges. In many countries, senior judges are appointed by politicians, and conservative politicians tend to appoint conservative judges while liberal politicians are more likely to appoint liberal ones. Nor are judges entirely immune from the social pressures of public opinion and the mass media. Most importantly, judges usually come from conservative social groups and deliver conservative political judgments. In short, it is claimed that judges are not, or cannot be, neutral.

2. In a democracy, so it is argued, the democratically elected legislature should have responsibility for interpreting the constitution, not an appointed and unrepresentative judiciary.

Judges are involved in more than constitutional law. The meaning of other laws may also be ambiguous and disputed, and sometimes this has political implications – electoral law for example, or tax law with implications that affect government's capacity to raise money for public services. In fact, some legislation is deliberately vague, because it was the only way out of political deadlock between competing groups. In such circumstances, it is the job of the courts to interpret the law and to decide how it should be applied to particular cases. In doing so, the courts may go beyond merely interpreting the law to modify or change it. In this respect, judges can play an important political role as the third branch of government.

Judicial activism

The role of the courts in government is tending to widen. The Supreme Court of the USA was not given power of constitutional review in the 1787 constitution, but successfully claimed it in 1803 when it ruled in the case of *Marbury v. Madison*. The USA then went through two notable periods of **judicial activism** in the 1930s (when it tried to stop Roosevelt's New Deal legislation) and again in the 1950s (when it promoted racial integration).

> **Judicial activism:** Involves the courts taking a broad and active view of their role as interpreters of the constitution and reviewers of executive and legislative action.

In the early 1960s the Court of Justice of the European Communities decided that individuals can invoke European regulations before national courts ('direct effect') and that their ruling had supremacy over decisions by national courts. There is a general tendency now for the courts to take a more active role in government across the democratic world where the judiciary has the right of judicial review. The five main reasons for this are:

- An increasing volume of legislation and government actions
- The increasing complexity of government machinery, which means that there is greater chance of conflict between branches and levels of government, especially in federal systems or when new supranational governments (e.g. the EU) are being developed
- An increasing emphasis on the rule of law and the rights of citizens, and the need to write these down in the legal form, such as in a Charter or Bill of Rights
- A willingness to use the courts (the 'culture of litigation') as a means or only means of resolving conflict
- Possibly, an unwillingness or inability of politicians to deal with difficult political issues; they may be happy to pass on some political 'hot potatoes', especially moral issues, to the courts.

There are problems with judicial activism as there are with judicial review of the constitution. Striking down legislation and choosing between different interpretations of the law can amount to policy making, and sometimes even small differences of legal interpretation of the law can have large policy ramifications. Should judges have this power? And when there is a conflict between elected government and the courts, who should win?

> **Ombudsman:** A state official appointed to receive complaints and investigate claims about maladministration.

Another quasi-legal development in modern democratic politics is the appointment of ombudsmen. An **ombudsman** is a 'grievance officer', or a state official to whom citizens can appeal if they feel wrongly treated by public bodies. Sweden, which invented the concept, has four ombudsmen covering different areas of public services. Although ombudsmen are found in many western European countries, most democracies (about 75 per cent) do not have them, preferring to use normal court procedures. For the most part, ombudsmen are not lavishly funded and their powers are usually limited, so they rarely have a big impact.

■ Unitary and federal states

We shall discuss **federal states** and unitary government at greater length in chapter 6, but it is appropriate to make an important constitutional point here. In federal systems, power is divided not only between the executive, legislative and judicial branches of government,

> **Federal states:** Federal states combine a central authority with a degree of constitutionally defined autonomy for sub-central, territorial units of government.

but also between territorial units of government. These territorial units – states, or regions, or provinces – often have substantial powers and rights that are guaranteed by the constitution.

In some ways, therefore, federalism is another form of the division of powers within the state – a geographical division between geographical areas, to complement the political division between the executive, legislative and judicial branches. Moreover, the territorial units of federal systems often repeat the division of powers found at the federal level because each unit has its own executive, legislative and judicial branches of government.

> **Unitary states:** In unitary states the central government is the only sovereign body. It does not share constitutional authority with any sub-central units of government.

This distinguishes federal from **unitary states**. In a unitary system, national government ultimately controls all layers of government below it, and can reform, reorganise, or abolish units of local or regional government without any constitutional restraint. In federal systems, the rights and powers and existence of the federal units are protected by the constitution.

■ The limits of constitutionalism

Constitutions are not like cookery recipes that produce exactly the right result if they are followed to the last detail. They are, after all, only legal words on pieces of paper. How they work in practice is a rather different matter. Constitutions are important documents, perhaps supremely important, but there are seven key reasons why they should not necessarily be taken at their face value.

- They may be completely unimportant simply because they are not observed. Most dictatorships have democratic constitutions, and politicians in established democracies have been known to try to flout, break, or go around them.
- They may be incomplete. They are general documents that may not even mention some of the more important aspects of the constitution – electoral systems, political parties, or even the office of prime minister.
- A full understanding of a constitution sometimes requires reference to other documents – supreme court judgments, historical documents, or the UN Declaration of Human Rights.
- Written constitutions are often supported by unwritten rules generally developed over a long period (**conventions**).

> **Conventions:** Unwritten rules that impose obligations on constitutional actors that are held to be binding, but not incorporated into law or reinforced by legal sanctions.

- Constitutions can develop and change, even if the documents do not. The American example of the Supreme Court simply taking upon itself the function of judicial review in 1803 is an example.
- Constitutions can be vague or fail to cover particular or exceptional circumstances.
- Constitutions can fail. History is full of failed democratic constitutions that have been supplanted by revolutions, autocrats and military dictatorships. The lesson is that successful democracy cannot be imposed by constitutional law, no matter how well thought-out this may be; democratic politics must also be accepted and practised by political elites and citizens alike. Constitutions are like fortresses – they must be well built and well protected by soldiers.

Constitutions are rather like maps or blueprints of the main institutions of government, but actual operations may differ – even differ radically – from the legal documents. This leads to the debate about how important institutions are, and to what extent they actually determine the operations of a political system and the behaviour of political actors within it.

■ Constitutional and institutional theories

The 'old constitutionalism'

The interest of political theorists in constitutions dates back at least to Aristotle's famous commentary on the constitution of Athens. In the late nineteenth and first half of the twentieth century, however, the lead in commenting on government was taken not by political theorists but by lawyers and comparative political scientists. At that time their work was largely legal, descriptive and historical, and confined to a few Western states, especially to the UK, the USA and France. After the Second World War this style of political science was fiercely criticised for being descriptive and legalistic rather than analytical, for its failure to theorise and generalise, for being culture-bound by its narrow Western origins and, above all, for its interest in formal and legal documents rather than 'going behind the scenes' to get at the real stuff of everyday politics and the actual practices of government.

Moreover, as we have already seen, constitutions do not always work as they are supposed to. As a result, many of the constitutions so carefully designed (mainly by constitutional lawyers for the newly decolonised and independent countries of Africa and Asia) collapsed and gave way to dictatorship and military government because they were not adapted to social, political and economic circumstances. Even if they had been designed for the needs of new and struggling ex-colonial states, they might have failed simply because those with power ignored them. The failure of these constitutions made it clear that democracy rests on more – far more – than constitutional design, no matter how good this may be on paper. Consequently, when an interest in constitutions was revived in the last quarter of the twentieth century, it went beyond the 'old' institutionalism of legalistic and descriptive studies of constitutions.

The 'new constitutionalism'

The 'new constitutionalism' tries to avoid the problems of the old by combining three things:

1. The protection of citizen rights and the limitation of government powers – in other words, the classical concerns of constitutional theory.
2. A concern with balancing the limited powers and maximum accountability of government, with the need for effective government action in a complex and fast-changing world. It is argued that constitutions are not abstract designs, but practical machines that need careful construction and engineering, and then to be judged by how effectively they work in practice.
3. An attempt to adapt the constitutional design of a country to its social and economic circumstances. It recognises that there is no single constitutional design that is best, but a variety of models to suit different conditions. Constitutional theory tried to solve the problem of how stable democracies could be established in previously undemocratic countries, especially in countries divided by ethnic, religious, linguistic and cultural cleavages. In central and eastern Europe, civil society theorists argued that it was vital that constitutions guaranteed the rights of citizen organisations, and their independence from government. Ethnically mixed societies, it was argued, needed a form of 'consensus' democracy that protected the rights of minorities and gave them effective power to participate in government. We will return to civil society theory in chapter 10 and to consensus democracies in chapter 7.

The 'new institutionalism'

Both the 'old' and the 'new' constitutionalism assumes that constitutions matter, and that they are not only a vital part of any democratic system but also an influence – perhaps even a decisive influence – on how political actors behave and how political systems work. This basic idea is expounded in what is known as the 'new institutionalism' (also referred to as 'neo-institutionalism'). 'The new institutionalism' is not so much a theory as a general approach that focuses on the organisations, structures and institutions of government and politics. There are variations on the general theme, but there is a common argument underlying them:

- Institutions are the framework within which individuals behave. Political institutions not only constrain what individuals do, but also what they think it is possible to do. As we have seen, actors in a system tend to take its basic structure and rules for granted – as given – and organise their behaviour accordingly.
- Institutions are the products of past political battles in which winners tend to create particular forms of organisation that work in their own interests, although they may be quite unconscious of this. Constitutions embody the outcomes of past political struggles over how the game of politics is to be played, and by whom.
- Institutions have a degree of inertia built into them. Once established, they will tend to persist, unless circumstances encourage attempts to change them, and sometimes they may be so firmly rooted that this is difficult.

In short, institutions matter. They have an influence of their own. They are partly the products of the society in which they are embedded, but they also help to shape society and its politics. It has therefore been argued that political science should 'bring the state back in' by combining a concern with the major institutions of a political system (not just constitutions) with an understanding of their historical development. The idea of 'constitutional engineering' is based on the premise that institutions are important and that whether it concerns reforming an existing constitution or designing a new one from scratch, getting the right mix of institutions for a society is important for its democratic stability and quality.

The mobilisation of bias

The idea that institutions matter was caught (some time before the 'new institutionalism') by the American political scientist E. E. Schattschneider (1892–1971) in the phrase 'organisation is the mobilisation of bias'. This means that all organisations (one kind of institution) have a built-in capacity to do some things better than others, which may well serve some interests better than others. Politics, therefore, is the organisation of bias in the sense that some issues and capacities are organised into politics, while others are organised out.

In some countries, second chambers are used to give membership of the upper house to geographical areas or to occupational groups. This means that some interests will find it easier to gain access to the highest levels of government than in a unicameral system. And since upper chambers tend to be conservative bodies (this is one justification for them), there is a tendency for bicameral systems, especially strong bicameral ones, to build a conservative bias into the political system.

Institutional influence, rules and inertia

In an important article published in 1984 in the *American Political Science Review*, James G. March and Johan P. Olsen argued that institutions are basically a collection of interrelated rules and routines that define how the members of an institution see it and their own role within it. These routines include stock responses to problems that are typically used before trying anything else. How people behave within the institution, therefore, is determined by institutional rules and routines that defined what was appropriate action in the circumstances. These routines have been called 'normal operating procedures' – not automatic but habitual. Legislative assemblies, especially old ones steeped in tradition, for example, have their own rules and ways of doing things. New members must learn and accept their customs to have a successful political career.

The economist Douglass North (1920–2015) spent much of his life exploring the ways in which economic institutions, once created, can have long-term effects on the content and impact of economic policy. The political scientist Peter Hall (1950–) also shows that institutions come to absorb and embody a set of policy ideas, such as Keynesian economic theories, that have a long life because they become institutionalised in particular structures which gives them a life of their own. To understand the policy choices made now, we have to understand institutional histories and the ideas they stand for.

Marxist structural theory

An early form of institutional and structural analysis was the account by Karl Marx (1818–83) of the capitalist state, which, he said, was simply a device that enabled capitalists to stay in power and exploit the workers. As he put it in the *Communist Manifesto* (1848), 'the executive of the modern state' is 'but a committee for managing the common affairs of the whole bourgeoisie'. According to Marx, capitalists create and use the institutions of the state for their own purposes: the police and the courts to protect capitalist property; schools, universities and established religion to indoctrinate people into a state of 'false consciousness' in which they cannot even recognise their own best interests; parliament to give an illusion of democracy; and the military to protect the empire as a source of profit. Marx thus employs a structural–historical approach that focuses not on the behaviour of individuals who happen to be capitalists or workers, but on the workings of the whole system and its historical development. He implies that capitalists are not to be blamed for their exploitation of the workers; they are simply following the logic of the situation in which they find themselves. The import of his work is that a constitution is a tool the ruling class uses to maintain the political power it needs to manage the capitalist system.

Governance

Recent forms of institutional theory revolve around the concept of **governance**. Although the term means rather different things to different people, its core idea is that government

> **Governance:** The act of governing; that is, the total set of government's activities in each phase of the policy making process.

no longer revolves around a few institutions of the central state, but consists of a much wider and looser network of organisations and institutions, some private, some public and some a partnership of the two. Political systems contain all sorts of organisations, not just the institutions of government with their constitutionally defined powers and functions, but also government departments and agencies, political parties, the media, international governments and agencies, quangos, and a huge number and variety of private organisations and associations. Governance is about bringing these together, trying to reconcile their competing interests and coordinate them politically. Government is no longer about a narrow range of organisations and institutions but about trying to give shape and direction to the complex multi-level activities of multifarious public and private political actors. In short, governance focuses not on a few institutions of the central state but on a wide variety of institutions, organisations and associations that blur the dividing line between government and the wider society.

■ What have we learned?

- Constitutions are a codified set of entrenched and fundamental laws (laws that determine the procedures to be followed in making other laws) that allocate powers between the main offices and institutions of the state.
- Democratic constitutions are designed to establish the rule of law and to limit government power so that it is accountable and responsive to the will of its citizens.
- The best way of doing this is by dividing power between different offices and bodies, so that each acts as a check on the other and has its power balanced against that of the others.
- In most democracies, power is divided between three branches of government – the executive, the legislature and the judiciary, each of which checks and balances the others. All democratic governments follow this principle to a greater or lesser extent, but presidential and parliamentary, unicameral and bicameral, general courts and special constitutional courts, and federal and unitary forms of government do it in different ways.

■ Lessons of comparison

- Democratic constitutions come in a great many shapes and forms, with many different institutions and many variations on their themes. All these forms can be democratic, and comparison shows that there is no single route to democracy but different pathways arriving at roughly the same place.
- Different institutions have different combinations of strengths and weaknesses. Each does some things well, other things less well. None is perfect, so choosing this or that institution is a matter of trading off between a package of 'goods' and a package of 'not so goods'.
- Political systems rarely operate in the precise manner outlined by their formal constitutions, but most democracies operate roughly as the formal constitution requires. To a greater or lesser extent they all operate a system of division of powers, with checks and balances between the executive, legislative and judicial branches of government, all provide a more or less free and fair electoral system, all have a set of institutions that ensure a greater or lesser degree of accountability of the government to its citizens.
- Institutions have a life of their own, and they have an effect on society independent of that of politics. Among other things, they influence and shape the behaviour of individuals within them, a fact recognised by 'institutional' theories of politics.
- The study of failed constitutions shows that a democratic constitution on its own, no matter how well framed, is not enough. To paraphrase the political theorist Karl Popper (1902–94), constitutions are like fortresses; they must be well designed and well protected by the people inside them.

Projects

1. Assume you are a consultant brought in to advise on the creation of a constitution for Iraq **or** Afghanistan. Would you recommend:
   1. A unicameral or bicameral legislature?
   2. A federal or unitary system?
   3. A special constitutional court?
   4. An ombudsman/ombudsmen?
   Explain the reasons for your decisions.
2. How can institutions have an influence of their own and constrain what people think and do?
3. If the French President visits the Netherlands, the Dutch Queen would normally welcome him, but the French Prime Minister will normally be welcomed by the Dutch Prime Minister. How do you explain this? Whom would you invite to a meeting of 'heads of government' of EU member states if the meeting was held in your country?

Further reading

V. Bogdanor (ed.), *Constitutions in Democratic Politics*. Aldershot: Gower, 1988: 1–13. This introduction to an edited volume of essays on constitutions and democracy provides a useful general discussion of constitutions.

G. Flanz, R. Grote and R. Weolfrum (eds.), *Constitutions of Countries of the World*. Oxford University Press (loose-leaf publication, undated).

R. L. Maddex, *Constitutions of the World*, 3rd edn. London: Routledge, 2007. Presents a summary of the constitutions and constitutional history of 100 nations.

P. M Shane, 'Analyzing constitution', and J. M. Colomer, 'Comparing constitutions', both in R. A. Rhodes, S. A. Binder and M. A. Rockman (eds.), *The Oxford Handbook of Political Institutions*. Oxford University Press (2008). Recent short and comprehensive commentaries on constitutional studies.

C. R. Sunstein, *Designing Democracy: What Constitutions Do*. Oxford University Press, 2001. Explores the idea that conflict and division in politics can be harnessed by the checks and balances of constitutions to bring about integration.

F. L. Wilson, 'The study of political institutions', in Howard J. Wiarda (ed.), *New Directions in Comparative Politics*. Oxford: Westview Press, 3rd edn, 2002: 189–210. A good discussion of why and how political scientists study institutions.

Websites

http://oxcon.ouplaw.com/page/about-ocw/about.
Translations and commentaries on the world's constitutions. Subscription only.

http://confinder.richmond.edu.
Provides the constitutions, charters, amendments and other related documents of the almost 200 nations in the world. Each country entry is linked to its constitutional text, and covers historical and regional aspects. In eleven languages.

https://www.constituteproject.org/content/about?lang=en.
Covers the constitutions of almost every country in the world in 2013 with updates as they are amended or replaced, and allows users to compare constitutions on a large number of different topics.

www.servat.unibe.ch/icl/.
The International Constitutional Law website with an extensive collection of constitutional documents.

5 Presidential and parliamentary government

We have seen in chapter 4 that each democratic constitution has its own particular and special features and each combines them in a different way. This might produce a severe problem for comparative politics, for if every system was unique then all we could do would be to describe them in bewildering and endless detail. Fortunately for students of comparative politics, this is not the case. The great majority of democracies combine their three branches of government in one of three general ways – most of them fall fairly neatly into presidential or parliamentary or semi-presidential systems. Of course, each particular democracy retains its own special features and there are a few democracies that do not fall neatly into one of these three categories (e.g. Israel, Switzerland and the European Union), but most conform to one of the three types, and can be classified accordingly.

The first task of this chapter is to map out the three systems and the main differences between them. Since each has its own strengths and weaknesses, the second task is to consider their respective merits and deficiencies. Third, since constitutions do not exist in a societal vacuum, the next job is to try to sort out the form of government best suited to each set of social and historical circumstances. Some forms of government are likely to work better in certain conditions than others, and it is also possible that countries might do well to shift from one form to another as they develop over time.

The five major topics in this chapter are:

- presidential systems
- parliamentary systems
- semi-presidential systems
- presidential, parliamentary and semi-presidential systems compared
- theories of parliamentary, presidential and semi-presidential government.

■ Presidential systems

In this section we discuss executive presidents who are both heads of state and heads of government, setting aside the non-executive type of presidents who are head of state but not of government. A great many executive **presidential systems** are modelled on the USA, and they reproduce many features of the American system, though not in every detail. The main point about this form of government is that its president is **directly elected** by the electorate as a whole and his or her executive power is balanced by a legislature that is independent of the president because it,

> **Presidential systems:** A directly elected executive, with a limited term of office and a general responsibility for the affairs of state.

> **Directly elected:** Election by the electorate as a whole (popular election) rather than the legislature, or another body.

too, is popularly elected. The president, alone among all the officials of state, has general responsibility for public affairs. He or she may appoint ministers or cabinet members, but they are responsible only for their own department business, and they are accountable to the president, not the legislature. To ensure a real separation of powers neither the president nor members of the cabinet can be members of the legislature.

Presidential government is marked by four main features:

1. *Head of state and government* Presidents perform the ceremonial duties of head of state and are also in charge of the executive branch of government: they are usually chief of the armed forces and head of the national civil service, and responsible for both foreign policy and for initiating domestic legislation. In most instances presidential office is held by a single person, but there are examples of dual and multiple presidential office holders. Switzerland is unique in having seven members of the Federal Council (Bundesrat), one being selected to be formal president each year.
2. *The execution of policy* Presidents appoint cabinets to advise them and run the main state bureaucracies.
3. *Dependence on the legislative branch* Presidents initiate legislation but depend on the legislature to pass it into law.
4. *Fixed tenure* Presidents are directly elected for a fixed term and are normally secure in office unless, in exceptional circumstances, they are removed from it by the legislature. Most are restricted to one or two terms of office, a few to three and most set a minimum age for candidates that is higher than for other public offices in order to get more experienced candidates.

The separation of executive and legislative, each with its independent authority derived from popular election, is a deliberate part of the system of checks and balances. In theory both have powers and are independent of each other, but in practice presidents and assemblies usually have to share power. They must cooperate to get things done, and the result is not so much a separation of powers as a complex mix of them, consisting of a separation of institutions but a mix of powers in the daily give-and-take of their political relations (see briefing 5.1).

This division of powers has an important effect on the way that presidents work, because they are ultimately dependent on their legislatures to get legislation accepted. It is said, for example, that the US president has little power over Congress other than the power of persuasion. Some in the White House have found this inadequate for the purposes of government. If Congress and the president are of a different political mind they may fight each other and

Briefing 5.1

The presidential system in Costa Rica
Costa Rica offers a typical example of the separation of powers in presidential systems. Its constitution provides for independent executive, legislative and judicial branches of government, with a clear division of offices and powers with checks and balances on each.

- The president is head of state and government and is elected by popular vote for a four-year term. The fifty-seven members of the legislative assembly – the deputies – are also elected for a four-year term.
- The executive branch (president, vice-presidents and ministers in the Government Council) has the power to tax and spend according to law, but the legislative branch (the Legislative Assembly) has the power to amend the president's budget, and appoints a Comptroller General to check public expenditure and prevent overspending.
- The president has the duty to maintain order and tranquillity in the nation and to safeguard public liberties, but the Assembly (provided it has a two-thirds majority) has the power to suspend individual rights if it believes there is a public need to do so.

- The president has the power to enter into agreements, public treaties and accords, and to enact and execute them according to the constitution, but the Assembly has the right to approve or disapprove international conventions, public treaties and concordats.
- The Legislative Assembly appoints members of the Supreme Court, which has used its right to enforce constitutional checks on presidential power.
- The Legislative Assembly appoints a powerful and independent Special Electoral Tribunal to oversee elections and ensure their free and fair conduct.
- The Constitutional Chamber of the Supreme Court reviews legislation and executive action when required and also receives appeals contesting the constitutionality of government action.
- A further set of independent state officials – a Comptroller General, Procurator General, and an Ombudsman – have powers to oversee government action and are active in reviewing, scrutinising and sometimes prosecuting elected and appointed officials of government.

get little done. One image likens the president, the House of Representatives and the Senate to participants in a three-legged race – difficult to move along unless they move together, and easy to fall over if they pull in different directions. The problem is heightened if the presidency is controlled by one political party, and one or both houses of the legislature by another. If, on top of this, the president is weak and the parties poorly coordinated or split, the majority party may be unable to pass its legislation. The result is that presidents who are powerful in theory are sometimes neutralised by elected assemblies.

For this reason, many presidential systems have failed the test of democratic stability and some experts believe that they do not make for effective government. The USA is probably the most successful example, although Costa Rica has successfully maintained its presidential system since 1949.

■ Parliamentary systems

In **parliamentary systems** the executive is not directly elected but usually emerges or is drawn from the elected legislature (the parliament or assembly) and, unlike a directly elected president, is often an integral part of it. This form of parliamentary executive usually consists of a prime minister (sometimes called chancellor or premier) and a cabinet or a council of ministers.

> **Parliamentary systems:** These have (1) a directly elected legislative body, (2) fused executive and legislative institutions, (3) a collective executive that emerges from the legislature and is responsible to it, and (4) a separation of head of state and head of government.

The cabinet or council is the collective executive body. Usually the most powerful offices of state are taken by the leaders of the largest party in the assembly or the governing coalition within it. Unlike presidents, who are the only officials with general responsibilities for government affairs, parliamentary executives share responsibilities among their members. This means that the cabinet, including the prime minister, is collectively responsible for all the actions of government, and the prime minister, in theory, is only *primus inter pares* (first among equals). In fact, prime ministers in many countries have acquired more power than this, as we shall see.

Whereas the executive and legislative branches in presidential systems are separated, this is not so clearly the case in parliamentary systems where:

1. the leader of the party or coalition of parties with most support in parliament becomes the prime minister or chancellor;
2. the prime minister or chancellor forms a cabinet usually – but not necessarily – chosen from members of parliament, and the cabinet then forms the core of government;
3. the government is dependent upon the support of parliament, which may remove the executive from power with a vote of no confidence. The executive is also dependent on the legislature because the latter can reject, accept, or amend legislation initiated by the government. Equally, the executive can dissolve the legislature and call an election (see briefing 5.2).

Briefing 5.2

The parliamentary system in Japan

- Japan is a constitutional monarchy with an Emperor who is largely limited to a ceremonial role as head of state. The Japanese system of government sets out to create the checks and balances of presidential systems, but with a different set of executive, legislative and judicial institutions to do so. The Japanese Parliament has two chambers: a lower house, the House of Representatives, and an upper house, the House of Councillors. Together they are called the National Diet and designated by the constitution as 'the sole law-making organ of the state', with powers to make laws, approve national budgets and ratify treaties. Both are directly elected by popular vote.

- The House of Representatives is the more powerful of the two. The House of Councillors can delay important matters such as a budget, a foreign treaty or the selection of a prime minister, and it has the power to veto other matters. But the House of Representatives can override the veto with a two-thirds majority.

- Both houses can conduct investigations into government and order the prime minister and cabinet members to attend inquiries and answer questions.

- The National Diet can also propose constitutional amendments, but these must be passed by national referendum.

- The prime minister is appointed (from among the members of either house) by the National Diet in order to establish its supremacy over the executive, but the House of Councillors has little power to oppose the nomination of the House of Representatives.

- The prime minister is the head of government, the cabinet, and the Japan Self-Defense Forces, with power to appoint and dismiss cabinet members, to initiate legislation and present it to the Diet to sign bills and declare a state of national emergency.

- In practice most proposals for legislation come from the prime minister and the cabinet, but the Diet has the power to accept, reject or amend them.

- The prime minister can dissolve the House of Representatives, but not the House of Councillors. The Diet can also dissolve the government if a vote of no confidence gains the support of fifty members of the House of Representatives.

- The Japanese Supreme Court is independent of government and has the power of judicial review of laws, regulations and acts of government.

This means that the executive in a parliamentary system is directly dependent on, and accountable to, the legislature (i.e. the parliament), which can veto legislation with a majority vote, and bring down the executive by expressing a lack of confidence. Since the executive has **collective responsibility** for government (unlike a president), it must stick together because public disagreement within the cabinet or council on a major political matter will almost certainly result in its being seriously weakened. The prime minister and the cabinet must be closely bound together by mutual dependence and 'collegiality' if

Collective responsibility: The principle that decisions and policies of the cabinet or council are binding on all members who must support them in public.

they are to have a chance of remaining in office. The prime minister appoints cabinet members and can sack them, but to remain in power the prime minister must also retain the confidence of the cabinet.

Presidential systems are usually modelled on the USA and often found in Latin America, while parliamentary systems are often modelled on the British system, and are widely found in the British Commonwealth, but also in western Europe. While, in theory, presidential and parliamentary systems operate in very different ways, in practice they tend to converge. Both depend on a close working relationship between executive and legislature. Although the power of a president is formally greater than that of a prime minister, in practice prime ministers in the modern world are said to be accumulating power so that they become more and more 'presidential'. For example, British prime ministers and German chancellors seem to have become progressively more powerful in the last decades. The process of **presidentialisation** can be observed in many countries implying a further concentration of political power in the hands of the executive in parliamentary systems, especially strengthening the power of the prime minister, premier or chancellor.

Presidentialisation: The process of increasingly concentrating political power and autonomy in the hands of the executive, especially its head.

One of the advantages of parliamentary over presidential systems is said to be that the former produce strong and stable government by virtue of the fusion of executive and legislature. This has generally been the case in Australia, Britain, Canada, Denmark and Japan. But just as presidential systems are sometimes weak, divided or deadlocked, so also are some parliamentary systems – in Italy and in the French Fourth Republic (1946–58). The difference between stable and unstable parliamentary systems may lie less in their constitutional arrangements than in their party systems. Where there is a strong, stable and disciplined party majority (either a single party or a coalition) the result is often strong and stable government, because the executive can usually depend on majority support in the legislature. Where parties are fragmented, factious and volatile, or where majorities are small and uncertain, the parliamentary system is likely to be weak and unstable. Equally, where party discipline in parliament is strong, prime ministers can also be strong and dominate their parties and parliament, thereby reducing the effectiveness of the checks and balances said to be built into parliamentary systems. This directs attention from constitutional arrangements to the role of political parties, a theme we will revisit, especially in chapter 13.

Parliamentary systems are most common in the older democracies of western Europe (including Austria, Belgium, Denmark, Ireland, Netherlands, Norway, Sweden and the UK), and half of them are in British Commonwealth countries, including Australia, Botswana (where the Prime Minister is confusingly called the President), Canada, India and New Zealand. A large proportion of parliamentary democracies are smaller states (India is an exception) and many are small island democracies. Of the newly democratised countries of central and east Europe, Croatia, Bulgaria, Hungary, Latvia and Slovakia are fully parliamentary.

In contrast to presidential systems, the prime ministers or chancellors of parliamentary systems do not have limited terms of office, and in recent decades some of them have had successive election victories and have held on to power for a long time – Gonzales (Spain), Kohl (Germany), Menzies, Fraser and Hawke (Australia), Thatcher, Major and Blair (UK) and Trudeau and Mulroney (Canada).

■ Semi-presidential systems

The French Fourth Republic suffered from chronic instability caused by party fragmentation and deadlock in the assembly, running through twenty-seven governments in thirteen years. To overcome this problem the French Fifth Republic created a **semi-presidential system** in 1958 with a strong, directly elected president with substantial powers to act as a stable centre for government. Often known as hybrid systems (i.e. mixed systems) or as dual-executive systems, semi-presidential government combines a directly elected president who shares power with a prime minister. The president has powers to:

> **Semi-presidential system:** Government consists of a directly elected president, the electorate, and a prime minister who is appointed by the president from the elected legislature and accountable to it. The president and prime minister share executive power.

- appoint prime ministers from the elected assembly, and to dismiss them;
- dissolve parliament and call a referendum;
- declare a state of emergency, and is given substantial powers to deal with it.

The prime minister, in turn, appoints a cabinet from the assembly (the president may do this if he is from the same party as the prime minister) which is then accountable to the assembly. In this way, the French system of semi-presidential government combines the strong president of a presidential system with a prime minister and the fused executive and legislature of parliamentary systems.

This system worked smoothly in the early years of the Fifth Republic when the president (de Gaulle) and the prime minister (Debré) were from the same political party. During this time the president was the dominant force. To the surprise of many, the system continued to work well later, when the president (Mitterrand) and the prime minister (Chirac) came from different parties – what the French call 'cohabitation'. In this period, the balance of power tended to swing in favour of the prime minister.

Semi-presidentialism is found in relatively few democracies: Finland, France and Portugal are alone in maintaining it for more than a quarter of a century, and Finland has changed so that it is now classified as a parliamentary system by some experts. Semi-presidentialism has been adopted by some of the new democracies of central Europe (the Czech Republic, Estonia, Lithuania, Poland and Slovenia), which have tried to blend parliamentary systems with a comparatively strong, directly elected president. The attraction of an elected president in the ex-communist democracies is to have a single strong public figure who can act as (1) a focus of national feeling, important in a newly independent state that needs a strong central figure, and (2) as the centre of executive power to help overcome extreme party fragmentation in the new legislatures.

There are indications of a tendency to move away from semi-presidentialism in some countries as political conditions change. In Finland, there have been attempts to reduce the power of the president. The central European states are still feeling their way, and if they develop strong party systems and consolidate their national identity, they may well move from a semi-presidential towards more purely parliamentary forms of government.

■ Presidential, parliamentary and semi-presidential systems compared

We are now in a position to compare all three types of government. The main points of comparison are laid out in briefing 5.3. It is clear that there are things to be said both for and against all three as forms of democratic

Briefing 5.3

The three major forms of democratic government: main features

Presidential	Parliamentary	Semi-presidential
• Citizens directly elect the executive for a fixed term	• The executive emerges from a directly elected legislature and is closely related to it	• Executive power is shared between a president (directly elected) and a prime minister who is appointed or directly elected
• Except for a few joint presidencies, the president alone has executive power	• The cabinet shares executive power and must reach compromises to maintain unity	• The prime minister appoints a cabinet, usually from the ruling party or coalition in the assembly
• The presidency is the only office of state with a general responsibility for the affairs of state	• The executive is a collegial body (cabinet or council of ministers) that shares responsibility, though the prime minister, premier or chancellor may be much more than *primus inter pares*	• The president often appoints the prime minister and has general responsibility for state affairs, especially foreign affairs
• The president shares power with a separate and independently elected legislature	• The office of the prime minister/premier/chancellor is separate from the head of state (whether monarch or president)	• The president often has emergency powers, including the dissolution of parliament

Presidential	Parliamentary	Semi-presidential
• Neither can remove the other (except in special circumstances such as impeachment)	• The prime minister and cabinet can dissolve parliament and call an election, but the prime minister and cabinet can be removed from office by a parliamentary expression of a lack of confidence	• The prime minister and cabinet often have special responsibility for domestic and day-to-day affairs of state
• The president is directly elected and therefore directly accountable to the people	• The prime minister and cabinet are responsible to parliament	• The president is directly elected and directly accountable to the people; the prime minister is responsible either to the president or to parliament
• Examples: USA, many states in Central and South America (Colombia, Costa Rica, Dominican Republic, Ecuador, Venezuela), Cyprus, Philippines and South Korea	• Most stable democracies are parliamentary systems – Australia, Austria, Belgium, Canada, Denmark, Germany, Greece, Iceland, India, Ireland, Israel, Italy, Japan, Netherlands, Norway, Spain, Sweden, Switzerland, UK	• Examples: Finland (until 1991), France and many post-communist states, including Belarus, Poland, Russia and Ukraine

government, and it is also clear that all three can work as effective democratic structures. Whether all three work equally well in countries with different social conditions and political histories is a different matter. One view is that presidential systems can be weak and ineffective, and run into problems of executive–legislative deadlock, leading to attempts to break through the problem by a 'strong man' who promises decisive and effective government. Not many countries have managed the presidential system as well as the USA.

At the same time, semi-presidential systems also have their problems. They can produce deadlock between presidents and prime ministers, leading to weak and ineffective government. Not many countries seem to be able to handle the problems of 'cohabitation' as well as France. Some parliamentary systems have also produced weak, divided and unstable government, while others have tended towards an over-concentration of power (see controversy 5.1). It is clear that we should look more closely at the arguments about parliamentary, presidential and semi-presidential government.

Presidential, parliamentary or semi-presidential government?

Presidential	Parliamentary	Semi-presidential
For		
• The USA is a model	• Most of the world's stable democracies are parliamentary systems	• In theory combines the best of presidential and parliamentary government
• Separation of the executive and legislative institutions of government according to classical democratic theory	• Fusion of executive and legislative can create strong and effective government	• The president can be a symbol of the nation, and a focus of national unity, while the prime minister can run the day-to-day business of the government
• Direct election of the president means direct accountability of the president to the people	• Direct chain of accountability from voters to parliament to cabinet to prime minister	
Against		
• Conflict between executive and legislation may be chronic, leading to deadlock and immobilism	• The fusion of the executive and legislative, and a large legislative majority, combined with tight party discipline, can produce leaders with too much power	• Conflict and power struggles between prime minister and cabinet, and between prime minister and president are not unusual
• Weak and ineffective presidents have sometimes tried to make their office much stronger	• Parliamentary systems without a legislative majority can be weak and unstable	• Confusion of accountability between president and prime minister
• Few presidential systems have survived long		

■ Theories of parliamentary, presidential and semi-presidential government

At the heart of debates about the three types of government lies one of the fundamental problems of any democracy: how can a political system balance the need for accountability to citizens and protection of their basic rights against the need for government that is strong enough to be effective? Too much government power means too little democracy, but too little government power means too little government. How do our three systems measure up to this dilemma?

At the outset, we have the problem of evaluating semi-presidential systems: there are too few of them, and only two examples in established democracies (France and Finland, which has moved towards a parliamentary system). Many of the new democracies of central and eastern Europe are semi-presidential, but these are rather special cases and some seem to be transforming themselves into parliamentary systems. Only time will tell whether they remain semi-presidential or for how long, and we have to set them aside for the time being at least.

A leading writer on the relative merits of presidential and parliamentary systems is Juan Linz (1926–2013). He claimed that presidentialism entails a paradox. On the one hand presidents are strong because they are directly elected and have popular support. They can rise above the petty in-fighting of parties and factions and speak for their country and its people. The president is also a single person who takes all the power of the presidential office. On the other hand, presidents are normally bound by all sorts of constitutional provisions that limit their power: they must have legislative support for actions, decisions and appointments; they have to deal with the independence of the courts; and they sometimes face a highly fragmented, undisciplined and ineffective party system that makes it difficult to shape and implement a coherent policy. Because presidents do not always have the support of the majority in the assembly, they may be unable to implement their policies. In a word, presidentialism is prone to **immobilism** (see briefing 5.4). In addition, unlike parliamentary leaders, presidents have a fixed term of office, which means it can be difficult to remove an unpopular president, but also means a sharp break in policies when a new one is elected.

Immobilism: The state of being unable to move (immobilised) or unable to take decisions or implement policies.

According to Linz, parliamentary systems are more conducive to stable democracy. They are more flexible and adaptable because they do not impose the discontinuities of fixed terms of presidential office. Since the political executive is rooted in the majority party of the assembly, or in a coalition of parties, it is based on compromise and bargaining within or between parties.

Briefing 5.4

The perils of presidential government
The outgoing president in 1952, Harry S. Truman, is said to have commented about his successor in the White House, the Second World War General, Dwight ('Ike') D. Eisenhower:

> He'll sit here, and he'll say, 'Do this! Do that!' And nothing will happen. Poor Ike – it won't be a bit like the Army. He'll find it very frustrating.
>
> *(Richard E. Neustadt,* Presidential Power and the Modern Presidents: The Politics of Leadership, *New York: Free Press, 1960: 9)*

And since parliamentary executives are not limited to one or two terms in office, they can maintain a degree of continuity – the party leader may be replaced but the party or coalition may continue in power.

How does the theoretical argument about the superiority of parliamentary over presidential government measure up to the empirical evidence? At first sight, the evidence is compelling. The USA and Costa Rica are among the few examples of long-lived democratic presidentialism, and there are a few notable failures – Argentina, Brazil and Chile. At the same time, a high proportion of west European democracies are parliamentary, as are many of the stable democracies of the British Commonwealth. It is estimated that of forty-three stable democracies in the world existing between 1979 and 1989, thirty-six were parliamentary, five presidential and two semi-presidential.

A second look at the evidence, however, suggests a more favourable evaluation of presidential government. First, while it is true that many presidential systems have failed, many of these are in Latin America, which raises the question of whether the explanation lies in inherent institutional design faults, or in the economic problems, lack of democratic traditions and fragmented parties of the countries which adopted the system in the first place. Would parliamentary government have worked any better in these countries? It is impossible to know, but it is important to note that parliamentary systems failed in Greece and Turkey, and have not performed well in France and Italy.

There are also different sub-types of presidential government, some giving the office great powers and others limiting them. Similarly, some presidents operate within a cohesive and well-organised party system. It may be that presidents with strong party support in the main legislative body have a better chance of producing stable democracy than presidents with weak party support.

■ What have we learned?

This chapter shows that:

- In spite of great constitutional variety, democratic states fall into one of three general categories – presidential, parliamentary and semi-presidential systems.
- Presidents in democracies are directly elected for a fixed term of office to serve as the executive head of government. The main examples are found in the USA and Latin America. Though often powerful executive heads must share power with elected legislative bodies and are subject to judicial review.
- In parliamentary systems the political executive (chancellor, premier, or prime minister and the cabinet or council of ministers) is not directly elected but emerges from the majority party or ruling coalition in the assembly and is accountable to it. The executive continues in office as long as it has the support of the assembly, so there is no fixed term of office. Parliamentary systems are found mainly in western Europe and the stable democracies of the British Commonwealth.

- The semi-presidential system is a hybrid of the other two types, consisting of a directly elected president and a prime minister who appoints a cabinet from the assembly. There are not many semi-presidential systems in the world, and the best known is in France.
- Most stable democracies in the world are parliamentary. Relatively few are presidential or semi-presidential.

■ Lessons of comparison

- There is no single best formula for a stable and vibrant democracy. Each of the three main systems has its advantages and disadvantages.
- Different systems may be suited to different national circumstances, and the same country may change its system as it develops. The best system for any given country at any given time may depend on its particular historical, social and economic circumstances.
- The semi-presidential system seems to be well suited to the circumstances of the new democracies of central Europe, but this may change as they develop.
- Comparing presidential and parliamentary systems around the world suggests that it may not be the basic constitutional arrangements of presidentialism that tend to create unstable democracies so much as the political, economic and social characteristics of the countries that adopt this form of government. It may be that presidents in countries with a history of democracy, a strong economy, and a stable and an organised party system can sustain stable democracy.

Projects

1. Assume you are a consultant brought in to advise a newly independent state that wishes to set up a democratic constitution. Would you recommend (a) a presidential, (b) a semi-presidential or (c) a parliamentary system? Explain the reasons for your decisions.
2. Why is there no single best institutional design for the relationships between the executive and legislative branches in a democracy?
3. How could we decide, using the comparative method, whether it is the basic design of presidential government or the weakness of party systems that causes democratic instability?

Further reading

R. Elgie (ed.), *Semi-presidentialism in Europe*. Oxford University Press, 1999. Explains variations in the structure and performance of semi-presidential systems.

A. Lijphart, *Patterns of Democracy: Government Forms and Performance in Thirty-Six Countries*. New Haven: Yale University Press, 2012, esp. ch. 7, 'Executive–Legislative Relations'. Presents a systematic comparative analysis of the advantages and disadvantages of these relations.

A. Lijphart (ed.), *Parliamentary versus Presidential Government*. Oxford University Press, 1992. The best collection of work on parliaments and presidents.

J. J. Linz and A. Valenzuela (eds.), *The Failure of Presidential Democracy*, Baltimore, MD: Johns Hopkins University Press, 1994. A critical commentary on presidential government.

S. Mainwaring and M. S. Shugart (eds.), *Presidentialism and Democracy in Latin America*. Cambridge University Press, 1997. A defence of some forms of presidentialism.

T. Poguntke and P. Webb (eds.), *The Presidentialization of Politics: A Comparative Study of Modern Democracies*. Oxford University Press, 2007. A comparative analysis of various developments stimulating the strengthening of executive powers in democracies.

A. Siaroff, 'Comparative presidencies: the inadequacy of the presidential, semi-presidential and parliamentary distinction', *European Journal of Political Research*, 42 (3), 2003: 287–312. Discusses the inadequacies of the three forms of government and presents a different typology.

Websites

http://info.worldbank.org/etools/docs/library/108383/session4h.pdf.
A detailed account of the three forms of government according to their separation of powers, removal from office and leadership.

http://encyclopedia.thefreedictionary.com.
Comprehensive accounts of parliamentary, presidential and semi-presidential systems of government.

www.ipu.org/dem-e/guide/summary.htm.
A long and detailed account of the role and functions of democratic parliaments in the world.

www.researchgate.net/publication/265101267_The_Politics_of_Semi-Presidentialism.
Introduces the concept of semi-presidentialism and explains why some countries might adopt it.

6   Multi-level government: international, national and sub-national

Government in all but the smallest countries is organised like a set of 'Chinese boxes', or 'Russian dolls' – one unit of government tucked inside another.

- The smallest units of community or neighbourhood government fit inside local government
- which is contained within higher levels of government variously called state/regional/provincial/county or city government
- which are parts of the national system of government
- which is a member of various organisations of international government.

For example, a resident of Wilmersdorf-Charlottenburg lives in one of the twelve *Bezirke* (boroughs) that form the City of Berlin:

- which is one of the sixteen *Länder* (states) that make up the Federal Republic of Germany
- which is one of the member states of the EU in Europe, of NATO in Europe and North America and of the UN across the entire globe.

Government is organised on different geographical levels in this way because no single centre could possibly do everything itself. It must be divided, not only into different branches at the national level (executive, legislative, judiciary) but also into smaller territorial units of local administration and policy making at the sub-national level. Nor can countries manage their affairs entirely on their own; even the largest and most powerful must deal with other countries to solve international problems of security, diplomacy, the environment and trade.

Dividing government into geographical layers in this way makes sense, but it also creates questions of its own:

- What should be centralised and what decentralised to lower levels of government?
- How do we ensure that the resulting system is as efficient and as democratic as possible?

We touched briefly on this topic in chapter 4 when we discussed unitary and federal states, but the topic of multi-level government is so important that we return to it in this chapter in greater depth.

There are usually three main layers of government within a country:

1. national, central, or federal government
2. a middle or meso-level that is variously called state, provincial, regional, or county government
3. local or municipal government, which may cover anything from quite small areas to large metropolitan cities or rural regions.

Often there is a fourth and lowest tier of government for local communities and neighbourhoods, but it is rarely of very great governmental significance and will not be discussed here. Layers of government below the national level are collectively referred to as 'sub-national' or 'non-central' government. In addition, there are many kinds of international and supranational organisations that have an important impact on the way that national and sub-national governments conduct their business, all the greater in an increasingly globalised world.

This chapter, therefore, discusses the multiple layering of government. It starts at the international level and works down to the most local level of subnational government, as follows:

- supra-national and international government
- the national level: federal and unitary states
- the interplay of multi-level government
- the arguments for and against centralisation and decentralisation
- theories of multi-level government.

In chapter 1 the general concept of the state was introduced, but in discussions about multiple layering of government the concept has three more specific meanings. It can refer to the whole apparatus of the government, as in the phrase 'the state apparatus', which refers to all branches and all levels of government. It can also refer to the national or central government of a country, as in the phrase 'the central state'. And third, in federal systems it can refer to the level of government below the central government, where the federal government is nationwide and states are sub-divisions of the federal territory, as in the state of California, or the state of North Rhine-Westphalia in Germany. Sometimes the meaning of the word is only clear from its context – as in 'state and local government' (middle and local levels in the USA), 'the Japanese state' (Japanese government apparatus), 'the Indian states' (regional units), and 'the federal states of the world' (national systems of government that are federal).

■ Supra-national and international government

Government above the national level is, for the most part, a matter of cooperation between countries that keep their national sovereignty but nevertheless set up organisations to deal with problems that spread across national boundaries. We could not, for example, organise international flights without international air traffic control. International cooperation of this kind between governments is replete with an 'alphabet soup' of inter-governmental organisations (IGOs), including the UN, NATO, the IMF, the ILO, the OECD, OPEC, Interpol, GATT, the IBRD, NAFTA, the OAU, the WTO. These are all agencies of government that are created by international agreements between countries, but they are not the same as governments or states. They are forms of confederation, so our first job is to distinguish confederations from their close cousins, the federations.

Confederations

The term 'confederation' is often confused with 'federation', because the terms sound similar and have much in common. **Confederations** are looser-knit than federations, and formed by organisations that want to cooperate with each other on a generally specific matter, but that also want to preserve their independent identity and not merge completely into a single, larger body. Confederations do not encroach upon the sovereign autonomy of their members, which can leave the confederation when they please, whereas federations are created by a pooling of sovereignty that binds their constituent units together. Confederations range from powerful and cohesive organisations to weak and loose-knit ones, and they can be involved in any kind of activity, political and non-political. The majority of international political confederations are weaker, less centralised and less stable than federal states and all have a narrow range of functions and duties. The short-lived American Confederation Congress (1781–89), that prefigured the USA's federal system formed in 1789, highlights the main problem of such groupings – they are often too loose and powerless to achieve much, and sometimes they fall apart.

> **Confederations:** Organisations whose members lend some powers to a body that manages affairs of common interest, while retaining their own independence.

Confederations are formed by all sorts of organisations for all sorts of purposes, and they operate at all levels of the political system, from the most

Briefing 6.1

The Dominican Republic: membership of international organisations
The Dominican Republic is a member of fifty-six major international organisations, including the Food and Agricultural Organisation, the Inter-American Development Bank, the International Labour Organization, the Inter-Parliamentary Union, the International Organization for Migration, the Permanent Court of Arbitration, the Rio Group, the United Nations, the Universal Postal Union, the World Customs Organization and the World Trade Organization.

local to the most global. Trade unions, for example, often form confederations around their common interests, as do business associations, professional organisations, churches and sports clubs. However, international confederations are particularly well suited to the needs of countries that want to retain their independent identity and autonomy while cooperating with other countries on specific matters such as economic development, defence, environmental policy or cultural affairs. The World Trade Organization (WTO), the International Monetary Fund (IMF), the World Bank, and the European Space Agency (ESA) are examples of international government confederations. Briefing 6.1 lists just a few of the international confederal organisations to which the government of the Dominican Republic belongs.

Supra-national government goes one important step further than international government. It involves the cooperation of countries that are willing to pool sovereignty, at least on certain matters, along federal lines. Since the international system has long been based on sovereign nations (the Westphalian system outlined in chapter 1), the creation of supra-national government is a rare thing. In fact, the European Union is the first and far and away the most advanced specimen of supra-national government in the world today.

> **Supra-national government:** Organisations in which countries pool their sovereignty on certain matters to allow joint decision making.

The European Union: federation or confederation?

The European Union is a hybrid of confederal and federal features. Its federal features are a Commission (a quasi-executive), a powerful European Court (ECJ) whose verdicts take precedence over national law, and some pooling of sovereignty on particular matters. Its confederal characteristics are an unwillingness of member countries to surrender sovereignty on some matters of economic, social or migration policies, a weak parliament and weak coordination of foreign policy. Members can leave a confederation at any time (Greenland left the EEC in 1985), but the deep integration of the EU along quasi-federal lines makes this difficult. France withdrew its troops from NATO military command (a confederal organisation) in 1966 but rejoined in 2009 after a period of participation without full membership.

It remains to be seen whether the EU strengthens its federal or its confederal nature. It has a choice between deep integration and shallow integration. As things stand at the moment, however, its nearest equivalent in the world is the North American Free Trade Association (NAFTA), but its limited concern with trade relations between the sovereign states of North America means that it is not contemplating the deep integration of the EU. NAFTA is unlikely to turn itself from an international body into a supra-national one.

■ The national level: federal and unitary states

At the national level, government is organised on either a federal or a unitary basis. As we saw in chapter 4, federal systems contain middle-level territorial units of government (states, provinces, regions – see table 6.1) which have a guaranteed status in the constitution that gives them a degree of independence and autonomy from the central government. In contrast, **sub-central** units of government in unitary states are the creatures of central government, which creates them and which can reform, restructure, or abolish them without constitutional limitation. How central government changes local government in a unitary system is a sensitive political issue, of course, and there may be severe limitations to what it can do, but this is a political, not a constitutional matter.

Sub-central government: All levels of government below central/national government.

Though they vary considerably in the degree to which power is concentrated, unitary governments are still more centralised than most federal systems. The advantage of federalism is that it combines a degree of national government unity with a constitutionally entrenched degree of independence for lower levels of government, variously named states, regions, or provinces.

Table 6.1 Federal states: names and numbers of regional units of government, 2000

State	Characteristics
Australia	6 states, 11 territories
Austria	9 *Länder*
Belgium	3 regions
Canada	10 provinces, 3 territories
Germany	16 *Länder*
India	29 states, 7 union territories
Mexico	31 states, 1 federal district
South Africa	9 provinces
Switzerland	20 cantons, 6 half-cantons
USA	50 states, 1 federal district

Sources:
http://en.wikipedia.org/wiki/Federated_state; www.regional.gov.au/territories/; www.nationsonline.org/oneworld/countries_canada.htm; http://knowindia.gov.in/knowindia/state_uts.php.

We can see this in figures 6.1 and 6.2 and table 6.1, which show that sub-central units of government in federal systems usually account for a greater proportion of public sector taxes, spending and employment, suggesting greater decentralisation of service responsibilities to lower levels of government.

Federal decentralisation is especially important where a country is large geographically, or where different social groups in the population are concentrated in particular regions.

Figure 6.1: Share of total government expenditure: central and non-central government, 2012, per cent

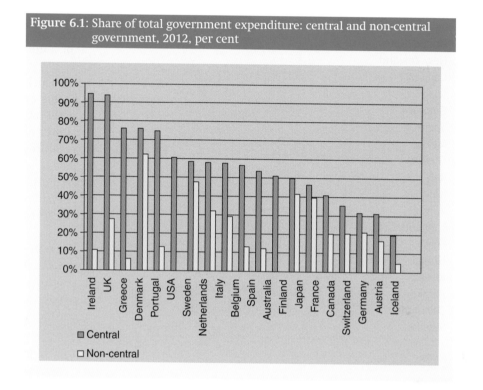

Figure 6.2: Share of total government receipts, 2012, per cent

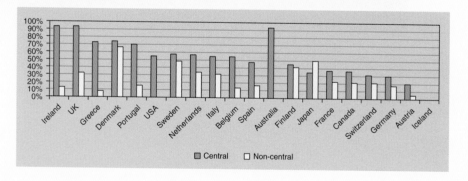

Table 6.2 Share of public employment, percentages, 2011

State	Central	Local	Social Security
Turkey	89.92	9.04	1.04
Luxembourg	71.90	26.43	1.67
Slovenia	58.95	38.24	2.82
Czech Republic	45.90	52.98	1.11
Estonia	47.78	52.22	0.00
Finland	22.92	75.37	1.71
Ireland	90.22	9.78	0.00
United States	12.93	87.07	0.00
New Zealand	89.13	10.87	0.00
Canada	12.89	87.11	0.00
Japan	14.85	85.15	0.00
Germany	12.86	78.47	8.66
Spain	19.71	80.29	0.00
Mexico	25.64	61.26	13.10
Greece	77.08	19.46	3.45
Italy	55.28	43.27	1.45
Israel	76.00	23.30	0.71
Portugal	71.01	26.52	2.47
Netherlands	23.43	74.12	2.45
France	45.18	32.29	22.53
Hungary	30.18	68.91	0.91
Norway	35.04	64.96	0.00
Belgium	16.17	80.19	3.64
Denmark	24.02	75.73	0.25
Sweden	18.03	81.88	0.09

Source:
International Labour Organization (ILO), LABORSTA (database)

Notes:

Data for Australia, Austria, Chile, Iceland, South Korea, Poland, Slovakia and the United Kingdom are not available.

Data for Italy, Netherlands and New Zealand are expressed in full-time equivalents (FTEs).

Social security funds are not separately identified (i.e. recorded under central and/or sub-central government) for Canada, Estonia, Ireland, Japan, New Zealand, Norway, Spain, Switzerland and the United States.

Germany, Ireland, Norway and Sweden: 2010.

Japan, Mexico, Brazil and the Russian Federation: 2009.

Greece, Hungary, Portugal and Switzerland: 2008.

Czech Republic: 2007.

France and South Africa: 2006.

Information on data for Israel:
http://dx.doi.org/10.1787/888932315602.

Geographically large countries

Large territories may be better organised as federations in order to give far-flung territories a degree of autonomy that reduces their dependence on a distant centre of government. One of the founding fathers of the American constitution, Thomas Jefferson (1743–1826), said: 'Our country is too large to have all its affairs directed by a single government.' Many of the largest countries in the world, in terms of area or population, or both, are federal (see briefing 6.2).

Countries with markedly different geographical regions

Many federal states have multi-ethnic or multinational populations that are concentrated in different geographical areas (e.g. Belgium, Canada, India, Switzerland and the USA). A country with deep political cleavages of any kind, whether based on language, ethnicity, religion, culture or history, may have severe problems with its unity, and these problems will be compounded if the cleavages coincide with geographical divisions. For example, in Canada the French-speaking part of the population is concentrated in Quebec. Federalism makes it easier to hold diverse areas together within a single country by giving regions a

> **Political cleavage:** A political division created when political organisations use social cleavages for their own purposes to mobilise support. Social cleavages are often more important politically if they coincide with regional divisions.

Briefing 6.2

Federal states

Of the 193 independent states in the world twenty-four are fully federal, many of them the largest in the world (e.g. Brazil, Canada, Mexico, India and the USA) covering some 40 per cent of the global population. Not all are large, however. The Swiss Confederacy, traditionally dated back to 1291, is the oldest in the world if one excludes the Archaean League of ancient Greece (251–146 BC). Belgium is one of the most recent, being created in 1993 out of three linguistic areas of Brussels (French), Flanders (Dutch) and Wallonia (French).

No truly federal system has ever evolved into a unitary system, but there are many examples of failed international federations (the West Indian Federation, 1962, the Central African Federation, 1963, the Malaysian Federation (Singapore left in 1965), the East African Federation, 1977, and Yugoslavia and Czechoslovakia, both 1992). Though technically a unitary state, Spain grants greater powers to its autonomous regions than some federal nations give to their states. And, curiously, though part of the unitary state of the United Kingdom, Scotland has its own education and legal system, issues its own banknotes, and has its own regional parliament with considerable devolved powers. Northern Ireland and Wales also have their own special and different devolved powers, and all three have their own flags and anthems and their own football teams for the World Cup, though not their own teams for the Olympic Games. In some respects, therefore, it is not unknown for unitary states to have some characteristics of federal ones.

degree of control over their own affairs. Belgium turned itself into a federal system in 1993 to prevent its three major regions (French-speaking Brussels, Dutch-speaking Flanders and French-speaking Wallonia) from falling apart.

Federal systems all have a constitutionally recognised territorial division of political powers, but there are different forms of federalism: some have many units of sub-central government, others only a few (see table 6.1); some reserve powerful functions for the centre (Canada, India), others give them to the states (Australia, Switzerland, the USA); some specify carefully the functions and powers of each level of government, others assume that powers and functions not specifically assigned to one level will be the responsibility of the other. In some federal systems, the upper legislative house is reserved for representatives of the states, regions or provinces (the Bundesrat for the German *Länder* and the Senate for American states), which gives them a powerful stake in national as well as regional and local politics.

In theory, there is a distinction between 'cooperative federalism' and 'dual federalism'. In the cooperative type, federal and state government share powers and, consequently, are required to cooperate closely with one another (Germany, Switzerland). In a dual system, there is supposed to be a clearer separation of functions and powers (Australia, the USA), with each level of government having its own sphere of competence. In practice, however, federalism of both kinds requires close and constant cooperation, negotiation and bargaining between federal and state government. In theory, the USA draws a line between the responsibilities of the federal government and the states, but in practice they cooperate closely in many areas of domestic policy. The metaphor of 'the marble cake' is often applied to the USA: a cake where the layers are not divided by clear, straight lines, but mixed and melded in a complex partnership of shared responsibilities. The key fact about any federal system, whether of the Swiss/German or Australian/US type, is not the separation of powers, but cooperation, inter-governmental relations and interdependence. The study of 'inter-governmental relations' and 'fiscal federalism' (the politics of shared taxing and spending powers) is important in federal systems because government is not so much layered as intertwined in a way that makes it difficult to understand how it works in practice.

Federal systems usually have three main levels of government – national government, local government and a middle level between them. To make life complicated the main middle-level units are often called 'states'. To distinguish 'states' in a federal system from central government the latter are often called 'federal' or 'national' governments. Local government is normally under the general oversight of the states, not the federal government. This means that each state or province can determine its own system of local government, with the result that they can differ in a bewildering variety of ways within a single country. The picture is often complicated further where large cities are given special powers of their own. Some cities in the USA have 'home rule charters', which give them a special degree of autonomy. In many countries (e.g. Brazil, Australia, the USA, India) the capital city is also treated as a special case.

Although federalism allows the degree of decentralisation and flexibility that is necessary for large and mixed populations, there is often a price to be paid for it. Inter-governmental relations between federal and state government can be complicated and sensitive, and special arrangements and understandings have to be created to allow them to operate effectively. These can be slow, complex and costly as different levels of government, each with its

Briefing 6.3

Canadian federalism in practice

Federalism is a central feature of the Canadian state and divides the government of the country into two constitutionally autonomous levels – federal and provincial – each with its own constitutional powers and jurisdictions, which they exercise independently. The federal government has its own national parliament, prime minister, cabinet and judiciary with full responsibility for twenty-nine policy areas – for example trade regulation, postal service, census and statistics, the military, navigation and shipping, fisheries, First Nations (Canadian indigenous peoples) and reserve land, criminal law, international treaties, declarations of emergency and any mode or system of taxation.

Each province also has its own elected legislative, premier, cabinet and courts. Provinces implement their own laws within their own territories and according to their constitutional powers, but they can be overruled by the Supreme Federal Court of Canada. The Canadian constitution gives each province sole jurisdiction over sixteen major areas of government (e.g. education, hospitals, asylums, charities, municipal institutions, prisons, property and civil rights). Agriculture and immigration, pensions and natural resources are matters of 'concurrent powers', meaning that they are shared with federal government. All powers not explicitly given to the provinces are retained by the federal government.

To have real power the provinces need money, which they raise from their own taxes and grants which they receive from the federal government. Some grants are subject to conditions laid down by the federal government and some are block grants which the provinces are free to use as they wish. These financial arrangements are matters of conflict. Some of the richer provinces want more discretion over their taxing and spending, and some complain that they should not be so dependent on federal grants, especially conditional ones. This sort of conflict, however, is often found in unitary states as well.

As in other federal systems, each unit of government is in daily formal and informal contact with all the others. They meet constantly to talk and argue, exchange information and opinions, and compare experiences, public policy innovations and experiments. Many units of governments, federal and provincial, have large departments of inter-governmental affairs with ministers in their cabinets who have responsibility for contacts with other government units and who report back to their own cabinet. The federal prime minister meets provincial and territorial premiers in the First Ministers' Conferences and provincial premiers meet formally in the Council of the Federation. Together they ensure a high level of horizontal and vertical communications within the federal system.

Source: www.mapleleafweb.com/features/
federalism-canada-basic-framework-and-operation#canadian

own powers and duties, work out a common programme of action between them. The growth of federal funding and regulation has often created a tangled mass of complicated inter-governmental relations.

Unitary states

To repeat, in unitary states the central government is the only sovereign body. It does not share constitutional authority with any sub-central units of government. In unitary states sub-central government is the creation and the creature of central government and has no constitutionally guaranteed powers of its own. Central government has the formal power to reform or abolish units of sub-central government at will, and can add or take away from its powers and duties as it sees fit. Among the democracies of the world with a population of a million or more, forty-four are unitary, including most of the old and new democracies of west, central and east Europe as well as Chile, Costa Rica, the Dominican Republic, Israel, Jamaica, Japan, Mali, Namibia, New Zealand, South Korea and Uruguay. Unitary states are usually smaller than federal ones, Japan being the largest (population 130 million) and Estonia, Mauritius and Trinidad and Tobago among the smaller, with populations of not much over a million.

In practice the differences between federal and unitary states are often not as clear as the constitutional definitions suggest. In the first place, unitary states delegate government functions to sub-central units of government. Indeed, they could not operate a modern state if they did not, because they depend on sub-central government to carry out their policies and to deliver a wide array of public services. Each has to negotiate and cooperate with the other to some extent, as in federal systems. In the second place, sub-central government has often acquired a legitimacy and a vested interest of its own, so politically central government may find it difficult to change the system. Third, in practice unitary and federal systems often have the same division of labour, with similar functions, duties and powers reserved for the central government, and similar ones for the sub-central levels.

Fourth, some unitary states have quasi-federal features such as a degree of 'home rule' for special areas. These include the island of Åland (Finland), Corsica (France), the Channel Islands and the Isle of Man (the UK), and the Faroe Islands and Greenland (Denmark). Special status is not reserved only for islands. Scotland, Northern Ireland and Wales have long had their own standing within the UK, as do the regions of Alto Adige and Val d'Aosta (as well as the island of Sicily) in Italy. Spain is a unitary state but it gives some regions (notably Catalonia and the Basque Country) so much autonomy that it might be called a semi-federal or regional system. In other words, unitary states can be rather variable and flexible, and not as highly centralised as they first seem In a word, they also **devolve** power to lower levels of government.

Devolution: Devolution occurs where higher levels of government grant decision-making powers to lower levels while maintaining their constitutionally subordinate status.

Fifth, federal systems are tending towards greater centralisation. As countries become internally more integrated, and as they face the pressures of globalisation, so federal governments have assumed greater control over some national affairs. Some have become more centralised in an attempt to reduce economic inequalities between regions and in order to implement national minimum standards of service provision. Because federal government has greater financial resources it is increasingly funding local services through grants and transfers of various kinds. In doing so, it is exercising greater control over local policies and services.

Although there is a tendency for federal and unitary states to converge, they still remain distinct. Figures 6.1 and 6.2 and table 6.1 show that central government in unitary states usually accounts for a higher proportion of public expenditure and employment than central government in federal states: compare France, Ireland, New Zealand, Portugal and the UK at the top of table 6.1 with Australia, Canada, Germany and the USA at the bottom.

Briefing 6.4

France: sub-central government in a unitary state

France has a semi-presidential form of unitary national government with three layers of sub-central government below it, namely regions, departments and communes. This makes it one of the few countries with four, rather than three, important layers of government. It is also one of the more highly centralised of the democratic states, although a decentralising law of 1982 introduced greater local autonomy.

Metropolitan France has twenty-two regions and another four for overseas territories. In the main the regions are concerned with planning, economic development and the costs and equipment of secondary schools (*lycées*). Each has an elected council, which elects its own chair, which works closely with an appointed consultative committee. Regions, in turn, are sub-divided into a total of 100 departments. They also have an elected council with a chair responsible mainly for health, social services, rural capital works, roads, and the costs of running colleges of further education. Departments, in their turn, are subdivided into a total of 37,000 communes, many more than most west European local government systems, some very small. In order to provide better services at lower costs the smallest are strongly encouraged to merge into larger urban communities or to cooperate in groups of communes. Communes have elected councils that lay down guidelines for municipal policy and administration, adopt the budget and manage primary school buildings and equipment.

Communes also have an elected mayor who has two special roles, one as their commune's elected executive officer and a second as the central state's representative in it. As the local executive and head of its administration the mayors carry out the decisions of the municipal council, propose and implement the budget, and have responsibility for the natural and build environment, security, and public health and having at their disposal the municipal administration, which they head. As the central state's representative the mayor has police, legal and other duties but is subject to control by the courts and by a prefect.

Prefects are appointed by the central government to act as their only representative in the departments and communes. In departments prefects ensure that the services of the state are properly administered and its policies implemented. In the communes, they are superior to the mayors when mayors act in their central state capacities.

In this way, mayors, with their central and local functions, and prefects, as appointed representatives of the state in local affairs, combine to ensure that the policies of the central state are implemented and to integrate central and local services. As in federal government the French system tries to combine elements of local autonomy and democracy with a degree of central and shared central–local control of public affairs. In this way federal and unitary governments try to achieve the same very general goals but by different means.

Source: www.citymayors.com/france/france_gov.html

■ Unitary, federal and confederal government compared

Having described the operations of federal, confederal, and unitary government in theory and practice, we can now compare their advantages and disadvantages. This is done in controversy 6.1. We can draw three general conclusions from this summary:

1. Choosing between them is not a matter of deciding between good or bad, or even between better and worse, but trying to decide which is better for what purposes and under what circumstances.
2. Federal systems are better suited to large countries, especially where minorities are concentrated in geographical areas that can be given a degree of independence from central government. Unitary states are better suited to small, homogeneous countries.
3. Confederations are good at dealing with specific policy areas where those who participate in the confederation want to retain their own formal independence.

Local government

Why do we have local government? Why not allow central government to run everything, or perhaps restrict the system to two levels alone – national and regional? The answer is simple: most countries are far too large and complex to be run by a single centre, or even by a few regional units of government. Government must **decentralise** some of its operations in the interests of both democracy and efficiency. It makes no sense, for example, to have bureaucrats in the capital city deciding when to close park gates in some distant

CONTROVERSY 6.1

Unitary, federal or confederal?

Unitary	Federal	Confederal
For		
• Central government is clearly accountable	• Another form of the separation of powers	• Permits states (or other autonomous political units) to cooperate while maintaining their sovereignty
• A single centre of power that permits coordinated and decisive state action	• Encourages consensus and compromise between federal and other state authorities	• Makes loose cooperation possible when tight integration is not wanted or needed
• Best suited to small states, or homogeneous states with similar regions	• Best suited to large states (either population or geographical area), and/or those with markedly different regions	• Best suited to cooperation in one sector or field of government activity – economic (IMF), diplomatic (UN), defence (NATO)
• Can help national integration by focusing on national politics	• Can protect the rights of territorially concentrated minorities	• May be the only form of cooperation possible
• Facilitates the equalisation of regional resources (through national tax system, for example)	• Can maintain the unity of the country by containing regional divisions, so deflecting and defusing potentially dangerous national conflicts	
• It is still possible to grant some areas special powers (e.g. Basque Country in Spain)	• Encourages small-scale experiment, innovation and competition between states: the efficiency argument	
• Helps the creation of a system of equal rights and duties for all citizens	• Creates opportunities to respond to the different needs and demands of groups in different regions	
Against		
• Can result in an over-powerful central state	• Can result in duplication, overlap and confusion of responsibilities and accountability	• Unstable – members can withdraw easily

Unitary	Federal	Confederal
• Can result in national majorities exploiting or repressing regional minorities	• May lead to conflict, inefficiency, or stalemate between levels of government	• Can be ineffective – when members cannot agree because there is no sovereign power
• Can result in a rigid and hierarchical form of government detached from local conditions	• Can result in complex, slow and expensive forms of government	
	• Can be inherently conservative	
• Over-centralisation can lead to break-away demands for local and regional autonomy	• Can strengthen tendencies towards national disunity and disintegration and deflect attention from national interests	
	• Can deflect political attention from national groups and interests to geographical interests	

town, or what books to buy for the local library. These are local matters that are best left to local hands. As a result, most countries rely heavily on local government to deliver a wide range of services.

The difficulty lies not in justifying either centralisation or decentralisation in theory, but in deciding exactly what and how much to centralise and decentralise in practice. As a general rule, the 'high politics' of state (e.g. international diplomacy, defence, economic development, the distribution of national resources) are handled by central government, while local government has its own core services (its general **functions such as** local planning, transport, refuse collection, sewage, local libraries, parks, fire services).

Fused systems: The system of local government in unitary states in which central officials directly supervise the work of local government.

Dual systems: The system of local government in unitary states in which local authorities have more independence than in fused systems but within the authority of central government.

Increasingly, however, there is a larger grey area of services that are shared or mixed between levels of government to various degrees (education, police, major highways, serious crime, and a variety of special services such as specialist research centres, housing policy, regional development, air traffic, national libraries and museums).

Local government in unitary states tends to fall into three broad categories. Ranging from the most to the least centralised, these are **fused systems**, **dual systems** and local self-government.

Fused systems

The clearest example of the fused model is the centralised and uniform system set up by Napoleon in France. He placed agents of central government (*préfets*) in each local government unit (*département*) to supervise their work and ensure that central government policies were carried out. The French state gave greater autonomy to sub-central layers of government in 1982. Variations on the centralised French system are found in Italy, Spain and Portugal and in their former colonies and spheres of influence in Africa, Asia and the Americas, as well as in Japan and South Korea. Fused systems are also found in many of the new democracies where sub-central political officials were traditionally appointed by the ruling central government.

Dual systems

The classic example of the dual system is Britain, where central government retains a good deal of power, though it does not directly control local government through an army of *préfets*. Rather, it 'manages' local government at arm's length, thereby giving it rather more autonomy. Many key public services (education, housing, health) are delivered by local councils but controlled and financed to varying degrees by central government. Local authorities are required by central government to provide some services and engage in some activities, but may have discretion over other services and activities. The British system has gradually become more and more centralised over the last 100 years. The dual system is found in the UK, the USA, Israel and India, and in many former British colonies in Africa, Asia and the Pacific. There was world-wide approval in the 1980s and 1990s of local self-government, but good intentions were not always put into practice.

Local self-government

The principle of local self-government with more freedom of local action characterises the Nordic countries. Local government is entrusted with the tasks allotted to it by central government, and has freedom of taxation within limits. As figures 6.1, 6.2 and table 6.2 show, local government in Denmark, Finland and Sweden accounts for a relatively high proportion of public expenditure and employment among the unitary states. Whatever the local government system, it involves a degree of decentralisation of government and a degree of autonomy and legitimacy for local government. This makes a lot of sense in many ways, but it also creates two special problems:

- central–local political conflict
- the dilemma of reconciling the needs of democracy and efficiency.

Central–local political conflict

Political conflict between central and local government is endemic in many states. If local government is to play its democratic role, it must be elected by, and accountable to, local citizens; but central government is also elected and accountable. Which level of government is to have the final word in decision making? The problem is likely to be aggravated if central and sub-central government are controlled by different political parties. This is often the case because local elections are usually held between national elections (mid-term elections), when there tends to be a reaction against the central government of the day. The result is that parties in opposition at the national level are often elected locally. Party political conflict is sometimes thus built into central–local relations. Usually this is resolved by negotiating, bargaining and compromising. In turn, this calls for a set of institutions which enable central and local governments to talk to each other and resolve their problems.

The problem of how best to fund local government is a permanent source of disagreement and conflict. On the one hand, central government is ultimately responsible for national fiscal policy and the level of public spending – both local and national. It also controls most of the taxes that raise money (income tax, business and sales taxes) and it is the rare local authority that can fund its own services from its own revenues. In addition, the demands of equality between areas mean that central government redistributes money from rich to poor areas, otherwise the latter would have unacceptably poor public services. Transfers of money from central government are often the largest source of funds for local authorities. On the other hand, democratically elected local councils naturally wish to control their own affairs, which means minimising financial dependence upon central government. The Japanese say that their local government is '30 per cent free' because 70 per cent of its money comes from central government.

The resulting tensions between financial centralisation and decentralisation were heightened in the second half of the twentieth century by the sustained growth of the welfare state and by the increasing amount of public money spent by sub-national government – money that was often provided by central government grants and transfers. The situation was then compounded by financial problems and cuts in services in the last part of the century, and even more by the tendency for central government to delegate new service responsibilities to the localities without funding them adequately.

Democracy, size and efficiency

The second dilemma for local government is how to reconcile the often competing claims of democracy and *efficiency*. There are eight main aspects to this problem.

Subsidiarity: The principle that decisions should be taken at the lowest possible level of government – that is, at the level closest to the people affected by the decisions. Usually the term subsidiarity is used in connection with the territorial decentralisation of government, but it is not limited to this form.

- Democracy in local government requires that it should be based, as far as possible, around small communities of people where participation is easiest and there is a common identity and set of interests among citizens. The **subsidiarity** principle requires that decisions are taken at the lowest possible level in the system.

- Some services are most efficiently provided on a small scale, some on a larger one. Parks, refuse collection, local libraries and local transport are small-scale, but refuse disposal, central reference libraries, higher education, urban transport, water and police services are larger-scale. This means that there is no single optimum size for multi-purpose authorities.

- Services are not isolated from each other. They need integrating so that, for example, residential areas, schools and hospitals are provided with public transport, and transport should be integrated with local economic development and environmental policies. This means that there is a need for a body that can plan and coordinate a wide range of services, some small-scale, some large.

- Some services are clearly not desired by very local communities, and citizens will use local democracy to block the construction of nuclear waste storage, jails, drug addict clinics or provisional housing for refugees in their communities. In general these services are desired, but citizens don't want to have them in their backyard **(NIMBY)**. Decisions about the location of such unwanted services cannot be taken by local authorities only.

  > **NIMBY:** (not-in-my-backyard) the principle that some government service is generally desired, but is not welcome in my own community.

- Local government units should be large enough to have a tax base adequate for their purposes, and they should probably be large enough to have a mix of rich and poor citizens so that the financial load can be equitably distributed.

- Some of the largest cities (Calcutta, London, New York, Tokyo) are bigger than some countries, and require large units of local government to run them, even if they have smaller sub-divisions nested within them. On top of this, there is a problem of where to draw the boundary around any large city. Should they be defined fairly narrowly to include only densely populated urban areas, or should they include the surrounding commuter suburbs and villages? Since suburban commuters use central city services for both work and pleasure, it seems sensible to draw wide boundaries around cities.

- Some features of local geography and history, such as rivers, mountains and historic divisions, suggest boundaries between local government units that may not fit neatly with the most efficient or the most democratic scale of service provision. Sparsely populated areas and groups of islands are often combined into geographically large units of local government with small populations.

- Optimum sizes change according to technical developments and ideas about how public services should be organised. Sometimes this reduces scale, but in other cases it increases it. Computer networks, for example, make it possible to decentralise some town hall functions and create many little local offices that are more accessible to the public. At the same time, the capital and environmental costs of refuse disposal and recycling make it necessary to operate on a larger scale than before. As city populations grow or shrink, so the optimum size of service-providing units also changes – small schools and those with a declining number of pupils are closed and their pupils sent to larger schools that are supposed to be more effective and efficient.

This means that there is no optimum size for units of local government, nor is there a 'natural' range of service functions for it: it is a matter of trying to balance economies and diseconomies of scale, and weighing up the often competing demands of large-scale efficiency and small-scale democracy. There are many different ways of organising local government, and the endless search for the best balance explains why local government across the Western world has been subject to constant reform. There is also little agreement about how best to measure efficiency in some local government services, so there is disagreement about the best size for them. Most countries have experimented with three forms of local organisation and service delivery to solve these problems of democracy and efficiency:

- general-purpose authorities
- joint bodies
- single-purpose authorities.

General-purpose authorities

These deliver a wide range of services and go under such different names as municipalities, communes, districts, prefectures, boroughs, councils and shires. They are invariably directly elected, but their function and population size vary enormously from one country to another. Local government in some large cities is sometimes split into two or more tiers each with different powers and functions according to their level.

Joint bodies

Rather than create new, larger authorities by merging two or more smaller ones, some countries have kept their smaller general-purpose authorities but created a range of joint bodies to provide a range of special mutual services (economic development, water supply). This practice is increasingly common across the world.

Special-purpose authorities

In some countries, particular services are provided by special single-purpose authorities. These include school boards, river authorities, water boards, urban transportation and police authorities. Special-purpose authorities are most frequently found in developing countries, in central and eastern Europe and in the USA.

The result of trying to match services and functions with different types and levels of local government units is often a complex and confusing structure of authorities. Such a structure may have a logic of its own, but one that is difficult to understand. The USA is an extreme case because it is fragmented into more than 85,000 units of local government in the shape of general-purpose authorities, special-purpose authorities, home-rule cities and cities without home rule and a bewildering range and variety of other agencies. The government of New York City, with its tangle of 1,500 local government and service units, has been called 'one of the great unnatural wonders of the world'.

Restructuring local government

For much of the twentieth century local government has struggled to keep pace with four key powerful social, economic and political changes.

1. *Social and economic changes* National and local political institutions have had to adapt to huge population movements, large shifts in working patterns, increasing interdependence of urban and rural areas, the growth of huge metropolitan areas and increasing national and global integration. Road transport, for example, has been transformed by the speed and volume of traffic, requiring much more government intervention, including national and international action.
2. *Financial pressures on central and local government* As the political demands and financial pressures on both central and local government grow, so both have to develop new modes of operating and relating to each other.
3. *Ideological pressure for decentralisation* Politics in the late twentieth century began to favour decentralisation and grass-roots participation.
4. *Technology* Transport, communications and computer technology have affected patterns of work, residence and leisure, and they have also made the decentralisation and devolution of local government easier, just as they have helped to centralise other public functions (central police records, national standards for schools and hospitals).

The result of these changes is that local government has been the object of constant restructuring, and few democracies have not altered their local government system at least once since 1945. Amid the huge variety of reforms and developments seven general trends stand out.

1. *Consolidation* In many countries small units of local government have been amalgamated and consolidated into larger units. Sometimes central government, especially in unitary states, has initiated reforms, but in other cases local units have voluntarily merged. Sweden, Denmark and the UK have reduced the number of their municipalities by up to 75 per cent. Consolidation has also occurred in Canada, New Zealand, Australia, and Japan, less so in France, Switzerland and the USA.
2. *Meso-government* Many unitary states have strengthened or created a middle level of regional government – **meso-government** – that fits between central and local government. In some cases this meso-level has been given substantial powers and service responsibilities so that it is the functional equivalent of state government in federal systems. In western Europe, France, Finland, Italy, Ireland, Greece, Spain and the UK have introduced important regional layers of government, while Austria, Canada, Denmark, Sweden, Switzerland and the USA have strengthened their middle levels of government and given them greater powers.

> **Meso-government:** A middle level or tier of government between central and local authorities, and often known as state, regional, provincial, or county government.

3. *Decentralisation* Local government in some unitary states has often been given a broader range of responsibilities and powers. Many new democracies

in central and eastern Europe in have done this in their efforts to democratise. Denmark, France, Hungary, Iceland, Ireland, Japan, Sweden, New Zealand and the UK have shifted some services from central to local levels. In some cases the powers and functions of cities have shifted downwards to the localities, communities and neighbourhoods – for example in Chicago.

4. *Centralisation* Both federal and unitary states have become more centralised in some respects. Sweden has shifted some powers from local to central government, and central control over local finances and services has increased substantially in the UK. In Australia, Canada and the USA the federal government has taken greater powers over state and provincial governments – over education in Australia, health services in Canada, and welfare, integration, minimum drinking age and speed limits in the USA.

5. *Politicisation* Local government became increasingly political in the late twentieth century. As local authorities enlarged their size and responsibilities, parties and ideological groups penetrate the corridors of power and contest local elections.

6. *Central–local conflict* Politicisation of localities has sometimes brought them into direct conflict with central government, especially where different parties are in power and both levels claim democratic legitimacy from their elections. This has occurred in many parts of the world where national political struggles have spread to the local level.

7. *Contracting out and privatisation* Almost all democratic states have contracted out, privatised or created public–private partnerships to some extent. This is further discussed in chapter 8.

Usually these reforms are justified in technological, modernising and efficiency terms, but in addition there is sometimes (or perhaps often?) a political agenda behind them as parties in power seek to change the system to their own advantage. This may involve making it easier to implement their policies but it may also deprive opposition parties of their political strongholds and undermine their organisational and voting strengths. Some right-wing governments have reduced the powers or even abolished units of big city government because they are controlled by left-wing parties. Conversely, some left-wing governments have reduced rural authorities or tied them to their nearest urban government in order to reduce the strength of the conservative countryside. As usual, politics often plays an invisible role in supposedly technocratic government.

■ The interplay of multi-level government: the case of the EU

We have seen how the changing world has brought about greater interdependence between levels of government, and nowhere is this clearer than in the EU. The mere existence of the Union as a developed form of supra-national government means, of course, a degree of centralisation in Brussels. At the same time, the EU pays careful attention to its regions (as federal systems do), putting regional policy and grants high on its priorities. Its Committee of the Regions (CoR) is only an advisory body but it gives regions a direct input into EU deliberations. As a result the EU can often bypass national governments – which can be a nuisance when they present obstacles to its policies – and deal directly with the meso-level of regional government. This enhances the power, importance and financial resources of the regions, and therefore represents a decentralising tendency. Consequently, the EU is both a centralising force, insofar as some national powers have moved upwards, and a decentralising one, insofar as it strengthens regional government, while encouraging regional dependence on Brussels for financial and political support.

■ The arguments for and against centralisation and decentralisation

The merits and difficulties of centralised and decentralised forms of government are presented in controversy 6.2. This makes it clear that the debate has many sides. It is not a question of whether to have either centralised or decentralised government, but rather a matter of what to centralise and how much, what to decentralise and how much, and what to share between higher and lower levels of government and how much. There are no clear answers to these questions and the debate is likely to continue.

CONTROVERSY 6.2

To centralise or decentralise?

■ Arguments for decentralisation

- *Democracy* Local government adds an important dimension to democracy by allowing people in small communities to participate in, and have some control over, their own local affairs. Because it is also closer to citizens, local government may also be more accessible and democratic.
- *Efficiency* Centralisation may be inefficient, as many large corporations and the highly centralised states of the communist era found, because it means that decisions are taken by people who are far removed from the implementation of the decisions and from first-hand knowledge of their effects. Centralisation may be too rigid and unresponsive to local needs and demands.
- *Adaptation to local circumstances* Should central government officials in the capital city decide what time to lock local park gates, or how to run local libraries? Such things ought to be decided by local people according to their wishes and knowledge of local circumstances.
- *Local minorities* Decentralisation allows geographically concentrated minority groups to control their own local affairs.
- *Training ground for democracy* Local government is a citizen training ground for democracy.

- *Recruiting ground for national politics* Local politics help to develop a pool of politically interested and talented people who can be recruited into national politics. Many national politicians start off in local government.
- *Experimentation and development* State and local government can experiment on a small scale with new services and new methods of delivering services. Successes can spread quickly; failures are not large-scale disasters.

■ Arguments for centralisation

- *Efficiency* Sometimes centralisation is more efficient because of economies of scale.
- *Indivisible services* Some services are indivisible. Regional planning of economies, housing, work, school, hospitals has to be integrated and carried out at both centralised and decentralised levels to be effective and achieve its goals.
- *Integrated services* Some services can only be done, or are best done, at a higher rather than a lower level of government – for example an integrated transportation system of road, rail and air, specialised health, education and research, serious crime and nuclear waste, among others.
- *Specialisation and cost* Specialised health, education and research, serious crime, among others. The Large Hadron Collider built by the European Organization for Nuclear Research (CERN) is the largest machine in the world and could only be financed and run with the collaboration of 10,000 scientists from over a hundred countries and with input from over a hundred universities and research institutes.
- *Redistribution* The redistribution of resources and the equalisation of public service quality between different areas can only be done by a central authority.
- *Minority protection* Some minority groups require a large political unit to reach a critical mass before they gain sufficient number to be politically influential.
- *Local elites* Decentralisation can protect entrenched local elites, often wealthy landowners and business leaders.
- *Disintegration of the state* Decentralisation may feed the desire of regional elites for further decentralisation or national disintegration – Basque separatism, Quebec, Scottish nationalism.

■ Theories of multi-level government

Theories of multi-level government tend to fall into three basic types: first, philosophical and political defences of decentralised government, including pluralist theory; second, rational-choice theories of federalism and local government; and, third, historical accounts of centre–periphery relations.

Philosophical and political theories: Mill and Tocqueville

The basic philosophical and political arguments for decentralised government were laid out by a French writer on American democracy, Alexis de Tocqueville (1805–59), and the English philosopher John Stuart Mill

(1806–73). Developing basic liberal values, Mill argued that local self-government was important because, as far as possible, political decisions should not be imposed from above, but developed and accepted from below. According to Mill, local government gives more people a first-hand experience of public affairs and a greater chance of direct participation in them and so it is the chief instrument for educating people about their citizen duties. Tocqueville argues a similar case, but his writing concentrates on the citizenship benefits of local parties and voluntary associations rather than local government, ideas we shall consider in chapter 10.

Pluralist theories

Modern pluralist theory builds on Mill and Tocqueville. It argues that democracies should not have a single, monolithic centre of power but require many centres of power so that many people and groups can exercise influence on different issues, in different ways and in different political arenas. Democracies divide power vertically (into executive, legislative and judiciary) and horizontally (into different layers of territorial government) in order to create a variety of political arenas. Groups that lose a political battle in one arena can turn to another, and so live to fight another day. If they fail to get satisfaction in, say, central government, they can take their causes to the courts, or local government, or perhaps international arenas.

Breaking the political system into geographical units with their own powers and responsibilities also has the advantage of decentralising political problems, and hence of not overburdening the centre with an accumulation of divisive issues. This is especially important where minorities (ethnic, linguistic, religious, or cultural) are geographically concentrated and where they have their own sub-central units of government to tackle their own problems in their own way. What makes local politics important is its very 'localness' – meaning that it is accessible to local people and that they are best placed to understand and deal with local issues.

Economic theories

Rational choice

Rational-choice theories borrow heavily from economics and assume that politics is based on the rational calculations of actors (individuals, organisations, governments) who are self-interested and who try to maximise their own preferences. Many rational-choice theories start from the position that the political world consists of individuals, as against institutions with a culture and a history, who make rational choices that maximise their own utility. The theory assumes that political behaviour is driven by calculations of self-interest. Rational choice is a high-level general theory and it has been applied to many aspects of government and politics. Here we are concerned with its use to explain (1) the origins of federalism, and (2) its defence of highly fragmented systems of local government made up of very small, competing, jurisdictions.

According to William Riker (1920–93), the origins of federalism lie in a 'bargain' between national and local leaders, to the benefit of both, which enables them to expand the territory under their control, and to defend it against external enemies. Federalism is a rational solution to the problem of how to maintain a balance between the interests of a central power and of geographical regions so that each maintains control of their own affairs but can cooperate to deal with a common, external threat, and thereby increase their own power. In his book *Federalism: Origins, Operation, Significance* (1964), Riker claims that evidence about the origins of federal systems supports his hypothesis that military security and territorial expansion are the driving forces behind the formation of federations.

William Riker, *Federalism: Origins, Operation, Significance* (1964)

It can be argued that much the same explanation accounts for the historical origins of unitary states as well. Many were forged historically from smaller political units, city-states and princedoms when these were threatened by large, efficient and powerful enemies. A single authority brought together by centralising leaders had a much better chance of developing the economic capacities and military power to compete effectively with external enemies. If so, the formation of both federal and unitary states is a response to external economic and military threats, and the need to create a larger and stronger political unit to deal with them. What distinguishes them is the historical circumstances of their development along either federal or unitary lines, something best explained by centre–periphery theory, discussed below.

Rational-choice theory of local government

Rational-choice theory also has its theory of local government, especially the highly fragmented and divided local government in the metropolitan areas of the USA. Splitting the government of a large urban area into many local jurisdictions, and giving each its own taxing and spending powers, means that citizens (the theory calls them 'consumer-voters') are provided with a choice of different 'packages' of public goods at different prices. Consumer-voters can move from one locality to another in search of their preferred 'package' of public goods, in much the same way that shoppers choose their supermarket for the goods it sells and the prices it charges. One municipality may have low taxes and few public services, another may tax in order to provide good education for young families, while a third may specialise in services for the retired.

This theory substitutes an economic logic for a political one: consumer-voters can move from one municipality to another to maximise their preferences, instead of using their vote to influence civic leaders and local public services. The economic argument is that a highly fragmented system of government is not inefficient, as many argue, but, on the contrary, produces a quasi-market that allows consumer-voters to vote with their feet. Some political economists find this approach helpful and insightful, but others doubt its value, for a string of reasons. First, consumer-voters are not free to move at will from one municipality to another. They are severely constrained by the needs of work, family, schools and house prices. Second, survey data shows that few people see local public services as very important when they are deciding where to live. Being near work, family and shops is much more important. Third, there is only a tenuous link between local taxes and services in many countries because financial transfers from higher levels of government pay a large proportion of the local service bill. And last, in most countries other than the USA, local government is not fragmented into many competing jurisdictions. It is consolidated and coordinated by higher levels of government which redistribute national tax resources and regulate local services in the interests of service quality and equality between municipalities.

Centre–periphery relations

Unitary states have typically emerged from old, centralised monarchies that kept their local government under the authority of central government as they gradually developed their modern democratic structures. Denmark, Finland, Japan, Netherlands, Norway, Sweden and the UK are examples. In contrast, federal states are often formed by the merger of established and autonomous political areas that come together to form a political union, while retaining a degree of their original independence. In the case of Switzerland, federalism is designed to accommodate a history of autonomous localities created by mountainous geography and reinforced by language and cultural differences. In the case of Australia, Canada, India and the USA, federal governments cover large geographical areas that were not previously united under a single (monarchical) centre, but brought together or created by a colonial power.

According to the widely quoted theory of Rokkan and Lipset (see chapter 1), the historical process of state and nation building involved, among other things, the centralisation of regions and territories under a common central rule. In many cases a powerful and modernising elite first conquered outlying areas and their local elites and then, by the processes of state and nation building, created a single political system with common political institutions and a common sense of national identity. The processes started many centuries ago in the case of some European countries, and took a long time to complete. Even so, one can often still see the historical imprint of centuries past in modern times, even in the most centralised and uniform unitary state, where the parties, voting and political/social patterns of peripheral regions are often rather different from the metropolitan centres.

133

However, the centre's attempts to incorporate the periphery has not always been altogether successful, as we can see from the nationalist movements in Italy (the Northern League), Spain (the Basque country and Catalonia), the UK (Scotland, Wales and Northern Ireland) and France (Corsica). In such cases, the unitary state may best be preserved by devolving powers to the peripheries. In the unusual case of Belgium, a unitary state turned itself into a federal one in order to maintain the integrity of the country.

Relations between the centre and the periphery are often relations between dominant and subordinate political groups. One variant of centre–periphery theory argues that the institutions of the central state were originally created by powerful interests (a class or ethnic group) that exploited the periphery for its resources, in much the same way that colonial powers exploited the natural resources of developing countries. According to some writers 'internal colonialism' of this kind exists in a subtle form in the UK (where England exploits Scotland, Wales and Northern Ireland) and the USA (where the north exploits the south), and in countries where the capital city region dominates and exploits the surrounding rural and agricultural areas.

■ What have we learned?

This chapter has dealt with the organisation of multi-level government. It argues that:

- The government and politics of the modern world consists of four main levels, with the lower levels nested in higher ones – local government nested inside middle or meso-government, nested in unitary and federal systems, and a layer of international and supranational government above them all.
- Most organisations at the international level are confederations that are looser than federations and do not encroach on the sovereignty of their members. The European Union is part federation, part confederation.
- Federal systems are more decentralised than unitary states, although to some extent federal systems have centralised and unitary states have decentralised since 1945.
- Federal systems are better suited to some circumstances (large countries with territorially concentrated minorities) and unitary states are better suited to others (small, homogeneous countries). There is a close association here between social and geographical circumstances and forms of government.
- Local government in all countries, federal or unitary, faces two insoluble dilemmas:
  (a) the conflict that often arises between different levels of democratically elected government;
  (b) the problem of how to reconcile the conflicting claims of democracy and effectiveness.

■ Lessons of comparison

- There is not a single or a simple solution to the democracy versus efficiency dilemma because there is no single, optimal size for units of sub-central government. Each country has its own solutions, each with its merits and deficiencies.
- Attempts to solve these democracy versus effectiveness problems can take different forms involving the consolidation of units of local government into a smaller number of larger units, a shifting of service functions both up and down the political system, the creation or strengthening of meso-government, a degree of decentralisation in federal states and centralisation in unitary ones.
- The centralist/decentralist debate revolves around the problem of what to centralise, and how much, and what to decentralise, and how much, and what to share between levels of government. In most countries, whether unitary or federal, there is a large area that is neither central nor local but involves close cooperation between central and sub-central government.
- Once again, there is no simple choice between unitary or federal systems of government. Both have advantages and disadvantages and are best suited to different national circumstances.

Projects

1. Draw up a table that assigns government functions in your country (international relations, education, pollution control, libraries, parks, economic development, housing, transportation, police) to different levels of the political system (international, national, regional, local, community). What general lessons can you draw from this exercise?
2. Sub-central government is responsible for varying proportions of total government expenditure and employment in different countries (see figures 6.1 and 6.2 and table 6.1). Would you draw the conclusion that the higher the sub-central share of public expenditure and employment, the more decentralised the country?
3. Suppose your country needs to find a place for the storage of nuclear waste but no community is willing to accept the construction of such a plant on their territory. How could a decision procedure look that is both efficient and democratic?

Further reading

B. Denters and L. Rose (eds.), *Comparing Local Government: Trends and Developments*. Basingstoke: Palgrave Macmillan, 2005. An account of local government in western countries.

P. John, *Local Governance in Western Europe*. London: Sage, 2001. A comprehensive and wide-ranging account of institutions and how they have changed local government in western Europe.

OECD, *Managing Across Levels of Government*. Paris: OECD, 1997 (also at www.oecd.org/dataoecd/10/14/1902308.pdf). Compares multi-level government in twenty-six member states of the OECD.

P. E. Peterson, *The Price of Federalism*. Washington: Brookings Institution Press, 2012. An analysis of the benefits and disadvantages of federal government in the USA.

R. A. W. Rhodes, S. A. Binder and B. A. Rockman (eds.), *The Oxford Handbook of Political Institutions*. Oxford University Press, 2008. Contains excellent reviews of the literature on federalism, institutionalism, and local government and many other forms of governmental and political institutions.

Websites

www.citymayors.com/government/aus_locgov.html.
A comprehensive website describing the local government systems of thirty-seven countries in the Americas, Europe, Asia and Africa, and Australia.
www.forumfed.org.
The Forum of Federations is an international network on federalism and related issues. General information about federalism, useful links and a list of countries with federal systems of government.
www.coe.int/T/Congress/Default_en.asp.
The website of the Local Government International Bureau from the Congress of Local and Regional Authorities of Europe. Covers forty-seven countries in Europe.
http://encyclopedia.thefreedictionary.com/Local%20Government.
Basic introduction to local government with links to related topics.
http://encyclopedia.thefreedictionary.com/Unitary%20state.
Basic introduction to unitary states with links to related topics. List of unitary states with links to general information about them.
http://encyclopedia.thefreedictionary.com/Federation.
Basic introduction to federation and federalism with links to related topics.

7   Policy making and legislating: executives and legislatures

Governments are there to get things done. At the highest level, the most important things are to formulate public policies and frame the laws of the land, and at the heart of the policy and law-making process lie the two main branches of government – the executive and the legislative assembly. This means that the study of the relations between executive and legislative branches is a topic that lies at the very core of comparative politics.

Sometimes the executive and the legislative branches cooperate and act together, sometimes they fight and struggle for power. Since democratic constitutions deliberately divide the powers of government between different branches, so that they check and balance each other, there is nothing wrong with the political struggle between them. However, some analysts argue that all is not well with the classical system of checks and balances because the golden age of legislatures, some time in the nineteenth century, has given way to the twentieth-century supremacy of executives. What were once powerful elected assemblies with a great deal of control over the affairs of state are now said to be little more than rubber stamps for decisions made by their executives. If true, this has obvious implications for democracy in modern executive-dominated government.

Others claim that presidents and prime ministers have not acquired such great power. They argue that legislative assemblies were never that powerful to start with, that the balance of power between executives and legislatures has not changed much and that executives are still dependent upon the support of their elected assemblies.

Another part of the discussion is concerned with correcting a common misperception about the actual role of legislative bodies, rather than how much power they have, or have lost. To 'legislate' means to make laws, and who should do this other than those who are elected to the legislative chamber? Do not our national assemblies sit in endless discussion – sometimes solemn debate, sometimes angry and heated argument – about the policies and laws of the government of the day? Yet law making is not actually the main function of legislatures, and may not even be one of their most important functions. The curious fact is that legislatures, in spite of their name, are not mainly there to legislate. To understand why this is the case, we must examine the main functions of legislative bodies.

Administration: (1) A term synonymous with government – e.g. the Obama administration, the Merkel administration; or (2) a term synonymous with the management processes of bureaucracies – e.g. the administration of the state through bureaucratic agencies.

Since things rarely ever remain the same, we will also examine recent efforts of legislative assemblies to modernise. Many of them are in the process of reforming and streamlining themselves for modern government **administration**, so that they can do their work more efficiently and acquire the political muscle necessary to exercise more control over their executives.

In this chapter, we analyse the relationship between executives and legislatures in the policy and law-making processes of modern democratic government; that is, we focus on the meaning of administration as the management processes of bureaucratic agencies. The major topics are:

- making laws: executives and legislatures
- the increasing power of executives
- the functions of legislatures
- the reform of legislatures
- theories of democratic institutions: consensus and majoritarian systems.

■ Making laws: executives and legislatures

Classical democratic theory divides government into three main branches – executive, legislative and judicial – and gives them different powers and functions so that none can become too powerful. Each should have powers of its own, and each should operate a system of checks and balances to ensure that they are dependent on each other. In this way neither can do its job without the agreement of the other if they are bound together in a relationship of perpetual, mutual dependency, as they should be according to the theory of the separation of powers (see chapter 4). In virtually all democratic systems legislation can be passed only when both the executive and legislative

Legislation: The body of laws that have been passed by the legislature. Legislating is thus the act of initiating, debating and passing such laws.

branches agree. Indeed, this condition is formally spelled out in some constitutions. For example, Article 81 of the Dutch constitution states, 'Acts of Parliament shall be enacted jointly by the Government and the States General.' It is this sort of formal requirement for agreement that tries to ensure that power is shared.

In real life, however, some democratic systems deviate to a greater or lesser extent from the classical formula. Because the two branches should work closely together there is inevitably some overlap and fusion of executive and legislative functions and powers, and it is more accurate to say that their powers are mixed rather than separated. This is most evident in parliamentary systems, but it also applies to presidential ones where, although there is supposed to be a clearer separation of powers, there is, as we saw in chapter 4, in reality a complex and subtle mix of executive and legislative powers.

Some have, however, argued that the classical system of executive and legislative checks and balances does not operate in modern government. They claim that modern executives have acquired so much power that they now dominate the processes of government, reducing legislative assemblies to the role of junior partners, even to little more than rubber stamps for executive decisions (see controversy 7.1). If this is true, then the lack of checks and balances may even pose a threat to democratic government itself.

CONTROVERSY 7.1

Parliaments and legislatures

■ What happened to parliaments?

Something has happened to parliaments. Parliaments were the key institutions of representative democracy. They translated the voice of the people into reasoned debate and ultimately into law. They also held governments to account; of all the checks and balances of power they were the most effective. They symbolised the constitution of liberty. For my father – and later for me – becoming a member of parliament was an affirmation of our deep belief in democracy.

Much of this, however, has to be said in the past tense today. A number of developments have conspired to weaken parliaments:

- Governments have increasingly used orders, regulations and other secondary legislation which is not subject to parliamentary scrutiny.
- There is also a tendency for governments to turn directly to the people – by referenda, but more ominously by relying on polls and the views of 'focus groups'.
- This process goes hand in hand with phenomena like celebrity politics (candidates have to be telegenic), and snapshot or throwaway politics (what counts is the moment, not extended debate).
- Self-elected crowds and groups, demonstrations in the streets, non-governmental organisations, increasingly claim to be the people, to speak for the people.

- All this happens at a time at which important decisions have emigrated to political spaces for which there are no parliaments anyway. This is as true for internal decision making as it is for the role of economic markets.

(Adapted from Lord Dahrendorf, speech at the Institute for Human Sciences, Vienna, Newsletter, 72, Spring 2001)

■ A decline of legislatures?

In what was the first truly empirical study of Western governments, James Bryce (1838–1922), devoted a chapter to the subject of the 'decline of legislatures'. He argued that legislatures were weak and legislators incompetent or even corrupt. The idea of the decline of legislatures seemed confirmed in the twentieth century by the weaknesses of west European parliaments, not to mention those of most developing countries.

While contemporary legislatures are often weak, there is some doubt as to whether they *declined* in quality and power during the period which preceded Bryce's investigation, let alone in the decades which followed. The view that there was a 'golden age' of legislatures seems at best exaggerated …

Legislatures are generally weak. Their weakness is due to general causes, many of which are structural and are connected with the complexity of matters and the need for urgent decisions. Only on a very few occasions did they realise the standards which Bryce, and, indeed, earlier, Locke and Montesquieu, would have wanted them to display.

(Adapted from Jean Blondel, Comparative Government, London: Prentice Hall, 1995: 250)

The rise of executives

There are good reasons for believing that the balance of power between executives and legislatures may have shifted decisively in favour of executives. Six stand out as particularly important.

1. *Government complexity* The growing complexity and interdependence of the social, economic and political world gives a new importance and role to executives. As technical problems grow ever more technical (nuclear power, the environment, the economy), as society becomes ever more complex and difficult to manage, as demands on government grow, as international and global pressures increase, so complex government increasingly requires a single centre of coordination and control. In addition, one of the major problems in modern government is to keep the multifarious agencies, departments and units of government moving in the same direction, and this increasingly difficult job of coordination is an executive rather than a legislative function.

2. *Delegated legislation* The nature of legislation also changes. It is no longer possible to frame laws for specific and known circumstances – these change

too quickly, in accordance with technological innovation, international forces and social pressures. It is necessary instead to devise more general laws, which inevitably leave much of the detail to be decided by executives. This is known as **delegated legislation**, and it gives executives more power.

3. *Organisational advantages of executives* Executives have significant advantages when it comes to organising for power. They are usually small in number – presidents and cabinets – which makes it easier for them to unite around a common interest, and to react quickly and decisively to events. They are often supported by large and well-funded staffs in presidential and prime ministerial offices, and they are headed by highly visible political leaders who are able to appeal directly to the population, over the heads of the members of the elected assembly.

> **Delegated legislation:** Law or decrees made by ministers, not by legislatures, though in accordance with powers granted to them by the legislative body.

4. *Mass media* Modern executives equip themselves with effective press offices to help them exploit every ounce of favourable publicity they can get from the mass media. To some degree, the debating functions of legislatures have also been transferred to the mass media because more public debate about politics now takes place in television studios than in parliamentary debating chambers. In contrast, legislatures are rather large and cumbersome bodies consisting of hundreds of elected representatives, divided along party lines, and often unable to act quickly or with a single voice. In such circumstances executives take the lead and acquire power.

5. *Party organisation* In modern legislatures elected representatives are often tightly organised and highly disciplined along party lines. This helps executives to maintain control of their parties and ensure that their policies and **bills** are accepted. By and large, the stronger the party system, the stronger the executive, and the weaker the legislature. The major exceptions to strong executive power are usually found in countries with comparatively weak parties. Switzerland is probably the best example, but in Israel, the USA and the new democracies of central and eastern Europe, weak and fragmented parties help to undermine the executive and strengthen the legislature.

> **Bill:** A formal proposal for a law put before a legislature but not yet accepted by it.

6. *Emergency powers* The threats of pandemics, natural disasters and terrorism require, some argue, greater power in the hands of political executives who are best able to respond quickly and effectively to emergencies, and if they do so effectively and decisively they are likely to gain popular esteem.

There is evidence to support these general arguments. First, some executives have been given greater law-making powers in recent years (Australia and France). Second, the executives in many countries have made increasing use of the power of delegated legislation, which gives them more decision-making autonomy. Third, some analysts argue that prime ministers in parliamentary systems have become so powerful that they have, in effect, assumed the powers and status of elected presidents. This is said to be occurring in Australia, the UK and Hungary, where a series of powerful prime ministers have accumulated decision-making authority that has transformed their office. Fourth, as we saw in chapter 6, power in federal systems, the most decentralised form of government, has become increasingly concentrated in the twentieth century, and in doing so has given the executive officers of their federal governments greater power than before.

Arguments about the rise of executives are strongly disputed by other political scientists, who claim that the trend is more apparent than real. They point to events that seem to show that even the strongest executives can be reined in by their legislatures. Nixon had to resign to avoid **impeachment**. Clinton was impeached, but not convicted of the charges. Thatcher was eventually toppled by her parliamentary party. The power of the 'imperial presidency' in Mexico has weakened, and in Norway the influence of parliament has grown in recent years. There are examples of coalition governments falling because they no longer had the confidence of their elected assemblies (see chapter 13). Consequently, it is said, the old executive systems of prime minister and cabinet continue to function more or less as they did in the nineteenth century, in the sense that power is shared and mixed between the two branches of government.

Impeachment: To charge a public official, usually an elected politician, with improper or illegal conduct in office before a duly constituted tribunal, usually an elected legislative body. Depending on the country, an official who is impeached may either be removed from office or be formally tried by another legislative body. Impeachment is not known much outside the USA, and not often used there.

Increasing power of executives?

Is it possible to resolve the dispute about the increasing power of executives by reference to some systematic evidence? The figures in table 7.1 show what proportion of bills in fifteen western European countries were introduced by executives, and what proportion of these were duly accepted by legislatures and passed into law. The figures show two things quite clearly. First, most bills are introduced by executives, not legislatures. Second, the overwhelming majority of bills introduced by executives are accepted by the legislatures and become law.

What can we conclude about the rise of executive power? Not much, some would say. The fact that legislatures invariably accept executive proposals for legislation simply shows how carefully executives sound out opinion in the legislative body before they present proposals. This argument is based on what Karl Friedrich (1901–84) has called 'The law of anticipated reactions'. This states that wherever there are mutually dependent power relations, those involved will try to anticipate the reaction of others and modify their own behaviour accordingly. In terms of executive–legislative relations, neither is likely to make a move or a proposal that is likely to be rejected by the

Table 7.1 The source of legislation: governments and legislatures

	Government bills as percentage of all bills	Government bills total	Bills total[a]	Percentage of government bills passed
Britain[a]	60.4	1,224	2,025	92.4
Denmark[e]	48.2	2,10	435	93.3
(West) Germany[a]	72.2	1,999	2,767	94.3
France[a]	60.6	3,311	5,466	98.5
Iceland[f]	64.0	110	172	67.3
the Netherlands[f]	94.3	249	264	94.0
Belgium[a]	53.2	2,710	5,096	84.3
Austria[c]	53.3	496	931	97.2
Ireland[d]	38.1	45	118	12.5
Finland[d]	–	939	–	87.1
Spain[b]	53.3	237	445	84.4

Sources:
[a]T. Bräuninger and M. Debus, 'Legislative Agenda-Setting in Parliamentary Democracies', *European Journal of Political Research*, 48(6) (2009): 804–39.

[b]www.congreso.es/portal/page/portal/Congreso/Congreso/Iniciativas and www.senado.es/web/actividadparlamentaria/actualidad/leyes/entramitacion/index.html#IN%20THE%20CONGRESS%20OF%20DEPUTIES

[c]www.parlament.gv.at/PAKT/RGES/ (Bills 2008–2013)

[d]www.oireachtas.ie/viewdoc.asp?DocID=-1&StartDate=1+January+2014&CatID=59 (Bills 2014)

[e]www.ft.dk/Dokumenter/Publikationer/Folketinget/~/media/Pdf_materiale/Pdf_download/Aarsberetning/Aarsberetning_2013_14/aarsberetningen_2013_14.pdf.ashx (Bills 2013–2014: page 28)

[f]Data from contacting the respective parliamentary information offices (Iceland:2013–2014; Netherlands: 2014)

other, so they sound each other out carefully before taking action. In fact, in most systems of government the two branches maintain an elaborate set of institutions and officials in order to maintain a constant dialogue to find out what each is prepared to accept. Unfortunately for the political scientist, much of this goes on behind the closed doors of party committee rooms, and we do not hear much about the endless process of mutual bargaining and adjustment – what is sometimes termed 'wheeler-dealing' or 'horse-trading' which usually involves compromise.

Others, however, argue a different story. They agree that a good deal of legislation is based on shared powers and mutual accommodation between executives and legislatures. Nevertheless, the fact that most legislation is introduced by the executive, and that a very large majority of it is accepted by legislative assemblies suggests, to them, that executives are very powerful, even that legislatures have been reduced to little more than 'rubber stamps' and 'talking shops'. A key factor here, it is said, is the presence of increasingly centralised and disciplined political parties. Because party unity is so crucial to modern politics, and because a divided party is unlikely to do well in elections, party members in assemblies are under great pressure to comply with the wishes of their leaders. Strong parties make for strong executives; weak parties make for strong legislatures.

It may well be that the controversy about executive dominance will not be resolved. The executive seems to have gained the upper hand in some (Britain under Thatcher and Blair seems to be a good example), but mutual dependence seems to characterise others, especially where party systems are weak or fragmented and legislative committees are strong (Denmark, Switzerland, the USA).

Whatever the strengths of executives, or some of them, we should not slip into the assumption that legislative bodies are powerless in the face of almighty executives. It is one thing to claim that executives are increasing in power, quite another to say that legislatures are powerless. Indeed, elected assemblies still have an important role to play in government, and they are organising themselves to increase their influence and efficiency.

■ The functions of legislatures

Elected assemblies play many roles and have many functions, but these may be conveniently grouped under four general headings:

- The representation of public opinion
- The legitimation of government and the political system
- Law making
- The scrutiny of the executive and the administration of the state.

Representation of public opinion

Legislatures are the main representative body in democracies, and therefore the main assembly must be directly elected in order to reflect public opinion and to be accountable to it at election time. In most cases, this means reflecting party political opinion, because most first chambers are elected along party lines. Some assemblies, however, represent the political interests of specific groups in society (farmers, workers, businessmen, churches, minority groups), or specific areas (cities, regions, or constituencies). No matter how they are elected or how they reflect public opinion, however, legislatures perform the common function of representing the electorate. In turn this means that legislative bodies must sort out and represent the main clusters of public opinion – a function known as **interest aggregation** – and then voice them in policy debates – a function known as **interest articulation**.

Interest aggregation: Sorting the great variety of political attitudes and opinions on a political issue, to reduce it to a simpler, more clear-cut and agreed 'package' of opinion.

Interest articulation: The expression of political demands in order to influence public policy.

Elected assemblies are often criticised for not being representative of society, and it is true that many are not a social microcosm of the population they represent. Most are dominated by what might be called the four 'Ms' – that is, middle-class, middle-aged, majority group, males. In fact many elected legislatures are drawn heavily from a rather restricted set of occupations and social groups, most notably the professions (especially lawyers), civil servants and the better educated sections of society. Politics is becoming more 'professionalised' in the sense that elected representatives, when first elected, have spent little time in ordinary life and jobs, going into politics as young adults and staying there as they climb the 'greasy pole' of a political career. In sum: elected politicians in national government are rarely a good cross-section of society.

Against this, it might be said that it does not particularly matter whether the elected assembly is a microcosm of society or not. In the first place, politicians can represent the views of social groups other than their own. For example, middle-class individuals can reflect and defend the interests of the working-class people, and, indeed, many of the early pioneers of socialism were middle and upper class. In the second place, it might be argued that what counts most is to represent the views of political parties, which is how the electorate most usually divides itself when it votes. Most popularly elected legislatures do this fairly well, although exactly how well depends in large part on the voting system, as we shall see in chapter 12.

Legitimation

Whatever its composition and method of election, the fact that parliament is directly elected by the population and that it meets regularly in public to debate political issues, is important for the **legitimation** of the political system. Elected legislatures give governments their democratic legitimacy, and help stabilise the political sys-

> **Legitimation:** The process of making something morally or ethically acceptable, proper, or right in the eyes of the general public.

tem. This means that they not only legitimate the government of the day, but also the whole political system and the rules by which it works. This is important because it means that those who oppose the government will accept it because it is elected. Oppositions can wait patiently for the next election when they have a chance of taking over government themselves and being recognised as legitimate by those who have just been turned out of office.

Law making

We have already seen that most legislatures do not initiate bills, but they do consider them at some length. In many cases they change and modify details – sometimes important details – and in some cases are able to throw out bills or alter their fundamental intent. The intense pressures on parliamentary time means that some bills, or parts of them, are not scrutinised in any great detail. All, however, are processed according to a complex set of rules governing the passage of bills through parliament before they become law. This usually involves a sequence of debates or readings in one or two chambers, and a series of hearings in legislative committees, also in one or two chambers. Bills normally shuttle backwards and forwards between these debates and hearings and are subject to modification along the way before they are finally accepted (see briefing 7.1 for a Swedish example). To this extent, the mutual dependency of executive and legislative branches of government is a major feature of parliamentary systems. The legislative body is more important and

Briefing 7.1

A legislature at work: the Swedish Riksdag

- The Riksdag takes decisions on government bills, and on motions from its members concerning legislation, taxation and the use of central government revenue.
- Meetings of the chamber form an important part of the work of the members, but much also takes place in the party groups and in the sixteen Riksdag committees. The committees, whose members are drawn from the various parties, are working groups with responsibility for a particular area of business.
- All proposals for a Riksdag decision must first be considered by one of its sixteen committees. The committee publishes its conclusions in a report which may then be debated and decided by a plenary session of the Riksdag.
- Decisions in the chamber are often preceded by a debate.
- When the debate is over, the matter is decided, either by acclamation, or (if there are dissenting opinions) by vote.
- Occasionally the chamber will refer a matter back to the committee. When this happens, the committee has to reconsider the matter and draw up a new report.
- Members of the Riksdag are allowed to submit an **interpellation** – a question to a minister about the performance of his or her duties. Such questions enable the Riksdag to scrutinise and control the work of the government, to obtain information or to draw attention to a particular issue.

> **Interpellation:** A parliamentary question addressed to government requiring a formal answer and often followed by discussion, and sometimes by a vote.

- Question time is held weekly for about one hour. The prime minister and six or seven other ministers answer questions put directly to them by members of the Riksdag.
- If a party group in the Riksdag wishes to debate a particular matter which is unconnected with other business under consideration, it may request a current affairs debate. In 1997–8 five were held.
- Occasionally the government provides the Riksdag with oral information on issues of current interest. This is often followed by a debate.
- Much of the work of the Riksdag is regulated by the Riksdag Act, which regulates the chamber and its meetings, the election of the Speaker and the way in which business is prepared and decided.
- The Riksdag board is responsible for the overall planning of parliamentary business, including the selection of work procedures. The board comprises the Speaker (chairman) and ten other members who are appointed by the Riksdag from among its members.

(Adapted from the Riksdag's website www.riksdagen.se/en/)

powerful in the law-making process of some countries (Italy, Switzerland and the USA), but in all democracies the legislature does discuss and criticise new legislation, with a view to modifying it, or even rejecting it outright. Yet in every system a proposal or plan can only become a law after being accepted by the majority of the legislature.

Scrutiny of the executive and the administration

A primary function of elected assemblies is to keep a close watch on the executive and on the administrative machinery of the state. Examining government bills is one method of doing this, but there are many others:

- *Veto powers* Some legislative bodies have powers to veto or modify policy proposals made by the executive.
- *Approving executive appointments* Appointments to high positions of state such as ministers, secretaries of state and national bank directors are involved here.
- *Question time* Most presidents or prime ministers are required to present themselves or explain themselves to their legislative bodies either in person or writing. Normally questions are routine parts of the parliamentary timetable (see briefing 7.1), but they can be special (impeachment proceedings against the American president, for example – see below).
- *Debate* Debates are an occasion to consider government policy and actions in some detail. Some debates are concerned with specific pieces of legislation and may be quite technical, others are on general political issues, and some about emergency matters. The advantage of debate is that it subjects governments to the glare of public scrutiny and criticism, and can help to improve the quality of the legislation. The disadvantage is that debates in public assemblies are often reduced to party political 'shadow boxing' – ritual events staged for the public.
- *Vote of no confidence or impeachment* The ultimate power of legislative assemblies is the ability to remove the executive by a vote of 'no confidence' or impeachment. In parliamentary systems the government of the day can remain in office only as long as it has the support of a majority in the assembly. If it loses a vote of confidence in the assembly, it can no longer continue in control and will have to resign so that a new government with majority support can be formed. In many parliaments the rejection of an important government proposal is sufficient to conclude that government has lost its confidence. The dependency of government on the confidence of parliament is the cornerstone of the relationship of mutual dependence between the executive and the legislature, and we shall discuss it again in chapter 13, which considers the formation of party and coalition governments.
- *Committees* Perhaps the most important single legislative development in recent times is the strengthening of committees. In fact, committee work is now such a significant part of legislative operations, and so crucial to the scrutiny of executives, that it needs to be considered in greater depth.

Legislative committees

Parliaments, including the European Parliament, are adapting to changing circumstances and trying to improve their effectiveness by streamlining their procedures, and by providing members with better facilities and resources (offices, secretaries, researchers, information). Most important they are increasingly concentrating on the scrutiny (sometimes known as 'legislative oversight') of executive and administrative action. They have tried to do this by creating more effective and more powerful committees (see briefing 7.2).

Legislative oversight: The role of the legislature that involves the scrutiny or supervision of other branches of government, especially the executive and the public bureaucracy.

Close scrutiny of government cannot be done in large meetings. It is better performed by small committees with the time, experience and technical expertise to delve into the great complexities of modern legislation. Committees can also avoid the worst aspects of ritual party conflict that is often found in the main debating chamber. Effective and powerful committees, in turn, require their own expert advice and information, bureaucratic support and time for detailed work. If they are to have a major impact they must also be powerful, which means having a loud bark as well as sharp teeth – in other words they need real powers which enable them to influence government action.

Briefing 7.2

Parliaments, executives and committees

[I]t is now becoming widely accepted that parliaments should be independent of the executive in the way they organise themselves, including control over their own timetable and the ability to recall themselves outside normal session if circumstances so require. This is one area where the constitutional difference between presidential and parliamentary systems is more clearly marked. In the former the typical challenge may be to achieve effective cooperation between legislature and executive; in the latter the challenge is rather to achieve a more robust organisational independence or autonomy …

Most of the work of a parliament is carried out in committees, whether legislative or oversight committees, or a combination of the two. It is an accepted practice in almost all parliaments that the membership of such committees is proportionate to the strength of the different parties or groups in the chamber as a whole …

The most systematic method for oversight of the executive is by parliamentary committees which track the work of individual government departments and ministries, and conduct specific investigations into particularly salient aspects of their policy and administration. Many parliaments have reformed their committee systems to enable them to parallel the respective government departments and their members to develop appropriate expertise accordingly. In many countries these are joint committees of both chambers of parliament. Although even specialist committees are unable to be comprehensive in their coverage of the respective department's work, it is sufficient for accountability that the department knows that they *could* investigate any aspect and do so rigorously, even if in practice they have to be selective.

Source: www.ipu.org/dem-e/guide/guide-6.
htm#P1144_264386

Many legislatures are trying to assert their power, or regain lost powers, by developing an effective committee system for the twin purposes of reviewing government bills before they become law, and oversight of executive action. This is often an uphill battle, because committees depend on executives to grant them powers and resources, and executives are usually unwilling to do this, because they know that these powers may well be turned against them. The clearest examples of powerful and powerless committees are in the USA and the French Fifth Republic. The former has a remarkably complex and powerful system of small and expert committees that can, and frequently do, exert a profound influence on executive appointments and policy. The French system is restricted to six committees, two of which have 120 members, and are therefore pretty ineffective. The Danish parliament also derives a good deal of its influence over government affairs from its effective committee system.

Effective committees tend to have a membership of fifteen to twenty-five or thirty people, with a good core of members who have served long enough to gain specialist knowledge and experience of a particular policy area. If there are enough of them, committees can cover a wide range of government business, including the close and detailed scrutiny of bills, public spending, foreign affairs, and all the main aspects of home affairs. In addition, many parliaments appoint committees to review exceptional cases or decisions (reviewing, for instance, the way government granted a huge army project or handled the consequences of a natural catastrophe). Each committee has a convener, or chair, who usually has a high standing and long experience in parliamentary affairs. The party composition of committees often reflects that of the assembly as a whole, with a majority of government members.

If they are to be influential and independent of the government, parliamentary committees will probably be constituted in the following ways:

- Their chairs should not necessarily be members of the governing party or parties.
- They should have their own staff and expert advisors.
- They should have powers to call witnesses and the right to question them closely, including leading members of the government.
- They should have had time to build up their own knowledge and expertise in the business handled by the committee.
- They should be able not only to issue public reports, which get publicity in the media, but also have the power to require government action following their recommendations.

Committees may not have all these powers in full, and hence they may not often operate at maximum strength, but nevertheless they are one of the most effective weapons that legislative bodies have in their battle with powerful executives.

■ Theories of democratic institutions: consensus and majoritarian systems

On many occasions in previous chapters we have pointed out that there is an enormous variety of formal democratic arrangements and institutions, and that each country combines them in its own unique manner. We have also observed that this great diversity of constitutional characteristics usually resolves itself, in practice, into only a few general patterns shared by many countries. For example, in spite of their differences in length, detail and content, constitutional documents normally fall into four distinct parts. Again, of all the different ways of combining executive–legislative relations, these usually revolve around only three types – presidential, semi-presidential and parliamentary. And although there are a great many different ways of organising territorial government within a country, there are only two main types in practice – federal and unitary – and only a few sub-types in each category. Fortunately for comparative political scientists, what might easily be a confusing mass of detailed country-specific differences turns out, in the end, to fall into a comparatively simple general pattern, albeit with exceptions to the general rule. This is good news for students of comparative government because it means that they can generalise about a number of similar democratic systems rather than point out the detailed differences between each and every one of them, although these undoubtedly exist.

In his ground-breaking comparison of thirty-six democracies, Arendt Lijphart (1936–) observes that despite their enormous variation, democracies tend to fall into two general categories. He calls these *majoritarian* and *consensus* democracies. Majoritarian systems, as the name suggests, give political power to the majority of citizens and the political parties that represent them, while consensus democracies try to represent as many people and groups as possible. The basic mechanism of the majoritarian model is to concentrate power in the hands of the political executive and to leave the exercise of this power relatively unconstrained. The majoritarian model concentrates executive power and places comparatively few restraints on its exercise, while the consensus model both disperses power and restrains its use.

The main characteristics of the two types of democracy are listed in table 7.2.

Majoritarian democracy, or the 'Westminster model'

This model

- concentrates executive power by giving it to whichever party (or, more rarely, combination of parties) controls a bare majority in the legislative assembly
- fuses executive and legislative powers in the classic parliamentary manner
- concentrates power by being either unicameral or, if, there are two chambers, by giving one assembly a clearly superior status

Table 7.2 The main institutional features of majoritarian and consensus democracies

Majoritarian democracy	Consensus democracy
Concentration of executive power	Executive power sharing
Fusion of executive and legislative power	Separation of powers
Single party government	Coalition government
Two-party system	Multi-party system
Simple majority electoral system	Proportional electoral system
Unitary government and centralisation	Federalism and decentralisation
Asymmetric bicameralism or unicameralism	Balanced bicameralism
Constitutional flexibility	Constitutional inflexibility
Absence of judicial review	Judicial review

- gives the courts no special powers to review legislation or decide constitutional matters, because this would diffuse power to another branch of government
- has a degree of constitutional flexibility by allowing the constitution to be changed by majority vote in the legislature
- is often a unitary state and gives central government considerable powers not only over its own business but also that of the territorial units of government below it
- has majoritarian and disproportional electoral systems favouring the emergence of two major parties, banks that are dependent on the executive and a pluralist interest group system.

We shall discuss interest groups, electoral systems and party systems later (chapters 10, 12 and 13) but can now consider the formal constitutional and institutional features of majoritarian government. It is no coincidence that the institutional characteristics of majoritarian government tend to go together, for they 'fit' with one another in a consistent and logical way. The British system is one of the best examples of majoritarian democracy, and it was based on the principle of parliamentary sovereignty, at least until membership of the EU changed this. If parliament is sovereign then it follows logically and inevitably that no other body or institution of government should be able to challenge parliament – not the courts, nor a written constitution, nor lower levels of government, nor a second chamber. The idea is to create a stable and effective government with power to get things done, but that is still accountable to the population through the elected legislature.

Consensus democracy

Consensus democracy also relies on majority government, but rather than concentrating power, it shares it. Consensus democracies

- Try to construct broad coalition government consisting not of a single majority party or a bare majority of them, but of a coalition of them.

- Separate and balance executive and legislative power.
- Are often federal – which, of course, means a degree of territorial decentralisation. In some cases safeguards may be built in for non-territorial language, ethnic or cultural groups, which are given a degree of governmental autonomy.
- Have two legislative assemblies (bicameralism), often with balanced powers.
- Have judicial review of political and constitutional matters, as a way of trying to sort out conflict between the different branches and levels of government.
- Have a degree of constitutional inflexibility, because they try to maintain their diffusion of power and to include a wide range of opinion in any attempt to change the system.
- Have proportional elections, multi-party systems, corporatist interest-group systems, and independent central banks.

These institutional features of government also 'fit' together logically, given the initial assumption that the job of democracy is to include and represent as many groups as possible. Such a government would share and separate power between the main parties and between two representative assemblies. It would also divide government territorially, especially if it were a large country in terms of geography, or population, or both. It would make sure that its arrangements were not easily changed by a few vested interests, and would reinforce the rights of all citizens by giving the courts the right to review constitutional matters and public policy. All this would be a particularly coherent package if the society in question were a culturally and ethnically mixed one, or what Lijphart terms a 'plural' society. These are particularly likely to be federal systems, and to have the other characteristics of consensus democracy. The basic idea is to create a form of government that is stable and effective, and works by distributing power, including most social groups in the political process and building a consensus acceptable to most of the organisations and parties involved.

Lijphart's study of democracy is widely discussed and has inspired much other research, but it is not without its critics. Some claim that the typology is too broad and general to apply to all cases, and that there are many exceptions that do not fit properly. The USA is neither majoritarian nor consensual, but a bit of both. Switzerland is a consensual system but it does not have judicial review. Canada is a consensus federal system in some respects, but has had dominant one-party cabinets.

We will return to majoritarian and consensus democracies later (chapter 13), after we have considered voting systems, and pressure group and party government, which are additional features of the two types of democracy not yet discussed.

■ What have we learned?

This chapter deals with the roles of the executive and legislative branches of government, whose relationship is at the very heart of policy and law making. It argues that:

- In democratic theory, the executive and legislative branches should be separate, and each should maintain a system of checks and balances on the other. In practice, there is more of a mix than a separation of powers.
- There is a controversy about whether executives have increased their power in recent decades in response to a variety of social, economic and political pressures.
- Legislatures still have an important role in government. They represent public opinion, help legitimate the political system, review bills proposed by the executive and watch over the executive and state bureaucracy.
- Legislatures have tried to improve their efficiency and authority in different ways, but especially by developing committee systems that enable them to perform their function of scrutiny and oversight more effectively.

■ Lessons of comparison

- Powerful legislatures often have comparatively weak party systems in the legislative body (and vice versa) and a comparatively strong committee system.
- Although each democratic system of government has a unique combination of particular features, they often combine their general characteristics in only a few ways, so creating some general patterns and only a few general types.
- In spite of their infinite variety of detail, democracies tend to come in two main types, majoritarian and consensual.
- There are clear links between the social conditions of a society and its system of government. Consensus democracies are often large and pluralist societies. Many majoritarian systems are members of the British Commonwealth and show their British heritage in their government.
- Large plural societies tend to be consensual, suggesting that there is an important social basis to consensus forms of government.
- Historical background is important. Many majoritarian systems are British Commonwealth countries and developed their majoritarian institutions at the time of the British Empire.

Projects

1. Does the composition of your own national parliament show that it is dominated numerically by the 'four Ms' – middle-aged, middle-class, majority group, males? What are the implications of your conclusion?
2. The website for your own national legislature is likely to have information about its committee system. What can you conclude from it about how the system works and how influential and important it is in the government of the country?
3. Has the power of the executive increased in your country over the past few decades?

Further reading

J. Denis and I. D. Derbyshire, *Encyclopedia of World Political Systems*, Vol. 1. Armonk: M. E. Sharpe, 2000: chs. 4 and 5. A comprehensive overview of the world's executives and legislatures.

P. Heywood, 'Executive Capacity and Legislative Limits', in M. Rhodes, P. M. Heywood and E. Jones (eds.), *Developments in West European Politics*, 2nd edn. Basingstoke: Palgrave Macmillan, 2002.

A. Lijphart, *Patterns of Democracy: Government Forms and Performance in Thirty-Six Countries*. New Haven: Yale University Press, 2012. A broader, deeper, expanded and updated version of the classic work.

L. Longley and R. H. Davidson (eds.), *The New Roles of Parliamentary Committees*. London: Frank Cass, 1998. A good book on the role and development of parliamentary committees.

A. P. Norton (ed.), *Parliaments and Governments in Western Europe*. London: Frank Cass, 1998. A useful set of essays on western Europe.

Websites

www.ipu.org.

Information on the structure and working methods of parliaments in the world (including the EU) with links to each country and the regional groups of parliaments.

www.ipu.org/dem-e/guide/guide-6.htm#P1144_264386.

A long and detailed account of how parliaments work in practice with national examples.

www.ecprd.org/

The European Centre for Parliamentary Research and Documentation deals with European parliaments.

8 Implementation: the public bureaucracy

Governments make policy and pass laws, but they are not and cannot be involved in the vast amount of routine implementation and daily administration of policy. For this, they rely on government ministries and the army of state bureaucrats who work in them. Like armies, the bureaucracy ranges from a small handful of very top officials down to office workers who carry out the routine work. The jobs of the highest officials sometimes called 'mandarins') are little different from those of the chief executive officers (CEOs) of multinational corporations in the private sector, while many of the lower ranks are known as '**street-level bureaucrats**' because they come into everyday contact with the general public.

Street-level bureaucrats: The bureaucrats who regularly come into contact and deal with the public.

Whether they are mandarins or filing clerks, state bureaucrats are sometimes seen as lazy and inefficient. But alongside this stereotype there exists a completely different one that views bureaucrats as ambitious empire builders who want to expand their own departments in the interests of their own status and salary, and who conspire to take over the policy-making function of politicians to make sure that things are run according to the bureaucrats' wishes. As often in life there are opposite and contradictory stereotypes.

Bureaucracy: A rational, impersonal, rule-bound and hierarchical form of organisation set up to perform large-scale administrative tasks.

There is another deep ambivalence that permeates the public **bureaucracy**. On the one hand, no democracy could even exist without effective bureaucracies to implement public policies and deliver public services. On the other hand, senior bureaucrats are often more experienced and highly trained than their political masters, and their role at the very heart of government gives them an enormous potential for power in the affairs of state. Yet they are supposed to be servants, not masters of the state.

In this chapter, we examine controversies about the role and power of public bureaucrats. The chapter outlines, first of all, the organisation of the state bureaucracy before looking more closely at the distinction between policy making and administration. It then considers the theory that it is permanent officials (bureaucrats) who run the state, not elected politicians. Politicians, of course, are fully aware of the potential power of their top civil servants, so the chapter continues by looking at how they try to counter this power. Finally, the chapter examines the wave of recent reforms that have tried to make the public bureaucracy more efficient and theories of public bureaucracies.

The major topics in this chapter are:

- The organisation of the state bureaucracy
- Policy making and administration
- The dictatorship of the official?
- The New Public Management
- Theories of public bureaucracy.

■ The organisation of the state bureaucracy

The administration of the state – that is, the day-to-day work of implementing policies – is carried out by the bureaucratic departments or ministries of government. These are usually organised around the major functions of the state: economic affairs, foreign relations, defence, home affairs, transport and communications, education, welfare, the environment and so on. There is no logical or best way of dividing these functions, so the list of ministries varies from one country to another. In some, education is grouped with family matters, in others it is organised with employment and vocational training. Similarly transport, the environment and planning may be combined in the same ministry, or remain separate. Sometimes there is a special ministry for women and children.

As a result, ministry sizes vary enormously from quite compact ones (ministries of justice are often separate and small) to huge super-ministries. Increasingly ministries combine a range of related functions under one umbrella in an attempt to integrate different aspects of policy – economic development, transportation and regional affairs, for example. The advantage is that related policy areas are combined under one organisational roof; the disadvantage is that the larger the department, the more cumbersome it may be.

The total size of the public bureaucracy also varies greatly from country to country. It is relatively small in Japan, Greece and Turkey, and relatively large in the advanced 'Nordic welfare states' of Denmark, Norway and Sweden (see table 8.1). But even when it is relatively small compared with other countries,

Table 8.1 Public employment[a] as a percentage of total employment, OECD countries, 2011

	'Limited' public sector[b]	'Extended' public sector[c]
Japan	6.7	7.9
Greece	7.9	20.7
Brazil	8.6	9.9
Mexico	8.8	10.0
Chile	9.1	
Germany	9.6	13.6
Switzerland	9.7	14.5
Poland	9.7	21.5
New Zealand	9.8	11.7
Slovak Republic	10.7	19.3
Turkey	11.0	12.0
Spain	12.3	12.9
Netherlands	12.6	21.4
Czech Republic	12.8	19.4
Italy	14.3	14.3
United States	14.6	
Slovenia	14.7	22.7
Ireland	14.8	16.7
Australia	15.6	
Israel	16.5	16.5
Canada	16.5	18.8
United Kingdom	17.4	18.6
Luxembourg	17.6	17.6
Estonia	18.7	22.4
Hungary	19.5	19.5
Russian Federation	20.2	30.6
France	21.9	24.3
Finland	22.9	22.9
Denmark	28.7	31.5
Norway	29.6	34.5

[a]The OECD warns that it is very difficult to define and compare public employment across different countries, and that therefore care should be taken in interpreting these figures. They refer to slightly different financial years in each country.

[b]The 'limited' public sector column covers central and federal government, regional and state government, and local government and the municipalities.

[c]The 'extended' public sector covers the limited sector plus public enterprises.

Source:
OECD 2013, *Government at a Glance 2011*, Paris: OECD Publishing.

Public sector: That part of social, economic and political life that is not private but controlled or regulated by the state or its agencies.

the **public sector** is often a rather large part of the economy in its own country. Japan, for example, has one of the smallest public sectors in the OECD countries, but it still accounts for an eighth of total employment. The largest public sectors account for a quarter of the workforce. Note, however, that the size of a ministry in terms of employment or its budget may tell us little about its power and importance. Japan's Ministry of International Trade and Industry (MITI) is closely integrated with the country's business and political elites, and has played a very important role in Japan's economic success, but it is not a specially large ministry.

The earliest empires had bureaucracies to help them run their large territories long before the French invented the word 'bureaucratie' in the eighteenth century to describe a form of government that was different from monarch and autocracy. The term 'mandarin' – referring to those at the very highest levels of the modern civil service – comes from the civil service of ancient China, but now every country has its modern equivalent whether they are called 'apparatchiks' in the Soviet Union, Eurocrats in the EU or *Beamte* in Germany. Being a top civil servant in many countries is very prestigious, perhaps most of all in France and Japan. The French administrative elite are known as 'Enarques' after the Ecole National d'Administration (ENA), while most of Japan's senior civil servants are, traditionally, the products of the University of Tokyo's Law School. Spain has its prestigious system of *cuerpos*, and the British have traditionally recruited from the universities of Oxford and Cambridge.

Although they perform the same administrative functions, countries recruit and train their top bureaucrats in one of two main ways. Some believe in 'generalists' of all-round ability and intelligence to work in a wide variety of top jobs. The UK, Ireland and, to some extent, Italy, Portugal and Spain tend to operate like this. In contrast, the 'specialist' tradition is more technocratic and trains people for particular departments or jobs – France, Germany, the Netherlands and the Nordic countries.

For all their power and importance in the affairs of state, departments and ministries are rarely even mentioned in constitutional documents, but nevertheless in the great majority of democracies they are governed by similar crucial principles. At the very top of each department or ministry – the terms are often used interchangeably – there is usually a politician who is ultimately accountable to the general public for its operations. They may be directly elected and senior members of the representative assembly, or they may be appointed by, and accountable to, an elected politician. In parliamentary systems ministers in charge of departments are usually elected members of the governing party or coalition, and they constitute the cabinet or council. In presidential systems, the heads of the most important departments of state may also constitute a cabinet, but they are usually appointed by, and accountable to the president, not drawn from the elected assembly or accountable to it.

In all cases, the theory is that the bureaucratic machinery of state should be under the control of elected politicians who are ultimately accountable to the general public, through the ballot box. Public sector bureaucrats are appointed to be servants of the state. They are not accountable to the general public but to their political masters. The policies of departments are supposed to be directed by elected politicians, and the day-to-day administrative work directed by professional bureaucrats.

The politicians in charge of departments work very closely with a relatively small group of the most senior bureaucrats in them. Although ministers are ultimately responsible for the work of their departments, they have to rely on the experience and specialist knowledge of their civil servants (bureaucracy), both to make policy and to manage the daily affairs of the department. Departments are vast machines, and because bureaucrats often know most about the complexities of both policy and its **implementation**, they advise their ministers on both these aspects.

> **Implementation:** The process of applying policies and putting them into practice.

There are three main types of senior bureaucrat with administrative and policy advisor functions:

1. *Permanent administrators* Some public bureaucracies are built on the idea that permanent officials – whether specialists or generalists – should faithfully and impartially serve their ministers, whether or not they agree on policy matters. Permanent administrators are supposed to be politically neutral. The British system is based on this 'faithful servant' notion of an impartial bureaucracy, and for this reason its civil servants are not allowed to take any public part in politics. One can see the sense in having a corps of trained, experienced and expert state bureaucrats, but the danger is that it becomes too powerful and stuck in its ways of doing things.

2. *Political appointments* Some countries are sceptical about permanent administrators. They clear out the very top layers of departments when a new government is elected, and appoint their own people. A new American president typically appoints 3,000 people to posts in Washington, though occasionally nominees are vetoed by the Senate. One can see the sense in having people sympathetic to the government running its departments, but there is also the danger of **clientelism** and of using public office for private gain. The practice of incoming governments appointing their own top layers of the civil service is an old one in Finland, France, Germany and the USA, but it is now spreading to other countries.

> **Clientelism:** A system of government and politics based on a relationship between patron and clients. Public-sector jobs and contracts are distributed on the basis of personal and political contacts in return for political support.

3. *Policy advisors* To counter the power of permanent officials, ministers increasingly appoint teams of their own policy advisors. They are distinct from appointed administrators because they are concerned with

policy, not day-to-day departmental matters. There are two main reasons for appointing policy advisors. First, civil servants may not always be impartial in their advice because they have their own professional and organisational interests and may develop fixed opinions about policy issues. Second, they may have worked so long and so closely with the private organisations they are supposed to regulate that they become 'captured' and 'domesticated' by these organisations and start representing their interests (see chapter 10). Outside policy advisors can bring a fresh approach to old problems. There have been comparatively few political appointments in Japan.

■ Policy making and administration

In theory, elected and accountable politicians should make policy; appointed officials should implement it. In practice, however, the line between policy and administration is not that clear. It would be exceedingly foolish to try to implement a policy that could not be sensibly administered; at the same time the best administration in the world cannot save a fundamentally flawed policy; the way in which a policy is administered might well influence its capacity to achieve its stated goals, as some studies show clearly enough. Policy and administration are intimately bound together and cannot be neatly separated, a point made effectively in briefing 8.1.

If there is no clear distinction between policy making and implementation, how do we decide whether one has stepped into the role of the other? This is one of the oldest and most hotly debated controversies in government and in political science – the power of public bureaucrats.

Briefing 8.1

Policy making and administration

The relations between senior politicians and their civil servants would not seem to be promising material for a successful television comedy, but it was the theme of the long-running *Yes Minister*, succeeded by the equally popular *Yes Prime Minister*, on British television. In one episode, the wily mandarin, Sir Humphrey Appleby, gives a lesson on policy making and administration to his new and inexperienced minister, the hapless Jim Hacker:

I do feel that there is a real dilemma here, in that while it has been government policy to regard policy as the responsibility of ministers, and administration as the responsibility of officials, questions of administrative policy can cause confusion between the administration of policy, and the policy of administration, especially where the responsibility for the administration of the policy of administration conflicts or overlaps with the responsibility for the policy of the administrative policy.

(Jonathan Lynn and Antony Jay, Yes Minister, *London: BBC, 1982: 176)*

■ The dictatorship of the official?

The power of the permanent official

Like many other political institutions, the state bureaucracy is (a) essential and (b) dangerous. On the one hand, public bureaucracies are essential parts of the state apparatus to implement policies and deliver public services. Can you imagine any contemporary government without a small army of bureaucrats to organise public elections, collect taxes, administer state pensions, run schools and hospitals, provide welfare services, draw up contracts for military hardware, inspect the roads, ensure that public health and safety regulations are observed, run police and fire services and answer queries about all these from the general public? Whether these are public or private operations makes no difference to the fact that bureaucrats of some kind are indispensable. Bureaucracies are also supposed to administer these services in a consistent, efficient and universal manner, rather than an arbitrary, idiosyncratic and corrupt one. In this sense, they are not only essential for the administration of large-scale government, but they promote equality and democracy as well.

At the same time, bureaucracies are also potentially powerful and anti-democratic. They have a reputation for being inefficient, rigid, bound by red tape, secretive and impersonal. They can nurture a 'bureaucratic ethos' that is managerial, technocratic, inflexible and undemocratic. Bureaucrats also have their own interests, which may conflict with those of politicians and the public. It is important, therefore, that public bureaucracies are controlled by elected representatives who, in turn, are accountable to the public. But are ministers in control?

According to the German social scientist Max Weber (1864–1920), it is the dictatorship of the official that is on the march, not that of the worker. He denies the Marxist theory that the workers can seize power by revolutionary action, and points to the enormous power of the permanent officials who actually run public bureaucracies whatever party is supposed to be in power. Among these, central government bureaucrats are especially important, although precisely the same argument applies to all forms of public and private bureaucracy – parties or large pressure groups (see chapters 10 and 13). Weber had three main reasons for claiming that civil servants are the masters rather than the servants of the state:

- *Qualifications and expertise* Politicians are not necessarily selected for their educational qualifications or managerial abilities. Senior bureaucrats are often hand-picked for their intelligence and ability and then highly trained.
- *Permanence* Politicians come and go as they move political jobs or lose elections, and their influence on any given ministry tends to be short-lived. Career administrators may stay in post for a long time and have a potential for exercising a long-term influence.
- *Experience* With permanence comes long-term and specialised experience as well as inside knowledge of how things work.

To these three considerations we can add two other factors that make it difficult for politicians to control their bureaucrats:

- *Secrecy* Civil servants sometimes protect themselves with powerful secrecy rules, which makes it difficult for politicians and the public to find out what is going on.
- *Fragmentation* We often think of the state bureaucracy as a single organisation shaped like a pyramid with power to control the smoothly working machine concentrated at the very top. In reality, it is often a highly decentralised – not to say ramshackle – structure of ministries, departments, agencies, commissions, units and offices, each with its own traditions, modes of operation, interests and powers. The 'ship of state' is not so much a huge oil tanker that takes a long time to change direction, as a whole fleet of ships and boats, all going in their own direction, and all handling the winds and tides in their own way. This makes it difficult to control and coordinate the public bureaucracies.

Mechanisms of control

To say that state bureaucrats may be difficult to control is not to say that they cannot be controlled. There are all sorts of ways of trying to enforce their compliance, if enforcement is necessary:

- *Politically appointed administrators and policy advisors* – see above.
- *Law* Bureaucrats are not above the law, and there is a rapid growth of administrative law regulating their behaviour, as well as a greater tendency to use the courts to overturn administrative action.
- *Recruitment and training* Training can be used to instil in bureaucrats a professional ethos of public service. However, this can cut both ways: intensive training can also result in a bureaucratic culture of isolation, secrecy and self-interest.
- *Representative bureaucracy* Some countries have tried to make their state bureaucracy representative of the general public rather than being a separate elite with interests of its own. The *Proporz* system which ensures a balance of recruits from the major parties is found in Austria. Another method involves **affirmative action** and equal opportunity policies that recruit from a broad cross section of the population and especially from women and minority groups. Many state bureaucracies now have affirmative action programmes of one kind or another.

> **Affirmative action:** Policies designed to redress past discrimination. Affirmative action may require state bureaucracies to increase recruitment from women and minority groups.

- *Scrutiny, auditing and regulation* Financial controls are increasingly used to regulate and limit bureaucratic operations, as are elaborate procedures for scrutinising, auditing and monitoring them. Ironically, modern public bureaucracies have sometimes created small teams of bureaucrats to ensure that the bureaucracy is kept as small as possible. Parliamentary committees are also increasingly involved and, as we saw in chapter 7, have increased their efforts to keep a 'watching brief' over state bureaucracies.

- *Open government* Bureaucratic secrecy can be reduced by 'sunshine laws' to promote transparency and public scrutiny. Sunshine laws aim to shine light into the dark corners of state activity so that we can see what is going on.
- *Ombudsmen* These have been appointed to protect the public against maladministration and abuse of power (see chapter 4).

It may well be true that civil servants can use their training experience and expertise to exercise undue power over public policies, just as it may be true that they can use all sorts of tricks to try to outwit or deceive their minister. They can present policy options in a biased way, withhold crucial information (be 'economical with the truth'), wear down their minister with a huge workload, place crucial documents at the bottom of the minister's in-tray, give them a pile of documents to read by early the next day with the most important item at the bottom, act as gatekeepers to block people and information from their minister. It is equally evident that elected politicians are often well informed about such devious behaviour and have their own ways of dealing with them. They may block promotions and pay rises, transfer untrustworthy people to boring jobs and employ the same tactics used against them against their civil servants.

It should be said, however, that it is extremely difficult to reach any firm conclusion about the Weber thesis about the power of (permanent) officials because we do not have, and probably never will have, the necessary information. Discussion between cabinet members and high-powered civil servants is usually behind closed doors and often protected by officially sanctioned secrecy. At the same time, politicians can find it handy to blame mistakes on their officials, even when they are blameless. So it is difficult to get information, much more difficult to get reliable information.

■ The New Public Management: reinventing government

It is clear by now that there are inevitable tensions between (a) the bureaucratic goal of efficiency and rationality and the democratic requirements of public participation and debate in policy making, and (b) the policy-making roles of politicians and the administrative jobs of state bureaucrats. In addition there is sometimes, rightly or wrongly, severe criticism of public bureaucracy on the grounds that it is either inefficient and lazy, or imperialistic and expansionist – sometimes both simultaneously. At any rate, state bureaucracies have tended to grow in size and cost over the past decades, and

New Public Management (NPM): Reforms of the public sector in the 1980s and 1990s, based mainly on what was thought to be private-sector practice and consisting mainly of privatisation, deregulation, business management techniques and 'marketisation'. Known also as 'reinventing government', it is said to have had the effect of 'hollowing out' the state.

are commonly criticised for failing to keep up with the latest managerial practices claimed for the private sector of the economy. The result has been a wave of **'New Public Management'** (NPM) reforms that has swept across democracies since the 1970s. These reforms have taken two main directions (often at the same time).

Privatisation and market efficiency

Many public services have been privatised, which is assumed to make them more competitive and efficient. Some government departments have been transformed into private, profit-making and semi-private agencies that are contracted by the state to deliver certain services at a fixed cost. The argument here has often been that the competitive nature of the market economy is inevitably associated with efficiency in delivering goods and services that are in demand. The CEOs of these new agencies are often not career civil servants but 'hired guns' on short-term, commercial contracts. Bureaucracies remaining in the public sector have often been decentralised, obliged to contract out some of their functions (e.g. computer maintenance and servicing), and adopt competitive internal markets in which divisions within the same bureaucracy 'sell their services' to each other. In other cases public-sector agencies have cooperated with private organisations to provide public services by public–private partnerships. The purpose of these different reforms is to privatise the routine bureaucratic operations of the state, so that they are driven by the competitive forces of the market (or quasi-markets) to become more efficient. Another purpose is to separate those who '*steer*' (think about policy and plan future developments) from those who '*row*' (carry out the routine tasks), on the grounds that those who steer ought not to have to worry about the business of rowing, and vice-versa.

After its initial success and broad acceptance of privatisation and the introduction of market regulation in many countries to improve the provision of government services, many countries have slowed down these reforms or even reversed their implementation. Apparently, private arrangements for health and education, for railways and roads, or for air control or maritime pilots sometimes failed to improve the availability, efficiency or costs involved. The replacement of public services by private arrangements, therefore, was viewed more critically by some at the end of the twentieth century.

Empowerment

A second set of reforms has been designed to change what were believed to be rigid, hierarchical, faceless and rule-bound public bureaucracies delivering 'one-size-fits-all' services into flexible, accountable and user-friendly agencies that are responsive to citizen demands. Users of public services have been defined not as 'clients' of professional services but as 'customers' of services who are no different from shoppers in supermarkets. Public participation in running public services has been encouraged by setting up school boards, customer complaint arrangements, computer communications and user groups. Street-level bureaucrats who interact with the public have sometimes been given more discretion over individual cases, making decisions more flexible and personal.

New Public Management reforms are highly controversial, and the evidence for and against them is inconclusive and ambiguous (see controversy 8.1). Moreover, their importance has been overtaken by the interest in electronic government and electronic democracy. This focuses on the potential for new forms of electronic communication to make it easier for citizens to inform themselves about and participate in politics, and easier for citizens to hold government accountable.

CONTROVERSY 8.1

The New Public Management
Defenders of NPM argue that:

- Specialised agencies and those delivering routine services can concentrate on their core activity – the efficient delivery of good and cheap services to their customers.
- Senior civil servants can focus on their main job of policy making, long-term planning and strategic thinking.
- A smaller and efficient public sector releases resources for private economic development.
- Market and quasi-market competition with a customer focus make public services more responsive to citizen demands.
- Released from public bureaucracy rules and constraints, agencies are better able to recruit the best talents to their workforce.
- NPM management has 'depoliticised' public services by taking decisions out of the hands of politicians.
- Most significantly, privatisation and market practices have replaced red tape and inefficiency with modern administration and efficiency.

Critics argue that:

- The benefits and impact of NPM have been exaggerated. The established civil service model continues to dominate and most government functions are still carried out by the hierarchical and centralised bureaucracies of government departments.
- Some public services may be improved by NPM, others are harmed. NPM is not a universal recipe for success.
- There are few accurate or reliable measures of public service efficiency before NPM changes, so we cannot know if NPM is more efficient now.
- NPM reforms are not as common in developing countries as advanced ones, and the benefits for developing countries are smaller.
- The costs of reform outweigh its claimed benefits.

- NPM has fragmented government into small pieces at a time when joined-up government is crucial to its success. Government is even less integrated and coordinated than before.
- NPM has sometimes resulted in public monopolies, and has not eliminated the mistakes and inefficiencies of either private or public sectors.
- Some privatised and deregulated services have had to be re-regulated and taken back into the public sector in all but name. Deregulation of banks and finance contributed significantly to the collapse of the financial system across the world in autumn 2008.
- **Privatisation** has replaced the ethos of public service and professional care with the profit motive.

> **Privatisation:** The process of converting public services and amenities to private ones.

- Economic efficiency is not the only or best measure of some public services. Fairness, justice and equity also matter. Judge public transport by its pollution, social services by their quality of care, refuse disposal by its recycling, and education by the development of individual talents and creativity.
- Agencies have not so much depoliticised services as made them more responsive to those who shout the loudest and apply the greatest pressures.
- NPM management has ignored other deep-seated problems, some created by governments that created NPM systems (see briefing 8.2)

Briefing 8.2

Musical chairs, ministerial activism and official reticence

No one seems to know how often senior civil servants, apart from permanent secretaries, move from one department to another or between unrelated or loosely related posts within the same department; but, if it is 'ridiculous' to rotate ministers 'really quickly', as the anonymous minister claimed, then the same must be said of rotating officials rapidly, especially as ministers inevitably rely heavily on those same officials. If both ministers and officials are rapidly rotating at the same time and in relation to one another, the results are almost certain to be suboptimal.

Our study of [government] blunders suggests that officials, at least in many government departments and in many policy areas, have become remarkably reluctant to speak truth to power. They do not want to speak largely because they believe that power does not want to listen. Objection is construed as obstruction. Again and again in our interviews, former ministers as well as retired civil servants commented on the fact that, even when officials had harboured serious reservations about ministers' latest bright ideas, they had failed openly to express their reservations ... Several of the blunders we describe undoubtedly resulted, at least in part, from this formidable combination of ministerial activism and official reticence'.

Source: A. King and I. Crewe, The Blunders of Our Governments.
London: Oneworld, 2013, 328–9, 335.

■ Theories of public bureaucracy

Theories of public bureaucracy (sometimes known as the **civil service**) take different views of the power of administrative agencies of the state. According to Weber, the bureaucracy is powerful, but he has little to say about how the bureaucrats will use their power. According to rational-choice theory, the bureaucracy is

> **Civil service:** The body of civilian officials (not members of the armed forces) employed by the state to work in government departments.

capable of controlling public policy, and does so to promote its own interests. According to clientelist theory, however, some bureaucracies are used by politicians for their own political purposes.

The rational-legal ideal-type

Max Weber argues that society modernises itself by becoming more bureaucratic. Bureaucracy itself expresses the ethos of modern society because it is based on legitimate power, and organised in a rational way according to formal rules. Weber defined bureaucracy as the most efficient method of performing large-scale administrative tasks, and created an **ideal-type** of bureaucracy with rationality, legality, hierarchy and formal rules as its core features. An ideal-type bureaucracy is characterised by its:

> **Ideal-type:** An analytical construct that simplifies reality and picks out its most important features, to serve as a model that allows us to understand and compare the complexities of the real world.

1. *Hierarchy* (or pyramid) *of command*, with authority based on official position (as opposed to personal characteristics such as age, gender, race, party membership or religion).
2. *Civil service* of salaried professionals appointed and promoted according to their specialised competence, training and experience.
3. *Formal rules* determining individual decisions and behaviour (rather than personal or arbitrary decisions) so that individual cases are treated in the same, predictable way.
4. *Rationality* – the choice of appropriate means to achieve given ends.
5. *Record keeping*, providing bureaucracies with an 'institutional memory' of what has been done in the past, and the rules and precedents governing this action.

It is often pointed out that no real-life bureaucracy can function in this way. In the first place, the mechanical application of rules is bound to create injustice and hostility if people feel themselves to be no more than numbers or cogs in a wheel. Life cannot be reduced to rules, precedents and routines, and a human element must almost always be recognised. Bureaucracies invariably develop an 'informal organisation' of short cuts, personal contacts and unofficial procedures that help smooth operations and improve efficiency.

In the second place, it is said that bureaucratic means will become ends in themselves if bureaucrats blindly follow rules and refuse to take initiatives or responsibility – something known as 'trained incapacity'. What sets out to be an efficient way of running the modern state may become inefficient; it may even be anti-democratic if trained incapacity prevents the efficient and responsive delivery of public services. As a result, real-life bureaucracies may work very differently from the ideal-type, something that has given rise to a huge amount of empirical research.

In the best of all possible worlds, public bureaucracies would come close to Weber's ideal-type but combine it with a degree of informal organisation to improve efficiency and responsiveness to clients. However, the informal element must not lead to corruption, such as bureaucrats taking bribes to 'ease' the way for clients, and it is easy to slip into practices that are not at all compatible with democratic principles. This is the problem in some of the new democracies that suffer from clientelism and patronage, where civil service jobs are rewards for political loyalty, not merit.

Clientelism

In contrast to the impersonal, politically neutral, rule-bound and universalistic Weberian model, clientelism involves the political use of public office for personal gain – power, or money, or both. The clientelist government acts as a patron that distributes favours and benefits in the form of public jobs, money, contracts and pensions in return for political support. Jobs in the state bureaucracy are filled not necessarily according to merit, professional training or experience, but by those who support the government in power. Contracts are given not according to cost and quality of work, but for material and political gain. Voters are rewarded for their support with jobs, money or gifts, and those who donate money to the party are rewarded with jobs, contracts and honours. In other words, clientelism is an institutionalised form of *patronage* summarised by the old adage: 'To the victor belong the spoils.' It can easily become corruption.

Clientelism in the public service is found to a varying degree in most states, but it is strong in some, especially in some of the less well developed democracies of Latin America, Africa and central Europe. It is also found in Italy, Greece, and the USA (where it is popularly known as 'the spoils system', or 'machine politics'). It is closely associated with poverty, inequality, corruption and the weak rule of law. In some countries it is more or less formalised and public, to the extent that it is known and accepted that members or supporters of a given party will get certain public jobs if that party is in power. In some countries, even professors in universities owe their job to the party they support. There are 'mass clientelist' parties in France, Italy, Greece and Mexico. Clientelism is found mainly in societies that are rapidly modernising, urbanising and industrialising, and in those that are struggling to throw off a recent history of authoritarian rule that rested on clientelism and patronage. Nevertheless, clientelism obstructs both democratic and economic development.

Rational choice and the New Public Management

Rational choice and bureaucracy

In his two influential and widely quoted books (*Bureaucracy and Representative Government*, 1971, and *Bureaucracy and Public Economics*, 1994), William Niskanen (1933–2011) argues that state bureaucrats are self-interested, like anyone else, and try to maximise their position by expanding their budgets and staff. The bigger their departments, the greater their power and prestige, the larger their salaries and the bigger their pensions. Their special knowledge and experience – Niskanen calls this the 'agency problem' – makes it difficult for politicians to resist these expansionist goals. As a result, public goods and services are over-produced at the public expense and the public sector grows fat.

The theory has been widely criticised for the oversimplified assumptions it makes:

- It assumes that bureaucrats are energetically self-seeking, but might we just as easily assume that they are lazy and want an easy life?
- It assumes that bureaucrats pursue their own self-interest, but might they not also be concerned about the public interest?
- It assumes that bureaucrats will not recognise or care about the problem of over-production, but might they equally be trying to combat this problem?
- It assumes that bureaucrats will not serve their political masters, but might they not have a professional ethic of public service?

Though it is an elegant theory, few attempts have ever been made to test it empirically. However, allied with the new right politicians and a revival of liberal free-market economics, rational-choice theory had a strong influence on the 'New Public Management'.

The New Public Management

Central to NPM theories of the public sector is the belief that bureaucracies are costly because they are not competitive, as the economic market is said to be, and because they interfere with the *efficient workings of the private sector*. Public bureaucracies should therefore be cut, privatised and decentralised, and market principles introduced wherever possible in order to reduce public spending and prevent government 'interference' with private enterprise. The incentives for public bureaucrats to maximise their spending should also be limited, to encourage small and efficient operations instead. Some government departments have been replaced by agencies that are supposed to be run along business lines to provide government with services and facilities under 'market-like' contractual arrangements. These are run not by career public servants but by business executives on fixed-term commercial contracts. The routine tasks of government (processing forms, emptying dustbins, maintaining public property, even running hospitals, schools and prisons) can be privatised and decentralised, leaving a small core of top civil servants to 'steer, not row'.

On the consumer side of public services NPM reforms have tried to reduce what are believed to be the serious problems of bureaucratic inertia, secrecy and unresponsiveness to the public. It redefines public-service clients as 'customers' and tries to make public bureaucracies more responsive to the needs of ordinary citizens.

The NPM wave swept across many democracies in the 1980s and 1990s, but we have yet to find out whether it has resulted in real gains for the public sector. It will take many years for the benefits and disadvantages to emerge, and even then they will not be clear because of all the problems of measuring and comparing public and private sectors and services, and of lack of evidence about the situation before and after NPM. Besides, there are many side effects and **externalities** of both market and public services, which are sometimes ignored in the political wrangling about them and are exceedingly difficult to quantify. More important, the failure of the deregulated financial market in autumn 2008 has resulted in a rethink of deregulation and privatisation and calls from some quarters for some re-regulation and public ownership. So while some claim that NPM has had its day, others believe that it has not gone far enough.

> **Externality:** A cost or benefit that does not fall on those who are responsible for the decision or action that creates the externality, and which they do not take into account when they take the action.

■ What have we learned?

This chapter deals with controversies about the role and power of public bureaucrats. It argues that:

- Policy making is the job of elected politicians who head government departments and ministries, but the day-to-day administration of government business is carried out by appointed officials (otherwise known as bureaucrats, civil servants, public servants, or permanent officials).
- Appointed officials are accountable to, and work under the policy direction of, their political masters, the elected politicians.
- However, the distinction between policy making and administration is not clear or unambiguous, and the considerable overlap between the two makes for a confusion of roles, especially since the senior bureaucrats (mandarins) work closely with politicians and act as their policy advisors.
- Appointed officials are said to be able to exercise power over their nominal political masters by virtue of their superior ability, qualifications and experience. State bureaucracies are also known for their secrecy and fragmentation, which makes it difficult for politicians to control them.

■ Lessons of comparison

- Aware of the potential for bureaucratic power, politicians have tried three general methods of controlling their bureaucrats: (1) trying to enforce rules and a culture of bureaucratic political neutrality; (2) replacing the top level of the bureaucracy with political appointees favourable to a new government; and (3) recruiting the bureaucracy from a broad cross section of the population to make it politically and socially representative.

- More specific methods for controlling bureaucrats include appointing political advisors, introducing scrutiny and auditing, applying principles of 'open government' and appointing ombudsmen.
- The New Public Management (NPM) practices that have swept across many states since the 1980s privatised many public services, deregulated many private businesses and introduced market or 'quasi-market' practices to try to make public services more competitive and efficient. Attempts have also been made to empower public service 'customers' to make public bureaucracies responsive to public demands.
- The reforms of public bureaucracies are controversial, and their effectiveness is difficult to judge. The recent crisis in the deregulated financial system has led to demands for re-regulation.

Projects

1. 'State bureaucracy is essential and dangerous.' What do you understand by this statement, and how can we reconcile these two characteristics of bureaucracy?
2. 'For the time being the dictatorship of the official, and not that of the worker, is on the march.' Has history proved Weber's claim about the dictatorship of the official? How can we know?
3. Is the new public management a technocratic and economic argument about the state bureaucracy or a political one? Would your answer be different if the more recent scepticism about NPM is considered?

Further reading

T. Christensen, and P. Lægreid, *Transcending New Public Management: The Transformation of Public Sector Reforms*. Aldershot: Ashgate, 2007. Analyses the NPM reforms in Denmark, Norway, Sweden, Australia and New Zealand.

E. Ferlie, L. E. Lynn and C. Pollitt (eds.), *The Oxford Handbook of Public Management*. Oxford, Oxford Handbooks Online, 2007. Twenty-nine chapters on every aspect of the NPM.

C. Hood and G. Peters, 'The Middle Aging of New Public Management: Into the Age of Paradox?', *Journal of Public Administration Research and Theory*, 2004. Explores some of the paradoxes and unanticipated effects of the NPM.

B. G. Peters, *The Politics of Bureaucracy*. London: Routledge, 2000. A general book on government and bureaucracy.

C. Pollitt, S. Van Thiel, and V. Homburg, 'New Public Management in Europe', *Management Online Review*, 1–6, 2007. Shows how the Anglo-Saxon model of NPM has been borrowed and adapted to different effect in different countries.

J. C. Raadschelders, T. A. Toonen and F. M. Meer (eds.), *The Civil Service in the 21st Century: Comparative Perspectives*. Basingstoke: Palgrave Macmillan, 2007. A global analysis of the civil service and the problems it currently faces.

Websites

www.britannica.com/EBchecked/topic/482290/public-administration/36942/Public-policy-approach. A general discussion followed by accounts of public management in different countries.

http://encyclopedia.thefreedictionary.com/.

Covers at length the topics of bureaucracy, public management, public administration and civil service, sometimes by country, with discussions of theories and links to related topics.

PART III

Citizens, elites and interest mediation

Part II of this book has discussed the formal institutions of government. Part III now looks at the politics of everyday life as practised by people – ordinary citizens and political leaders. The division between parts II and III implies a distinction between the structures and institutions of government, on the one hand, and the political attitudes and behaviour of individuals, on the other. A similar distinction is drawn between government institutions and structures, which are relatively fixed, and political processes, which are dynamic. At other times, a distinction is drawn between macro- and micro-analysis. Macro-analysis is concerned with large-scale phenomena, and often compares countries or broad sweeps of historical change. Micro-analysis deals with parts of the whole, usually the smallest 'unit' of political analysis – the individual. For this reason much micro-analysis often studies individual behaviour, or uses survey analysis to study attitudes and behaviour.

The separation of institutions from behaviour, structures from processes and macro from micro, is useful for studying government and politics because it is impossible to study everything at once, but we must always remember that they are simply different aspects of precisely the same thing. Structures and institutions set a framework for everyday political life; political attitudes and behaviour help to shape structures.

Part III starts with an account of the political attitudes and behaviour of individuals. If we understand what people think and believe about politics we are better able to understand their behaviour, even though they do not always do what they say. Or perhaps we should put it a different way: unless we understand political attitudes and values, we will never understand why people behave the way they do, even if words and deeds do not necessarily correspond. Besides, what people believe and how they behave can have an impact on what governments do, and they can also help to shape the structures and institutions of the state itself. So the study of attitudes and behaviour is important in its own right and because of the impact they have on governments and the state. Chapter 9 is therefore about political attitudes, values and behaviour.

However, few of us have much political significance as individuals on our own. Most of us join with others in voluntary organisations, pressure groups, social movements and new social media in order to achieve our political goals. What we cannot do as isolated citizens we can try to achieve through trade unions or professional associations, pressure groups or social movements, which try to exercise organised influence over government. Chapter 10, therefore, looks at the politics of pressure groups.

The mass media are crucial in political life because they are the means by which citizens, groups and leaders acquire political information and try to influence each other. The mass media are also thought to be powerful political actors in their own right. Accordingly, chapter 11 turns to the politics of the mass media and their influence.

Elections determine who is to take control of government. They are vital to the conduct of politics and tell us a lot about how ordinary citizens relate to politics. Electoral behaviour is probably one of the best topics for research on mass politics and an important part of comparative politics. Chapter 12 therefore pays attention to voters and elections.

And, last in part III, chapter 13 deals with a very special and particularly important type of voluntary organisation – political parties. Parties have a chapter of their own because they are so important.

The five chapters in part III examine the key aspects of political attitudes, institutions and behaviour:

• political attitudes and behaviour
• pressure groups and social movements
• the mass media
• voters and elections
• party government.

9   Political attitudes and behaviour

Everyone has their own view of politics, and their own interests and ideas and ways of behaving. But individuals do not exist in isolation and nor are they unique. If this were the case it would make no sense to talk about social groups such as 'the working class', 'minority groups' and 'youth cultures', or to make generalisations about 'left-wing intellectuals' or 'right-wing business interests'. At a still more general level, citizens of the same country usually share similar assumptions and views about politics, which makes the Swedes different from the Chileans, the Spanish different from the South Africans and the South Koreans different from the Irish. Political scientists find it useful to label these shared patterns of beliefs and attitudes the '**political culture**'. The first part of the chapter discusses the political values and attitudes of individuals and groups, and examines how modern research has tried to understand and explain political cultures.

> **Political culture:** The pattern of attitudes, values and beliefs about politics, whether they are conscious or unconscious, explicit or implicit.

Values and attitudes are important in their own right, but they are also significant because they tell us something about how people are likely to behave, and behaviour has a big and direct impact on political life. In order to understand what people do, and why they do it, it is necessary to understand what they think. For example,

> **Values:** Basic ethical or moral priorities that constrain and give shape to individual attitudes and beliefs.

it is not enough to know that someone did not vote in an election: we need to know whether their inaction was caused by apathy, alienation, or contentment. In the right circumstances, the alienated may take to the streets in revolutionary action, leaving the apathetic at home watching television.

There is another good reason for trying to understand political cultures. The structures and institutions of government rest, it is argued, on cultural foundations. If most people are satisfied with the way their system of government works, then it is likely to be stable over time. If a large proportion is dissatisfied and engages in protest action, then the system may come under pressure to change. Democratic political institutions rest upon democratic cultures, and a combination of democratic cultures and institutions produces stable democracy. In other words, there are two good reasons for studying political culture: it helps to explain individual behaviour and it helps to explain the persistence of democratic institutions and structures of government.

In this chapter, we examine the political attitudes and behaviour of citizens and political leaders. The major topics in this chapter are:

- Political attitudes
    Interests and identity
    Political culture
    Materialism and post-materialism
    Political cleavages

- Political behaviour
    Modes of behaviour
    Conventional and unconventional behaviour
    Patterns of behaviour.
- Theories of political attitudes and behaviour.

■ Political attitudes

Political interests and identity

We know from our own experience that political attitudes and behaviour are not random. People with the same background often have a lot in common politically: manual workers differ from managers and professionals, students from their parents and men from women. Individuals build their political ideas around their personal circumstances and interests, and when we talk about political interests we mean two sorts of things:

- *Material* interests – money, promotion, taxes, security
- *Ideal* interests – political values and ideals, such as a sense of justice and freedom, religious beliefs, or a left/right political position.

We should not underestimate the importance of ideal interests and values in trying to understand what people think about politics, and why they act the way they do. Many of the most important events in political history have been brought about by people prepared to fight and die for material and ideal interests, and this means political beliefs and values that may have nothing to do with their own material circumstances.

How people define their material and ideal interests is, in turn, closely connected with who and what they think they are. They may define themselves as a member of a social class, or an ethnic or religious group, or perhaps as part of a gender, or age, or regional group. How people see the political world depends on how they believe they fit into it, and how they see their own **political identity**. According to this approach, politics is a struggle between people and groups whose material and ideal interests vary according to their class, region, ethnicity, age, gender, language or nationality.

> **Political identity:** The way in which people label themselves as belonging to a particular group (e.g. nation-state, class or caste, ethnic group, religious group).

Political culture

One of the most influential approaches to the study of political attitudes, values and behaviour since 1945 involves political culture. The concept is an elusive and complex one, and it can be loose and vague, but we can best see political culture as a sort of map of how people think and behave. A map is not the real thing; it deals only with selected and general features of the world, but it can be a useful guide to the real thing. In the same way, political culture does not reproduce every detail of what citizens know and think and feel about politics, but it can be a useful and simplified guide to the most important features of individual beliefs, values and attitudes (see briefing 9.1).

Briefing 9.1

Political cultures

Political cultures consist of values, attitudes, beliefs and assumptions about government and politics. Culture in this sense does not refer to the 'high culture' of art, music and literature but to social attitudes and behaviour and how people think and relate to politics in everyday life. Some social scientists prefer to talk of 'norms' (standard of expected behaviour) or 'orientations' (way of seeing or mentally approaching things) or simply of patterns of attitudes and behaviour.

Perhaps the best way of capturing the idea of political culture is to list some of its main components:

- *National pride and identity* Are citizens proud of their nation and its achievements?
- *Social and political trust and co-operation* Do citizens believe that most other people are trustworthy and willing to co-operate? Do they trust their political leaders? Do they express confidence in the main institutions of society – parliament, the cabinet, political parties, businesses, banks, the Church, the media?
- *Competence* Do citizens believe that they can have an influence on public life politics, either as individuals or in association with others (subjective competence or efficacy). Do

they believe that the political systems are effective in achieving its more important goals (system efficacy)?

- *Political support* Do citizens believe that democracy is the best form of government and that their own political system is sufficiently democratic?
- *Citizenship* Do citizens believe that they should participate in political life, keep informed, vote and join with others in community action? Do they talk to others about politics or do they avoid politics and religion? Are they polite, helpful and considerate with others?
- *Alienation.* Do citizens have a sense of fraternity with others or are they isolated and alienated from society?

This list shows that some aspects of political culture refer to the political role of individuals, others to political institutions and the system as a whole. Some are conscious attitudes and values, others are unconscious and at first sight may appear to have little political relevance. Some aspects of political culture are common to large proportions of citizens in a given culture, but others are found in the subcultures of regions, social groups or generations.

Used well, the concept helps us to focus on what is important and to see patterns in what might otherwise be a confused jumble of individual particularities (see controversy 9.1). Studies of political culture also tie in with other areas of comparative political research, particularly studies of political socialisation, historical explanations and general patterns of political attitudes and behaviour.

CONTROVERSY 9.1

Political culture as a tool of political science: for and against

■ For

- Studies of political culture have produced important empirical findings about political attitudes and behaviour – e.g. the role of education and the family, and the importance and origins of competence, social trust and national pride. These were often overlooked or underestimated in previous studies.
- Political culture is claimed to be a 'bedrock' factor – it changes slowly compared with the more changeable political attitudes discussed by newspapers and opinion polls.
- Political culture is a key concept linking (1) the micro-politics of individuals with the macro-politics of institutions and states; (2) subjective (values and attitudes) with the objective (e.g. voting behaviour); and (3) history and traditions with current circumstances and events.
- Sample surveys reveal differences in attitudes and behaviour that may be better explained by 'soft' cultural factors (values, religious background, education) than by 'harder' factors (social class, wealth) or by structural factors (election rules, government powers).

- Political culture does not explain everything but helps to explain quite a wide range of phenomena, from economic development and political stability to democratic development and political behaviour.
- The study of political cultures is often based on 'hard' and extensive quantitative data drawn from surveys.

■ Against

- Political culture is said to be a 'soft', 'residual', 'dustbin', or 'fuzzy' concept that can be used to explain everything and therefore nothing, especially where it is used as a last resort variable when others have failed. Culture can be used a *post hoc* (after the event) explanation that is not put to an empirical test.
- Political culture explanations risk circularity: we infer what people believe from how they behave, and explain their behaviour by what they believe. For example: people behave democratically because they hold democratic values, and we know that they hold democratic values because they behave democratically.
- Cultural explanations of behaviour are trivial when they refer to attitudes or preferences only (for instance: people with left-wing attitudes tend to vote for left-wing parties). Political scientists should search for causes that are further away in the causal chain – e.g. historical, or economic, or psychological.
- Cultures and structures are mutually interdependent and tend to go together. It is not surprising, therefore that cultures and structures are associated, but which is cause and effect?
- Some argue for a 'bottom-up' explanation in which the system is shaped and moulded by mass opinions and behaviour, others for a 'top-down' explanation in which structures shape or constrain attitudes and behaviour. If both processes operate, as they well may, how can we ever sort them out?
- Research shows the existence of subcultures, but not their relative importance. For example, is the elite culture of the political class more important than the mass culture, and how can we tell? Similarly, how much citizen participation is necessary to describe a national culture as 'participant' – 33 per cent, 40 per cent, 50 per cent, or perhaps 66 per cent?
- Where does the political culture come from? It may be useful to describe a nation's culture as 'participant' or 'alienated', but why is it like this?
- Political culture deals with the *last* link in a long chain of causes of political behaviour. The basic causes of behaviour may be historical, or economic (Marxist or class theory), or personality.

Political socialisation

Culture is not innate: we are not born with a genetic imprint of a political culture in our brains. Rather, we absorb the political culture of our social background, through the process of **political socialisation**, which passes on culture, with modifications, from one generation to the next. This transformation can be intentional and

Political socialisation: The process by which individuals acquire their political values, attitudes and habits.

manifest (as in civics courses), but usually takes place unnoticed and without explicit goals (as in daily contacts in families and peer groups). Political socialisation is an important specialism in political science.

History and persistence

Political cultures are strongly influenced by major historical events – winning or losing a war, severe economic depression, a period of economic affluence, a colonial past – so political culture as an explanatory variable is directly linked to historical explanations. And since political cultures usually change rather slowly, explanations in terms of political culture are also explanations of how the past influences the present and why political systems are persistent over time.

Pattern

Political cultures are patterned because members of the same social groups tend to be socialised into the same set of attitudes and values and because beliefs are often connected in a systematic way. For example, those in favour of minority group rights are likely to approve of aid to developing countries, and to have liberal social attitudes as well. Those who are alienated and distrustful are unlikely to participate and cooperate in the community. The patterned nature of political cultures leads us into research on what has been called the 'civic culture'.

The civic culture

The first and most influential study of political culture was *The Civic Culture* (1963) by Gabriel A. Almond (1911–2002) and Sidney Verba (1932–). They define political culture as a pattern of **political orientations** to political objects such as parliament, elections or the nation. They then divide orientations into three dimensions:

Political orientation: A predisposition or propensity to view politics in a certain way.

- cognitive
- affective
- evaluative.

Cognitive

To participate in politics, citizens must be aware of, know about and understand something about their political system – its main institutions, historical events, election system, political figures and national background.

Affective

To participate in politics, citizens must believe that politics is important enough to take up their time. It is significant, for example, that two out of three citizens in Austria, the Netherlands and Norway claim an interest in politics, compared with fewer than one in three in Argentina, Chile and Spain.

Evaluative

To know how they should participate in politics, citizens must also evaluate the system:

- Should it be supported or reformed (political support)?
- Do ordinary citizens have enough influence (**subjective or internal efficacy**)?
- Does the system operate as it should (**system or external efficacy**)?

Subjective or internal efficacy: The extent to which ordinary citizens feel that they can make their views and actions count in the political system.

System or external efficacy: The extent to which ordinary citizens feel that political leaders and institutions are responsive to their wishes.

According to Almond and Verba, to measure a political culture requires collecting systematic information from a random sample of the population about the most important aspects of these three dimensions. On the basis of their study of (West) Germany, Italy, Mexico, the UK and the USA, they identified three pure types of political culture, and showed that these were combined in different proportions in the countries they surveyed. They also identified a fourth type that, they said, was the mixture that came closest to a democratic culture:

- *Parochial cultures* have a low level of awareness, knowledge and involvement with government. They are usually developing countries and rural societies with poor education, low economic development and poor communications, but there are pockets of parochialism in developed countries as well. In *The Civic Culture*, Mexico came closest to the parochial model.
- In *subject cultures*, people are aware of government and what it does (its outputs) but do not participate much (citizen inputs). Subject cultures are mainly found in non-democracies that emphasise the power of government rather than citizen rights and duties. Subject cultures do not encourage enough democratic participation. *The Civic Culture* found West Germany in the 1950s to have elements of a subject culture.
- In *participant cultures*, citizens are knowledgeable about politics, attach an importance to them and participate because they feel competent and knowledgeable. *The Civic Culture* found the UK and the USA closest to this culture. The danger is democratic overload, in which too much participation produces too many political demands.

Therefore, the best political culture for a democracy is:

- The **civic culture**, in which subject and participant cultures are mixed to produce neither too much nor too little participation. Citizens are active and elites respond to their demands, but citizens also trust their political leaders and give them a degree of independence. Almond and Verba found that the UK in the late 1950s came closest to the civic culture.

Civic culture: The term used by Almond and Verba to signify the balance of subject and participant political cultures that best supports democracy.

The Civic Culture argued that political culture was a crucial theoretical concept that mediated between the micro and subjective properties of a political system, and its macro, institutional features. Culture is shared by individuals, so aggregate individual statistics (i.e. national averages) describe the properties of the system as a whole. Cultures and structures are also mutually interdependent, so they must 'fit' each other. As we saw in chapter 4, democratic constitutions are like fortresses – their institutions must be well designed and well built, but they must also be well manned by democrats who believe in them. When the culture matches the structure they are said to be congruent, but when they do not fit, the culture is said to exhibit **political alienation**. According to Almond and Verba, Italy in the 1950s had an alienated culture because the democratic attitudes and behaviour of citizens were not matched by a sufficiently democratic structure. Alienated cultures are likely to produce a demand for change and a degree of political instability. In extreme cases they could generate mass pressures for political change, perhaps even revolution, as they did in central and eastern Europe in the 1980s.

> **Political alienation:** A feeling of detachment, estrangement, or critical distance from politics, often because the alienated feel there is something basically wrong with the political system.

Materialism and post-materialism

Almond and Verba's work had a huge impact in its time and stimulated many similar studies in the 1960s, but the approach lost favour in the 1970s and 1980s. It was revived, in large part, by Ronald Inglehart (1934–) who conducted a series of social surveys in many countries over several decades of what he calls materialism and post-materialism. Whereas Almond and Verba were mainly concerned with the persistence of political cultures over time and their relationship with stable democracy, Inglehart is interested in cultural and political change. His work starts from two basic propositions:

- Rapid economic development in the last hundred years has taken care of the basic material needs of most people in the West. Consequently, their values are shifting from material concerns (food, health, physical safety, social order) to post-material ones (civil liberties, the environment, job satisfaction, political and community participation, self-expression and the quality of life). Rising levels of education and wealth have caused a fundamental transformation of political values from material to post-material cultures.
- The shift from material to post-material values is gradual because most people acquire their political culture in early socialisation and change only slowly after that. The clearest signs of the shift show up in the younger, wealthier and better-educated generation.

Inglehart's culture shift is slow and silent, but he argues that it has profound effects because it results in broader changes involving participation, equality, community and self-expression. Post-materialism also involves greater tolerance of abortion, divorce, euthanasia, sexual minorities, single parents and minority groups, and opposition to nuclear energy and weapons and to the exploitation of the environment.

Post-materialism first appeared in young, wealthy and well-educated groups in the most affluent parts of the USA and western Europe in the 1960s. Early signs appeared in the generation that produced the student revolutionaries of 1968 in Berlin, California, London and Paris. The shift towards post-material values therefore helps to explain the remarkable fact that the increasing affluence of the 1960s did not induce a sense of satisfaction with society but, on the contrary, resulted in a wave of political protest that tried to change the political system.

Post-materialism, Inglehart says, is spreading to other parts of the developed world as these grow more affluent. As older, more materialist generations are replaced, so the proportion of post-materialists in these countries is rising. Among the democracies, the highest proportions of post-materialists are found in Australia, Austria, Canada, Italy, the Netherlands and the USA, the lowest in Estonia, Hungary, India, Israel and Latvia. Moreover, as the younger generation rises to positions of political power, so post-materialists will gain control of governments. Nor is post-materialism limited to the Western club of affluent nations. It is now found in developing countries such as China, Poland and South Korea as they grow wealthier and better educated. In his 1995 book *Modernization and Postmodernization*, Inglehart finds a close association between democracy and an emphasis on trust, tolerance, participation and a sense of personal well-being. In contrast, populations with material and survival values centring on money, safety and job security are likely to have authoritarian governments.

Six far-reaching consequences of the shift to post-materialism are said to be:

1. **Cognitive mobilisation** Education and wealth bring greater awareness of politics and better skills to participate.

   > **Cognitive mobilisation:** The process by which increasing knowledge and understanding of the world helps to activate people to play a part in it.

2. *Replacement of class with cultural cleavages* Materialist versus post-materialist divisions based on political cultures will gradually replace the left–right divisions based on class.
3. *Increased religious conflict* Because post-materialists tend to oppose traditional religion, there may be a religious backlash against them, especially from religious parties of the right.
4. *More political participation* The cognitive mobilisation of post-materialists results in greater demands for grass-roots participation.
5. *New forms of participation* Post-materialists favour 'new forms' of direct participation, community politics and new social movements, which means the decline of 'old' forms of participation organised around bureaucratic and hierarchical parties and pressure groups (see chapters 12 and 10).
6. *New political issues* Post-materialists are less involved in left–right politics, and more interested in the environment, community politics, feminism, individual freedom and racial equality.

The post-materialist thesis is supported by a good deal of survey evidence from around the world, but not all the findings are consistent with it. Some research on value change in western Europe in the postwar period shows a rather different pattern:

1. *Persistent left–right divisions* The old left–right divisions have persisted, although they have changed and weakened in some respects.
2. *Fusion not replacement* Post-materialism has not replaced materialism. Rather, elements of the old have been fused with elements of the new.
3. *High tide of post-materialism?* The evidence suggests that the drift towards post-materialism among the youngest generations in western Europe may be slowing, as economic conditions get harder. Research suggests that post-materialism has declined since the economic crash of 2008.
4. *A missing ingredient?* Most post-materialists are young, well-educated and middle class, but most young, well-educated, middle-class people are not post-materialist. Is there something else that helps to produce post-materialism?

Subcultures and elite cultures

No country has a single political culture, and there are often variations between sub-groups and regions. Indeed, the existence of materialist political cultures side by side with post-materialism in the same country is evidence of the existence of subcultures. Members of a subculture share in the larger culture, but they also have their own characteristics. For example, the Canadian political culture differs in some important respects from that in Finland and South Africa, but at the same time French- and English-speaking Canadians have their own political subcultures. Subcultures are typically aligned with important divisions in society such as class, gender, generation, religion, region or race. One of the most important subcultures in any society, however, is that of the **political elite**, sometimes called the 'political class' although it is not, strictly speaking, a class.

> **Political elite:** The relatively small number of people at the top of a political system who exercise disproportionate influence or power over political decisions. If powerful enough it is a 'ruling elite'.

Elite cultures are normally different from other subcultures, partly because elites are often drawn from the best educated and more middle- and upper-class sections of the population, and partly because they interact so closely with each other over such long periods of time that they tend to develop their own world view. Compared with mass cultures, elite cultures are:

• *Abstract* They tend to be organised around abstract political ideas and ideals as well as dealing with the concrete policy issues of everyday political life.
• *Complex* They are more elaborate and systematic.
• *Informed* They are based on a good deal of information.
• *Broad* They cover most of the general and particular issues in politics.

Because of this, political elites are said to be 'ideologues' who have a broader, more sophisticated and better-informed view of the political world, compared with most ordinary citizens.

> **Ideologues:** Those with an informed, broad, sophisticated and more or less consistent (systematic) view of politics.

Some political scientists argue that the social background and education of Western elites make them more democratic and tolerant, and with more liberal and fewer **authoritarian attitudes** than the general population. According to this view, democracy relies on the civilised

> **Authoritarian attitudes:** Attitudes based on obedience to authority, usually accompanied by prejudice, dogmatism, superstition, low tolerance for ambiguity, and hostility to out-groups (anti-semitism and racism).

and democratic values of educated elites and their capacity to compromise and accept the rules of the democratic game. Others argue, on the contrary, that elites are more conservative than the masses, and that their liberal, democratic rhetoric simply disguises an interest in keeping power. This view argues that elites prevent the mass from developing political skills and interests because this would bring an end to elite power. We shall return to this theme at the end of the chapter.

Political cleavages

We discussed the concept of 'cleavage' in chapter 1, but we return to it now because it is important for an understanding of political attitudes and behaviour. The importance stems from the common observation that particular social groups (distinguished by class, religion, ethnicity, language, region, or some other social feature) often tend to be similar in their political attitudes and behaviour. However, social differences do not always produce political differences and political differences do not always produce political cleavages. For a difference to become politically important, three conditions must be met:

1. *Objective social differences* Differences must be socially important and recognised by society – race, religion or language for example.
2. *Subjective awareness* It is not enough for objective differences to exist – social groups must be aware of their identity and express them in their social life.
3. *Political organisation* It is not enough for objective and subjective differences to exist. There must also be a capacity and willingness on the part of political organisations such as parties and pressure groups to organise those who are objectively different and subjectively aware of their identity, and to represent them and fight for their interests.

There is no automatic progress from (1) to (2) to (3). Tall people meet the first criteria but not necessarily the second, and certainly not the third. Women meet the first two criteria but not necessarily the third. Objective differences must produce a shared identity, and these identities must produce organisations that defend collective interests before a social cleavage is transformed into a political one. This leaves plenty of room for political activists and political entrepreneurs to use social divisions for political purposes, and it may even be that social cleavages will not take a political form until and unless political activists exploit them.

All this leaves us with the question, under what sorts of conditions do social divisions become cleavages? The answer is that there is a big difference between divisions in society that are superimposed one on top of the other (**reinforcing cleavages**), and divisions that cut across each other (**cross-cutting cleavages**). Where lines of class, religion, education and ethnicity coincide they are more likely to create deep social differences between groups such that conflict breaks out. The deep divisions between the black and white populations of South Africa is a case in point. But where social divisions overlap, they sew society together by its own internal divisions (see briefing 9.2). For example, if a working-class person belongs to a church or a sports club that has both working- and middle-class members, the church and sports club will build bridges that cut across class differences. This will tend to moderate working-class opinions because class influences will pull in different directions. But social cleavages will be reinforced and polarised in the case of a working-class person who belongs to a working-class church and a working-class sports club. This will tend to reinforce and polarise political differences, so forming the basis for political attitudes and behaviour, party membership, voting and political action in general.

> **Reinforcing cleavages:** Cleavages that are laid one on top of the other, making them potentially more important.

> **Cross-cutting cleavages:** Cleavages that are laid across one another, thereby reducing their capacity to divide.

Different cleavage lines

Historical developments in various countries resulted in different cleavages and in different combinations of these cleavages. Important cleavages are:

- *Religion* Religion has a close association with politics. The Protestant Reformation in western Europe in the sixteenth century has been described as a critical juncture in its political history, and the Catholic–Protestant divide remains a factor influencing political attitudes and behaviour in Europe and in parts of Latin America to the present day. In a similar way, developments and conflicts in the Arab world can only be understood by taking distinctions between Shiites, Wahhabis and Sunnites into account.
- *Ethnicity* Ethnic differences, often linked to religious, national, language and cultural differences, are often the basis of political cleavages, especially where they are associated with economic inequality.
- *Spatial separation* A social group that is concentrated in the same area is more likely to generate its own political identity than groups that are

mixed together in the same place. Spatial separation reinforced the **centre–periphery cleavage** in the early development of Western states in which modernisers and centralisers of the state, usually in the capital and other big cities, came into conflict with local elites and landowners of rural areas and the periphery. The modernisers wanted to subject peripheral elites to the power and taxes of the centralising state, and the peripheral elites wanted to keep their power and wealth. Later this division was overlaid by the industrial–agricultural cleavage, where the interests of new, rich, industrial and commercial capitalists in the cities conflicted with the interests of the more traditional rural landowners and farmers in poorer rural areas.

> **Centre–periphery cleavage:** The political cleavage between the social and political forces responsible for creating centralised and modern nation-states, and other interests, usually on the periphery of the state, which resisted this process. Centre–periphery cleavages are often, but not always, geographical.

Briefing 9.2

Reinforcing and cross-cutting cleavages: Belgium and Switzerland

■ Reinforcing cleavages

Belgium is divided between Flemish-speaking (Flemish is a version of Dutch) Flanders in the north (57 per cent), and French-speaking Wallonia (42 per cent) in the south (reinforcing language–regional cleavages), with Brussels, the capital city, a contested area in the middle. Belgium is about 75 per cent Catholic (a cross-cutting cleavage) but the north is wealthier than the south (a reinforcing cleavage) and the socio-linguistic/regional cleavage is so important that parties are split along regional lines (reinforcing cleavages) creating highly fragmented party systems and great difficulty in forming stable governments. The linguistic conflict became so intense in the 1970s and 1980s that constitutional reform produced a decentralised federal system of government in 1993. After severe political crises the autonomy of the three regions was strengthened even more in 2008.

■ Cross-cutting cleavages

Switzerland is divided by both language (German 65 per cent, French 23 per cent and Italian 8 per cent) and religion (38 per cent Catholic, 27 per cent Protestant). All but four of the twenty-six cantons are linguistically homogeneous (a reinforcing cleavage) but the same language groups have different regional dialects (a cross-cutting cleavage), and most cantons are of mixed religion (a cross-cutting cleavage). Different language and religious groups often have the same economic interests in tourism or banking (a cross-cutting cleavage). There is no dominant city – Basel, Bern, Geneva, Lausanne and Zürich share capital city functions – and most Swiss identify with their nation (which cuts across the cleavages). Switzerland (a federal system) is a highly stable and integrated nation.

Spatial separation that entails the concentration of ethnic, religious, linguistic or cultural groups in geographical areas is often associated with separatist political movements that want self-government for their own area. We see this in the Basque and Catalan regions of Spain, in Scotland, Ireland and Wales in the UK, in the French-speaking population of Quebec in Canada, the Sikh population and Khalistan in India, the Flemish and Walloon regions of Belgium, the division of Czechoslovakia into Czech and Slovak states in 1993, and the dissolution of the Yugoslavian state amid horrific bloodshed and genocide in the 1990s. Political conflict can erupt into violence and civil war in places where social divisions coincide with spatial separation, and it is often difficult (though not impossible) to develop and sustain democratic government. In these instances, deep cleavages are the active ingredients that turn conflicting political beliefs into action. Federalism then becomes an important way of tackling the problem (see chapter 6).

Democratic countries show a great variety of cleavage patterns. Some countries have been relatively cleavage free. Japan and the Nordic countries of Denmark, Norway, Sweden and Finland all have relatively homogenous populations and few deep cleavages. Other countries have been divided politically along class and status lines (Australia, New Zealand and the UK), but these did not coincide with either religious, urban–rural or regional differences. Class cleavages in America have been blurred by race and region (the North–South divide of the Civil War). In spite of mass poverty, class and economic cleavages have not undermined Indian democracy and unity because the population is also fragmented by race, religion, language and caste. Religion has played a major role in the Netherlands but has been managed peacefully with its own special political arrangements. The superimposed cleavages of language and region in Belgium and Spain have been managed by federal and quasi-federal means.

■ Political behaviour

Political behaviour comes in a great many forms, including reading a paper, talking about politics and joining voluntary organisations that play no political role for much of the time (see briefing 9.3), as well as the most common of all, which is voting in elections. If we include actions that have an unintended effect on politics, the range broadens further to include such things as not paying taxes and not voting. After all, a large minority of non-voters is a cause for concern in democracies, and tax evasion has a direct effect on government policies. Even clothes, music and food can have a political connotation, as students know.

Political behaviour: All political activities of citizens, including sporadic political activity, inactivity and behaviour with indirect political consequences.

Modes of political behaviour

Research in the 1950s and 1960s suggested that the population of Western democracies could be divided roughly into three groups, according to their level of political participation:

- *Gladiators* These are the leaders and activists who run parties, political organisations and campaigns, and who hold political office. About 5–8 per cent of the population falls into this group.
- *Spectators* The great mass of the population is not engaged in politics beyond voting in elections, reading a paper, watching television news and occasional political discussion.
- *Apathetics* The politically inactive who know and care little about politics, and do not vote.

Briefing 9.3

Varieties of political behaviour

■ Conventional

- Voting
- Reading newspapers, watching television news
- Talking about politics
- Joining a political group (voluntary organisation, party, or new social movement)
- Involvement with a client body or advisory body for public service (consumer council, school board)
- Attending political meetings, demonstrations, rallies
- Contacting the media, elected representatives, or public officials
- Contributing money to a political group
- Volunteering for political activity (organising meetings, election canvassing)
- Standing for political office
- Holding political office

■ Unconventional

- Unofficial strikes, sit-ins, protests, demonstrations
- Civil disobedience
- Breaking laws for political reasons
- Political violence
- Boycotting products or a producer
- Buying products for political reasons ('buycotting')

- Posted links on social media (Facebook, Twitter, YouTube, etc.) to political stories or articles for others to read
- Commented on social media on political issues

Figure 9.1 is a stylised representation of how political participation repertoire has developed since 1940

Figure 9.1: Expansion of the political participation repertoire agenda since the 1940s

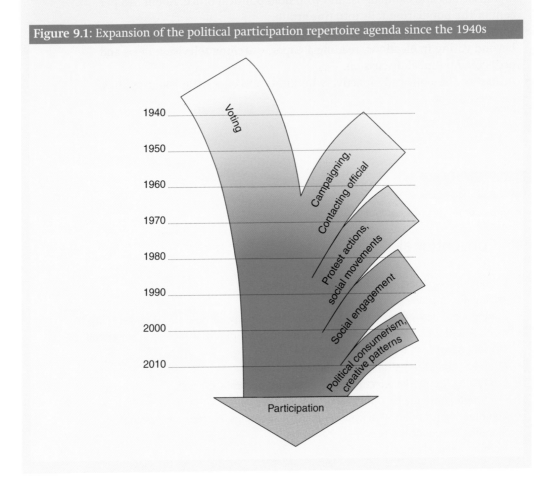

Later research on comparative political behaviour confirmed the existence of a small group of political 'gladiators' (leaders) and a larger group of 'apathetics', but it also found something surprising about the great mass of people in the middle. Their political behaviour could not be placed on a single continuum of political activity ranging from the simple act of voting at one end to the most demanding and time-consuming forms of political

Briefing 9.4

Modes of political behaviour

Inactives	Rarely vote or engage in any form of political participation
Passive supporters	Vote regularly, support the nation, tacit support for the political system
Contact specialists	Contact political and public office holders about personal matters
Community activists	Cooperate with others in their community, join local organisations, contact local officials about public matters
Party workers	Join parties, volunteer for campaign work, canvass at elections, give money, attend meetings, stand for election
Leaders	Fill major political and public offices – elected representatives in national and sub-national government, party leaders, leaders of pressure groups and social movements, political commentators
Protestors	Specialists in protest and unconventional behaviour

activity at the other. Rather, citizens tended to specialise in different modes of behaviour. Individuals usually concentrated on a group of similar sorts of political activity that clustered together (see briefing 9.4), according to the goals and values of the individuals, and according to the demands that the type of behaviour made on them. Political activity was not cumulative, and knowing what type of behaviour a given individual specialised in could tell us nothing about what other type of activity they might be involved in. For example, community activists were no more or less likely to vote than protest activists, and protest activists were no more or less likely to be party members than those who made contact with specialists.

Conventional and unconventional political behaviour

Democratic political participation has traditionally been confined to voting, attending political meetings, signing petitions, joining a party or political group and so on. These are sometimes known as 'conventional' forms of behaviour, but in the late twentieth century the political repertoire expanded to include 'unconventional' activities such as protests, demonstrations, boycotts, occupations and unofficial strikes (see briefing 9.3). Surveys show that this type of behaviour is much more widely accepted now, though it is still not widely practised. Fewer than 5 per cent in Hungary, Latvia, Japan and Argentina have been involved in the occupation of a building. By comparison with this low figure, election turnout in these countries is more than 70 per cent.

Internet participation

The latest expansion of political behaviour is related to the use of Internet-based technologies, especially social media such as Facebook, Twitter or YouTube. These technologies have become increasingly important for political behaviour because they facilitate:

- *Communication* On all kinds of platforms, websites, blogs and political opinion and information can immediately be communicated to an unrestricted number of people. Even more important is the fact that the Internet allows everybody to produce their own political information and make it available without limitations (see Chapter 11).
- *Mobilisation* Using the Internet makes it very easy to approach many people individually and to mobilise them to participate, for instance by inviting them to join a demonstration or sign a petition. The use of Internet in the Arab Spring or the Spanish *Indignados* shows the power these technologies can have for political action.

Internet technologies also make it easier to participate in conventional politics. by means, for example, of electronic petitions and voting, or spreading news about boycotting Internet retailers. In addition the Internet has made it possible to participate in new ways, such as posting a link on social media, clicking 'like', 'share' or 'tweet' on websites or writing a blog. Some authors expect these technologies to change completely the way people will be engaged in social and political activities. Others are more sceptical and point to the fact that Internet participation hardly requires any serious commitment or personal effort and that more people are writing comments than reading and exchanging arguments. In this view pushing a button to support a political cause or forwarding a political message is mere '**slacktivism**' that seems to be mainly important for the good feelings of the people involved and does not accomplish much.

Slacktivism: The act of showing support for a cause that requires minimal personal effort, and has little effect.

Patterns of political behaviour

There are many different types of political behaviour, and these combine in varying proportions in different countries according to their political structures, cultures and histories. However, there are also some striking patterns in participation in the democratic countries of the world which enable us to advance some reliable generalisations.

Most people are not political
Most people do not know or care much about politics. Many vote, the least demanding form of political activity, and they become active when the need

arises. But these people are not necessarily 'apathetic', because there are other reasons for being politically inactive:

- *Marginals* Those who are disenfranchised (including criminals, illiterates; immigrants; those who do not speak the majority language and the severely mentally ill; handicapped) and those who are enfranchised but have difficulty in voting (including the very old and infirm). Students often do not vote if they are registered to vote in their home town but are at university in a different place on election day.

  > **Political marginality:** Being on the fringes of politics and therefore having little influence.

- *Conflict avoiders* Some people avoid politics because it can lead to disagreement, conflict and bad feeling.
- *Alienated* Some people do not get involved because they believe they have no influence in the system (low subjective efficacy or competence), or think the political system is not democratic enough (system efficacy or competence). Confidence in parliament is comparatively high in some countries (e.g. Norway, the Netherlands), but much lower in others (e.g. Japan, Italy).
- *Loss of political salience* With the huge expansion of income and education since 1945, many people have the personal resources to deal with the problems and opportunities of their daily life. This makes them more independent as individuals. Politics, on the other hand, is a collective activity, and is thought to be less important in a world where individuals have their own money and personal skills to handle their lives. Politics is no longer **salient**: it becomes 'background noise' or 'elevator music'. This is not to say that politics is of no importance, but it does mean that, in comparison with other activities – work, family, leisure – some citizens treat it as less significant.

  > **Salient:** Something that is relatively important, significant, or prominent in people's minds.

- *Apathetic* Those who are simply not interested in politics. The term 'apathetic' is often used as a critical value judgement, which means it should be avoided, quite apart from the fact that many are politically inactive for reasons other than apathy.

Sporadic political involvement

Though most people are not politically active most of the time, many are involved some of the time: they read a paper, watch television news and talk about politics. They participate in one way or another when they feel the need, usually because their personal interests are affected. These sporadic acts of participation cover a substantial percentage of the population, and, as table 9.1 shows, more than half and as many as three-quarters of the population of most western European democracies have been politically involved in some way, beyond the simple act of voting.

Table 9.1 Rates of political participation,[a] western Europe, 1974–2012

	1974	1981	1990	2012
Britain	31	66	77	77
Sweden		58	74	74
Norway		58	68	67
Denmark		48	59	57
(West) Germany	34	48	57	67
France		52	57	55
Italy	34	50	56	44
Iceland		40	55	84
Netherlands	28	37	54	46
Belgium		27	51	46
Ireland		32	46	40
Finland	26	40	38	68
Spain		32	32	-

Note:
[a]Entries are percentages of the adult population who engage in some form of political participation beyond voting.

Sources: 1974, 1982 and 1990: Richard Topf, 'Beyond electoral participation', in Hans-Dieter Klingemann and Dieter Fuchs, **Citizens and the State** (Oxford University Press, 1995: 69); 2012: European Social Survey and World Values Survey.

Participation rates are rising

As table 9.1 also shows, rates of political activity are tending to rise in the Western world, contrary to the common claim that democracies are increasingly apathetic and alienated. Many parts of the democratic world show a decline in the 'old' politics of parties and elections, but an increase in the 'new' politics of referendums, petitions, community groups, citizen lobbies and single-issue groups.

Substantial variations in participation

The percentages involved in political activity often vary greatly from one country to another. This is true of particular forms of participation as well as of overall rates of activity, as the figures in table 9.1 show. Participation in the highest-ranked country in 1981, 1990 and 2012 is about twice as high as in the lowest-ranked one.

Continuous expansion in forms of participation

The rise in the rate of specific forms of political participation is not the only indication of the spread of political behaviour in democratic countries. As already shown in figure 9.1, new forms of participation have been invented in the last decades resulting in a continuous expansion of the repertoire of participation. Recent additions are individual acts that people use to express their discontent, such as boycotts. As a result the nature of political participation has changed. Older forms are specific activities devised and used to influence political processes: casting a vote, joining a demonstration, or supporting a candidate are all examples of such activities. As such, refusals to buy a specific brand of coffee or athletics shoes are not forms of political participation, but non-political activities that can be used for political aims. These activities do not require any organisation or collective action. To be effective, a large number of people must behave in a similar way, but they can all act individually, separately, and with distinct aims and motivations. Obviously, the spread of Internet-based technologies strongly helps the rise of these forms of participation. In this way, the expansion of the repertoire of political participation with **individualised forms of participation** (also called 'creative' or 'personalised' forms) differs clearly from previous expansions. By now, almost every form of behaviour can be seen as an act of political participation in specific circumstances.

> **Individual forms of participation:** Forms of behaviour used by single citizens aimed at expressing political opinions. These activities are usually driven by ethical and moral reasoning rather than by the wish to influence political decisions.

Voters are not fools

Some political scientists emphasise how little people know about politics, how little they are involved and how poorly prepared they are to perform their citizen duties. Some survey research concludes that voters are often ignorant, irrational and inconsistent and that, as a result, opinion polls and surveys are not to be trusted. Asked about a matter on which they have no opinion or information, many come up with a **'doorstep' response**, saying the first thing that comes into their head, or something that they think they should say. Contradicting this dim view of the electorate, the American political scientist V. O. Key (1908–63) argued that 'voters [are] not fools'. He produced evidence showing that American voters switched votes between candidates and parties according to their judgement of the political circumstances. They judged candidates and parties according to their past records and future promises. Subsequent research has tended to confirm this, in two ways:

> **Doorstep response:** Where those with no opinion or information respond to polls and surveys with the first thing that comes into their head (sometimes known as 'non-opinion' or 'non-attitudes').

- Electoral behaviour can be explained in terms of real political trends and events, especially taxation, inflation, unemployment, economic performance, and social policies, war, and international events. Support for NATO declined after the collapse of the Soviet Union in 1989 because people thought that there was no longer a great need for military defence of the NATO type, but when other military conflicts occurred they revised their views again.
- Some research argues that citizens use **'low information rationality'** or 'gut rationality' in deciding how to vote and behave. It is not necessary to have full and detailed information to make sensible judgements; a rough

> **Low information rationality:** Where citizens without a great deal of factual political information have a broad enough grasp of the main issues to make up their mind about them, or else they take cues from sources they trust (sometimes known as 'gut rationality').

idea is sufficient. If the issue is a complex technical one, people can take their cues from those they trust – party leaders, political commentators, friends, newspapers.

The 'standard model' of political participation

The 'standard model' applies across a wide variety of countries and times. It shows that class and status, plus the closely related factors of education, income and family background, have strongly influenced rates and types of political participation. Those with high class and status often have the education to be able to acquire political knowledge and skills, and they are likely to understand the relevance of politics to their own circumstances. They are more likely to have the resources (education, cars, computers, email, office support, money) to become effectively involved in politics, they have the social prestige to be influential and they often have family backgrounds with a political interest. Class and status is often abbreviated to 'SES' or '**socio-economic status**', where class is closely associated with occupation and income, and status with prestige in society. Some people make a lot of money but have low status (the owner of a string of porn magazines) while others have high status though not much money (aristocrats fallen on hard times). SES is a combination of these two things. Most research on political participation finds systemic differences along cultural and ethnic lines, as well as between religious groups. Family activism also tends to be passed on from one generation to the next. For the most part, different rates of participation reflect unequal access to resources, with money and education being the most important.

Status: A form of social stratification determined by social prestige rather than economic factors or occupation. At their simplest, class is determined by wealth and income, status by such things as social backgrounds, accents, dress, manners and interests.

Socio-economic status (SES): A combination of class (how people make their money) and status (how people spend their money) to form a single measure of social stratification. *See also* 'Class', 'Status'.

■ The 'civic voluntarism model' of political participation

The 'standard model' is often modified, though usually only to a small degree, by gender, age and length of residence in a community. In many countries, politics is still regarded as something of a 'man's game', and women tend to participate less. Young and old people are less active than the middle-aged, whose involvement with their children's schools, their colleagues at work and their community tends to draw them into politically related activities. The longer people live in their community, and the stronger their social networks, the more they tend to be engaged.

Ever since its development in the late 1940s and 1950s the 'standard model' has proven to be a strong predictor of political behaviour. In fact, not a single study showed that political participation did not depend on SES! In spite of this unique empirical success, it proved rather difficult to present a satisfactory theoretical interpretation of this relationship. In their study *Voice and Equality* (1995) a group of American political scientists led by the master in the field, Sidney Verba, solved this puzzle by presenting a modified 'standard model': the 'civic voluntarism model' (CVM). This distinguishes three ways in which SES can have an impact on political behaviour: (1) the chances to become politically active are low if resources such as time, money, or abilities are scarce or missing, (2) when people are not interested in politics or see no reasons to become involved, or (3) when none of their acquaintances, friends or colleagues invites them to join some action. In their famous conclusion the authors state that people do not participate politically 'because they can't; because they don't want to; or because nobody asked'.

Political elites

Following on from the last point, it is generally true that the leaders of the political West are overwhelmingly of the '3-M' variety – middle-aged, middle class and male. Most have a university education, and many have come from three professions – law, teaching and the civil service, although the trend towards the professionalisation of politics often means that increasing proportions of elected representatives at the national level have little or no work experience outside politics.

Changing attitudes and behaviour

The political attitudes and behaviour of the twentieth century are changing. New economic forms and technology, globalisation, population movements, social mixture and heterogeneity, secularisation, changing class structures, increasing affluence, higher levels of education, greater mobility, democratic reforms, different ways of making political decisions and electronic means of communication have created different social and political patterns. The class divisions that were important in many urban–industrial societies of the nineteenth and twentieth centuries are being weakened or replaced by new social cleavages, new forms of political activity and the new political interests of minority groups – women, Greens, the young, nationalists and post-materialists.

Where once attitudes and behaviour were associated with stable, structured and homogeneous social groups living in their own communities (mining villages, ship-building towns, middle-class suburbs, inner-city working-class areas), they are now associated with socially mixed, shifting and changing populations with a greater and less stable variety of political interests. According to some research the collective politics of centralised and hierarchical parties, trade unions and business associations are being replaced by fragmented **issue publics** that are formed around individual attitudes and opinions, that combine and re-combine in different patterns according

Issue publics: Groups of people who are particularly interested in one political issue (or more), are well informed and likely to take action about it.

to changing issues and political circumstances. There is a greater variety of issue publics and of life-style politics, greater volatility and greater demand for grass-roots and community participation. The new electronic media have made access to political opinion and information easier and cheaper than ever. Growing numbers of citizens use their shopping power to express their opinions or to exert political pressure when they refuse, for instance, to buy shoes or sweaters produced by child labour. Political attitudes and attachments are becoming weaker and less predictable and the standard socio-economic model organised around a few variables (class and status, religion, education, family background) now work less well. Whether fragmentation, variation and constant change are to be the hallmarks of the new world, or whether this will precede the emergence of a new and stable social and political order, remains to be seen. We return to this topic in chapter 12.

A note of warning – the ecological and psychological fallacies

This chapter has discussed attitudes and behaviour in terms of high-level generalisations. Although social groups may generally behave in their own way and may generally hold to a particular set of values and beliefs, it does not follow that every member of the group does so. Therefore it is not possible to assume that because a given individual is a member of a particular social group that they will behave as other members of the group do. To take a non-behavioural example, let us say that the first 100 swans you saw in your life were all white. Can you assume from this that all swans are white?

The white swan assumption can lead to false conclusions being drawn from statistically valid research about social phenomena such as political culture, attitudes and behaviour. Ecological research deals in the characteristics of groups of people, a usual form of social science analysis, but open to misuse of statistics. An example of this kind of error is the growing success of the British Union of Fascists in the East End of London in the late 1930s. The Fascists were anti-Semites and it happens that many Jews also lived in the East End at the time. The patently absurd conclusion is that this combination of facts, all true, shows that Jews are anti-Semitic. The reverse pitfall is the **psychological fallacy** whereby conclusions about a group are drawn from individual members of it. This morning I saw a woman driver cause a road accident. Should I conclude from this that all women are bad drivers?

Ecological fallacy: Drawing false inferences about individuals from valid evidence about groups.

Psychological fallacy: Drawing false inferences about groups from valid observations about individuals who are members of those groups.

The ecological and psychological fallacies are a misuse or misunderstanding of statistical evidence. They sometimes appear in the social sciences and are more common in general bar-room discussion and political debate. What we can conclude from them is not to dismiss statistical research, because that would be throwing the baby out with the bathwater, but to be careful about how we use the evidence to draw inferences about the political world.

Briefing 9.5

Political behaviour in the USA

Three features of the electoral system in the United States help to explain the low voting turnout in the country. First, an estimated 521,000 officials are elected in the USA, ranging from the president in Washington to local mayors, council members, county commissioners, sheriffs, auditors, judges and treasurers. American citizens may suffer from a degree of election fatigue. Second, registration as a voter can be a difficult and cumbersome process, especially for minority groups. Third, parties are weak and are not as effective in mobilising voters as some of their European counterparts.

Individual factors also play a part. As one source comments,

> Research underscores the significance of personal characteristics in motivating a person's decision to participate on election day. Education is the most critical variable. As their educational level increases, individuals develop a stronger sense of civic duty and a greater interest in, and knowledge of, politics. But education alone is not a sufficient explanation, since voting rates have continued to decline despite the proliferation of college degrees in recent decades. Another characteristic that correlates with voting is age; older voters are more likely to participate. But here again, overall voting rates have diminished while the population has aged. Something other than personal characteristics therefore seems to play a role in election turnout: the characteristics of the election itself. Most recent elections have presented voters with uninspiring candidates who failed to stimulate interest or excitement. The lack of a realigning issue has made politics boring. However, turnout reaches notable peaks in certain elections, as in 1964 (a sharp ideological choice between candidates) and 1992 (an economy in recession and the charismatic candidate H. Ross Perot). Voters participate when aroused to do so.

Considering how few tangible rewards participation produces, it is not surprising that over 40 per cent of Americans either do not participate at all or limit their participation to voting. Compared to citizens of other democracies, Americans vote less but engage more in communal activity.

Although voter turnout has decreased over the past twenty years, it seems that other forms of participation, such as writing letters to public officials and engaging in demonstrations, have increased. There are many ways in which Americans can participate in politics – ranging from voting, which a majority do with some regularity, to belonging to a political club or organisation, which only a few do.

Source: www.socialstudieshelp.com/APGOV_Participation.htm.

■ Theories of political attitudes and behaviour

Marxist and class theory

Marxist theories argue that political attitudes and behaviour are shaped by capitalist institutions that ensure that the system 'reproduces' itself, and that the masses are indoctrinated into a state of **false consciousness**. Education conditions the workers to fulfil their economic function; religion, 'the opiate of the

> **False consciousness:** The state of mind of the working class induced by the ruling class to conceal the real nature of capitalism and the real interests of the workers.

masses', teaches people their place in life and emphasises spiritual matters rather than the physical conditions of life; the mass media indoctrinate people with a mixture of political propaganda and popular distractions (sport, game shows, films, soap operas, gossip). Political culture is, therefore, largely the creation of the ruling class and designed to protect their economic interests. The Italian philosopher, Antonio Gramsci (1891–1937) used the term **hegemony** to refer to the way the ruling class exercised power not by force, but by subtle influence over the hearts and minds of ordinary people. Political culture, viewed this way, is merely a 'superstructure' built on the material substructure of the capitalist mode of production and its class system.

> **Hegemony:** A situation in which a class, political interest or country is so powerful that it does not have to rely on force or power to maintain its rule because its values and attitudes have been accepted or because people dare not oppose it.

Rigid and 'vulgar Marxist' theories (that is, crude and over-simple Marxism that simply presumes specific interest behind every expression) have nothing to recommend them. They are 'over-determined' in the sense that they do not allow for the many individual and group variations that exist within any political system. The concept of false consciousness also has its difficulties; who can tell others that they do not see the world correctly, or understand their own best interests?

At the same time, there is clearly more than a small grain of truth in the class theory of attitudes and behaviour. Empirically, the 'standard model' that combines class and class-related variables explains a good deal of the variation in political attitudes and behaviour, and it seems to have applied to a broad variety of countries and circumstances for much of the nineteenth and twentieth centuries. However, it certainly does not explain everything, and its explanatory power declined in the late twentieth century. The class model, though far from defunct, seems to be on the wane. Instead, the 'civic voluntarism model' gained rapid and widespread approval.

Rational-choice theory

Marxist theory concentrates on social circumstances, particularly economic ones, as determinants of political thought and action. Even the capitalists who create and run economic and political systems act according to the 'logic of situation' they find themselves in. They pursue the ever renewed searches for profits because there is an imperative about the way that the market systems work. If they acted in any other way their businesses would perish.

Rational-choice theory uses an economic approach that explains political attitudes and behaviour in a different way. One of the earliest and most influential books of this kind, *An Economic Theory of Democracy* (1957), written by Anthony Downs (1930–), argues that voters are rational and self-interested people who support the party most likely to represent their individual preferences. Political parties in a similar way try to maximise their power by appealing to the voter who guarantees them election victory. Remarkably this is not the average voter but the median voter. Usually, but not necessarily, the median voter also holds the typical, middle-of-the-road attitudes and preferences of the great majority of people.

Early rational-choice theory, following economic models in which consumers were assumed to have perfect knowledge of the market, assumed that individuals were well informed about politics. Since this is obviously implausible, given that many people know rather little about politics, later versions relaxed this assumption and accepted that most people had little political information, but perhaps enough to make political judgements. Indeed, rational-choice theory turned its earlier assumptions about perfect knowledge into a strength, arguing that it is not rational to spend a lot of time gathering political information. The chances of any ordinary citizen having the slightest effect on any given political outcome (e.g. an election result) is close to zero, so the costs of being well informed far outweigh any likely gain. Indeed, from a rational self-interested point of view even voting is a waste of time, since it is much more sensible to **free-ride** on others. The theory thus comes logically to the conclusion that very few people will bother to vote. Such a theory is best suited to explain why people do not vote. Since large numbers do turn out on election day, this is a problem for the theory. They bother to vote, in part at least, not because of rational self-interest but because performing civic duties is part of a culture that emphasises civic responsibility as an end in itself.

> **Free-ride:** To extract the benefits of other people's work without putting in any effort oneself.

Another difficulty of using rational-choice theory to explain political behaviour concerns the discussion of what is rational and what is self-interest (see briefing 9.5). Was it rational and self-interested for the early Christians to allow themselves to be thrown to the lions? If you define 'self-interest' in terms of the soul and salvation, the answer is 'yes', but then everything can be rational self-interest. Whatever people believe and do is evidence of their behaving in their own interests and maximising their preferences. Besides, some seem to vote for the public interest rather than self-interest. They are, in the jargon, not '**pocket-book voters**' who are motivated by their own material self-interest but **sociotropic voters** who take account of the general interest and the public good. They may even vote for increases in their own taxes for the general good – as middle-class socialists do.

> **Pocketbook voting:** Deciding which party to vote for on the basis of economic self-interest.

> **Sociotropic voting:** Deciding which party to vote for on the basis of general social or economic circumstances.

However, rational-choice, social-choice and public-choice theorists can argue that it is rational and self-interested to vote in the public interest because this helps to maintain the social and political conditions of security and stability that enable people to achieve their personal interests. Once again, if it is rational self-interest to vote for the public interest then perhaps everything is rational self-interest.

Social and psychological theories

There are three other main theoretical approaches to political attitudes and behaviour, but two of these are particularly relevant to voting studies which are discussed at greater length in chapter 12. The third is social capital theory, which is tied up closely with research on voluntary associations, the topic of chapter 10. Therefore we will not discuss these theories here but pick them up in the chapters to come.

■ What have we learned?

This chapter deals with the political values and attitudes of individuals and groups, and examines how modern research has tried to understand and explain political cultures. It argues that:

- Although every individual has a unique set of political attitudes and values, and a unique pattern of political behaviour, people tend to show the typical forms of attitudes and behaviour of their social and economic group.
- Political attitudes and values are built around the material and ideal interests that individuals derive from their sense of identity. Hence attitudes and values are generally strongly linked to class, ethnicity, language, religious and territorial identities. Another way of saying this is that attitudes and values are closely associated with the social, economic and political characteristics of individuals and groups. Different theories stress different characteristics.
- The concept of 'political culture' is claimed to be important empirically (it is associated with many important empirical findings) and theoretically (linking subjective and objective, and macro- and micro-features of the political system). Critics claim that it is a vague and unsatisfactory explanatory variable.
- An important distinction should be drawn between reinforcing and cross-cutting political cleavages. The former are associated with political integration and stability, the latter with conflict and violence.
- People tend to specialise in a particular mode of political behaviour (clusters of similar forms of activity). With the exception of a minority of political activists, most individuals do not cover the full range of activities, but combine them in their own particular ways.
- Forms of behaviour used by single citizens aimed at expressing political opinions are spreading, especially facilitated by Internet-based technologies. These activities are usually driven by ethical and moral reasoning and not with the intention of taking part in decision making.
- Voters are not fools.

■ Lessons of comparison

- Most people are not political: sporadic political activity rather than persistent or regular engagement is the norm.
- Research on materialism/post-materialism argues that younger generations in affluent societies are shifting their values from material ones (jobs, money, etc.) to post-material ones (self-expression, job satisfaction, the quality of life, etc.). Critics observe that this culture shift has slowed down, and that post-material values have not replaced material ones but have been combined with them.
- Participation is often associated with different forms of social stratification (class, status, caste) and stratification-related variables (education, religion, ethnicity), and to a lesser extent with gender, age and length of residence in the community.
- Across the Western world, class differences in attitudes and behaviour appear to be declining and other forms of social difference are becoming more important, notably religion and, some claim, political values.
- Protest behaviour has become a normal part of the political repertoire, though still much less common than conventional types of political activity. Direct political engagement in the community is increasing; participation in the traditional and hierarchical organisations of representative democracy (parties and trade unions) tends to decline.

Projects

1. Read the section in this chapter on materialism and post-materialism, and then assess the extent to which you and your friends are materialists or post-materialists.
2. Critically assess Marxist and rational-choice approaches to political attitudes and behaviour. Which do you prefer, if either, and why?
3. Political attitudes are said to be determined by material and ideal interests. Which do you think is most important and why?

Further reading

G. A. Almond and S. Verba, *The Civic Culture: Political Attitudes and Democracy in Five Nations*. Princeton University Press, 1963. The original and classic study of political culture, followed seventeen years later by G. A. Almond and S. Verba (eds.), *The Civic Culture Revisited*, Princeton University Press, 1980, an appraisal of the concept of political culture and the research done on it. The most recent publication in this tradition is R. J. Dalton and C. Welzel (eds.). *The Civic Culture Transformed: From Allegiant to Assertive Citizens*. Cambridge University Press, 2015.

R. J. Dalton, *Citizen Politics: Public Opinion and Political Parties in Advanced Industrial Democracies*, 6th edn. Thousand Oaks: CQ Press, 2013. The best general introduction to political attitudes and behaviour. It covers France, Germany, Britain and the USA.

R. J. Dalton, 'Citizenship norms and the expansion of political participation', *Political Studies*, 56 (1), 2008: 76–98. An examination of changing patterns of participation.

R. J. Dalton and H. D. Klingemann, (eds.), *Oxford Handbook of Political Behavior*, Oxford University Press, 2007. A definitive collection of essays on theories and cross-national research on political culture, political attitudes and behaviour.

R. F. Inglehart, 'The renaissance of political culture', *American Political Science Review*, 82, 1988: 1203–30. Marks a revival of interest in political cultures.

C. Welzel, *Freedom Rising: Human Empowerment and the Quest for Emancipation*. Cambridge University Press, 2013. The most extensive attempt to explain human history on the basis of cultural developments.

Websites

www.socialstudieshelp.com/APGOV_Participation.htm.
A brief account of political participation in the USA.

http://pprg.stanford.edu/wp-content/uploads/2009-Handbook-of-Social-Psychology.pdf.
A thorough and comprehensive account of the psychological basis of political behaviour.

www.europeansocialsurvey.org/docs/findings/ESS1_5_select_findings.pdf.
A wide-ranging account of public attitudes and public policy in Europe 2002/3–2010/11.

www.nationmaster.com/country-info/stats/Lifestyle.
Country comparisons of political attitudes and behaviour including, for example, social trust, political action and confidence in institutions.

10   Pressure groups and social movements

Few of us have much influence in politics as individuals on our own; we have to combine with others to have any impact. And that is exactly what people do in democracies. Using their rights of assembly and free association, they organise themselves into a huge number and variety of voluntary organisations – professional and business organisations, trade unions, charities, social clubs, environmental groups, veteran associations, churches, women's groups, welfare organisations, community associations, youth clubs, consumer groups, and arts, science, leisure and sports clubs. In recent decades, they have also developed an additional weapon in the struggle for political power, namely social movements, which are not the same as pressure groups but have a lot in common with them.

Voluntary organisations and associations, clubs and social movements play an enormously important role in social and political life, and are said to be one of the main foundations of modern democracy. Politically active groups voice the demands of their members and defend their interests in the political arena, as any peaceful group in a democracy is entitled to do. Many groups play a direct role in the consultative machinery of government. Even if they are not politically active, or only rarely so when circumstances require, groups help to create a peaceful, integrated and stable social order in which democratic government can operate effectively.

Voluntary associations organise themselves around the interests of social groups and strata, which makes them another example of the way that government and politics are deeply rooted in social life. In fact, they play a special role in politics as mediating organisations. They organise individuals into groups, and then link these groups with the political system by expressing and defending their political interests when the need arises. In this sense, they act as 'input' agencies in the political system that express the demands and concerns of individuals, but they also act as 'output' agencies that help to implement public policy. This means that groups are mediating agencies in a two-way process that links society and government – a function they share with parties and the media, which have their own chapters in this part of the book (chapters 11, 12 and 13).

Voluntary associations and organisations are thus crucial to an understanding of government and society: they express the social and political interests of their members, they try to influence the public by putting pressure on government, they often play a direct role in the consultative machinery of government and they play a crucial role in democratic politics by organising, integrating and stabilising society.

The main topics in this chapter are:

- Political connections
- Pressure groups and social movements in action
- Determinants of power
- Corporatism, para-government and tri-partism/pluralism
- International NGOs
- Groups, pressure groups and democracy
- Theories of voluntary organisations.

■ Political connections

Voluntary organisations and pressure groups

Modern government is often big government, with activities that extend into almost every corner of life and have an impact on the daily lives of citizens in many different ways. Therefore social groups have an incentive to organise themselves to defend their interests and to influence government policies that affect them. Perhaps the most conspicuous are the business associations and professional associations and trade unions that represent people in their working lives. These are often large, wealthy, active and powerful. Known as **interest groups**, many of these groups are constantly trying to shape government economic policies and matters that affect their occupations.

Interest groups: Sometimes known as 'sectional' groups, interest groups are the type of pressure group that represent occupational interests – business and professional associations and trade unions.

The professional associations and trade unions representing state bureaucrats can also be powerful interest groups, and in most countries the army, although not organised as an interest group, often exercises a powerful influence over defence policy.

Occupational groups are not the only form of pressure group. Far from it. In addition there are huge numbers and a vast variety of other groups known as **cause groups** that fight for their non-occupational goals. Churches are active on moral, educational and social issues, community associations deal with a wide range of local matters. Environmental groups have their special causes, as do arts and cultural groups, sports clubs, youth clubs, scientific associations, pensioners' organisations, women's groups, arts and cultural associations, welfare organisations, transport groups, consumer associations, humanitarian groups and so on. The list is almost endless, and it is difficult to exaggerate their number and variety (see briefing 10.1).

> **Cause groups:** Sometimes known as 'promotional' or 'attitude' groups, cause groups are a type of pressure group that do not represent organised occupational interests, but promote causes, policies or issues of their own.

Briefing 10.1

■ Pressure groups in the European Union

It is estimated that there are some 15,000 lobbyists and more than 3,500 active groups in Brussels. The vast majority represent business interests. The European Commission actively supports groups of many kinds and integrates them into the policy-making process. This is partly to achieve a more balanced representation of interests and partly to engage groups in its own activities. The groups can use two types of strategy, sometimes both but usually one rather than the other. The inside strategy tries to use influence policy from within by joining the formal policy-making process of the EU. The outside strategy involves trying to influence policy by staging public protests and getting publicity in the media. The inside strategy is more common because it is difficult to organise Europe-wide protests in Brussels, because EU policymakers are less vulnerable to public opinion than national legislatures and executives, and because EU policies are more remote from daily life.

The success of group pressure depends on three things: the characteristics of the groups; the system they operate in, and the issues involved. The most important group characteristics are expertise and political support. Campaign financing is less important than in the USA because money plays a smaller part in elections. Groups are most successful when their issue is confined to a few participants and others with an interest in the outcome.

Source: H. Lelieveldt and S. Princen, The Politics of the European Union, *2nd edn, Cambridge University Press, 2015: 149–50.*

■ Pressure groups in India

The main interest groups in India are organised around the traditional identities of caste, religion, language and region, but increasingly there are groups for students, professionals and local communities. Unlike in other democracies, caste and religious groups play a major part in Indian politics. Given the multi-party nature of politics most groups try to maintain their non-aligned status, but parties also organise their own sectional groups to act as pressure groups for students, professions, industries, castes and tribes. There are also new organisations for women, the environment, civil liberties, regional autonomy and grass-roots communities, and a new class of social mediators who are professional and wealthier people representing the interests of scheduled castes, ethnic minorities and the destitute. The new movements and mediators have forced their issues on to the political agendas of the old parties.

Groups use the traditional methods of linking with regional, caste and religious loyalties and modern ones of lobbying, funding parties and candidates, and using the media. Unconventional and direct forms of civil disobedience and protest are also popular, including strikes and their opposite, in which workers surround a place of work or a government office and prevent its employers from leaving the building until demands are met. Some observers claim that conflict between traditional political parties and the new pressure groups and movements has resulted in a tension between amorphous population and authoritarian government. India had a period of national emergency from 1975–7 followed by a peak in rioting in 1980–1.

Sources: www.nios.ac.in/media/documents/SecSocSciCour/English/Lesson-21.pdf; www.indiastudychannel.com/resources/152696-Pressure-Group-role-function.aspx

The result is that at any given moment and on any given issue organised groups and associations are likely to be engaged in a political struggle with each other and the government for influence over public policies. This is hugely important in political life, because organised political action is one of the main ways in which citizens can influence their governments, hold them accountable and make them responsive to public demands.

Democracies vary greatly in the number, variety and influence of their **pressure groups**. Established democracies with a long history of freedom of association and decades of social and political stability tend to have a greater density of politically active voluntary associations than new democracies, where free association has not been allowed or encouraged by authoritarian or totalitarian governments. For example, the World Values Survey shows that in eleven of the best established democracies of western Europe and north America, 5.5 per cent of the population are members of local political action groups, compared with 2.4 per cent in the newer Mediterranean democracies (Greece, Italy, Portugal and Spain), and 2.2 per cent in eight of the ex-communist democracies in central Europe, and 3.7 per

Pressure groups: Private and voluntary organisations that try to influence or control government policies but do not want to become the government. It is a general term to cover interest groups and cause groups. They are sometimes referred to as advocacy groups, campaign groups or lobby groups.

cent in the four of the third-wave democracies of Latin America (Argentina, Chile, Mexico and Peru).

From the point of view of governments there are three main types of pressure group:

- *'Episodic' groups* Most voluntary associations are not at all concerned with public issues and avoid politics if possible because they are controversial and cause difficulty between people. A local football club or film club has no need to get involved in politics in normal circumstances, but if their football pitch or cinema is due for demolition to make way for a road, they may campaign to protect their amenities, but only as long as the issue lasts. Such groups are known as **'episodic' groups**. Their importance lies in the fact that, while most groups are not political most of the time, they are already organised and can be mobilised quickly to defend their interests if these are threatened.

  > **'Episodic' groups:** Groups that are not usually politically active but become so when the need arises.

- *'Fire brigade' groups* Some citizen organisations, known as **'fire brigade'** groups are set up especially to fight a particular political campaign and disbanded when the issue is settled. For example, a local action group might be set up to keep a park as an open space, but fade away when the issue is won or lost.

  > **'Fire brigade' groups:** Groups formed to fight a specific issue, and dissolved when it is over.

- *Political groups* Some groups are created to engage in politics. One major purpose of trade unions and business associations, for example, is to engage in politics and to influence the wide range of public policies that affect their interests.

At this point, it would be helpful to clear up a purely verbal matter. This chapter refers to voluntary organisations of all kinds that play a political role as **'pressure groups'**. It uses the term 'interest groups' to refer to those kinds of pressure group that represent the interests of people in their occupational capacities – that is the business, professional and trade unions. All groups other than occupational groups are called **'cause groups'**. Interest groups and cause groups together make up the whole of the 'pressure group world'. This is not how the terms are used in some studies, which refer to politically active groups of all kinds as 'interest groups'. This, however, rather confuses matters because it leaves us with no way of distinguishing between occupational and other groups. We shall see later why this distinction is so important.

This still leaves us with other problems of definition. We have already mentioned that pressure groups and social movements are alike in some respects, and in addition that pressure groups are like political parties in some ways. All three are voluntary organisations and all are political. How, then, are we to distinguish between them?

Pressure groups and political parties

The pressure group world overlaps with political parties, but it is helpful to draw lines between them because they usually play a different role in politics:

- Pressure groups want to influence government, parties want to become government. Trade unions and business organisations want to keep a foot in the door of government, but they do not want to be part of it.
- Most pressure groups are interested in only one policy area, party programmes cover all (or almost all) of them. Welfare groups are concerned with welfare, art groups with art. Neither have any particular interest in foreign policy.
- Parties are primarily political, most pressure groups are not. Parties are set up to win power by contesting elections. Rose growers' associations are not interested in politics unless they have to be.
- Parties fight elections, most pressure groups do not.

These are not hard and fast differences. The Labour parties of Australia and the UK were created by socialist, workers' and trade union pressure groups. Rural and agricultural interests have played such an important role in Scandinavia that they created their own agrarian parties. Some groups are naturally **aligned groups** – business organisations with right-wing parties, trade unions with left-wing parties – and some are integrated into parties or have been set up by them (see briefing 10.1 on India) and some contest elections, though often for the publicity this brings rather than the hope of winning. But most groups stick to their own particular interests and try to maintain a neutral political position so that they can work with whatever party or coalition is in power, as the occasion requires.

> **Aligned groups:** Pressure groups that ally themselves with a political party, the best examples being trade unions and left parties, and business organisations and right parties.

Social movements

Social movements also have much in common with parties and pressure groups, but differ in some respects. Social movements:

- Bring together a range of different organisations and associations to work loosely together. They are not organised into a single bureaucratic structure like pressure groups and parties.
- Have a broader range of political interests than most voluntary associations, but a narrower range than most political parties.

Probably the best single example of a social movement is the working-class coalition formed in many countries in the nineteenth century to protect and promote working-class interests. Formed by trade unions, cooperatives and collectives, savings clubs, worker educational organisations and socialist organisations of all kinds, they initially formed a broad coalition of forces.

Later, many of them formed their own political parties, so they made the transition from groups to movements to parties. The suffragettes were another early social movement, though they rarely formed their own parties.

In the modern world, we hear much more about '**new social movements**' (NSMs). These differ from voluntary organisations and parties in several ways. They have:

> **New social movements:** Loosely knit organisations ('networks of networks') that try to influence government policy on broad issues, including the environment, nuclear energy and nuclear weapons, economic development, peace, women and minorities.

1. A different sort of political agenda insofar as they are often counter-cultural, anti-politics and anti-state.
2. A broader range of interests (human rights, minority groups, the environment, peace) than most groups, but a narrower range than parties.
3. A broader range of members than most groups, but a narrower range than the largest parties. Some social movements have been called 'rainbow coalitions' because they try to link rather disparate social groups and organisations under a single political umbrella.
4. A looser and more decentralised form of organisation than groups or parties – they have been described as 'networks of networks'. The 'old' organisations are hierarchical, bureaucratic and professionally run, the 'new' ones are more dependent on the grass-roots participation of volunteers.
5. Political methods that are often innovative and unconventional, involving direct political action, community involvement and sometimes protest action or even violence.

Environmental movements illustrate many of these features. They often pursue a self-consciously different style of politics from conventional parties and pressure groups, and they have a wider agenda than most groups, as well as attracting a broader range of social types. Most groups appeal to specific kinds of individual for specific kinds of activities – they are sports clubs or choirs or mountain walkers' clubs. Environmental movements are often networks of interests that come together as loose-knit coalitions, rather than hierarchically organised and bureaucratically centralised organisations. That is why they are called 'movements'. They often use unconventional political methods, including direct action, grass-roots participation and eye-catching protests.

However, social movements, including 'new' social movements, are not particularly new. The Abolition (of slavery) movement and the Chartist and the Suffragette movements of the nineteenth century were followed in the 1950s in Britain by the Campaign for Nuclear Disarmament (CND). However, the 1960s and 1970s saw a wave of social movements concerned with the environment, peace, women's rights, nuclear power and weapons, minority rights, animal rights and racism. Examples include Friends of the Earth and Greenpeace, the Black Power movement in the USA, peasant and land reform movements in South America and the loose alignment of right-wing and racist groups in Europe.

Initially it seemed to some observers that these new social movements threatened the established order of the state, and its conventional parties and pressure groups. It was claimed that they undermined the established institutions of government – parties and pressure groups, overloaded the political system with non-negotiable demands, and threatened the established order with unconventional forms of protest behaviour. But, as it turns out, new social movements have quite a lot in common with 'old' social movements, political parties and groups. Each has tried to steal the other's clothes. The old parties adopted some of the policy goals of the new groups and movements, while groups and movements have sometimes adapted and compromised with the world by adopting the more conventional and pragmatic methods of the parties. The Greens formed political parties to fight elections, and while they initially opposed the formal hierarchies of the old parties and tried to work with a rotating leadership, some gradually succumbed to the old ways of doing things and kept the same leadership. Meanwhile, the old parties, realising which way the wind was blowing, started to adopt modified Green policies and parts of the feminist agenda in order to head off electoral threats and criticism.

■ Pressure groups and social movements in action

Pressure groups and social movements perform two main political functions:

- *Interest aggregation* The formation of a single policy programme from a set of rather different interests and views. Student organisations have to aggregate the interests of different students – first- and higher-degree, arts and social science and natural science, home and overseas, young and mature, wealthy and poor. Pressure groups have the important role of sorting and sifting opinion and presenting it as a single package.
- *Interest articulation* Expressing and publicising policies in order to influence government action. This is their 'voice' function, in which they try to make their views heard amid the great confusion of noise made by all groups equally concerned to stress their own point.

Groups and movements use many different methods of articulating their interests – from lobbying politicians and bureaucrats, producing pamphlets, doing research, producing websites and organising petitions, to organising strikes, sit-ins, non-cooperation, rioting and violence, and staging publicity events. There are two general rules in choosing any one or combination of these methods:

- First, try to get into the policy formation process as early as possible, because this is when options are open, when parties have not yet taken a public stand and when government is still undecided.
- Second, operate at the highest possible level of government to which you have access, because this is the best way to achieve the greatest amount of influence with the least possible expense and effort.

This, of course, is easier said than done, because groups have to take account of two sets of powerful constraints that determine how they operate in the political system and how much power and influence they have in it. The first set of constraints concerns the nature of the group and its interests; the second, the nature of the political environment they are working in.

Groups and issues

Some groups have a privileged 'insider' status that gives them direct access to high-level government officials. **'Insider' groups** and governments are sometimes heavily dependent upon each other and are in close and constant contact: groups want to influence policies and receive advance warning about them; governments sometimes depend upon groups for their technical information and expertise, and for their cooperation in the smooth implementation of policy. A great

> **'Insider' groups:** Pressure groups with access to senior government officials, often recognised as the only legitimate representatives of particular interests and often formally incorporated into the official consultative bodies.

deal of the business between groups and government does not involve major policy issues but technical matters and details; some groups are routinely consulted about these, but to preserve their 'insider' status, they must not disturb the relationship by making extreme demands or attacking the government in public. A professional association of doctors may be very concerned about a health issue and have important information that it wants to feed into government policy-making circles, for example. Equally, doctors are a prestigious group that governments have to listen to and need in order to implement their health policies. Consequently, doctors are most usually included in special consultative committees on health matters.

Many 'insider' groups represent business and professional interests – business interests, farmers, doctors, bankers, supermarket and shopping chains – which play a key role in the economy. This gives them political influence. In some countries close relations between government and private interests are promoted by similar elite backgrounds – Oxford and Cambridge universities in Britain, the Grandes Écoles in Paris, the Tokyo Law School and the Law and Business Schools of Harvard and Yale. In many countries it is not uncommon for ministers and senior civil servants leaving public service to work for the very businesses and organisations they were regulating when in office – the so-called 'revolving door' in the UK and the USA, or 'the descent from heaven' in Japan.

'Outsider' groups do not have this special relationship. They are excluded from close consultation because they lack bargaining power, are

> **'Outsider' group:** Group with no access to top government officials.

too critical of government, are generally unpopular, or because they prefer to be outside and independent of government. While 'insider' groups rely heavily on their close government contacts, outsider groups use other methods of protest, direct action and publicity-attracting demonstrations. One of

Briefing 10.2

A life of pressure: Peter Jenkins, a public affairs officer with the British Consumers' Association

I wish I were taking people out to lunch all the time but it's not really like that. The Consumers' Association is different from most lobbying organisations in that we are here to represent consumers' interests and we don't have large budgets for entertaining in the same way as some of the private lobbying firms.

I campaign on food and communication issues and work as part of a team made up of specialist advisers, lawyers and staff from our policy unit. Between us we form, draft and carry out strategies on a variety of issues. At any one time I might be working on V BSE, GM crops, food poisoning or consumers' problems with the utility companies.

An example of the lobbying work we do would be the work we carried out in the run-up to the formation of the Food Standards Agency. The CA had long campaigned for such an agency to be put in place, and once it was announced the focus of our efforts changed. During the drafting of the White Paper we were in contact with civil servants writing the legislation; once it was published we worked in Parliament to produce amendments that we felt were in the public's best interest.

Because the present government has such a large majority in the House of Commons we have found it easier to work in the Lords. It's a case of lobbying sympathetic peers, explaining what the impact of the legislation will be if it is unchanged, and persuading them to table amendments.

Sometimes it involves stalking the corridors of parliament late at night; mostly it's about knowing the right person to call, and picking up the phone.

The other side of my job is representing the organisation to the media. Part of the campaigning involves writing press releases and being on call to do radio and television interviews. On Monday I came into work thinking I had a quiet day, only to be told there was a car waiting to take me to ITN. The thrill of the job is when you are working on a campaign that is getting MPs excited and there is the perceptible feeling that things are really happening.

(Adapted from the Guardian, *12 May 2001)*

the ironies of pressure group politics is that powerful 'insider' groups can operate most smoothly and quietly out of the public eye, while the 'outsider' groups, for all the noise of their demonstrations and protest campaigns, are less powerful and effective: protest politics is a weapon of the less powerful. Perhaps the best-known 'outsider' protest politicians in the world were Nelson Mandela (1918–2013) and Martin Luther King (1929–68), which makes the point that protest politics can sometimes be both peaceful and successful.

The nature of government

The way pressure groups operate is strongly influenced by the nature of the political system they are dealing with, and the location of power within it.

Direct routes

As far as they can, groups start with the most powerful actors:

- *Executives* In presidential systems it is best to approach the president or a staff member, and in parliamentary systems the prime minister or the cabinet. Since only a few, special, groups have such high-level access, the rest must approach the less powerful points that they can reach.

- *Legislatures* Groups without access to their political executives may start with their legislature, which usually attracts a good deal of pressure-group activity, especially in the USA, where parties are weak, elections frequent and elected representatives are sensitive to special interest campaigns and funds. Powerful groups do not need to waste time in the **lobby** of the legislative body. They have privileged contacts with officials and in committees and consultative bodies of government. There is little sense in walking the corridors of power when it is possible to pick up the phone and talk to a contact. Members of legislative bodies are often associated with a wide circle of interest groups of various kinds. As elected representatives they have clear policy goals of their own on many issues but they are also bombarded with huge amounts of information from groups trying to get their attention and support. Groups without easy access to the political executive, however, may have the funds to employ professional lobbyists (see briefing 10.2) and some 'buy' influence by contributing to campaign funds. The issue of private contributions to election campaign funds has become an acute concern in many democracies.

  > **Lobby:** A popular term for pressure groups (based on the mistaken belief that pressure group representatives spend a lot of time in the 'lobbies' or ante-rooms of legislative chambers).

- *Government departments* It is often effective to start with the top bureaucrats in government departments, especially if the political system is blocked by weak and fragmented parties, or by conflict between the executive and legislature. It is probably also best to start with bureaucrats on technical matters because they will probably handle them in the end. Having a friend or ally who is (or was) a top public servant is exceedingly helpful.

- *State and local government* Many pressure groups deal with local matters, so their natural target is state or local government.

- *International and supra-national government* Given the global nature of the modern world increasing numbers of interest groups are operating at the international level (see briefing 10.3).

Indirect routes

Since many groups do not have good access to either elected or appointed government officials, they try more roundabout routes to gain influence (see briefing 10.2).

- *Political parties* Aligned groups have special, friendly connections with political parties that have similar interests and political goals. Sometimes this friendly relationship is sealed by donations to party funds. At the

Briefing 10.3

International peak organisations

International NGOs such as Amnesty International and environmental groups are often regarded as key organisations in international governance, but they are only a small part of a huge number. They attract a lot of media attention but it does not mean that they are as influential or powerful as some other NGOs that are able to work effectively without much publicity, especially those in the economic, farming, business, health and labour areas. The following gives a flavour of the vast range and breadth of international NGOs.

- The *World Council of Churches* represents about 500 million Christians, bringing together more than 345 churches, denominations and fellowships in 110 countries and territories (https://www.oikoumene.org/).
- The *International Confederation of Free Trade Unions* is the world's largest trade union body, with 224 affiliated organisations and 176 million members in 161 countries on six continents. It maintains close links with other international labour organisations, such as the European Trade Union Confederation (ETUC) and the International Trade Secretariats.
- The *Olympic movement* consists of the International Olympic Committee (IOC), sixty-five International Sports Federations, 204 National Olympic Committees, the Organising Committees for the Olympic Games, national sports associations and clubs and their athletes and other organisations recognised by the IOC (www.olympic.org).
- *Rotary International* is a world-wide organisation with some 1.2 million members in more than 34,000 clubs in 180 countries (www.rotary.org).
- The *World Association of Girl Guides and Girl Scouts* has over 10 million members in 146 countries (www.wagggsworld.org). The World Scout Movement has more than 30 million members in 161 countries and territories (www.scout.org).
- The *Union of International Associations* is a clearing house for information about more than 67,685 international non-profit organisations (www.uia.org). Its list of organisations includes: Disinfected Mail Study Circle, International Group of Priests for Circus and Showmen of All Confessions, European Council of Skeptical Organisations, International Goat Association, International Institute for Andragogy, International Union of Private Wagon Owners' Associations, Proutist Universal, Society of Indexers, Toy Traders of Europe, United Elvis Presley Society and World Association of Flower Arrangers.

same time, parties that have already taken a public stand on an issue will be hard to shift, so it is best to get in early before they have thought about the matter.

- *Public campaigns* Modern methods of advertising, desktop publishing and computer mail shots have made public campaigns more attractive, but they are still relatively expensive, time-consuming and uncertain in their effects. There are so many groups in the political arena that it is difficult for any one of them to have a big effect, but if a group has public opinion on its side then governments are more likely to treat it with respect.

- *Mass media* Many groups court publicity with press briefings and events (see chapter 11). News reports may be cheaper and more effective than advertising, but the channels of mass communication are overcrowded and it is often difficult to get media attention. A big demonstration or an eye-catching publicity stunt may do the trick, but that may alienate the public and officials so it can be a risky strategy.
- *Internet and social media* By offering information on their websites and stimulating discussions on their special platforms many groups try to reach a broad audience and to mobilise support for their cause. Besides, groups use new social media (Facebook, Twitter etc.) to spread their opinions and responses immediately to their followers.
- *Courts* Groups can achieve their goals through the courts, especially since they now play an increasingly important political role. The litigious nature of American society means that pressure groups are constantly in court, but in other countries the courts can be a last resort because the legal process is slow, expensive and uncertain.
- *International and multinational government* Pressure groups are increasingly operating at the international level, lobbying bodies such as the UN and the EU. The distinction between 'insider' and 'outsider' groups operates here as well.

Groups often use different combinations of access points into the political system, depending on their resources, characteristics and political connections, and they will often look for allies and build coalitions with like-minded groups. It is helpful to have other groups as allies in the struggle and this sometimes produces strange bed-fellows: militant groups of alternative life-style ecologists have sometimes formed an alliance with conservative landowners to protect the environment. There may also be a price to pay for coalition building if partners want help with their own campaign as the cost of support. Some groups refuse to fight with others if they think they are too militant and extremist, especially if they use violence. Cooperation and coalition building help to moderate group demands.

■ Determinants of power

An obvious and important question to ask about pressure groups is 'How much power do they have and how effective are their campaigns?' As so often this question is difficult to answer. Many factors are involved. Environmental groups have had some success in recent years, but they have been helped by a shift in public opinion, changes in government and media coverage of nuclear accidents, oil spills and global warming. Has government policy changed because of environmental campaigns or because of a combination of these other factors? Environmental groups have certainly helped to change opinion, just as they have used their media skills to publicise environmental disasters to bring pressure to bear on governments. But circumstances have also changed and the different factors are so closely intertwined that it is virtually impossible to sort them out and say how much is due to environmental groups and how much to other things. Group influence does seem, however, to depend on two groups of considerations – the internal features of groups and their issues, and the political environment in which they operate.

Group features

Eight group characteristics, often interrelated, seem to influence the power of any given group.

- *Income* Some groups are wealthy and have offices and a large staff, others are poor and rely on a few voluntary workers. By and large, interest groups are wealthier than cause groups, because they represent the economic interests of their members, who have material and work-related incentives to join and pay a subscription.
- *Membership size* Large groups can collect membership subscriptions from many people, and then use this income to pay staff to raise more money. Nevertheless, size is not always an advantage. Small but cohesive groups can defeat large and divided ones and some small groups are remarkably wealthy.
- *Organisational advantages* Some groups are easier to organise than others because potential members work or live in the same place, because they have the time and resources to contribute to group efforts or simply because they are not disadvantaged by age or personal disabilities. Compare adults and children, producers and consumers, doctors and patients, the healthy and chronically ill, professors and students, rich and poor, home owners and the homeless, majority and minority groups, the employed and the unemployed.
- *Membership density and recruitment* A group representing almost all its potential members is likely to have more influence than one representing only a small proportion. Professions (doctors, lawyers, dentists, musicians) often make membership of their association compulsory, so they have membership density of 100 per cent. Farmers' associations often have a high density. At the other end of the scale, organisations for the homeless, the mentally ill and handicapped, children and the very old rely on dedicated activists, most of them not themselves homeless, handicapped, very young or old.
- *Divided groups* A united group is likely to have more influence than a divided one, and a group that holds the field on its own more influence than one with a rival that competes to represent the same interests. Groups that are united by common interests are sometimes coordinated by a single **'umbrella' organisation** or 'peak associations'. Though unity is generally an asset, some moderate groups benefit from

'Umbrella' organisation: Association-of-associations that coordinates the activity of their member organisations.

having radical or extremists groups separate from them but with similar goals. When it comes to negotiating, governments would sooner deal with moderate groups and may be forced into doing so by the activities of the extremists. In some cases the moderate group has set up its own extremist 'shadow' wing to help the process.

- *Sanctions* Some groups have powerful sanctions. Businesses that can move their capital abroad, professional bodies that can withdraw cooperation with the government and groups with public sympathy and can influence voters. Other groups have weak sanctions, or none – children can't go on strike, hospital patients don't refuse treatment or engage in protest 'lie-ins', the homeless can't withhold rent, the poor may not have access to lawyers. Often this boils down to how important the groups are in the economy, and their structural power within it.
- *Leadership* A charismatic leader (Nelson Mandela, Martin Luther King) is a great asset.
- *The issue* Governments and parties often have set opinions about big, controversial public issues, so many groups choose to work on policy details and technicalities.

The political environment

There are five key features of the political environment that can affect pressure group success:

- *'Insider'/'outsider' status* 'Insider' groups are more likely to be powerful than 'outsider' groups. Their access to top decision makers gives them a 'voice' and influence at high levels of the political system.
- *Public opinion* Governments are more likely to take note of groups with strong public support. To do otherwise is to risk losing electoral support.
- *Legitimacy* Groups representing what are seen as legitimate interests in society (doctors, lawyers, teachers, businessmen, farmers, church leaders) often have more influence than marginal ones (drug addicts, prostitutes, ex-criminals, minorities and radical groups of many kinds).
- *Party alignment* Groups that are aligned with the party in government can have 'inside' influence – only to lose it, of course, when their party is out of office.
- *Countervailing powers* Groups with the field to themselves are likely to be more influential than those which face opposition. Sometimes groups cancel each other out by competing on different sides of the issue (they veto each other). One theory argues that the pressure group world is a 'veto-group system', in which few groups can get what they want because other groups have a capacity to stop them encroaching on their own interests.

It is not difficult to think of an imaginary case to illustrate the influence of a group and political factors on the success of a pressure group campaign.

Imagine that students are campaigning higher maintenance grants from the government:

- The student body in most countries is quite large, but since many students are not wealthy their representative associations do not have a great deal of money, although they may have a small, experienced and enthusiastic permanent staff to organise a political campaign.
- Student bodies are often divided internally because they represent groups from diverse social and political backgrounds, different political interests, and varying types and levels of study.
- Students have few sanctions. Their strikes are symbolic; they cannot threaten to move their capital investments, shut down factories or paralyse the economy. Withdrawing cooperation with the government and its officials would have no effect.
- On the political side, student representative bodies may not be 'outsider' groups, exactly, but there are many 'insider' groups with more prestige and power. Their image in some countries is often not one that wins them much public sympathy.
- Students support a wide assortment of political parties and positions and, in any case, it is doubtful if their representative body swings many votes in public elections.

■ Corporatism, para-government and tri-partism/pluralism

Corporatism

In some countries, the relationship between government and economic interest groups representing employers and workers was so closely organ-

> **Corporatism:** A way of organising public policy making involving the close cooperation of major economic interests within a formal government apparatus that is capable of concerting the main economic groups so that they can jointly formulate and implement binding policies.

ised within formal government structures that a special term, 'corporatist', has been invented to describe them. **Corporatism** in democratic states (sometimes called neo-corporatism or liberal corporatism) can only work under specific circumstances, however:

1. A small number of hierarchically organised 'umbrella' or 'peak' associations to speak authoritatively for all their members.
2. Such groups are recognised, licensed or even created by the government to ensure that it deals only with a small number of dependable, official representatives.
3. A wide array of formal decision-making and consultative government bodies that cover all groups and issues in the policy area.
4. An ability to produce policies that are binding on all parties, and implemented by them.

Corporatism was strongest in the economic sphere where the main interests could be coordinated:

- Trade unions agreed to limit wage and other demands in return for full employment.
- Employers agreed to maintain full employment in return for industrial peace and cooperation.
- The government promised low inflation and social benefits in return for economic stability.
- All were willing and able to impose these agreements upon their own members. They came together within formal government institutions to hammer out a compromise public policy which all accepted and stood by.

One danger of corporatism is that groups not in the system – students, immigrants, peace and anti-nuclear campaigners and (initially) the Greens, as well as extremist right-wing and racist organisations – are excluded from these closed circles of power, and hence may explode into direct action in order to make their voice heard. Some student and worker protest movements have referred to themselves as 'extra-parliamentary opposition' to stress the point that they are outside the formal arenas of power. Corporatism developed in the 1970s and 1980s in western Europe as a method of managing economic growth, but tended to break down in the 1990s under the pressures of economic stagnation. Strong corporatism was found in Austria, Denmark, Luxembourg, Norway and Sweden. Weaker forms were found in Belgium, Finland, Ireland, the Netherlands, Switzerland and West Germany. A different form of corporatism is found in new democracies, where pressure groups are often weaker and less well organised, and where, traditionally, they have been controlled by authoritarian governments (see briefing 10.4). The new democracies are usually moving towards more open and pluralist systems.

Para-government

In some countries, large institutional groups play the role of *para-public agencies* that provide public services with financial and other help from the state. The result is an area of government that is neither purely private nor public, but a third sector that is a mixture of both:

- The Catholic and Protestant churches in Germany collect taxes through the state, and provide social services in return.
- Scandinavian housing associations are para-public organisations that cooperate closely with public authorities and receive money from them.
- Farmers, business organisations, professional associations and churches are involved in close cooperation with the state in Germany and Scandinavia, in order to resolve conflict, regulate society and provide services.

Briefing 10.4

Corporatism, interest groups and democracy in Latin America

Although democracy has a firm grounding in some Latin American states it should not be assumed that they follow the same political processes as the democracies of North America and western Europe. Latin America's politics is rooted in corporatist systems in which leading social and economic groups had a privileged place in the political system – traditionally the aristocracy, the church and the military. Countries such as Costa Rica and Uruguay have succeeded in expanding the opportunities for political participation for new groups, but in other countries political power is more likely to be more tightly controlled by a few charismatic leaders, the socio-economic elites and the military.

Latin American politics is more pluralist than before, but there are far fewer organised interest groups than in the USA: tens of thousands of interest groups are represented in Washington; far fewer are found in Latin American capitals. And whereas American groups are independent of government, in Latin America they are sometimes co-opted or organised by the state or by the ruling party.

However, there has been an explosion of interest groups in Latin America in the past thirty to forty years. They now cover not just the elites of the army, the church and business, but also the middle class, professionals, workers, peasants, women, indigenous groups, students, government workers and international NGOs. Nevertheless, interest group pluralism still tends to be under-developed. Many new groups are poorly organised and weak, and the system typically favours the privileged few, rather than the many. Among the democracies, Argentina, Chile, Costa Rica, Brazil and Uruguay have achieved a low level of pluralism, but other countries have yet to approach this standard.

Based on Communications in Latin America, 'Report on Latin America:
Politics and Economics' (http://iml.jou.ufl.edu/projects/
Spring2000/Calcote/latam_la.html)

Tri-partism: A looser and less centralised system of decision making than corporatism involving close government consultation – often with business and trade union organisations.

Policy communities: Small, stable and consensual groupings of government officials and pressure group representatives that form around particular issue areas.

Policy networks: Compared with policy communities, policy networks are larger, looser (and sometimes more conflictual) networks that gather around a policy area.

Tri-partism/pluralism

Some countries without corporatist structures use a less centralised and coordinated system of economic policy making known as **tri-partism**. Here, the three corners of the 'economic triangle' cooperate in a much looser manner through a variety of different formal and semi-formal committees, consultative bodies and meetings. In such systems it makes more sense to talk about **policy communities** or **policy networks** than about corporatism. France, Italy, Japan and the UK are examples, and have been joined by some of the new democracies of central Europe, and by Mexico and Chile in Latin America.

Canada, India, New Zealand and the USA tend to be less centralised and co-ordinated, and more pluralist and open in their approach. Nonetheless, the relationships between government and private interest groups in some policy areas of the USA are sometimes so close that political scientists talk of the **'iron triangles'** formed by executive agencies, congressional sub-committees and pressure groups. For example, the farming lobby in the USA is wealthy and well organised and has close, intimate working relations with government policy makers.

> **'Iron triangles':** The close, three-sided working relationship developed between (1) government departments and ministries, (2) pressure groups and (3) politicians, that makes public policy in a given area.

■ International NGOs

Pressure groups have never been confined to domestic politics, but international groups are now more visible and active than ever before. Barely a week passes without a major news story that involves Amnesty International, Greenpeace, Médecins Sans Frontières, Transparency International or the Red Cross. Organisations like these form an increasingly dense network alongside the growing number of agencies of international governance such as the OECD, the UN and the WTO (see briefing 10.3). As with domestic pressure groups, the international NGOs we hear about most are not necessarily the most powerful. Environmental groups and Amnesty International are certainly not weak, but they can rarely match the power of business organisations. We will return to them in the concluding chapter of the book.

■ Groups, pressure groups and democracy

Freedom of assembly and association are essential parts of any democratic system, and all groups have a right to be heard and to try to influence public policy in a peaceful manner. Besides articulating demands (the input function) in the open political arena, they also play an indispensable role within government itself on official consultative committees, working parties, advisory groups and commissions. Most democratic political systems have an elaborate array of these, and rely heavily on groups for advice, information, specialist expertise and help with implementing policies. Groups also have an output function in producing services for their members and the general public. They deliver meals to the ill and the old, run community centres, raise money for schools, hospitals and overseas aid, provide sports facilities and organise exhibitions. In some countries they run schools, hospitals and a wide variety of social services, sometimes with government support and money, sometimes independently of any public agency.

For these reasons groups play a central part in **pluralist democracy**, which is based on free competition between a plurality of organised

> **Pluralist democracy:** A democratic system where political decisions are the outcome of the conflict and competition between many different groups.

Mass society: A society without a plurality of organised social groups and interests, whose mass of isolated and uprooted individuals are not integrated into the community and who are therefore vulnerable to the appeals and manipulations of extremist and anti-democratic elites.

interests and on mutually beneficial relations between groups and government. The opposite of pluralist society is **mass society** which has a weak foundation of organised groups and which, it is said, is particularly susceptible to extremist politics because the population is not well organised into groups that can defend their interests.

At the same time, pressure groups can also present a threat to democracy. They are often not particularly democratic internally, although some are more democratic than the parties in government. Most represent narrow sectional interests of their own, not the public interest. If they become too powerful, and if they get too close to the top levels of government, they may 'capture' and control government policy in their own interests. This is the wrong way round: governments are supposed to control private groups when they threaten the public interest (see controversy 10.1). Policy areas often claimed to be under strong private influence (even control) include agriculture (e.g. genetically modified (GM) crops), health (e.g. smoking for much of the twentieth century), the defence industry (e.g. arms manufacturers), business (e.g. finance capital, manufacturing and commerce). One particular difficulty is the 'revolving door' or 'descent from heaven' practice of senior elected or appointed officials who leave their

CONTROVERSY 10.1

Do pressure groups sustain or undermine democracy?

■ Sustain

- Groups perform the essential democratic functions of aggregating and articulating public opinion.
- Voluntary organisations are indispensable ways of organising minority interests.
- Voluntary associations are the 'free schools of democracy', teaching people political and organisational skills.
- Groups are recruiting grounds for local and national political leaders.
- Groups encourage the politics of accommodation, understanding and compromise by bringing together different people with different backgrounds and opinions in the same organisation.
- Overlapping and interlocking networks of organisations tie society together, counteracting internal divisions and superimposed cleavages.
- Groups give people a sense of belonging, community and purpose.
- Groups act as channels of communication between citizens, and between citizens and government.
- Groups provide a network of organisations outside and independent of government. They are a ready-made organisational basis for mobilising public opinion against unpopular government action.

- Groups provide governments with technical information and specialist knowledge, and can help implement public policy efficiently and effectively.
- Mass societies are prone to extremist politics and totalitarian political movements.

■ Undermine

- Narrow, sectional interests may conspire against the public interest.
- Some groups – typically the wealthy, prestigious and insider ones – are very powerful. Others – typically the poor, minority, outsider ones – are virtually powerless.
- Groups can be exclusive, keeping out some sections of the population and not representing their views (e.g. women, minorities). Corporatism and policy communities are also exclusive and work with a limited number of groups.
- Private organisations are often oligarchic, representing the interests of leaders, not members.
- Pressure groups are responsible only to their own members, but governments are responsible to the whole population. If pressure groups have too much power, then representative and responsible government will have too little.
- Close cooperation between groups and government risks two dangers. (1) Groups may become too 'domesticated', losing their critical independence of government. (2) Governments may be 'captured' by private interests, losing independence and accountability to the public interest.

> **Hyper-pluralism:** A state of affairs in which too many powerful groups make too many demands on government, causing overload and ungovernability.

- Too many powerful groups making too many demands on government may result in government overload and **hyper-pluralism**.
- Groups tend to fragment public policy, preventing governments developing coherent policies.

public post to become advisors or consultants for private organisations. There is nothing necessarily wrong with this but it can lead to corruption, which is why it is often regulated by law.

The most serious problem presented by pressure groups is money. Wealthy groups usually (not always) have an advantage over poor ones, so creating inequalities in political power. Wealthy groups are also able to contribute to the election funds of parties and candidates. Once again, there is nothing necessarily wrong with this, but it can also lead to corruption, which is why it is controversial and often the subject of complicated laws and a need for transparency. The problem is an extreme one in the USA where billions of dollars are donated to parties and candidates. It should not, however, be assumed that political influence necessarily or inevitably follows these donations or that they are given only to right-wing and conservative causes (see table 10.1).

It seems that a successful pluralist democracy depends on a balance of power between government and groups. Too much pressure group power results in private interests running government; too little results in autocratic government that pays insufficient attention to legitimate citizen demands. It is a matter of debate where one draws the line between 'too much' and 'too little'.

Table 10.1 Donations to parties and candidates, USA, 2013–15

	Total to parties and candidates (US$ billion)	Democrats (per cent)	Republicans (per cent)
Finance, insurance, real estate	344.5	37.4	62.4
Ideology, single issue	234.1	50.1	49.7
Other	233.1	53.3	46.3
Miscellaneous business	181.6	38.2	61.5
Lawyers and lobbyists	140.4	65.2	34.6
Health	131.3	43.0	56.8
Communications, electronics	90.7	59.9	39.8
Energy, natural resources	88.72	21.0	79.0
Agribusiness	64.1	24.9	74.7
Labour	60.6	88.9	10.9
Construction	59.8	28.4	71.4
Transport	56.6	28.3	71.6
Defence	25.2	40.1	59.8

Source: www.opensecrets.org/industries/

■ Theories of voluntary organisations

The very large body of literature on groups and movements in politics tends to fall into one of three major theoretical camps – pluralist theory, Marxist/elitist theory and social capital/civil society theory.

Pluralism

Pluralists argue that:

- Many political issues are fought over by competing groups. Rarely is one of them so powerful that it can get its own way. Most have to compromise, but they often get something they want, even if it is only to prevent other groups encroaching on their interests. This is called **veto-group** power.

> **Veto-groups:** Groups with the power to prevent other groups or the government implementing a policy, although they do not necessarily have the power to get their own policies implemented.

- All groups have some resources to fight their political battles – money, numbers, popularity, 'insider' status, leadership skills, popular support, votes. Resources are not distributed equally, but nor are they distributed with cumulative inequality. Some groups have voting strength, some money, some organisational skills, some have the ability to attract publicity, some have charismatic leaders and some have public support. Most groups have one or more of these but few have all of them. As a result no group is powerless and no group is all-powerful.
- Power is fragmented, fluid, or 'mercurial'. It depends on the issues, the political circumstances, the parties in power and the constellation of groups

involved. There is no fixed power structure or power elite, but different configurations of shifting coalitions and power according to the issue and the circumstances. Today's winners will be tomorrow's losers, and vice versa.

- Groups that fail in one political arena (national government) may be successful in others (local government, the courts, international arenas).
- Groups often look for political allies, which obliges them to compromise and cooperate with others.
- Groups cannot always get what they want, but they can often veto other group proposals they do not like.
- The main exponent of pluralist theory, Robert Dahl (1915–2014), argues that pluralist democracy does not work in a perfect 'textbook' manner, but it works reasonably well, 'warts and all'.

Marxist/elitist theory

Pluralist theory is opposed by Marxist and elitist theories which claim that the pressure group system undermines democracy:

- The 'iron law of oligarchy' (chapter 13) means that groups are controlled by a few, unrepresentative leaders, because they are the people with the skill, knowledge and experience to run them, and because leaders make sure they control group resources and the means of communication.
- The group world is dominated by educated, wealthy and upper-class 'joiners'. Survey research shows that people of higher socio-economic status are more likely to join voluntary associations and that the leaders of such associations are generally dominated by the upper strata.
- Some social groups are weakly organised, or largely unorganised. The very poor, children, the homeless, the mentally and physically ill and minority groups have to rely upon those with political resources to defend them, which puts them in a vulnerable position.
- Group resources are distributed with cumulative inequality. The class-based nature of the group world ensures that wealthier groups have most of the resources necessary to fight political battles.
- Groups with structural power in the economy (especially business interests) are particularly powerful.
- Groups fight within a political system that is systematically loaded in favour of wealthy groups and business interests. Government is not a neutral 'referee' in the group battle, but part of a system that favours the wealthy and well organised.
- The group world reflects and reinforces the power structure in which wealthy interests with structural power in the economy dominate the political system.
- Some elite theorists argue that a '**military–industrial complex**' controls key decisions, leaving less important issues to pluralist competition.

> **Military–industrial complex:** The close and powerful alliance of government, business and military interests that is said by some to run capitalist societies.

Social capital and civil society theory

Social capital: The features of society such as trust, social norms and social networks, that improve social, economic and government efficiency by encouraging cooperation and collective action.

Social capital theory has a lot in common with pluralist theory. Drawing on Alexis de Tocqueville's (1805–59) influential study of *Democracy in America* (1831), and on modern social science evidence, the American political scientist Robert Putnam (1941–) argues that:

- Voluntary associations – particularly 'bridging' associations that bring different social groups together – are crucial for the development of democratic attitudes, such as trust, reciprocity and satisfaction with democracy, and for democratic behaviour, such as civic engagement, voting and membership of parties. The social trust and the personal and organisational networks that groups create form the social capital on which democracy rests.
- Voluntary organisations teach the political skills of a democracy – how to organise, how to run meetings, how to compromise and how to work and cooperate with others for collective goals.
- Not all social organisations generate 'good' social capital that is beneficial to society as a whole. The Italian Mafia, for example, generates 'bad' social capital that benefits the Mafia.
- Putnam's research on Italy and the USA suggests that economic success and democratic stability is rooted in networks of voluntary associations. Democratic malaise (falling election turnout and party membership, declining trust in politicians and government institutions, cheating on taxes, political fear and cynicism) is caused, in part, by a decline in the voluntary organisations that generate social capital.

Among the many possible causes of the collapse of civic engagement in the USA, television is often said to be important because it pulls people out of their community and its voluntary associations, and isolates them in their homes. television is said to be responsible for many of the signs of civic and political malaise – distrust, fear, cynicism, alienation, apathy, low political interest and understanding.

Social capital theory has aroused a great deal of interest and controversy. Its critics claim that:

- The definition and treatment of the concept of social capital is vague and all-inclusive.
- Some survey evidence shows that voluntary organisations have rather little effect on political attitudes and behaviour. In any case, which is cause and which is effect? Do the trusting join voluntary associations or do associations generate trust in their members?

- Some research suggests that television is not particularly responsible for eroding social capital – on the contrary, television news and current affairs programmes can inform and mobilise people (see the next chapter).
- Some social capital theory assumes a 'bottom-up' process in which individuals who join organisations are trusting and strengthen social capital. Others emphasise the 'top-down' importance of the collective culture as an influence on the attitudes and behaviour of individuals whether or not they are members of voluntary associations. A 'top-down' approach also points out that governments help to create the conditions in which both voluntary organisations and a climate of trust can flourish. Institutions also matter, in that a fair and just legal system, corruption-free police and courts, an impartial state bureaucracy and the rule of law are a foundation of social capital.
- Social capital theory attracted much attention in the late 1980s and early 1990s, which was a period in which the expansion of government activities appeared to be increasingly problematic. Critics claimed that social capital was used by politicians to mask 'state failures' by blaming problems on politically inactive and disengaged citizens. These critics claimed that when trust in politicians and political institutions is falling, politicians should look at their own behaviour and policies and not try to deflect blame on to citizens, voluntary associations and the mass media.

Writing on **civil society** has much in common with pluralist and social capital theory. It has flourished in the new democracies of central and eastern Europe where the importance of free and independent citizen associations not controlled by the governing regime is emphasised as a basis of democracy. Historians have also studied the role of middle class and professional groups (the burghers) in creating a civil society of groups that have an independent influence on government and had a vital role in converting autocracy to democracy. Civil society theory argues that:

> **Civil society:** That arena of social life outside the state, the commercial sector and the family (i.e. mainly voluntary organisations and civic associations) that permits individuals to associate and act freely and independently of state control.

- Strong and vibrant private organisations are essential both for a satisfying social life and as a counter-balance to the power of the state.
- Transition to democracy depends on building autonomous, private organisations and creating a culture and tradition to sustain them, especially in societies where such organisations have been controlled or suppressed by the state.
- So far, civil society in central and eastern Europe has tended to develop in a different way from Western pluralism, in that organisations in some countries have formed most readily around nationalist, ethnic and religious interests that have become a force for division and conflict, rather than compromise and integration.

■ What have we learned?

This chapter deals with the key modern pressure groups and social movements. It argues that:

- A dense network of voluntary organisations is the social basis of pluralist democracy. Politically active groups mediate between citizens and government by aggregating and articulating political interests. Politically inactive groups help to integrate and stabilise society, permitting democratic government to operate effectively.
- Western democracies are marked by a high density of overlapping and inter-locking voluntary organisations that are built around virtually every conceivable human interest and activity.
- Some associations are created to engage permanently in political activity, some are created around a particular issue and dissolve when that is settled one way or another, and some are rarely active politically.
- Pressure groups are similar to political parties and new social movements, but not identical.
- Pressure groups and governments are mutually dependent on one another. Groups need government support to attain their goals and governments need groups for support and help in implementing their policies.
- Although a vibrant group life is essential for democracy, groups that are too strong are a threat to it. They can 'capture' policy areas and make public decisions that favour their private interests. Strong group pressures from every side may also cause hyper-pluralism and overloaded government.

■ Lessons of comparison

- The ways in which pressure groups work and the influence they exercise are determined by the nature of the groups (their own resources, the issues they pursue, their public support and insider/outsider status) and the government environment in which they operate (the locus of power in presidential and parliamentary, federal and unitary, and centralised and decentralised government).
- It is difficult to establish the power and effectiveness of groups because there are usually many factors at work at the same time.
- In most countries, groups have a close relationship with government, ranging from highly formalised and institutionalised corporatist arrangements, to para-government systems, the 'iron triangles' and tight policy communities of tripartite politics and to the more open ad hoc policy networks of the most pluralist systems.
- There are arguments both for and against pluralist, Marxist/elitist, social capital and civil society theories of pressure group politics, but all agree that organisations and associations that aggregate and articulate interests are vitally important for democracy but can, under certain circumstances, threaten it as well.

Projects

1. Each student in the group should take a daily paper of their own country and read it for a few days, picking out news items mentioning voluntary organisations and pressure groups. Classify the groups according to whether they seem to be interest/cause, insider/outsider, peak organisations, episodic/fire brigade, aligned/non-aligned. What, if anything, does this tell you about the likely power of the groups?
2. Voluntary organisations and pressure groups often have good websites. Search the websites in your country for examples of, say, a dozen groups (or for some of the groups mentioned in this chapter), and see what you can find out about the political activity or inactivity of the groups, how they operate and with what success.
3. Do you think pressure groups are good for democracy or help to undermine it?

Further reading

R. Chari, H. John and G. Murphy, *Regulating Lobbying: A Global Comparison*. Manchester University Press, 2012. A comparison of regulatory laws in the USA, Canada, Germany, Poland, Lithuania, Hungary, the EU, Taiwan and Australia.

M. Diani, *The Cement of Civil Society: Studying Networks in Localities*. Cambridge University Press, 2015. Analyses voluntary associations, civil society, conventional and protest groups, insider and outsider groups and how they interlink and relate.

M. Edwards (ed.), *The Oxford Handbook of Civil Society*, Oxford University Press, 2011, and M. Edwards, *Civil Society*, 3rd edn. Cambridge: Polity Press, 2014. Both volumes present a number of up-to-date and comprehensive essays on civil society.

J. Goodwin and J. M. Jasper (eds.), *The Social Movements Reader: Cases and Concepts*, 2nd edn. London: John Wiley & Sons, 2014. A set of articles providing a basic introduction to classic texts and accounts of the recent Arab Spring, Occupy and Global Justice.

H. Lelieveldt and S. Princen, *The Politics of the European Union*, 2nd edn. Cambridge University Press, 2015, ch. 6. An up-to-date, succinct and comprehensive account of the pressure groups in the EU.

L. Zetter, *Lobbying: The Art of Political Persuasion*. Petersfield: Harriman House Limited, 2012. Examines and explains interest group politics in the USA, Japan, the UK, Brussels, Asia and the Middle east.

Websites

www.britannica.com/EBchecked/topic/290136/interest-group/257774/
   The-regulation-of-interest-groups.

A long and comprehensive review of interest groups (what are termed
   pressure groups in this chapter) containing a section on pluralism and
   neo-corporatism.

www.newworldencyclopedia.org/entry/Social_movement.

A brief but useful introduction to social movements around the world.

http://en.citizendium.org.

A website with introductory articles on civil society and social capital.

www.politicalresources.net/.

Lists organisations in many countries, and has a long list of international
   organisations.

www.uia.org/ybio?name=.

An open yearbook with detailed information about 68,000 international
   organisations, covering 300 countries and territories and including inter-
   governmental organisations (IGOs) and international non-governmental
   organisations (INGOs).

11　The mass media

In theory, the news media should be the watchdogs of democracy, but, in practice, some believe they are as much a threat to democratic government as a protector of it. The media are not just channels of communication that simply convey news but major political players in their own right with power and, in some cases, political agendas of their own. This raises all sorts of problems and questions. What is their proper role in a democracy and do they perform it properly? How should they be organised? They should certainly not come under the control of government, because that would turn them into a propaganda machine, but should they be left to the economic forces of the commercial market? How much influence do they wield over public opinion and behaviour and over elected politicians and governments? Are they biased in their treatment of the news? What impact has the new digital technology had on political communications?

The major topics in this chapter are:

- The mass media and democracy
- Regulating the media
- Ownership and control
- The new digital technology
- Theories of the mass media.

■ The media in theory and practice

We rely on the news media for a lot of our knowledge of the political world, and if we are to be informed citizens capable of making our own political decisions, we need to be supplied with news that is comprehensive, accurate and impartial. How is this best done? Classical pluralist theory argues that it demands a free press that is independent of state agencies and governments and not dominated by any single political and economic interest. Instead, the news media should be in the hands of a multiplicity of sources of news and opinion that cover politics from a wide variety of political positions. In this way, all main political interests will have a voice and in the resulting competition of ideas and opinions, citizens will be able to make up their own minds.

In practice, however, there are many obstacles to the creation of a pluralist system in the modern world.

- Economic forces have created a few huge multinational, multimedia corporations that have drastically reduced pluralism.
- It is not just the news media that matter, because the vastly larger entertainment and advertising industries may also exercise a strong influence on political life.
- The evidence suggests that many are easily bored by the news media and its political discussion. They prefer films, game shows, soap operas, celebrity gossip and sport. The result is that news budgets have been cut, and news programmes shortened and broadcast at off-peak hours, when they attract smaller audiences.

None of this is made any easier by the fact that the news media face contradictory demands that make it difficult for them to do their job:

- There is so much news flowing in from around the world that journalists have to make hard choices about what to report and what to ignore.
- It is extremely difficult to maintain high standards of journalism given increasingly tight news deadlines. Besides, a great deal of politics is conducted in confidence or in secret, so it can be difficult for investigative journalists to find out what has actually happened.
- News should be detached and objective, but political opinion is engaged and subjective. How can the political media be both? The usual answer is that they should separate facts (the news) from opinion (editorial, analysis and opinion pieces), but this can be extremely difficult, if not impossible, since values permeate political news and the language we use to discuss politics.

Spin-doctors: Public relations specialists employed to put the best possible light on news about their clients. The term implies that they are people whose job is to manipulate the news.

- It is quicker, easier and cheaper for journalists to rely on the nicely packaged press releases provided by **spin-doctors** than to probe behind for other information and opinion.
- The mass media should be critical of politicians when they feel it necessary, but they are often criticised by politicians for not being 'fair and impartial'.

The problem is that journalists may feel that being 'fair and impartial' means getting to the truth of the matter, while politicians feel that it means reporting accurately and fully what they say.

In sum, the mass media are very important in democratic politics, but their role is riddled with dilemmas and problems. This raises the crucial question of how they are best organised in the modern world so that they deliver comprehensive, accurate and unbiased news. Should they be controlled or regulated in the public interest, or should the invisible hand of the market determine how they are run and perform?

■ Regulating the media

The public service model

There are two main answers to the question of how best to organise the mass media – the **public service model** for electronic communications, and the commercial model that favours a competitive economic market for all forms of communication. Their merits are hotly debated (see controversy 11.1).

> **Public service model:** A system of granting broadcasting licences to public bodies, usually supported partially or wholly by public funds, for use in the public interest rather than for profit.

The media differ between the print and electronic forms. The print media consists mainly of newspapers, books, journals and magazines, while the electronic media are mainly radio, television, email, text message (social media such as Facebook and Twitter) and the web (such as news websites and blogs). In principle, anyone can publish a paper, magazine or newsletter (many organisations do), and desk-top publishing has made this easier. Electronic communication is different. Until recently, radio and television broadcasting was limited by the technical limitation of **spectrum scarcity** which meant that there were very few wavelengths for competing television channels and radio stations. In the

> **Spectrum scarcity:** The shortage of terrestrial broadcasting frequencies for radio and television, which meant that there could be only one or a few channels.

1950s few countries had more than two television channels, if that, which meant that broadcasting, unlike the print media, did not form a competitive, pluralist market. Since broadcasting wavelengths were regarded as a public asset of great importance it was agreed that they should be used and regulated in the public interest. Consequently, most democracies controlled and regulated broadcasting according to the public service model. This has six main characteristics:

1. *Market regulation* Spectrum scarcity makes a competitive market in electronic broadcasting impossible, so the state regulates radio and television markets, usually by giving broadcasting licences to a few organisations that are required to operate under public interest rules.

> **Market regulation:** The regulation of the media market by public bodies.

Public service versus commercial media?

■ For the public service model

- The market does not ensure that truth or the best ideas will prevail, only that consumer demand is satisfied.
- News and political opinion is not a commodity, like soap powder, or something that can be road-tested, like motor cars. It is not subject to the same laws of supply and demand as consumer durables or commercial services.
- Regulation in the public interest is the best way to ensure comprehensive, accurate, and impartial news reporting. To leave the news media to the market is to hand it over to a few multi-millionaire media moguls and multinational corporations (MNCs) whose economic interests result in systematic news bias.
- The twin dangers of the news media being in the control of the state or of big business can be avoided by using agencies that are independent of state and business. Known as QUANGOs (see below), these are used all over the world to run important public services.
- Bad media drive out the good, or force the good to adopt low standards in order to compete in the market. Public service news reporting is more professional and reliable in public service countries (Germany, Scandinavia). The news is often more politically biased and of a lower standard in commercial systems.
- The state must step in to exercise market and content regulation where market failure or spectrum scarcity results in oligopoly or monopoly. Some countries have prevented foreign business from buying their main news agencies.
- The commercial media are not necessarily politically free. They can be subject to powerful commercial and political pressures.

■ For the market model

- Regulation of the political media is not consistent with free speech.
- The public service model stifles innovation and is patronising – it gives the public what broadcasters think it should have rather than what it wants.
- Whatever their faults, market forces are better than government or public service regulation of the media.
- The end of spectrum scarcity means that the electronic media are the same as the print media, and should be subject to the same regulatory principles – minimal or no content regulation (other than the normal laws of the land) and market regulation only to avoid market failure.
- In a globalised world it is difficult or impossible to regulate satellite broadcasting and the web.
- Media QUANGOs are susceptible to 'backdoor influence' of governments which they enforce by controlling budgets.
- Commercialisation of the media saves public money.
- Low standards of journalism and political bias are the price to be paid for the absence of government control and regulation.

2. *Content regulation* In the absence of a market for broadcast news broadcasters were also subject to **content regulation**, requiring them to produce high-quality news that was balanced and impartial.

> **Content regulation:** Regulation of the content of the media, especially news programmes, in the public interest.

3. *Self-regulation, or regulation by QUANGOs* If public broadcasting agencies were to avoid the danger of state regulation of the news, they should be self-regulating and under the control of public bodies that are independent of government. Such bodies, known as 'QUANGOs', operate at arm's length from government. Quangos are used all over the world to run public services that should not be directly under the control of the government – universities, the agencies to decide election rules and draw election boundaries, regulating and watchdog agencies.

> **QUANGOs:** Organisations that are partially or wholly funded by the government to perform public service functions but not under government control. QUANGO is an acronym for 'quasi-autonomous non-governmental organisation' – neither state nor market, but a third type of organisation.

4. *Public funding* Public service broadcasting is funded, partially or wholly, by public funds and not dependent upon profit.

5. *To educate, inform and entertain* Public service broadcasting involves a wide range of programmes, including news and current affairs and educational and cultural programmes, as well as entertainment. It serves the public interest, rather than responding to market forces.

6. *National broadcasting* Public broadcasting should serve the nation, including its minorities (linguistic, religious, cultural and regional), and act as a focus for national identity.

Broadly speaking, the public service model of radio and television operated in many Western democracies from the start of radio broadcasting in the 1920s up to the 1970s, when technology started to erode spectrum scarcity. In the twenty-first century, the public service model is strongest in Austria, Denmark, Finland, Norway, Sweden, Switzerland and Germany.

The market model

Since the print media are not subject to spectrum scarcity and since, in principle, anyone can enter the market, newspaper content in democracies has not been subject to regulation. The principle of freedom of speech means that they can print whatever they wish within the general laws of the land. They are subject to market regulation only when there is danger of oligopoly or monopoly, although newspapers are subsidised or protected by the state in some countries (see briefing 11.1).

In the 1960s, the distinction between the print and electronic media started to break down. First, there was an increase in the number of available wavelengths for terrestrial television and radio broadcasting, at which point commercial licences were granted. Then digital technology ended

Briefing 11.1

Mass media systems: Finland, Norway and Japan

■ Finland – a pluralist system

Finland has a tradition of an independent and pluralist press dating back to the late eighteenth century, and for a country of 5.2 million it has an amazingly large and diverse media system – two hundred newspapers (30 dailies), a mixed set of public and private television channels (12) and national and local radio stations (76), 12,000 book titles a year, and high use of the Internet. Finland has one of the highest newspaper circulations in the world. More than 80 per cent of Finns read a newspaper every day, and 60 per cent say that they are their main source of news. The state helps with tax concessions for publishers and subsidies for party newspapers and other quality magazines. There is increasing concentration of ownership and control of the media, especially of newspapers. Two large newspaper chains had emerged by 2000. As more media outlets are created, so the audience for each one has declined and the total media market has become more fragmented. There is a variety of news agencies, public, private and party affiliated. Audiences for public television are large by international standards, but all television and radio stations devote a good deal of their time to news and current affairs. Citizens who feel injured by press reports can appeal to the Council for the Mass Media, which has the power to fine and order a rejoinder. International comparison suggests that Finland's media are of a high quality and reflect the main current of Finland's political life. The tone is perhaps best described as consensus seeking and civilised rather than aggressive and muck-raking.

■ Newspaper subsidies in Norway

Daily newspapers are considered an essential commodity in Norway, in their contribution not only to the workings of democracy, but also to cultural life. In relation to its population, Norway has a large number of papers with high circulations sustained by public financial support in the form of subsidies, government advertising, direct grants, loan arrangements and cheap distribution. In addition, the Norwegian daily press is exempt from value added tax VAT. It has been calculated that subsidies to the press as a whole account for about 20 per cent of all newspaper income.

Source: www.reisenett.no/norway/facts/culture_science/culture_under_int_pressure.html

■ Japan – pluralism with self-censorship

Japan has one of the very highest newspaper readerships in the world and a rapidly diversifying media system, including six major national papers, over one hundred local papers, and many public and private television channels and radio stations. Television and radio coverage of news is comprehensive, and the public stations are balanced and factual, avoiding editorialising and commentary. The private print media can be critical of the government and it reports corruption among politicians, bureaucrats and businessmen, but at the same time the free reporting of news is restricted by the tight organisation of 'kisha clubs', which are private (and often, it seems, secret) clubs in government, business and politics. They exercise strong informal pressures on their members that amount to systematic self-censorship. Investigative reporting is comparatively rare and mostly done by journalists outside the main media corporations and kisha clubs.

Sources: compiled from a variety of sources including Reporters Without Frontiers (www.rsf.org/), the Federal Research Division of the Library of Congress (http://countrystudies.us/), BBC Country profiles (http://news.bbc.co.uk /2/hi/country_profiles/default.stm), Pressreferences.com (www .pressreference.com/) and individual country reports.

spectrum scarcity, so that some countries decided to commercialise their public services. There are now great numbers of public and commercial radio stations and satellite and cable television channels. Moreover, desk-top publishing has made print media easier and cheaper to produce. And if one adds the vast amount of global political news and opinion available on the Internet, the communications system of modern democracies is more pluralist than ever before. Since the market for electronic news is the same, in principle, as the newspaper market, there is no longer need for market and content regulation, at least on the basis of spectrum scarcity. Besides, it is difficult, though not impossible, for states to regulate the flow of some global news.

This transformation of the communications system has resulted in rapid proliferation and globalisation of news sources, to the point where there is, some argue, less need for public service broadcasting, or no need at all. As a consequence, most countries have changed their broadcasting system to create either a wholly commercial one, or a mixed model that combines both commercial and public service elements (see briefing 11.2). The market model is strongest in Belgium, the Czech Republic, Greece, Japan, the Netherlands, Portugal, Turkey, Greece, Italy and the USA. Some new democracies have reacted against the state-controlled system of their anti-democratic past and commercialised completely, but many of the old democracies have retained a large public service element.

Even in the most commercial systems, however, there is still a fair amount of public regulation, which takes two main forms:

1. *Regulation to ensure market competition* **Cross-media ownership** and **multimedia conglomeration** are often restricted, parts of the mass communications system thought to be essential to national interest are kept in national hands and attempts are made to prevent

Cross-media ownership: When the same person or company has financial interests in different branches of mass communication – for example when they own a newspaper and a television channel, or a publishing house and a television network.

Multimedia conglomerates: Single business organisations with financial interests in different branches of mass communications – for example when they own or control a newspaper and a television channel, or a publishing house and a television network.

Briefing 11.2

The new media in the UK

The number of television channels, radio stations, newspapers and other printed media in any given country has mushroomed so fast in recent times that it is difficult to keep up with the growth. In addition, it is now possible to use the Internet to access television channels, radio stations and printed matter from almost every corner of the globe. Consequently, sources of news and political opinion of almost every conceivable kind are now so large that they are impossible to count. The following figures, therefore, are approximate. The figures refer to the UK because this is a well-documented case, but the same pattern could be observed for most Western countries.

In 2015 in Britain, it was possible to access more than 600 television channels on television sets,[1] including around 100 or so foreign channels.[2] Over forty domestic channels cater specifically for minority groups and there are special channels for local government, the health services and the armed forces. Many television channels carry little, if any political news, but those dedicated to news and discussion include BBC News, Sky News, Star News, and BBC Parliament, and those from abroad include Al Jazeera, Bloomberg, CCTV (Chinese), CNBC Europe, eNCA Africa, EuroNews, Fox News, France24, RT (Moscow), NDTV (Delhi), NHK (Japan), and CNN.

The UK has about 800 home-grown radio stations, of which more than 40 are national and semi-national, 350 local and the rest mostly regional and community.[3] There are about fifteen radio stations for minority ethnic groups, although there is a constant turnover, and many more for students and hospitals. Like television channels, most radio stations carry little if any political news, but those with in-depth news coverage and discussion include Radio 4, Radio 5 Live, the Asian Network and Bloomberg Live Radio. The BBC World Service broadcasts news and analysis in twenty-seven languages, and there are a dozen or so other news and talk stations.

In addition to eleven national daily papers, there are some 1,500 regional and local papers, including more than 100 for special language, ethnic, national and religious groups. About 2,000 magazines and reviews are published in the UK, most without any political content, but a growing number is produced by political groups of many kinds. Desk-top publishing has made it easier than ever before to produce political newsletters, pamphlets and broadsheets.

The web carries a vast amount of political news and opinion. Some of this is produced by the old media (the television channels, radio stations and newspapers that existed before the electronic media) and some by 'digital natives' whose numbers have multiplied many times over to take advantage of the new technology. There are now hundreds of thousands, perhaps millions, of digital natives on the net covering news and opinion from every corner of the globe, in almost every language and from almost every political perspective under the sun.

Sources: [1] http://media.info/uk/television/channels. This number includes time-shift channels with the same content.
[2] www.international-satellite.com/channels/foreignchannels.aspx
[3] www.mediauk.com/

monopolies and oligopolies. The rules have been progressively relaxed because of economic forces.

2. *Content regulation* Some commercial broadcasters are required to follow strict rules about balanced and impartial news reporting, and there is still content regulation of things such as cigarette advertising, pornography and the amount, content and distribution of advertising throughout the day.

However, in spite of these two forms of regulation, the commercialisation of the media across most of the Western world has strengthened a trend that started in the early twentieth century and is the cause of much concern among many media experts. This is the increasing concentration of ownership and control of the media in a small number of huge multinational, multimedia corporations.

■ Ownership and control

Since the 1950s, the mass media market has developed in five related ways, with far-reaching implications for the workings of democratic government:

1. *Concentration of ownership and control of the mass market* The development of a global market has vastly increased the capital costs of production and distribution and, in turn, encourages mergers and take-overs that have increased the concentration of ownership and control of the media industry. Pluralist and competitive markets are increasingly replaced by a small number of giant media empires.
2. *Multimedia conglomeration* Many media companies have collected media concerns that span the range of publishing, music, films, radio, television and the net. This result is cross-media ownership or multimedia conglomeration.
3. *Horizontal and vertical integration* Conglomeration entails the vertical integration of the communications industry, in which the same company controls all aspects of the financing, production, distribution and marketing of its products. It also means horizontal integration of television, radio, film, music, DVD, radio, newspaper, the web and magazine businesses, which feed off and support each other economically. Some media conglomerates have also expanded into related businesses such as theme parks, entertainment, hotels, leisure centres, sports clubs and chains of shops.
4. *The integration of the media with other business activities* There is nothing new about a few media moguls dominating press or television, but in the past they have usually confined their interests to the communications business. In contrast, multimedia conglomerates are now increasingly incorporated into a wide range of industrial and commercial activities, making it difficult to distinguish between the media market and big business in general. For example, General Electric is involved in television (twenty-eight television stations and networks in the USA, Europe and Latin America), film

companies; leisure, entertainment and sports; film rights, production and distribution; military hardware; commercial finance companies; energy and water; health care; and aviation.

5. *Internationalisation* Media conglomerates are no longer limited to countries or continents. In a borderless world they span the whole globe.

Among the largest of giant media corporations are General Electric, AT&T, Sony, Liberty Media, Vivendi, Viacom, Time Warner, Walt Disney Corporation, and 21st Century Fox. Many are American.

■ Cultural imperialism and soft power

The market model assumes pluralist competition and diversity, but this is in decline as far as the mass media are concerned. There has emerged, over the past fifty or so years, a handful of huge multinational, multimedia conglomerates that control large portions of the media market. These business corporations, it is argued, can use their control over large portions of the mass entertainment and political media to promote their own political and economic interests. Consequently, they have 'power without responsibility', and, in any case, as international organisations they are beyond the regulation of democratic states.

> **Cultural imperialism:** The use of cultural products, particularly films, books, music and television, to spread the values and ideologies of western culture. One version labels this the 'McWorld' theory, after the fast food chain and other American products that are claimed to undermine the cultures of developing areas.

> **Soft power:** In contrast to 'hard power', based on military and economic force, soft power uses popular culture and the media to influence the way that people think and feel and behave.

One result of the growth of multinational media conglomerates is what is termed '**cultural imperialism**'. In the nineteenth century, imperial nations enforced their rule with gunboats. Now, it was said, the Western world, especially the USA, uses the '**soft power**' of its films, television and fashions in clothes, music and sport to extend its economic and political influence. The global spread of CNN news, Hollywood films and Western advertising would, it was claimed, be a powerful force that replaced indigenous cultures with American values.

There are reasons for believing that cultural imperialism and soft power may not be so powerful. In the first place, it may underestimate the strength of cultures in developing countries. Popular opposition to Western power and culture in some parts of the Third World suggests that drinking Coke and wearing baseball caps and jeans does not mean that people think and feel like Americans. Popular opposition to Western power and culture in many parts of the developing world suggests that they do not. Besides, the prediction that the world would become a global village tuned into the same soap operas and news channels has not been confirmed by events. Since the 1980s, the trend has been to broadcast television news in local languages and to mould it around the values and interests of local populations. National television has also resisted globalisation. There are some international blockbusters, but most television audiences still watch their own national programmes, especially national news, and most national television stations still schedule more domestic programmes than imported ones. Some ideas and themes for television programmes are contagious and spread quickly across countries, but as often as not, they are remade to suit local tastes and interests. Bollywood has a huge film industry, different and separate from Hollywood, and *Avenida Brasil*, a home-grown soap opera in Brazil, has a national audience of around 40 million. The global reach of communications technology does not yet have an equally large global grasp.

It is also wrong to assume that commercial news sources will automatically display a pro-business bias. Most Western countries have at least one commercial newspaper of record which is widely recognised to be an impartial and trustworthy source of news. These include, among others, *Le Monde* (France), *El País* (Spain), *Frankfurter Allgemeine Zeitung* (Germany), *De Standaard* (Belgium), *The Globe and Mail* (Canada), and *The Times of India*. Content analysis of the main terrestrial television channels and a sample of local papers in the USA finds that they provide reliable and impartial news about presidential election campaigns. It seems, therefore, that commercial media markets are not all the same. Local papers in the USA may have to be politically impartial in order to attract a large enough readership to keep them in business.

■ The new pluralism

Perhaps the most important development in modern communications, and the trend that has done most to undermine the power of media corporations, is the wildfire spread of digital technology that has transformed the news and entertainment systems of the Western world beyond all recognition in only two decades. A generation ago, each country had a small handful of television channels, a few more radio stations and an assortment of newspapers and political magazines and journals. Now, anyone with a television set and connection to the Internet can access a dozen or more cable news channels, hundreds of television channels, thousands of radio stations, and hundreds of thousands of political websites (see briefing 11.2). Like the old pre-digital communications systems, most of the new media are devoted to non-political matters, but the absolute number of sites dedicated to news and political commentary is large and growing exponentially. The American portal, BlogCatalog, lists thousands of political blogs in the USA, and most other Western countries have them in their hundreds or thousands as well.

The digital revolution has had four main consequences for news reporting. First, it has produced a virtually instantaneous flow of news around the world. Whereas it used to take days to get news about important foreign events, it can now be instantaneous. Second, a wide diversity of news and opinion can be accessed more cheaply and more easily than ever before on radios, television sets, computers, tablets and smartphones. Third, the pluralist diversity of political communications is now vastly larger than anything that could be imagined only twenty years ago and probably larger than at any previous time in human history – in spite of the growth of huge multinational, multimedia corporations.

Fourth, and perhaps most important, whereas most people used the old media to *receive* information, the new media allows them to *receive, produce* and *exchange* information. Many groups and citizens have their own websites and blogs providing the world with opinions, facts, photos, and videos about anything that interests them. The social websites carry a huge amount of information traffic and while much of it is of little or no political relevance, they have added to the absolute volume of political information and opinion that is being produced and exchanged. The production of news is no longer limited to the mass media – everybody is able to produce their own.

This seems to have revolutionised and democratised the way mass media function in our society. It seems that while the mass market for news and opinion is becoming less and less pluralist, the specialist market is rapidly becoming more so, driven by the technological revolution in digital communication.

■ Theories of the mass media

The nature and the pace of technological change is clear for all to see, but its impact on daily political life is highly controversial and not at all obvious. In fact, the effects of both the new and the old media have always been unclear and difficult in the extreme to pin down. Media research of this kind has always been faced with severe problems.

1. The mass media are only one of the many influences on our lives, which include the family, education, work, income, gender and age. Media effects are closely tangled up with these other influences, so it is exceedingly difficult to sort out their independent influence. For example, the wealthier and better educated sections of the population are generally more trusting politically and tend to pay more attention to trusted sources of news. Are they more trusting because of their income and education, or because they are regular consumers of reliable news?

2. It is impossible to generalise broadly about the impact of 'the media' because there are many different media and they probably have different effects on different kinds of people. Watching television news might have one effect, violent movies another, and comedy and soap operas a third. To complicate matters, different kinds of people watch different kinds of television.

3. It is exceedingly difficult to isolate causes and effects in media research. The media target particular audiences and tune their messages to appeal to them. Equally, audiences select the media they attend to. For example, there is often a close correspondence between the politics of individuals and

the papers they read. Do we conclude from this that the paper influences or determines political opinions, or that individuals self-select a paper that is in tune with their own politics? What is cause and what is effect?

It is no surprise, therefore, that media effects are a matter of great controversy in political science. There are three main schools of thought.

1. Mediamalaise

Mediamalaise theory argues that the media, especially television, exercise a strong influence that often tends to undermine democracy, and does so by a combination of news, entertainment and advertising. The news, it is said, is often sensational and superficial and concentrates on the worst in the world – disasters, conflict, scandal, terrorism, crime, corruption and failure. Journalists are often critical of politicians (attack journalism), which undermines trust in leaders, perhaps even trust in democracy itself. The entertainment media add to this effect with heavy doses of crime, disaster, horror and violence in its films and television drama. The advertising industry is claimed to create a culture of 'me-first' individualism and

> **Mediamalaise:** The attitudes of political cynicism, despair, apathy, distrust and disillusionment (among others) that some social scientists claim as caused by the mass media, especially television.

materialism that is not conducive to citizen responsibility and civic engagement. In short, the modern media are said to create a 'mean world effect' that gives politics a bad name and creates a mood of political cynicism, distrust and apathy.

Moreover, the media are said to exercise a strong influence on political life by virtue of their power to set agendas and to prime and frame the news in a way that influences how audiences receive it. **Agenda setting** theory argues that the media cannot determine what we think but can and do strongly influence what we think about, because

> **Agenda setting:** The process by which political issues are continuously sorted according to the changing priority attached to them.

they cover some issues intensively over a long period of time. Persistent media coverage of crime, for example, is said to make people more afraid of it than the figures justify.

Priming and **framing theories** argue that the media have a subtle and indirect influence over public opinion by virtue of the way in which they present news stories. If party A is thought to be better on domestic affairs and party B better on foreign affairs, then an emphasis on domestic affairs will prime people to think about the issue that favours party A. Framing sets a news item within a context that affects

> **Priming:** The idea that the news media can lead us to focus on certain things in certain ways by highlighting a matter that is linked to another.

> **Framing:** The theory that the way news stories are set up (framed) influences how audiences interpret them.

how it is perceived. For example, a television documentary about homelessness might present it as a policy issue that is linked with unemployment and housing policy, or it might be presented in human interest terms and linked to individual problems with alcohol, the family or laziness. The first presents homelessness as a public issue for government attention, the second as a problem of personal histories and personality defects.

2. Reinforcement

Contrary to mediamalaise theory, **reinforcement theory** argues that the mass media have minimal effects, because of the supply and demand characteristics of the media market. On the demand side, individuals tend to self-select media messages that fit their opinions and interests, while neglecting, forgetting, distorting or suppressing other messages. One obvious example is that individuals with strong political opinions tend to select a newspaper or a television news channel with the same views. Another example is that many voters have clear opinions about the party they support and have decided which way they are going to vote before the election campaign. The voting patterns of these 'core voters' are not much affected by the election campaign or the news coverage of it.

Reinforcement theory: The theory that the mass media can only reflect and reinforce pubic opinions, not create or mould it.

On the supply side of the media equation, the commercial media have powerful economic reasons for supplying their audiences with what they want to read, see and hear. Audience and circulation figures are crucial, because they determine profits and advertising revenues, and so the media tailor their content around the opinions and interests of the audiences they most want to attract. The commercial media, in other words, are no different in principle from supermarkets that sell goods that shoppers want and are willing to pay for. Media consumers choose, and media producers respond by following, not leading.

3. The weak force and virtuous circle

A third theory is beginning to emerge from empirical research that usually, not always, finds the media to be a weak force. Extensive experimental work in psychology laboratories shows that the attitudes and opinions of individuals can be exceedingly hard to change and that misunderstandings and misperceptions of facts can be exceedingly hard to correct. People with opinions, especially strong ones, tend to stick to them by using a wide range of psychological mechanisms and short cuts, known variously as **cognitive bias**, or **heuristics** to preserve their beliefs. And they can do this successfully, even in the face of overwhelming evidence to the contrary. Survey research in the USA finds that around a third of adult Americans reject evolutionary theory – the creationists – and about the same number believe that weapons of mass destruction were found in Iraq after the invasion of the country. The power of the

Cognitive bias: A way of thinking about a topic that leads to systematic misunderstanding and misperception of it. Sometimes this kind of bias can be used to protect beliefs that run contrary to logic, evidence and argument.

Heuristics: Mental shortcuts and rules of thumb that enable individuals to make quick judgements about matters, often when there is a lack of time, information and interest that is necessary to reach a considered opinion about a complex matter.

media is limited when it comes to public opinion that is deeply rooted and based on personal values of a social or political kind. These are common in politics when they touch on issues such as peace and war, nuclear energy, the death penalty, abortion, nationalism, party politics and voting, the free market versus socialism, and the 'bread and butter' issues of education, health, housing, employment and taxation.

The weakness of the media is often reinforced by the **hostile media effect**, which often leads individuals to reject media reports because they are biased against their own political position. Left-wingers are inclined to believe that the media in general have a right-wing bias, but right-wingers believe it is biased in favour of the left, and both are convinced of this even when the media in question can be shown by content analysis to be balanced and impartial. Distrusting a medium because it is believed to be hostile will usually lead to rejecting its message.

> **Hostile media effect:** The belief of people with views on a matter that media reports on it are biased against their own position, irrespective of how objective and balanced those reports may be.

At the same time, research shows that attention to the news media usually has a positive impact on democratic attitudes and behaviour, although a comparatively modest one. Holding constant the obvious variables (education, income, age, sex, religion and ethnicity), those who regularly attend to the news are usually well informed and more understanding of politics, and display stronger patterns of democratic attitudes and behaviour. There is, it seems, a **virtuous circle** whereby those who regularly follow the news know more about politics, are more trusting, more likely to vote and more supportive of democratic leaders and institutions. Public service news programmes have been found to have stronger effects of this kind than commercial news.

> **Virtuous circle:** A tendency for those who are politically engaged and trusting to follow the news regularly, which then feeds back to increase their levels of trust and engagement.

■ What have we learned?

- Pluralist theory argues that democracy requires a news media system that delivers a comprehensive, accurate and impartial account of the news that presents a full range of political opinion. Therefore the system should be free from government control and not dominated by any particular set of political and economic interests.
- The print media are presumed to form a pluralist commercial market with freedom of speech and minimal government regulation being its organising principles. In the days of spectrum scarcity, the broadcasting airwaves meant that radio and television broadcasting were natural monopolies. As public assets they were run as public services with both market regulation and regulation of news content.
- When electronic and digital technology ended spectrum scarcity the electronic media were deregulated and commercialised in most countries.

Some opted for wholly commercial systems, others for a mixture of public and private broadcasting.

- Economic forces have resulted in increasing concentration of the mass media in a few multimedia, multinational conglomerate corporations, mainly American. The result is concern about a loss of democratic pluralism.
- However, technological developments have resulted in cable and satellite television, local and community radio, desktop publishing and the computer and the Internet, and a larger number and variety of specialist news sources than ever before. New technology also makes it possible for individuals not only to receive information and opinions, but also to produce and exchange it.
- The mediamalaise school of thought claims that the media are such a powerful influence on government and politics that they undermine democratic attitudes and behaviour. Another theory claims that the main effect of the media is to reinforce existing attitudes. A third points out that the media are usually, not always, a weak force because individuals use cognitive bias and heuristics to defend their own attitudes and values.
- Controversy about media effects results from great difficulties in pinning down the impact of the media, because the media and their audiences are mutually intertwined in a tangle of cause and effect relationships.

■ Lessons of comparison

- Ownership and control of the media have become increasingly concentrated in the hands of a few giant, multimedia, multinational companies with markets in every corner of the globe.
- The new media technology has had a huge impact in some respects (the spread of global news, increasing pluralism of digital news outlets, ease of access to news), but less effect in others (the resilience of local news, languages and cultures, the slow progress of E-politics in some countries).
- There is no necessary connection between democracy and either a free market or a public service media system. Some advanced democracies have a wholly commercial system, some a mixed public/private system.
- Nor can it be assumed that commercial news media will automatically be biased in favour of business interests. In some countries they are, but others have commercial newspaper and television stations that deliver balanced and impartial news.
- Comparing countries suggests that the extent to which the media generate mediamalaise, if at all, depends on the kind of media system it has. Attention to the news media, especially public service news, is associated with better-informed and less alienated citizens.

Projects

1. Think of five reasons why the mass media may have rather little impact on politics, and then think of five reasons why they may have a big impact.

2. Classical pluralist theory argues that sources of political news and opinion should be independent of the government, should not be controlled by any one set of political and economic interests and should cover the news from a broad variety of political positions. Would you say that the news system of your country is more or less pluralist according to these criteria?

   Or

   Using whatever websites you can find, replicate briefing 11.2, so far as possible, for the news sources in your country. What conclusions would you draw from the material you collect about media pluralism, or lack of it, and about political bias, or lack of it, in your country?

3. Examine the following figures and discuss what conclusions they suggest about the impact of newspaper reading on voting.

	% reading left paper	% reading right paper	% reading no paper	% Total
Left voters	50	25	25	100
Right voters	15	70	15	100

Further reading

J. Downing, A. Mohammadi and A. Sreberny (eds.), *Questioning the Media: A Critical Introduction*. Thousand Oaks, CA: Sage, 1995. A useful set of essays on the mass media.

C. Fine, *A Mind of its Own*. London: Allen & Unwin, 2007. A comprehensive and highly readable account of how cognitive bias and heuristics enable individuals to protect their beliefs.

R. Gunther and A. Mughan, *Democracy and the Media: A Comparative Perspective*. Cambridge University Press, 2000. Useful and informative essays on politics and the media in Britain, Germany, Italy, Japan, the Netherlands, Spain and the USA.

P. Norris, *Virtuous Circle: Political Communications in Post-industrial Societies*. Cambridge University Press, 2000. An excellent and wide-ranging investigation of media effect on mass democratic attitudes and behaviour.

M. Prior, 'Media and political polarization', *Annual Review of Political Science*, 16, 2013: 101–27 (available through Google Scholar at www.princeton .edu/~mprior/Prior%20MediaPolarization.pdf). An in-depth and closely argued analysis of the effect of the new media (the Fox cable news channel, in this instance).

Three useful research articles, all available online, that compare media systems and their different effects are:

T. Aalberg, P. Van Aelst, & J. Curran, 'Media systems and the political information environment: A cross-national comparison', *International Journal of Press/Politics*, 15 (3), 2010, 255–71 (available on Google Scholar at http:// eucenter.wisc.edu/Media%20System.pdf).

F. Esser, C. H. de Vreese, J. Strömbäck, P. van Aelst et al., 'Political information opportunities in Europe: a longitudinal and comparative study of thirteen television systems', *International Journal of Press/Politics*, 17 (3), 2012, 247–74 (available at http://uahost.uantwerpen.be/m2p/publications/ 1351591980.pdf).

S. Soroka, B. Andrew, T. Aalberg, S. Iyengar et al., 'Auntie knows best? Public broadcasters and current affairs knowledge', *British Journal of Political Science*, 43 (4), 2013, 719–39 (available at http://usir.salford .ac.uk/27294/1/AuntieKnowsBest_complete.pdf).

Websites

The Columbia Journalism Review (www.cjr.org/resources/), State of the Media's Dashboard web pages (www.stateofthemedia.org/media-ownership/) and Think and Ask (www.thinkandask.com/news/media-giants.html) contain information about global media ownership and control.

The EU4journalists website contains detailed information about the media systems of the European Union's 27 member states and 14 neighbouring states (www.eu4journalists.eu/index.php/dossiers/english/C98/442/index .html).

And last, YouTube contains many different presentations on the media – pluralist, Marxist, conflict, dominance and postmodern theories, media freedom, the new media, media bias and manipulation, and more. You can sample these and make up your own mind about the many conflicting views and theories.

12   Voters and elections

Elections determine who is to take control of government. No other form of political participation has such clear consequences and few have more important ones. For these reasons elections are treated as a distinct and very important topic. Given their importance in any democratic system of government, a great many questions can be asked about voting and elections: How are democratic elections best organised? What is the best voting system? Who votes and why, and should we worry about declining turnout? Who votes for which party and why? How have voting patterns changed in recent decades?

Quite apart from their importance in their own right, elections also have the research advantage of involving a large number of citizens and of producing a large volume of reasonably reliable statistics. This makes them one of the best topics for studying mass political behaviour and participation. They tell us a lot about how ordinary citizens relate to politics, what they think is important and how they make up their minds about parties, governments and political issues.

In this chapter we tackle these questions in the following sections:

- Democratic elections
- Voting systems
- Voter turnout
- Party voting
- Theories of voting.

■ Elections

Democratic elections

The preconditions for democratic elections are demanding, and we should not take them for granted, not even in advanced democracies. They include universal adult **suffrage**, a secret ballot, impartial administration of voting and vote counting, free and equal access to the polls, freedom for candidates and parties to contest elections and an absence of **gerrymandering**. Free elections also require basic democratic rights, including freedom of speech, association and assembly, access to accurate and fair news reporting and parties that are not too unequal in resources. Relatively few countries meet all these requirements. Indeed, the American presidential election in 2000 suggests that registration and vote-counting practices are far from perfect in the USA.

Suffrage: The right to vote.

Gerrymandering: Drawing electoral boundaries to favour a particular party or interest.

Referendum: The submission of a public matter to direct popular vote.

Voting comes in two main forms: elections for different levels of the political systems, and **referendums**. Referendums are particularly useful for expressing public opinion on a particular issue, and they often involve either a constitutional change or a major policy issue, often one that is morally and emotionally charged. A few democracies do not hold referendums at the national level – Germany, India, Japan and Israel – but most have had at least one in recent years and some are making increasing use of them, especially Australia, Denmark, France, Ireland, Italy and New Zealand. Switzerland stands out with twenty-eight national referendums held between 2010 and 2014. Nevertheless, referendums are far less frequent than general elections and most of this chapter will be about general elections to national executives and legislatures.

■ Voting systems

One of the most basic decisions for any democracy is what **voting system** it should have. Many have been invented (the main types are outlined in briefing 12.1), but it is no simple matter to say what is the best and most democratic. Each has its advantages and disadvantages, and the choice depends on what one wants from a voting system. Those who value **proportionality** more than anything else choose a proportional representation system (PR), but others say that the system should, above all, produce stable and effective government. Some emphasise clear lines of government accountability to the majority of citizens, and others argue for adequate minority representation, on the grounds that democracies are to be judged on how they treat their minorities. Consequently it may be less a matter of choosing the best voting system than of selecting one of them, knowing what its strengths and weaknesses are in the light of what is

Voting system: The arrangements by which votes are converted into seats on representative bodies.

Briefing 12.1

Main voting systems

■ Plurality-majority

1. *Simple plurality/first-past-the-post* (FPTP) The candidate with most votes (a simple plurality) wins the seat no matter how many candidates and how small the winning margin. Usually used in conjunction with **single-member districts**, so the combination of single member and simple plurality is often known as the SMSP system. Its advantage is simplicity and direct democratic accountability, because each district is represented by *one representative*. SMSP is likely to produce single-party governments with stable majorities, and this also favours clear lines of *political accountability*. The disadvantage is **disproportionality** in election results. The SMSP system favours large parties and discriminates against small ones, which are often seen as a 'wasted' vote. A variation on SMSP is the *block vote*, which combines first-past-the-post counting with **multi-member districts**.

> **Single-member districts:** One elected representative for each constituency.

> **Proportionality:** The ratio of seats to votes. The more proportional the closer the ratio.

> **Multi-member districts (MMD):** Constituencies with two or more elected representatives for each area.

   Plurality-majority countries include Bolivia, Canada, India, Jamaica, Mauritius, the UK and the USA. Italy adopted a mainly SMSP system in 1994.

2. *Second ballot* The second-ballot (SB) system tries to avoid the disproportionality problem of SMSP systems by requiring the winning candidate to get an *absolute majority* of the votes (i.e. 50 per cent + 1) in the first round – or if not, a second run-off ballot is held between the two strongest candidates. The advantage is simplicity, the disadvantage the need for a second ballot shortly after the first. The French use this system in presidential elections.

3. *Alternative vote* (AV) Voters mark their first and subsequent preferences among the candidates for their own constituency. If no candidate receives an absolute majority of first-preference votes on the first count, the candidate with the smallest number of first-choice votes is eliminated, but their second-choice votes are redistributed among the remaining candidates. This process continues until one candidate has an absolute majority. The system is simple to understand, but its results are no more proportional than the SMSP system, and it can produce unpredictable results. It is used only in Australia.

■ Proportional representation

Proportional representation (PR) tries to ensure the proportionality of votes to seats. The three main forms are:

1. *List PR system* One of the simplest ways of ensuring proportionality is to distribute seats on a *national basis* or on a large regional one. Parties rank their candidates in order of preference, and they are elected in proportion to the number of votes for that party, starting from the top of the list. A party getting 25 per cent of the poll will fill 25 per cent

of the seats from the top of its list. The advantage is simplicity and proportionality. The disadvantage is that voters cast a preference for a party, though they may prefer to vote for an individual candidate. The system also gives power to party leaders, who decide the rank order of candidates on their lists. Because list PR voting requires multi-member districts, it also breaks the direct and simple link between representatives and their districts. List PR is highly proportional and can encourage small parties and fragmentation of the party system. An electoral threshold can overcome this problem, but this increases disproportionality.

> **Electoral thresholds:** A minimum percentage of the poll required to be elected (to discourage small parties).

Many democratic countries have adopted the list PR system, including: Argentina (compulsory voting), Belgium, Chile, Costa Rica (compulsory voting), Cyprus (compulsory voting), Czech Republic, Denmark, Dominican Republic (compulsory voting), Estonia, Finland, Greece, Israel, Italy (before 1994), Latvia, Netherlands (compulsory voting before 1970), Norway, Poland, Portugal, Slovakia, South Africa, Spain, Sweden and Switzerland.

2. *Single transferable vote* (STV) Voters rank candidates according to their order of preference, and elected candidates must either get a specified number of first preferences or else the second preferences are taken into account. If no candidate has an absolute majority, the third preferences are counted, and so on until all seats are filled. STV must be used in conjunction with multi-member constituencies. The advantage of the system is its proportionality and the avoidance of 'wasted' votes. The disadvantage is the complexity of the STV formula (although this is now easily and quickly done by computers) and the fact that multi-member constituencies do not create a direct link between constituencies and a single representative. The system is used only in Australia, Estonia (1989–92) and Ireland.

3. *Mixed-member proportional* The mixed-member proportional system runs two voting systems at the same time. Plurality-majority districts are used to keep the link between representatives and constituencies, but a list PR system is added for a certain number of additional seats (usually 50 per cent) in order to compensate for any disproportionality that arises from the plurality-majority system. In Germany, half the additional seats are allotted at district and half at national level, and citizens have two votes, one for their district and one for the national list. MMP is found in Germany, Hungary, New Zealand (since 1996) and Uruguay.

■ Semi-proportional representation (Semi-PR)

1. *Parallel systems* Like the MMP systems these use the plurality-majority system with a PR system but, unlike MMP, the PR system does not compensate for disproportionality resulting from the plurality-majority system. Used in Japan (from 1994), Lithuania and South Korea.

2. *Single non-transferable vote* (SNTV) The SNTV system combines multi-member constituencies with simple majority vote counting, and one vote for each elector. Used in Japan (before 1994) and Taiwan (for 78 per cent of seats).

expected of it. In the democracies of the world the most favoured systems are the simple plurality system, which is believed to produce stable and accountable government, and the list PR system, which results in more proportionate election outcomes (see table 12.1).

The summary accounts of the three main voting systems presented in briefing 12.1 show that the overriding problem with the simple plurality/first-past-the-post system is the unfairness it can produce in the discrepancy between votes and seats (disproportionality). However, this depends on the particular context of the country concerned. Disproportionality is generally large in the UK, sometimes very large, but much less so in India where seats and votes were roughly matched across the country as a whole. Nevertheless, simple plurality systems are widely used by many democracies (see table 12.2), perhaps because it is the simplest system based on the idea that the person with

Table 12.1 Liberal democracies: voting systems

		%
Non-PR		
	Simple plurality	44
	Second-ballot	5
	AV	1
	Sub-total	50
PR and Semi-PR		
	List PR	36
	Additional member	8
	STV	3
	Limited vote (semi-PR)	2
	Sub-total	49
	Total	99

Source: Derived from J. Denis Derbyshire and Ian Derbyshire, *Political Systems of the World.* Oxford: Helicon, 1996).

Table 12.2 Proportionality and disproportionality, India and UK

India, 2004	% of votes	% of seats
Congress and allies	37	41
BJP and allies	36	35
Others	28	24
UK, 2005		
Labour	36	55
Conservatives	33	30
Liberal Democrats	23	10
Others	8	5

Source: www.ipu.org/dem-e/guide/guide-2.htm#P289_39876.

the largest number of votes wins the election, although this may mean that barely more than a third of the national vote can produce an absolute majority of seats in parliament.

■ Election turnout

Voter turnout varies substantially in democratic countries, from more than 85 percent in Belgium, Denmark, Iceland and Sweden down to 55 percent or less in Japan, France and Switzerland. However, it must also be remembered that these voting figures refer to the percentage of those on the electoral register who vote, which takes no account of those who are of voting age but not on the register. This is important because it is easier to register in some countries than others; in some cases any citizen of voting age is automatically added to the register when they first pay taxes. In other countries registration may take time and trouble, perhaps even effort and determination for some social groups. In such cases, voting as a percentage of the total voting age population is usually lower, sometimes much lower, than voting as a percentage of the register. The extreme case is the USA, where about two thirds of those on the electoral register vote, but since barely half of the voting age population is on the register, only a third of those entitled to vote actually do so. In Belgium the comparable figure is 87 per cent.

Voter turnout: The number of citizens casting a valid (i.e. not a spoiled ballot) vote expressed either as a percentage of those eligible to vote (adult citizens), or as a percentage of those on the electoral register.

Two sets of factors explain these country differences – system and individual considerations.

System factors

1. *The importance of the election* Citizens are more likely to vote if they think the election is important. They turn out in larger numbers for national than for local government elections, and for the election of executive presidents and lower chambers rather than upper chambers and weak assemblies. The **democratic deficit** of the institutions of the EU, especially the European Parliament (EP), is said to be partly responsible for the low turnout in the EU.

Democratic deficit: The idea that the institutions of the European Union are not fully democratic, or as democratic as they should be.

2. *Democracy* Turnout in established democracies with entrenched political freedoms and civil liberties is higher than in non-democracies and new ones.

3. *Electoral system* PR voting systems have a higher turnout than other systems. Average voting turnout in PR systems (68 per cent) is higher than in semi-PR systems (59 per cent) and in plurality-majority systems (59 per cent). This, in turn, is linked to the idea that each vote counts and there are fewer 'wasted votes' in PR systems. Consequently, turnout is 10 per cent higher where the largest party wins fewer than half the votes compared with less competitive elections where the largest party wins more than 50 per cent of the poll.

4. *Close, competitive elections* Close elections, where every vote counts, tend to have a higher turnout, as do competitive elections (where the largest party wins less than 50 per cent of the vote).

5. *Left parties* Elections that manage to mobilise sections of the population with a low voting turnout will usually register a higher turnout – for example, where left-wing parties appeal to working-class voters.

6. *Frequency of election* Citizens who are often called out to vote seem to suffer from 'election fatigue'. Switzerland, which makes frequent use of referendums, has comparatively low election turnouts, although in referendums it is usually around 45–55 per cent.

7. *Founding elections* It is often believed that 'founding elections' (the first democratic elections after authoritarian rule) have high turnouts. One thinks of the long queues at polling stations in the first democratic election in South Africa in 1994. An examination of election statistics, however, shows that this turns out to be true of central and eastern Europe, but not generally of Africa, Asia, the Middle East and Oceania.

8. *Presidential and parliamentary elections* In parliamentary elections in the second half of the twentieth century turnout was a good 20 per cent higher than presidential election turnout, but by 1997, the two were virtually identical. At the same time, presidential elections increased from 30 per cent of all elections to more than 50 per cent in 1999, so it is not clear whether presidential turnout has changed, or whether presidential elections are now held in a different set of countries which normally have low turnouts (see table 12.3).

9. *Community characteristics* Socially homogeneous communities (predominantly in terms of class, religion, language or ethnic group) with a sense of solidarity often have high levels of social and political participation.

10. *Human Development* Turnout is not closely related to national wealth or population size, but it is closely associated with the UN **Human Development Index** (HDI). Countries with the highest HDI ratings have an average turnout of over 70 per cent, those in the world with the lowest are closer to 55 per cent. Among the most advanced democracies average turnout (as a percentage of the register) is close to 80 per cent.

> **Human Development Index:** A UN index of national development that combines measures of life expectancy, educational attainment and wealth into one measure.

11. *Compulsory voting* In some countries citizens have to appear at the polling station on election days – a practice rather imprecisely labelled **compulsory voting** (no democracy would make actually casting a vote compulsory). In this sense, voting is technically compulsory in countries including Australia, Belgium, Costa Rica, Cyprus, Italy, Peru and Netherlands (before 1970). But even in these countries turnout is only about 4–5 per cent higher on average than in countries where it is not compulsory, partly because compulsory voting is not enforced in practice. Where compulsory voting has been abolished or fallen into disuse, voting tends to maintain a comparatively high level.

> **Compulsory voting:** The legal obligation for citizens to appear at polling stations on election day.

Table 12.3 Average voter turnout as a percentage of those registered, selected democratic countries, 2004–2015

	Parliamentary election	Presidential election
Argentina	74.6	75.6
Australia	93.9	
Austria	77.4	62.6
Belgium	89.9	
Brazil	81.0	80.2
Canada	61.6	
Czech Republic	62.2	
Finland	66.2	71.5
France	57.7	82.2
Germany	73.3	
Greece	69.6	
Hungary	64.6	
Ireland	68.5	56.1
Israel	65.3	
Italy	79.8	
Japan	62.2	
Latvia	61.0	
Mexico	55.3	60.8
Namibia	78.4	78.6
Netherlands	76.8	
New Zealand	77.3	
Norway	77.3	
Peru	86.2	85.3
Poland	47.8	53.2
Portugal	60.7	54.0
Slovenia	60.3	50.3
South Africa	75.8	
Spain	73.3	
Sweden	84.1	
Switzerland	48.7	
United Kingdom	63.5	
USA	54.4	75.6

Source: International Institute for Democracy and Electoral Assistance (www.idea.int/vt/survey/voter_turnout4.cfm).

Individual factors

1. *The standard model* The standard model of political participation, described in chapter 9, applies to voting turnout as well. The higher an individual's socio-economic status, the more likely she is to vote. Though still generally true, the associations between class, status and income and voter turnout have generally declined in the past decades in Western democracies.

2. *Age, gender, length of residence and race* The standard model of voter turnout may be modified by other variables. Young and old people are less likely to vote, so also are women and members of minority groups – unless minorities are mobilised by their own political organisations or political issues relevant to them. Long-term residents with roots in the community are more likely to vote than more mobile people.

3. *Party identification* Individuals with a strong **party identification (party ID)** are more likely to vote. There is also evidence that the strength of party ID is declining in some democracies, perhaps because of changing social structures, increasing population diversity, different working experience and increasing levels of education.

> **Party identification:** The stable and deep-rooted feeling of attachment to and support for a political party.

4. *Values* Post-materialist values, it is said, promote participation and civic responsibility.

5. *Voting culture* There is something of a cultural habit about voting and some evidence that low turnout among the young and first-time voters will tend to persist in later life. If so, turnout will continue to decline, perhaps even at a greater rate.

6. *Protest voting* History suggests that sudden and large increases in turnout may indicate widespread dissatisfaction with the political system and its leaders. The sudden jump in voter turnout in Germany in 1933, when Hitler's Nazi Party won, was the result of alienated people deciding to cast a **protest vote**. Equally, the arrival of an unusually popular candidate or party can mobilise voters (Obama in the USA in 2008).

> **Protest vote:** Voting for a party not so much to support it, but to show opposition to another party or parties, usually those in government.

Do low and declining turnouts mean democratic dissatisfaction?

In the established democracies (countries that have been democratic for twenty years or more) average turnout as a percentage of the voting-age population rose from around 70 per cent in the 1940s to around 75–80 per cent in the 1950s. This figure remained fairly constant over the 1960s and 1970s and then declined slightly to around 65–75 per cent by 2009. This does suggest decline although about 70 per cent of the population continues to vote. The rise and fall of the figures raises the question of whether the higher figures of the 1950–1970 period were unusual and the lower ones of the 1940s and 1990–2010 are more normal. They also raise the question of whether the era of decline was due to changing socio-demographic patterns, or to growing apathy, alienation and political dissatisfaction.

Voting in national elections is the simplest and easiest task of the citizen, and the fact that it is low and/or declining in some countries is often taken as a sign of democratic failure and dissatisfaction. A look at the seventeen factors just listed suggests that this is not necessarily the case, though it may well be in some instances. Many of the variables are system or structural considerations with little or no immediate connection with feelings of democratic dissatisfaction. Old class lines and allegiances are eroding, social and geographical mobility increasing, the number of old and chronically ill people who are unable to get to the polling stations rising, populations are more mixed, work experience changing, social groups more fragmented and the number of ethnic minorities and immigrant groups who have brought their non-voting culture with them has risen. A second look at the seventeen factors also shows that few necessarily are connected with apathy. In fact, some research finds that young people are less interested in elections or the conventional politics of mainstream political parties than in direct community participation and unconventional politics.

This is not to say that alienation and apathy do not play a part in declining election turnout, only that these are not the only or main explanations. There is hard evidence of dissatisfaction with parties, leaders and the political system, which goes with protest voting for minor and extremist parties. We return to this in chapter 17.

■ Party voting

As with voter turnout, there is a great deal of variation in party voting across the democratic world, but there are also patterns to be seen and generalisations to be derived from them about the determinants of party choices on election day.

Economic voting and stratification

Economic issues are intimately linked with some of the most basic conditions of daily life – not just money but housing, health, education and family prospects. Therefore there is often a link between the economy and voting, as in the commonly observed tendency for working-class and poor social groups to vote for parties of the left, and for wealthier groups to favour the centre or the right. There is also a tendency for voters to punish governments that perform badly on economic matters. But the link between class and voting is dependent on four other factors.

Class: A group of people sharing certain attributes determined by economic factors, notably occupational hierarchy, income and wealth.

1. Non-economic cleavages may override economic ones. A large working-class, left-wing party has not emerged in India, in spite of widespread poverty, because of the strength of race, religious, language and regional cleavages. In contrast, class voting was particularly strong in the UK and Australia, when class was the dominant cleavage and there were few other social divisions to confuse it. In comparison, the link between class and politics in the USA is considerably weakened by race and the north–south divide.

2. The extent to which voters reward or punish their government for a weak economic performance depends on how clear it is that the government is

responsible for economic conditions: government coalition partners blame each other for failures; higher levels of government blame lower levels and vice versa; presidents blame legislatures and vice versa; and poor government performance may count for little if voters believe that opposition parties would do worse.

3. Voters learn about government (economic) performance in different ways, at different times and with different effects. They are more likely to forgive the poor performance of parties they identify with and vote for (the 'home team' effect).

4. Social class is mainly defined by how people make their money, whereas social status is decided by how they spend it. Class is an objective way of grouping people based on income, while **status** is more subjective, based on social background, behaviour, education, speech, clothes and life-style. People from high-status backgrounds who have fallen on hard economic times can retain their high status even though they are impoverished, and equally those from poor backgrounds who have made a lot of money may be regarded as vulgar and nouveau riche. A combined measure of class and status is referred to as 'socio-economic status'. Voting may have as much to do with status as class, so that those who regard themselves as middle class, even if they lack the income, may vote accordingly. Equally, those who are strongly attached to their working-class origins may retain their class solidarity.

> **Status:** A form of social stratification determined by social prestige rather than economic factors or occupation. At their simplest, class is determined by wealth and income, status by such things as social backgrounds, accents, dress, manners and interests.

For much of the late nineteenth and the twentieth century class voting was strong and widespread in western Europe. It is argued that by 1920 the party systems of most of these countries had frozen around their main class cleavage and largely remained that way until the 1970s. During this period the left–right dimension was the most important in their politics (see briefing 12.2). However, when economic changes brought about a change and weakening of class structures, other social divisions became more important for voting. One of the most important is religion.

Briefing 12.2

The left–right dimension in politics
At the heart of the left–right dimension in politics lies a profound difference between (1) the left, which favours the welfare state and government intervention in society and the economy in order to achieve a degree of equality of opportunity, and (2) those on the right, who favour less government intervention and a market economy, although they often favour strong government in the interests of domestic law and order and national security. The left–right dimension is becoming less important with the decline of class differences in many democracies, but more important in some industrialising democracies, where a rapidly growing urban working class is combining with poor agricultural workers.

Religious voting

Religion has been a major source of political conflict for most of the world's history, and it remains a major, if not *the* major, social and political division in some democratic countries. In India, conflict between Muslims and Hindus is an acute political issue, and Hindu fundamentalism is the basis of the Bharatiya Janata Party (BJP), which has played a major role in opposition or government since 1998 and won an overwhelming election victory in 2014. Religious issues and voting patterns were strong in much of Europe and are still important in the USA.

While it is not surprising that religion is a basic foundation of political life in religious societies, it also continues to be a major influence on voting behaviour even in the secular parts of western Europe, where churches and the state came to a formal settlement centuries ago (see chapter 1). Both class and religious voting are tending to decline but religious voting less rapidly and, as a result, religion is becoming relatively more important (table 12.4). However,

Table 12.4 Country variations in class, religious and value voting, 1990s

Correlation with party preferences	Class voting	Religious voting	Materialist-postmaterialist voting
0.37		Netherlands	
0.30		Belgium	
0.29		Denmark	
0.27		Finland, Italy, Norway	
0.26		Austria	Netherlands, Finland
0.25		Spain	Denmark
0.22	Norway	France, West Germany	
0.21	Denmark		Britain, (West) Germany
0.20	Austria	Sweden	
0.19	Iceland		France, Iceland
0.18	Britain, Netherlands		Italy, Norway
0.17		Iceland	Spain
0.16	Belgium, Finland, Sweden	Ireland	
0.15	France, Italy, Spain	Japan	Sweden, Austria
0.14	Ireland		East Germany, Japan
0.13	(West) Germany		Belgium, Canada
0.12		Britain, Canada	
0.11	Japan		Ireland
0.10	Canada, USA		
0.09			USA
0.08		USA	

Note: Entries in the first column show the strength of the statistical association (the correlation) of party preference with social class, religion and post-materialism in the 1990s

Source: Russell J. Dalton, *Citizen Politics*, 2nd edn. London: Chatham House, 1996: 171, 180, 190).

religious voting is often more complex than class voting, since there is no simple working-class–middle-class/left–right cleavage. Instead, there is a more complex set of divisions between many different churches and faiths – including the formation of secular parties in opposition to religious ones, in some countries. While there is pressure on political parties to maintain their unity and voting strength, there is not the same need for churches in this regard.

In the predominantly Catholic areas of western Europe (in Austria, Belgium, France, Ireland, Italy, Spain and southern Germany) the largest centre-right party is a Christian Democratic one that relies heavily on Catholic votes. Catholics voted overwhelmingly for the centre-right candidate (Sarkozy) in the French presidential election of 2012. In Protestant western Europe, however (Scandinavia, the UK and the north of Germany), the main centre-right party is a secular one.

Other voting patterns

Few things consistently rival class and religion as the major influences on party voting across the broad sweep of modern democracies, but other factors can play a significant role (see briefing 12.3).

- Most countries have urban–rural differences and, more especially, regional variations in party voting. The latter are particularly likely to be associated with ethnic, religious, class or language differences, as they are in Belgium, Canada, Spain and India. Other countries have significant regional differences. Italy, Germany, the USA, and the UK have north–south differences, and Germany and the UK also have their regional divides between east and west and Scotland and England respectively.
- There is a slight gender gap in some societies, and although it is rarely as important as religion or class it can be large enough to determine an election outcome. In presidential elections in the USA 55 per cent of women and 45 per cent of men voted for Obama and, in the UK, Thatcher attracted a majority of female votes.
- Race and ethnicity, important in some of the newer democracies, has also gained in importance in the older ones as a result of global migration patterns.

New party voting patterns

Social and economic changes (some brought about by government policies) have had a strong influence on voting patterns. In the industrialising democracies, the decline of the agricultural sector and the growth of the cities populated by the working class and the poor have had a profound impact on political organisation and the development of socialist parties. The **left– right division** between working-class, socialist

The left–right continuum: The observation that parties and voting could be located on a single continuum ranging from communist and revolutionary socialist ones on the political left, to conservative and fascist groups on the right.

Briefing 12.3

Cleavages and politics: Chile

Republican political institutions were able to take root in Chile in the nineteenth century before new social groups demanded participation. Contenders from the middle and lower classes were gradually assimilated into an accommodating political system in which most disputes were settled peacefully, although disruptions related to the demands of workers often met a harsh, violent response. The system expanded to incorporate more and more competing regional, anti-clerical and economic elites in the nineteenth century. The middle classes gained political offices and welfare benefits in the opening decades of the twentieth century. From the 1920s to the 1940s, urban labourers obtained unionisation rights and participated in reformist governments. In the 1950s, women finally exercised full suffrage and became a decisive electoral force. And by the 1960s, rural workers achieved influence with reformist parties, widespread unionisation and land reform.

As Chile's political parties grew, they attracted followers not only on the basis of ideology but also on the basis of patron–client relationships between candidates and voters. These ties were particularly important at the local level, where mediation with government agencies, provision of public employment and delivery of public services were more crucial than ideological battles waged on the national stage. Over generations, these bonds became tightly woven, producing within the parties fervent and exclusive subcultures nurtured in the family, the community and the workplace. As a result, by the mid-twentieth century the parties had politicised schools, unions, professional associations, the media and virtually all other components of national life. The intense politicisation of modern Chile has its roots in events of the nineteenth century in spite of later twentieth-century developments including military coup, dictatorship and democratisation.

(For a more detailed analysis of Chile's cleavage politics, see http://workmall.com/wfb2001/chile/chile_history_historical_setting.html.)

parties and middle-class, conservative ones which emerged in the early twentieth century began to change towards the end of the century, partly as a consequence of the long economic boom (the economic miracle) that started in the 1950s. In the older democracies of western Europe, the old pattern of class politics showed clear signs of 'unfreezing'. Class became less important as **class de-alignment** and **partisan de-alignment** started to break the old voting patterns which were now less settled and more **volatile**. Minor parties tended to grow in number and strength, the green movement emerged as a political force, and there was, for a time at least, a tendency for some citizens to vote according to a particular issue – feminism, peace, anti-nuclear,

Class de-alignment: Decline in the class-based strength of attachment to class-based political parties.

Partisan de-alignment: Decline in the strength of attachment to political parties.

Volatility: The opposite of stability, volatility involves change in voting patterns from one election to another. Some refer to it as 'churning'.

immigration, minority rights and, in Europe, the issues surrounding European integration and the European Union.

The causes of these changes were many and varied, but include several common developments:

- Industrialising societies have often mixed old stratification factors based on caste, religion and ethnicity with new class and status distinctions. In post-industrial societies, the working class has shrunk and the larger middle class has fragmented into smaller sub-groups according to lifestyles or occupations (service, manufacturing or finance). This has weakened class voting.
- Urban–rural differences have declined with a shrinking agricultural sector, particularly where the urban and rural poor have formed a political alliance in industrialising countries.
- Education has created a more independently minded electorate that is less bound by class identities. Social mobility between classes has strengthened this and geographical mobility has weakened some local ties.
- Media, especially television and Internet-based technologies, have become more important.
- New parties have emerged and old parties have shifted their policies in an attempt to broaden their appeal and to respond to the demands of new social groups. In some cases, the old parties have stolen policies from the new parties and social movements in their attempt to maintain their electoral appeal.
- The basic bread-and-butter issues of poverty, work, health, housing and education have become even sharper in industrialising democracies, whereas the environment, nuclear issues, gender and minority rights, and (in Europe) European integration have often cut across the old politics of class in post-industrial societies.

The result of these far-reaching changes in socio-economic patterns is increased volatility and unpredictability in voting patterns in both new and old democracies. Nevertheless, talk of revolutionary and radical transformation is often exaggerated. Changes are usually gradual and involve fusions of the old and the new, and shifts of degree rather than kind. In some cases, even **partisan re-alignment** can be observed. Social stratification and religion

Partisan re-alignment: Change of old party identifications in favour of new ones.

remain the basic sources for political mobilisation, even if the nature of the stratification is shifting.

Tradition and change in Mexico

We can see the interplay of tradition and change in the electoral politics of Mexico, where economic inequalities of class are superimposed on old ethnic divisions. The Mexican social and political elite is composed of the *criollos*, people of pure Spanish ancestry dating back to the invasion of Mexico in the sixteenth century by the Spanish conquistador, Hernán Cortés. The middle layer of society is made up of people of mixed blood, the *mestizos*, with Spanish and indigenous Mayan and Aztec backgrounds. For sixty years, Mexico had an authoritarian system of government based on electoral manipulation and the ability of the Institutional Revolutionary Party (PRI) to unite the interests of these groups and those of the lowest class, the *indigena*, by bringing them together in a corporatist structure (see chapter 10). The structure however, largely excluded the interests of the very poorest section of society, the rural farmers who were concentrated in the south of Mexico and consisted mainly of people of Mayan background.

On New Year's Day 1994, the revolutionary National Liberation Front (NLF, the Zapatistas) burst into armed guerrilla activity that shook the foundations of the state and the governing PRI. Zapatista demands were economic, regional and ethnic. They wanted a better economic deal for poor farmers, who were mainly of Aztec origin and concentrated in Chiapas in the south of Mexico. Two remodelled parties emerged to challenge the hegemony of the PRI, both representing class interests. The Democratic Revolutionary Party (PRD, founded in 1989) is supported mainly by poor urban and rural people, and the National Action Party (PAN, founded in 1939) mainly by upper-income groups. PAN captured the presidency in 2000.

The Mexican case illustrates several points about changing voting patterns:

- Change is usually mixed with tradition.
- Voting is based on a mixture of factors involving social stratification and inequality, ethnicity and regional and urban-rural differences. Religious differences are not important in Mexico because it is 90 per cent Catholic.
- History is important. The Zapatista movement is the result of the subjugation of the Mayan and Aztec populations in the sixteenth century, and the 1990s movement named itself after the revolutionary leader Emiliano Zapata (1879–1919), who fought for the rights of poor farmers. Politics is important. Poor farmers lived in Mexico for centuries, but it was the charismatic leader 'Subcomandante' Marcos who organised a rebellion in 1994, which had a subsequent influence on the formation of new parties.

■ Theories of voting

The major theoretical approaches of political behaviour as introduced in chapter 9 are also valid for the explanation of voting behaviour. Due to the importance of voting in democracies a few approaches have been specifically developed to deal with voting (or more generally with electoral behaviour). The three main ones are:

- sociological/political sociological approaches
- psychological/social psychological approaches
- rational-choice/economic approaches.

Sociological approaches: the Columbia school

Paul Lazarsfeld (1901–76), a sociologist at Columbia University in New York, in 1944 carried out an early American election study which showed that people vote according to their membership of social groups, and that social groups vote for the party that best serves their interests. This makes class, religion, race, language, urban–rural differences and sometimes gender, generation and occupation the most important determinants of voting behaviour.

The strengths of the sociological school are that it relates politics to broad social and economic patterns and, as we have seen so often in this book, there is often a close connection between society and its government and politics. Indeed, research shows a close relationship between voting and factors such as class, religion, age, gender, education and ethnicity. However, the theory is not good at explaining the causal links between politics and society. To understand why, for example, the working class votes for left-wing parties, we have to introduce political elements – such as values, ideology and party policy – into the explanation. Working-class people do not vote for working-class parties naturally or automatically, any more than members of a religious group generally vote for a given party because of instinct. They do so because they see a link between the interests (material or ideal) of their social group and the things that the party stands for.

The sociological approach works very well in some cases – religion and voting in Northern Ireland, for example – but there are always exceptions to the social patterns, and some of them are so large they cannot be overlooked. Working-class people do not always vote for left-wing parties, just as some middle-class people do not vote for right-wing ones. Ethnic groups are rarely 100 per cent solid in their voting patterns. Sometimes they are split between two or more parties, sometimes divided down the middle. And, as we have already seen, the sociological model seems to be losing some of its power, with the emergence of the 'new' politics based not on group membership but on values and issue areas.

The cleavage model is a more complex version of the sociological approach. It also argues that voting is organised around social groups, but points out those cleavages are not the automatic outcome of social divisions. Indeed, many social divisions, such as age or gender, do not normally take on the importance of political cleavages. Social divisions become politically potent only when political interests (elites, parties, movements) manage to give them a political and symbolic significance, and build organisations around them. In other words, parties do not merely respond to cleavages; they play on them and develop them in their attempts to win support. Parties would find it difficult to mobilise voters without cleavage groups to appeal to, but social cleavages would have little political significance without parties to mobilise them and articulate their interests and values.

While cleavage theory can explain the historical origins of parties and party systems, it is less successful in explaining changing political alignments. The theory tends to take cleavages as given, and works out their political implications from there. It is rather less interested in why different societies have different cleavages or how and why they reconfigure themselves over time. Since the old cleavages appear to be fading a little, and new ones emerging, this is important to contemporary politics.

Psychological approaches: the Michigan school

Starting with Angus Campbell (1910–80) and his collaborators, the Michigan school of election studies emphasises the psychological orientations of voters. Whereas the sociological school emphasises social groups, psychological approaches concentrate on individual characteristics, particularly the role of party identification (party ID). This is a relatively stable and enduring feature that individuals acquire as a result of childhood and adult socialisation. Party ID is more than identification with a party, because it acts as a prism through which individuals perceive politics and interpret policies, issues, parties and candidates. It affects voting, and it also helps to mould the way in which citizens relate more generally to government and politics.

Campbell and his colleagues developed what they call 'the funnel of causality', in which all the variables affecting voting behaviour are organised according to the theoretical order of their influence. At the 'wide end' of the funnel is a set of the most general constraints on voting, such as social background and socialisation. As the funnel narrows, so variables constrain the voting decision more tightly. At the narrowest point are factors closest to the circumstances of particular elections, including attitudes towards party policies, candidates and election issues. This is a useful way of organising the many different variables that seem to affect voting behaviour, but at the same time it is a complicated model that is difficult to test as a whole.

The psychological school introduces specific political elements (party ID) into voting studies that are lacking in the sociological approach. It picks out the significance of political issues (unemployment, public services, economic development), party programmes (left–right dimensions, ethnic, religious, language and regional parties) and the images and appeal of political leaders as influences on party ID. There is also a close relationship between party ID and party voting. However, this is scarcely surprising, since party ID and party voting are almost the same thing: if people are asked in surveys which party they identify with, they are likely to think of which party they vote for. In the long causal chain of explanatory variables explaining voting patterns, party ID and the vote are practically next door to each other, so of course we find that they are closely correlated. The problem is not to understand the causal links between ID and voting, but to understand who develops what sort of ID, and why. In addition, survey research shows that the strength of party ID is fading in many Western countries (party de-alignment), although it is alive and well in countries such as South Africa, where black South African identification with the African National Congress (ANC) is widely and strongly held.

Rational choice

The rational-choice theory of voting originates with Anthony Downs's (1930–) book, *An Economic Theory of Democracy*, published in 1957, a work that starts with the assumption that citizens are rational and vote on the basis of a calculation of which party is most likely to satisfy their own self-interested preferences. Voting decisions are similar to those of consumers (voters) in the economic market who calculate the costs (taxes) and benefits (public services) of choosing one commercial product (political party) rather than another. Voting for a party is rather like choosing a basket of goods in a supermarket, in that voters select the 'package' of party policies that best fits their preferences at a price they can afford. Similarly, parties are like business competing for customers in the market place. In order to win the election they try to locate themselves and their policies close to the **median voter** – that is, close to the voter with equal numbers of voters to the left and the right. Usually, but not necessarily, this voter represents the position of the typical middle-of-the-road voter. Rational choice, in short, claims to explain the behaviour of individual voters and the strategies and policies of political parties in terms of an economic theory of the consumers (voters) and producers of public policies (parties).

> **Median voter:** Median voters have equal numbers of voters to their left and right, and are usually, but not necessarily, typical, middle-of-the-road voters.

Rational-choice theory – sometimes known as formal modelling because it can be expressed in terms of symbols and formulae – is said to have opened up many promising lines of research by virtue of its deductive and logical powers. It claims, first, that candidates in elections must locate themselves close to the median voter, in order to maximise their chances of election victory, and, second, that most citizens have little incentive to vote because among millions of others their vote counts for virtually nothing. For this reason, voters also have little incentive to inform themselves about election issues.

Rational choice has problems with explaining why people bother to vote at all. Logically, the most rational course of action for the voter is not to bother, not to vote, join a party or participate in collective actions because the costs in time and effort of acquiring the necessary information and then following up with action exceed whatever benefits are produced. Better by far to stay at home in warm and comfort watching the television, leaving others to do the work – what is known as **'free riding'**. However, people do vote, and they vote in large numbers even when the election result is a foregone conclusion and the winning candidate is expected to win by a very large majority. The reason is that voting seems to be a symbolic act in part, and people feel obliged to perform their citizen duty. This is not a matter of the rational calculation of self-interest, but a collective sense based on the value of democracy and the importance of exercising the right to vote. The act of voting then, needs explanations rooted in norms, values and social expectations.

> **Free ride:** To extract the benefits of other people's work without making any effort oneself. The free-rider problem is acute in collective action when individuals can benefit from a public good without paying taxes or making any effort of their own.

The claim that all voters act in their own self-interest can easily be circular, non-falsifiable or tautological. How can we tell when people are not acting in their own self-interest, and what counts as non-rational behaviour? Are middle-class socialists running against their own class interests? Were the Christians who chose to be thrown to the lions rather than recant their religious beliefs defying their own self-interests? Perhaps not: some people define their preferences in terms of the public good and are prepared to lay down their life for others and their own beliefs. But then it is difficult to see what 'self-interest' means, other than what individuals say it is. In this case whatever they do, no matter how altruistic or concerned with the public interest, is a rational calculation of self-interest.

Issue voting: Voters choosing one issue rather than a total party programme (or some other aspect of the party) as the basis of their voting decision.

Rational-choice has helped stimulate an interest in **issue voting**, which occurs when voters choose one issue rather than a total party programme as the basis of their voting decision. Traditional issues are unemployment and the economy ('it's the economy, stupid'), but it has also been suggested that race, human rights, the environment and peace have emerged in many countries as the focus of single-issue voting. However, research shows that the importance of issue voting may not be as great as some have suggested and that, in any case, voters do not always choose the party with the best policies on the issues they think are important. The voting decision is a trade-off, a package deal that is not simply the net balance of issue-based calculations but involves, in addition, a broader set of values and ideological considerations: voters use their hearts as well as their heads. Rational choice tends to avoid issues of the heart, or takes them for granted.

■ What have we learned?

This chapter deals with elections, which are vital in every democracy. It argues that:

- Democratic elections require a large number of preconditions. They should not be taken for granted even in advanced democracies.
- Election turnout in the post-war period has declined a little in the democracies, probably because of socio-demographic change as much as increasing voter apathy or disillusionment with democracy.
- The voting decision is the result of an interplay between social (group membership), economic (class and inequality) and political (party appeals and policies) factors. Inequalities based on class, status and caste are often tangled up with race, religion, language, education and region, and sometimes with age and gender as well.
- Although economic and political factors play important roles, voting behaviour is also based on normative, social considerations and ideologies (left–right placement).

■ Lessons of comparison

- Although every country has a unique electoral system, they fall into three main types: plurality-majority, proportional representation and semi-PR systems. The first two are the most common.
- There is no simple answer to the question: what is the best voting system? Each has its advantages and disadvantages. It is necessary to decide what one wants from an electoral system and choose accordingly.
- History matters. Once again we see that history and tradition cast a long shadow over contemporary events, and changing voting patterns are usually a mixture of the old and new rather than a transformation.
- Institutions matter. The electoral system of a country and, more broadly, its system of government, has an impact on voting behaviour. We will see in the next chapter how voting systems can affect party systems.

Projects

1. Was turnout in the last national election in your country high or low by national and international standards? What sorts of factor explain this level of turnout?
2. What is the best voting system? Why do you prefer it to other systems?
3. What are the strengths and weaknesses of (a) the rational-choice approach to the explanation of turnout and party voting, (b) the sociological approach (Columbia school) and (c) the psychological approach (Michigan school)?

Further reading

R. J. Dalton, *Citizen Politics. Public Opinion and Political Parties in Advanced Industrial Democracies*, 6th edn. Los Angeles: Sage and CQ Press, 2014. Compares electoral behaviour in France, Britain, the USA and West Germany.

M. Gallagher, M. Laver and P. Mair, *Representative Government in Modern Europe*, 5th edn. Berkshire: McGraw-Hill, 2011. The best short introduction to cleavage systems, voting and coalition governments in western Europe.

L. LeDuc, R. G. Niemi and P. Norris (eds.), *Comparing Democracies: Elections and Voting in a Changing World*, Thousand Oaks, CA: Sage, 2014. A good comparative study of voting and elections, covering a wide range of the literature.

P. Norris, *Democratic Phoenix*. Cambridge University Press, 2002. Discusses the rising level of political interest and activity in the established democracies, with chapters on voter turnout around the world.

C. van der Eyck and M. Franklin, *Voters and Elections*. Basingstoke: Palgrave Macmillan, 2009. A broad overview of electoral behaviour and the role of elections in democracies.

Websites

http://electionresources.org.

Links to internet sites around the world which provide detailed information about national and local elections, as well as other election resources.

www.fairvote.org/research-and-analyis/voter-turnout.

For data on electoral turnout.

www.libraries.ucsd.edu/resources/data-gov-info-gis/ssds/guides/lij/index.html.

Website of the Lijphart Election Archive, which is a research collection of district-level election results for approximately 350 national legislative elections in twenty-six countries.

www.idea.int/publications/vt/index.cfm.

An excellent account of voter turnout in over 170 countries.

https://sites.google.com/site/electoralintegrityproject4/home.

Website of the Electoral Integrity Project, providing excellent data on elections and the opportunities to improve electoral processes.

13   Party government

Democratic government is party government: electoral competition is largely party competition; parliamentary politics is invariably party politics; and government is rarely anything but party government. For better or for worse, **political parties** pervade all aspects of government and politics in democracies and are central to them. They help to integrate the political system from top to bottom, and to integrate from side to side across a wide span of political interests and social segments of society. From top to bottom they create two-way lines of communication between party members and the mass of ordinary citizens at the bottom of the political pyramid and the political elites and decision makers at the top. Large parties are 'broad churches', bringing together a wide variety of people with similar political interests but often different social backgrounds. They help to integrate across lines of class, gender, religion, ethnicity and region and they form alliances with a variety of voluntary associations and pressure groups. Parties do this in different ways according to their times and circumstances, so the first task of comparative studies is to identify the different types of party and the ways in which they operate.

> **Political parties:** Organisations of politically like-minded people who seek political power and public office in order to realise their policies.

In recent decades, however, the old parties have been challenged by new ones and by other forms of political organisation. It was said that the newcomers would replace the old parties with broader, looser, less bureaucratic and more flexible 'rainbow coalitions' of political interests. The old parties are still with us, however, and, moreover, those parties in any one country often bear a striking family resemblance to those in other countries. There are socialist parties with similar policies and appealing to similar social groups in many countries across the globe, just as there are conservative, liberal, nationalist, Christian and green parties operating in many countries.

Parties compete with each other for power, and sometimes one of them wins enough votes to take control of government on its own. More usually a combination of parties must form a coalition to form a government. This generally involves a good deal of bargaining and horse-trading to get an agreement on a set of policies for the new governing coalition, and to decide which partners in the coalition are to hold which positions in the cabinet. For some political scientists such secret wheeling and dealing behind closed doors shows that coalition government is inherently undemocratic and unstable. Others claim that coalitions can not only form durable governments but more democratic and effective ones as well.

The major topics in this chapter, therefore, are:

- Party organisation
- New parties and movements
- Party systems and party families
- Coalition government
- Coalitions and government effectiveness
- Theories of parties.

■ Party organisation

Public policy: A general set of ideas or plans that has been officially agreed on and which is used as a basis for making decisions.

Parties in democracies have two central purposes: to gain power by winning elections; and, once in power, to implement their **(public) policy**. Organisation is vital for both. In one form or another, it is essential for raising money, getting the party message to electors, getting out the vote and, once in power, party discipline and co-ordination are the backbone of a united government that can carry out its policy programme. Parties have passed through three main stages of organisation since their appearance in anything like a modern form:

Caucus: A small but loose-knit group of politicians (notables) who come together from time to time to make decisions about political matters.

- *Caucus parties* (also known as elite parties or cadre parties) In the eighteenth and nineteenth centuries, when few people had the vote, political parties were little more than loose alliances (a **caucus** or a clique) of like-minded people. They were led by a few elite 'notables', aristocrats or wealthy public figures.
- *Mass parties* In the twentieth century, with the coming of the universal franchise, parties broadened their electoral appeal by turning themselves

into mass parties, with a large membership and a bureaucratic, centralised and hierarchical form of organisation.

- *Catch-all parties* Since the 1970s, the 'unfreezing' of old cleavages and the development of 'new politics' have pushed parties towards 'catch-all' organisations, or rainbow coalitions that try to appeal to a wide variety of social groups and interests. Catch-all parties are widespread in Latin America where, although now run along more democratic lines, they have something in common with the clientalist parties of authoritarian governments which bought support from a mixture of different social groups with money, contracts and jobs.

> **Catch-all parties:** Parties that try to attract a broad range of supporters by advocating rather general policies.

In the last few decades analysts have argued that political parties are entering into a new, fourth stage of development but it is not yet clear how they will evolve and so they are described in different ways as media parties, cartel parties or electoral–professional parties.

- *Media parties* The spread of the mass media and Internet technologies means that party leaders can now appeal directly to voters, which reduces the need for a mass membership, a cumbersome organisation and mass meetings. State funding also relieves financial pressures. Media parties do not need such deep roots in society and depend less on mass organisations to raise money, organise meetings, mobilise voters, distribute party political leaflets and put up posters. It may even be that ordinary party members with views of their own about politics make life more difficult for leaders who want to respond rapidly and flexibly to fast-changing political developments in the world.
- *Cartel parties* Political parties in the late twentieth century have adapted to declining participation, it is claimed, by turning themselves from mass, competitive parties into cartel parties that collaborate with each other for state resources (money and patronage) as well as career stability and continuity for their leaders. Politics used to be a more 'amateur' affair for people who started their careers in ordinary jobs, mainly in business and the professions, before moving to politics. Now parliaments are full of career professionals who have done nothing but politics all their life. They have little working experience of the wider world, interact mainly with political professionals, and try to secure their own political jobs by colluding with each to exclude the smaller and newer parties.
- *Electoral–professional parties* Drawing from Michels's 'iron law of oligarchy' (see the end of this chapter), it is argued that modern parties have been 'captured' by professional career politicians who run highly centralised and technically skilled party operations and election campaigns.

Party policy and organisation, it is said, are now as much a technical and professional matter as an ideological one. They involve opinion polling, focus groups, spin-doctors, carefully planned public relations and money-raising campaigns, Internet technologies, mastery of the mass media, social networks, and new social media. Party conferences are no longer policy-making events, where the party faithful debate party policy to reach a decision, but stage-managed public relations events organised around photo-opportunities and sound bites designed to confirm the policy of the leaders. At the same time, parties still need a core of supporters and workers to get the vote out on election days and to raise money. Party organisations and grass-roots members are still required even in the media age, although possibly in new forms with different roles. In general, the role of party members has been reduced, and in some countries new parties do not even allow for membership and are completely organised and ruled by a few persons.

■ New parties and movements

New forms of organisation are not the only challenge that modern parties have to face. We have already seen how old voting patterns in western Europe have changed to some extent, causing party de-alignment, electoral volatility and the 'unfreezing' of the old party system. The result has been the appearance of new parties and movements that differ from the old parties in three main ways:

- They are based on the 'new' issues of the environment, peace, feminism, nuclear weapons and energy, animal rights, community participation, and minority group rights, but also on regional separatism, nationalism and immigration policies.
- They are supported mainly by the young, well-educated and relatively affluent sections of the population, so are found mainly in the most affluent democracies rather than industrialising countries.
- They use different political methods, often direct and grass-roots community action, protests and demonstrations and sometimes even violence.

The new parties have been called 'anti-party parties' or 'anti-politics movements', because they oppose the ideas and methods of the traditional and conventional parties and pressure groups. The first flowering of them is often said to have been in 1968, when a new generation of student activists, intellectuals and workers took to the streets in many Western countries to protest against conventional politics. According to some, these new parties are closely associated with the emergence of post-materialism (chapter 9) and they also overlap with the new social movements (chapter 10).

More recently many democracies have seen the rise of nationalist parties which oppose immigration and are especially against the spread of Islam. In Europe these parties are usually also against the EU and they want to reverse the process of European integration. Examples of these parties are the Front National in France and the Party for Freedom in the Netherlands, which have both been very successful in recent elections. Although the new parties of this type clearly belong to the right wing of the political landscape, they are frequently depicted as populist parties.

Originally there was speculation that the new parties and movements would cause a crisis in democratic politics by replacing the old party and pressure groups, or at least undermining them by destabilising conventional politics. This has not happened, partly because the new parties have usually remained quite small, and partly because the old parties have adapted to them by stealing some of their new policies. In fact, some of the old parties have long advocated aspects of the 'new' policies, though not usually placing them at the top of their agendas. They have now polished them up and pushed them closer to the front of their political stall to try to outflank the new organisations.

The result of the rise of new parties, as we saw in terms of voting in chapter 12, is not the replacement of the old politics by the new, but rather a fusion of the old and new. Few of the old parties have disappeared, although they have adapted their policies and organisation to fit new conditions, and they have sometimes declined in voting strength and power. At the same time, few new parties have displaced the old, although some have forced old parties to shift their political agenda. However, there has been a tendency for **party systems** to fragment as new parties have entered the arena, and for some increase in electoral volatility as the electorate changes its voting habits. Western elections have always attracted a large number of candidates, including many from minor parties with negligible chance of success, but the past few decades has seen the rise of small parties that can attract enough votes to threaten the major parties and perhaps win seats in parliament. The lengthening list of minor parties has created a need to measure the **number of effective parties** which reveals the extent to which the party system has fragmented in real rather than small and insignificant ways.

> **Party system:** The pattern of significant parties within a political system, especially their number and the party families represented.

> **Number of effective parties:** The number of parties with significant political strength either in terms of votes in elections (effective number of electoral parties) or in terms of parliamentary seats (the effective number of parliamentary parties).

In spite of increasing fragmentation of the party system, the pattern today is one of change mixed with continuity rather than the transformation of the old system. In large part this is because parties set out to appeal to sections of the population according to their social, economic and political interests. Since the social and economic structure does not change rapidly nor do the political parties, and since the social and economic structure of advanced societies are often rather similar, so also are their political parties. This leads us to a discussion of party families.

■ Party systems and party families

Most democracies have many parties, and each country has its own unique combination of them. Nonetheless, the parties of democratic countries have two major features in common:

> **Party families:** Groups of parties in different countries that have similar ideologies and party programmes.

- They often group into **party families**.
- They form party systems which can be explained with a few simple rules.

Party families

Although parties come in all shapes and colours, they often cluster into types because parties of the same sort in different countries often bear a striking family resemblance to each other. Because the main parties are built around the main social cleavages in society, and because urban-industrial societies tend to have similar cleavages, there are usually a few main parties that appeal to similar social groups and have similar core values and policies that express similar goals. There are seven main party families and, to simplify our task of classifying parties even more, most can be arranged fairly neatly on a left–right scale. We shall look much more closely at the beliefs and pro-grammes of party families in chapter 14; here it is enough simply to identify the types and show how they fit into government coalitions. Starting with the left the families are as follows.

1. Socialist parties are found around the world, from Chile to New Zealand and from Canada to Japan, and virtually everywhere in between. They include social democratic, Labour, new-left, left-socialist and ex-commu-nist parties.
2. Christian Democratic parties and Christian Socialist parties are found mainly in Europe and Latin America.
3. Agrarian parties, variously called Farmer, Peasant, Agrarian or Centre parties are mainly found in Europe (and India), and are usually of declin-ing importance. In other places agrarian and rural interests are often organised into powerful interest groups with close links to government ministries.
4. Liberal parties, often known as Radical, Progressive, Liberal or Freedom parties. Liberalism is strong in Europe, Canada, Australia and New Zealand, but weak in Africa and Asia and most of Latin America.
5. Conservative parties often go under the name of Conservative, National or Moderate parties.
6. Nationalist, populist, regional or minority ethnic parties. These take all sorts of political positions from radical parties of the left to those of the right. Some want complete national independence for their region, some stop short of independence but want more devolved powers (see chapter 6) from their central government. Regional parties are strong in India and regional politics are built into the structure of the state in Belgium and Spain, for example.
7. Green parties come in different left–right colours but are often centre-left, and all stress environmental protection and sustainability.

Briefing 13.1 lists these types, and provides examples of the parties in each family and the countries in which they are found. As already mentioned, their ideological positions and policies are discussed in chapter 14.

Briefing 13.1

Party families

Family	Country	Example
Socialist	Brazil	Democratic Labour
	Canada	New Democratic Party
	Czech Republic, Denmark, Estonia, Finland, Germany, Iceland, Japan, Lithuania, Sweden, the Netherlands	Social Democratic Party
	Australia, Ireland, Mauritius, New Zealand, Norway, UK	Labour Party
	Argentina, Austria, Belgium, Chile, France, Greece, Hungary, Japan, Portugal, Spain, Uruguay	Socialist Party
	Costa Rica	National Liberation Party
	Dominican Republic	Dominican Revolutionary Party
	Jamaica	People's National Party
	Peru	Peruvian Aprista Party
	South Africa	African National Congress
Christian Democrat	Argentina, Australia, Chile, the Czech Republic, Germany, Hungary, Latvia, Lithuania, the Netherlands, Portugal, Slovenia, Sweden, Switzerland Romania, South Africa	Christian Democratic Party
	Denmark, Norway	Christian People's
	Belgium	Flemish Christians and French Christians
Agrarian	Estonia, Finland, Norway, Sweden	Centre Party
	Latvia	Farmers Party
	Australia	Country, National Party
	Poland	Peasants' Party
Liberal	Canada	Liberal, Social Credit Party
	Sweden	People's Party
	Finland, Japan, Taiwan	Progressive Party
	UK	Liberal Democratic Party
	France	Left Radical Party

Family	Country	Example
	Germany	Free Democrats
	USA	Democratic Party
	Philippines	Liberal Party
	South Africa	Democratic Alliance
Conservative	Canada, Denmark, Norway, UK	Conservative Party
	Japan	Democratic Liberal Party
	New Zealand	National Party
	Sweden	Moderate Party
	Finland	National Coalition
	France	Gaullist Party
	Austria	Freedom Party
	USA	Republican Party
Regional, ethnic parties	Finland	Swedish People's Party
	Belgium	Flemish, Flemish Nationalist Party
	Spain	Basque Nationalist Party, Catalan Nationalist Party
	UK	Irish Nationalist (Unionist, Social Democratic and Labour Party), Scottish, Welsh
	Italy	Northern League
	Canada	Quebec Nationalist Party
New parties	Australia, Austria, Belgium, Canada, Finland, France, Ireland, Italy, Israel, Japan, Poland, South Africa, Sweden, Switzerland	Green Party
	New Zealand	Values, Greens and Alliance Parties

Party systems

Party families are closely linked with party systems because both are based on the same features of the social and economic structure of society:

1. Parties are built around social differences and reflect the interests of social groups. In the past the most important social differences were the cleavages based on class, religion, ethnicity, language and region, and so there is a close connection between the number of cleavages in society and the number of parties. Countries with one main cleavage – usually class – tend

to have two main parties, one on the centre-left and one on the centre-right. Countries with two main cleavages – class and religion, for example – tend to have three main parties, one to represent the middle class and its main religion, and two others to represent the working class and its different religious or secular values. This association between the number of cleavages and parties is sometimes expressed by the simple formula:

$$P = C + 1$$

where P stands for the number of parties and C for the number of cleavages.

2. Because there is usually room only for one major party to articulate one side of a cleavage, we rarely find more than one large party on the same side. A large social democratic party is not often found alongside a large communist party, and a large Christian democratic party is unlikely to be opposed by a large conservative party, or a major agrarian party found with a major liberal party. This, of course, is only another way of formulating the $P = C + 1$ rule.

3. Most social cleavages are old, so many of the main parties date back to the late nineteenth and early twentieth centuries, when the modern industrial system was developed and voting rights were extended.

4. Across Western nations the social democrats are usually the largest single party because the working class is the largest, though their strength has declined a little as the social structure has changed to reduce the working class and increase the middle-class population. They are followed by the conservatives, Christian democrats, liberals and agrarian parties, in that order.

Most discussion of party systems distinguishes between dominant one-party, two-party and multi-party systems. **Dominant one-party systems** are relatively rare and have mainly occurred in India (Congress Party), Japan (Liberal Democratic Party), South Africa (African National Congress) and Sweden (Social Democratic Workers' Party). **Two-party systems** are not much more frequent, with the main examples to be found in Canada, New Zealand (until 1966), the USA and the UK. **Multi-party systems** are the most common in the democratic world. Party systems are important because they have a big impact on government formation in most democracies – that is, whether they have single party, multi-party or minority governments.

> **Dominant one-party system:** A party system in which one party dominates all the others.

> **Two-party system:** A party system in which two large parties dominate all the others.

> **Multi-party system:** A party system in which several main parties compete, often with the result that no single party has an overall majority.

One-party and coalition government

Democratic accountability in democracies is supposed to be maintained by the fact that free elections allow voters to choose their political representatives. They can either reward good governments with another term of office or kick them out. The overwhelming majority of representatives are elected as party candidates, and it is the party distribution of seats in a parliamentary system that determines the composition of the government. As long as the government can muster the support of a majority of elected representatives in the assembly, it can continue in government.

In dominant one-party systems government formation is straightforward – there is no alternative to the dominant party (see briefing 13.2). However, one-party government is the exception rather than the rule in most democracies, and have been found mainly in India (Congress Party), Japan (Liberal Democratic Party), South Africa (African National Congress) and Sweden (Social Democratic Workers' Party). In two-party systems, it is usually also straightforward because the majority party will form the government if it has an absolute majority of seats in parliament, and if it does not it can probably govern with the legislative support of one or more of the other parties, usually minor ones. As a result, two-party systems generally produce one-party government in which the other party forms the main opposition. Two-party systems are also relatively unusual, found mainly in Canada, New Zealand (until 1966), the USA and the UK.

Briefing 13.2

Government formation: parliamentary systems

Party system	Assembly	Government
One-party dominant	One-party majority	Dominant party government – Japan, Sweden, South Africa
Two-party system	One-party majority or near-majority	One-party government with swings between the two main parties – Greece, Norway, Spain (1982–95), the UK
Multi-party system	Multi-party assemblies	Coalition government
Electoral alliance		Coalitions formed before election
No electoral alliance	Coalition government formed after election	Coalition government formed after election
		Minority government – common in Denmark and not uncommon in Finland, Italy and Sweden
		MWC – quite common in many coalitions
		Oversized coalition – quite common in Finland, Italy and Netherlands
		'Grand' coalition found in Austria, Bulgaria, Canada, Switzerland, (West) Germany, Portugal

Most government in most countries is by coalition simply because they have electoral and multi-party systems that do not usually produce a single party in parliament with an absolute majority of seats. This makes it important to understand the process of government formation and maintenance in multi-party systems with **coalition** government.

> **Coalition:** A set of parties that comes together to form a government.

■ Coalition government

If no single party is large enough to form the government, then a party coalition will have to be formed. Most democracies have parties that are important enough to claim a position in government, either because their voting strength in parliament makes it difficult to overlook them, or because their place in the party system gives them a pivotal role in government formation. The creation of such a coalition often involves long, hard and complex negotiations between party leaders. In some cases, alliances are negotiated before elections (electoral coalitions), but more normally coalitions are constructed after elections, when the parliamentary strength of the parties is known (see briefing 13.2). This process of bargaining between possible coalition partners is usually a hidden form of horse-trading, taking place late into the night behind closed doors, but there are some informal rules governing the process:

1. Normally, the leader of the largest party in the parliament/assembly has the first chance at trying to form a governing coalition, and as such is known as the formateur, but if this fails the job passes to the leader of the second largest party.
2. Some constitutions give the head of state the right to nominate the formateur, though there is often little choice given the first rule.
3. The job of the formateur is to find agreement among coalition partners on government policy and the division of cabinet posts between the parties. Policy agreements can be very specific indeed and result in thick and detailed policy documents. This may take months of hard bargaining.
4. As one would expect, the parties most likely to form a coalition are those with the most similar policies. In other words, left parties are most likely to co-operate with other left or centre parties and right parties most likely to team up with other right or centre parties. This sometimes makes centre (liberal) parties pivotal favourites in coalition government, but if natural coalitions of parties with similar outlooks is not possible, then coalition politics can make for strange bedfellows and possible government instability. Equally, grand coalitions of disparate parties are sometimes formed in response to war or national crisis.
5. Cabinet positions in a coalition are usually distributed roughly in proportion to the strength of the coalition partners in the assembly, and the leader of one of the largest parties usually becomes the prime minister.

Which politicians end up with which cabinet posts is usually a matter of tough negotiation, and pivotal parties (the smaller parties of the coalition that can form a coherent ideological partnership, or which have won enough seats to help make up a majority of parliamentary votes) in the coalition can drive a hard bargain.

6. If a governing coalition is formed it is then formally invested in office by the head of state, and sometimes parliament must give its formal assent as well.

7. A coalition government that loses a **vote of confidence** in the parliament/assembly is normally required to resign, but remains in office as a caretaker government until a new government is formed. In many countries no special vote is required: if it is clear that the government lacks confidence in parliament, its days in power are over (see chapter 5).

Vote of confidence: A vote of confidence (or no confidence) tests whether the government of the day continues to have the majority support of members of the assembly.

Early theory predicted that coalition governments would usually take the form of **minimum winning coalitions** (MWC) because these are the smallest that can count on a majority of votes in the assembly. Anything larger than a MWC has more votes than strictly necessary, and the more coalition partners there are the greater the chance of difficulties between them. Anything smaller than a MWC means that the government cannot count on a majority of votes in the assembly.

Minimum winning coalition: The smallest number of parties necessary for a majority of votes in parliament.

However, an examination of coalition governments shows that a large proportion is either smaller or larger than a MWC. A **minority government**, often consisting of one party, is quite common. The reason is that opposition parties can sometimes exercise a great deal of influence within parliament through its committees, or outside it through affiliated pressure groups (trade unions, business organisations). In such systems, it is not essential to have a position within government in order to wield political influence. In other cases, minority governments persist simply because the opposition majorities are not sufficiently united to be able to remove the minority from power.

Minority government: A government or coalition that is smaller than a MWC.

Quite a few coalitions are larger than necessary. '**Oversized' coalitions** often exist where the 'surplus' parties have policies that are similar to those of the other parties in the coalition. There is a political logic to this. Parties excluded from a coalition might join the opposition to it, so it may be best to bring them inside the tent. In some cases, '**grand' coalitions** are formed, consisting of all the most important parties. This is not common, but has occurred in Austria, Switzerland and Germany, and even in the UK at times of national crisis.

'Oversized' coalition: A coalition that is larger than a MWC.

'Grand' coalition: An oversized coalition that includes all parties or the largest of them.

Across the democratic world governing coalitions have taken many different shapes and sizes. About 10 per cent of all governments formed in western Europe between 1945 and 1995 were single-party governments, about a third were MWC, another third minority governments and one in six were surplus majority. Coalition government is common in the Nordic and Benelux countries, Germany, Switzerland, Israel and India. Grand coalitions have often ruled in Austria and Switzerland, and sometimes in Germany, but equally MWCs have survived well in Austria, Germany and Norway, and minority governments have done well in Ireland, Sweden and especially Denmark. Coalitions of all kinds have fared poorly in Belgium, France (1945–58), Portugal and Finland.

The general rule seems to be that coalition formation is very much a matter of particular political circumstances and election outcomes. Even countries which are supposedly clear-cut examples of two-party systems and single-party government turn out not to fit the expected pattern. The UK is often said to be the clearest case and yet of its twenty governments in the twentieth century, only a half were formed by a single party, five were coalitions and another five were minority governments. There were ten consecutive years of grand coalition between 1935 and 1945 in response to the Great Depression and then the Second World War, followed by minority governments or coalitions, most recently in 2010–2015.

■ Coalitions and government effectiveness

It used to be thought that two-party systems were preferable because they tend to result in stable, moderate and accountable government. They often produced clear and stable working majorities in parliament. Moreover, if only one party is in power it can be held clearly accountable for government actions, whereas coalition partners often blame each other for their failures in government. In two-party systems also there is a strong incentive for both parties to try to hold to the middle ground and hence pursue moderate policies. The inter-war Weimar government in Germany, and the frequent collapse of coalition governments in the Fourth French Republic and in post-war Italy were often wheeled out as examples to make the point about the instability of coalition government. It is also claimed that the process of forming coalition government gives too much power to politicians and their wheeler-dealing and secret horse-trading. The outcome of their bargaining may not reflect the preferences of voters, it may also give too much power to pivotal parties, whose support is necessary for successful coalition formation, even if they are small and unrepresentative.

It is true that some coalitions have been unstable and short-lived and have sometimes required the reconstitution of government between elections – that is, the formation of a new coalition: hence some countries have more governments than elections. But this has not been a problem for many coalition governments, most of which have survived a full term in office. The presence of the same party (or parties) in successive coalitions often gives continuity, and the cautious, inclusive and consensual nature of much coalition government discourages rapid swings of policy from one single-party government to the next. It is also easy to exaggerate the instability of coalition governments. Experience shows that they have been as stable as one-party government in Germany, the Netherlands, Scandinavia and Switzerland. While single-party governments are generally the most long-lasting, MWCs survive well in some countries, just as surplus majority ones do in others. By and large, coalitions made up of a small number of parties are most stable, especially if they are ideologically close on the left–right continuum. Finally, coalitions are not unrepresentative of electoral opinion. They often have to be moderate to stay in power, and their frequent inclusion of a centre party as a partner means they tend to be representative of the middle ground of politics.

■ Parties and democracy

Competition between parties for governing power is at the very heart of democracy. The peaceful transfer of power between parties at election time is a hallmark of successful and stable democracies, and all of them, including those with dominant single parties, have organised oppositions ready to step into office if they win elections. Democratic government was maintained without undue disturbance in Sweden, Japan and India when a long period of one-party government came to an end. Parties were also crucial in the second and third wave of democratisation where leaders acted on their willingness to accept (many or most of) the democratic rules of the game, including a willingness to relinquish power if they lost a properly conducted election.

Losers' consent: The willingness of parties and party supporters to accept the outcome of democratic elections when they have lost the election, thus contributing to the peaceful transfer of power that is an essential of democratic government.

Authoritarian governments and dictators often try to hold on to power at any price. Democratic politicians and their voters comply with election outcomes that are peaceful and fair, recognising the legitimacy of elected governments they are personally opposed to. This vital aspect of democracy is known as **losers' consent**.

Nevertheless, party politics is often attacked as harmful and unnecessary in a democracy (see controversy 13.1), especially when they are corrupt or where party leaders handle themselves and public affairs badly. There can be much truth in these criticisms, but there is also much truth in the counter-argument that whatever the faults of parties and party government, democracies of all kinds have yet to come up with anything better. If parties did not exist, someone would have to invent them.

It remains the case, however, that parties across the democratic world, and especially in the older democracies, are losing members and that fewer people are identifying with them. This means that parties are more dependent on sources of money other than individual subscriptions, which has raised

CONTROVERSY 13.1

Parties and democracy

■ Parties are bad for democracy because:

- Parties involve faction and conflict, and politicians should search for consensus and national unity.
- Parties represent the interests of particular sections of society (classes, religious groups, regions, ethnic groups, and the like).
- There is no need for party politics because common sense tells us there is only 'one way to lay a sidewalk'.
- Parties are inherently undemocratic, being run by small cliques and elites of self-interested and untrustworthy politicians.
- Therefore society should be run and important decisions taken not by factious, self-interested politicians but by a small group of wise people with the public interest at heart – the 'philosopher kings' advocated by Plato, or the 'good and the great' of society, or a group of experts and technocrats.

■ Parties are good for democracy because:

- Faction and conflict are unavoidable in politics. Disagreement and incompatible interests are the reason for politics in the first place, and democracy is a way of settling these differences in the most peaceful and least unsatisfactory manner.
- Society is, whether we like it or not, divided according to class, religion, region, gender, age, ethnicity, and so on. Democracy involves parties representing group interests trying to resolve their differences.
- There is not 'only one way to lay a sidewalk'. There is not and never has been anything but a variety of approaches to all public matters – who should pay for them, at what cost and standard, and why use scarce resources on sidewalks at all when the money should be spent on education or health or housing or art or public transport or …? The 'only one way' argument is used by people who believe theirs is the only 'true' way, something they usually call 'common sense'.
- We can rarely agree on who are the best people to run society and make important decisions, so we have elections. Therefore we have political parties of like-minded people to run for office.
- Parties perform vital political functions: interest articulation and interest aggregation, the communication of opinion and information between masses and elites, providing party cues and political information for those who need them in elections; the mobilisation of citizens and voters at appropriate times; the coordination of the machinery and policy of government; recruiting citizens for political office and training party activists for high positions of government; the formal organisation of a political competition for power at election time.

Not all parties are good. Some are anti-democratic. But a competitive party system stands the best chance of producing a stable democracy based on majority voting.

the issue of whether to allow them to raise more from private (business?) sources or to subsidise them with public funds. This is a highly controversial matter, much discussed when parties run into severe financial problems or find themselves in the hands of wealthy donors to their funds. In short, political parties do not solve all the many problems facing democratic systems of government, and they present quite a few of their own, but it is difficult to imagine how democracy could work without them.

■ Theories of parties

The 'iron law of oligarchy'

In *Political Parties*, published in 1911 and one of the most influential books on the subject, Robert Michels (1876–1936) argues that parties are, and always will be, run by minorities. Michels's famous 'iron law' claims that all large-scale organisations – parties, pressure groups, trade unions, churches, universities – are controlled by a few leaders, no matter how democratic they try to be. There are several reasons for this:

- Organisationally, leaders are best informed about the business of the organisation and control its internal means of communication. They are also likely to have better organisational skills (or experience) than ordinary members.
- Psychologically, the masses rely on leaders because they have neither the time nor the ability to master the affairs of the organisation, and because they feel the need for leadership 'direction and guidance'. Leaders generally have better pay and status than followers, so they try to hang on to their jobs.

Oligarchy: Government by a few.

A more recent version of Michels's theory of **oligarchy** is the electoral–professional interpretation of modern political parties discussed earlier in this chapter.

Oligarchy in organisations might not matter so much if it were not also believed that leaders inevitably betray their organisation, using their position either for their own interests – personal power, glory, or money – or following policies that are not approved by rank-and-file members. They may do the latter not because they are corrupt or untrustworthy, though this may be true in some cases, but because being leaders of their organisations who frequently come into contact with leaders of other organisations, they take a wider view of matters. They may also follow longer-term and more strategic policies.

Max Weber (1864–1920), a contemporary of Michels in Germany, argued a similar case when he said that 'for the time being the dictatorship of the official and not that of the worker is on the march' (see chapter 8). Michels and Weber argue that full-time, experienced and trained professionals will always dominate part-time, untrained and inexperienced amateurs. Although Weber applies his theory to the power struggle between bureaucrats and politicians, rather than party leaders and followers, the principles are the same.

There are two possible responses to the Michels–Weber thesis. The first argues that the law, though it may be generally true, is not 'iron' because there are examples of private organisations that are not oligarchical. The second claims that it does not particularly matter if organisations are internally oligarchic if competition between them produces democracy. Business associations and trade unions may not be particularly democratic internally, but competition between them may be. For democracy it is important that voters can choose between distinct alternatives presented to them and much less how these offers function internally and it matters much less how these organisations operate internally.

Duverger's law

The 'iron law' deals with the internal organisation of parties, while another classic 'law' of the French political scientist Maurice Duverger (1917–2014) is concerned with the relationship between electoral systems and party systems. He argued that states with non-proportional elections (specifically single-member, simple plurality systems – SMSP) favour two parties, while proportional elections favour multi-party systems. Non-proportional elections usually discriminate against small parties because they fail to turn their votes into a proportional number of seats. The electorate knows this, and is less inclined to vote for small parties because it may be a 'wasted vote'.

Many years of debate about Duverger's law have tended to concentrate on two issues:

- First, what is cause and what is effect? Belgium, Denmark, Germany and Norway were multi-party systems before they opted for PR, and they may have done so because it was in the interest of small parties to have PR, or because it was the only electoral system that was acceptable to most parties, including the small ones. On the other side of the coin, the USA and the UK seem to keep their SMSP system because it is in the interests of the two main parties. They are put into power by the SMSP system so they have no interest in changing it and are the only parties with the power to do so.
- Second, in spite of exceptions to the 'law', there is in general a good deal of truth in it. The most proportionate voting systems are more likely to be multi-party than the most disproportionate. Of seventy-three democracies in the 1990s, thirty-six had PR electoral systems and thirty-seven had non-PR systems. Of the thirty-six PR countries, 81 per cent were multi-party and the remaining 19 per cent were either dominant one-party or two-party systems. Of the thirty-seven non-PR countries, 50 per cent were either two- or dominant one-party systems, and 13 per cent were multi-party. The link between voting systems and party systems, in other words, is not an invariable 'law' but a general tendency.

However, there is some evidence that this general tendency is weakening. As voting patterns become more volatile, party identifications weaken, party membership declines, and as new and smaller parties appear on the scene to fragment party systems, so single-party governments may become less common and coalitions more so. In Europe in 2015 Austria, Belgium, Cyprus, the Czech Republic, Denmark, Estonia, Finland, France, Germany, Greece, Iceland, Ireland, Italy, Latvia, Lithuania, Luxembourg, the Netherlands, Norway, Portugal, Slovenia, Sweden, Switzerland and even the UK had coalition governments. So also did India, Israel, Japan, Australia and New Zealand.

Coalition theory

The early and influential work on coalition formation by William Riker (1920–93) predicted that coalitions would be just big enough to ensure a majority in the assembly, but no bigger or smaller. It was assumed that politicians were motivated primarily by a desire for power or prestige, in which case there was no sense in sharing cabinet posts among more parties than was strictly necessary. Consequently, coalitions would be MWCs.

It might also be assumed that politicians seek office not exclusively for power, prestige or government office, but also in order to influence public policy. Such politicians might consider a course of action that gave them influence over public policy even if it fell short of government office. Minority governments may thus be successful if there are politicians outside government who are prepared to support their policy. Similarly, surplus majority governments may be formed if they help to achieve policy goals. If it is policy, rather than office-seeking that counts, one might assume that the limits on coalition formation will be set not necessarily by coalition size but by the ideological 'closeness' of parties. If so, according to the theory proposed by Maurice Axelrod (1943–) in his book *Conflict of Interest* (1970) coalitions might be the smallest ideological span necessary to drive policy in a particular direction. Coalitions will be formed by the closest set of parties capable of forming an effective alliance.

Evidence over the post-war years in the democracies provides support for both the Riker and Axelrod theories, but there is not overwhelming support for either:

- The largest group of government coalitions are MWC, but it is also true that they are outnumbered by oversized and minority governments together.
- It is also the case that nearly a half of all coalitions are MWC, but this means that half are not.
- In short, most situations that could result in MWCs have not produced them, although, of all kinds of coalition, the MWC are most numerous.

Giovanni Sartori (1924–) argues that both the number and the ideological distance between parties are important for understanding how multi-party systems work and how governments are formed. He distinguishes between moderate and polarised pluralism. The moderate type usually has three to five main parties, which tend to compete for the centre ground, and therefore tend to be moderate. Polarised systems normally have six or more main parties, which tend to move to the extremes in order to find votes in an overcrowded political arena. This makes it difficult to form and sustain coalition cabinets.

Perhaps the only safe conclusion to draw from this discussion of coalition theory is that politicians are not exclusively self-interested (office-seeking), and that they may opt for either surplus majority or minority governments, if this helps them achieve other goals. Alternatively, they may opt to work outside the government if the system allows them to influence policy in this way. This is consistent with the conclusion that voters are not always self-interested, but pay some regard to the public interest. It does not follow that politicians are only interested in power and office, nor that they are only interested in the public good, but it does seem to be the case that they can and do pursue both kinds of goals at different times according to circumstances.

Majoritarian and consensus government revisited

At the end of chapter 7 we presented Arend Lijphart's account of majoritarian and consensus government, but did not complete the discussion, having covered only the formal institutions of government at that point. We can now deal with the rest of the majoritarian–consensus typology, having also discussed its other characteristics in chapters 9–12 dealing with electoral systems, party systems, government formation and pressure groups.

Majoritarian governments tend to concentrate power in the hands of the political executive and are associated with the fusion of executive and legislative powers, a unicameral legislature (or a weak second chamber), unitary government, and courts with no special powers to review constitutional matters or legislation. In the classic 'Westminster system', built around the principle of parliamentary sovereignty, these features of government fit together in a logical and consistent manner, given the initial purpose of concentrating a good deal of political power in the hands of the party that wins most seats in parliament.

We can now add four more key features of majoritarian democracies that concern electoral systems, party systems, governments and pressure groups that also fit the logic of majoritarian government.

1. *Majoritarian and disproportional electoral systems* Majoritarian democracies tend to favour single-member districts and first-past-the post voting systems. This favours large over small parties and magnifies the size of the winning party's majority of seats compared with its votes.
2. *Two-party systems* The winner-takes-all nature of parliamentary systems, as well as their electoral discrimination against small parties, encourages the formation of two large parties that alternate in government.
3. *Single-party government* The winning party with a majority of seats becomes the government. All other parties form the opposition.
4. *Pluralist pressure group systems* Pressure groups in society are loosely integrated in the decision-making structure of government, sometimes forming policy communities but more usually taking the form of competitive policy networks.

Consensus democracies, in contrast, try to represent not the electoral majority and its party but as many people as possible, including minorities. They therefore try to distribute executive power more broadly and are associated with the separation and balancing of executive power, bicameralism, federalism, independent central banks and judicial review. They are also characterised by four further features of the electoral system, party system, government and pressure group system that distinguish them from majoritarian systems, namely:

1. *Proportional electoral systems* These systems distribute seats in more or less the same ratio as votes.
2. *Multi-party systems* Multi-party government and proportional electoral systems are less likely to discourage small parties than first-past-the-post elections.
3. *Coalition governments* The formation of broad coalition governments can involve sometimes oversized or 'grand' coalitions.
4. *Corporatist pressure group systems* Major pressure groups are formally incorporated into the decision-making machinery of government, where they cooperate on policy issues.

This typology of majoritarian and consensus government not only describes the political systems of democracies, but also helps to explain their performance in five important respects:

1. *The distance between governments and voters* Consensus democracies have governments that are closer to the policy preferences of citizens than majoritarian systems.
2. *Citizens' satisfaction* The citizens of consensus democracies are more satisfied with the democratic performance of their countries than those of majoritarian democracies. In part, this is because the losers in consensus systems are more satisfied than the losers in majoritarian systems, because they acknowledge that the electoral system is fairer and they have not been discriminated against and because, even as electoral minorities, they can still have influence over government policies if their party is part of the governing coalition.
3. *Election turnout* Consensus democracies have a higher voting turnout (by about 7.5 per cent) than majoritarian ones.
4. *Women in parliament* Consensus democracies have about 6.5 per cent more women in the main legislative chamber.
5. *Effective number of parties* Consensus democracies not only have a larger number of parties contesting elections but, because of their proportional voting systems, they also have a larger number of effective parties – that is, parties that are large enough to play a significant role in the assembly.

On the basis of this evidence, Lijphart concludes that the majoritarian and consensus systems have extremely important practical implications for the performance of democracies. The performance of consensus democracies is superior.

It should be noted that although some democratic systems of government may conform in general to one of the two types, many countries do not conform in all particulars. As chapter 7 has already pointed out, the USA, Switzerland and Canada are mixtures of both. Moreover, one of the few examples of pure majoritarian democracy disappeared when New Zealand radically changed its constitution in 1986. Even the 'Westminster' model in the UK became a diminished form of majoritarianism when parliamentary sovereignty was relinquished on joining the EU, the Bank of England was made independent of government and the two-party system became a two plus two or more minor parties system.

What have we learned?

Politics is about the struggle for power, and this chapter deals with how parties are at the very centre of this struggle in their attempts to win elections and gain government office. It argues that:

- Parties have passed through three main phases of organisation – caucus, mass parties and catch-all parties. Now they are said to be moving into a new phase of media parties, or cartel parties, or electoral–professional parties, which have strong leaders and few members.
- Just as old patterns of voting have tended to persist, albeit with some changes, so the old parties, formed in the late nineteenth and early twentieth centuries, have persisted, albeit with changes induced by new parties and movements. The result is continuity of historical patterns with change, in which the new has combined and fused with the old, rather than a transformation of party systems.
- Democracies have one-party, two-party or coalition government, but coalitions are most common.
- Contrary to early theories, most coalition governments do not take the minimum winning coalition (MWC) form. Minority governments, surplus majority governments and (occasionally) 'grand' coalitions are more common.

Lessons of comparison

- There is not much evidence to support the claim that coalition government is unstable, unaccountable or unrepresentative compared with single-party governments.
- In the past, non-proportional elections (notably single-member, simple plurality elections) have generally been associated with two-party systems, and proportional elections have been associated with multi-party systems, although there have been some notable exceptions to this 'law'. In recent times, however, the unfreezing of the party systems, changes in the economy and class structure, and electoral volatility have resulted in a greater number of effective parties and a tendency towards coalition government.

- The evidence suggests that politicians are not exclusively interested in prestige or the power that goes with government office (office-seeking). They may support surplus majority or minority governments, and they may choose to work outside government if this helps them influence government policy.
- The evidence suggests that the democratic performance of consensus democracies is superior to that of majoritarian systems.

Projects

1. Collect a list of all the main political parties in your country and try to sort them into the seven main categories discussed in this chapter. What difficulties do you meet in trying to classify your parties, and why do you think your country produces parties that do not fit the scheme?
2. Are you persuaded that the democratic performance of consensus democracies is superior to that of majoritarian systems?
3. Are parties good or bad for democracy?
4. Does the literature on coalition formation in government suggest that political leaders are mainly interested in their own power and office or in the public good and national interest?

Further reading

C. Boix and S. C. Stokes, *The Oxford Handbook of Comparative Politics*. Oxford University Press, 2007. Contains excellent overviews of research on parties, party systems, parties and voters, interest aggregation and articulation and coalition formation,

E. Haute and A. Gauja (eds.), *Party Members and Activists*. London: Routledge, 2015. A set of comparative essays on party members and activists in Europe and Canada.

A. Ware, *Political Parties and Party Systems*. Oxford University Press, 1995. An introduction to parties and party systems in liberal democracy, focusing especially on the UK, Germany, France, the USA and Japan.

P. Webb and S. White (eds.), *Party Politics in New Democracies*. Oxford University Press, 2007. Examines the development and performance of parties in the new democracies of Latin America and central Europe.

Websites

www.gksoft.com/govt/en/parties.html.
Provides links to political parties in the nations of the world.
www.nationmaster.com/country-info/stats/Government/Political-parties-and-leaders.
Names of parties and leaders in countries of the world.

www.nationsencyclopedia.com/.
Details of the history and present composition of the party system of the
   world.
www.britannica.com/EBchecked/topic/467631/political-party.
A comprehensive account of the origin of parties, party systems, and their
   future.
www.idea.int/parties/.
The Institute for democracy and Electoral Assistance (IDEA) website with
   links to publications on parties, how they are financed and organised and
   how they relate to direct democracy.
www.politicalresources.net/.
Website with links to all the parties of the world, by country.

PART IV

Policies and performance

Most people are not interested in political institutions and processes. What interests them about politics is what governments do to them and for them. How much tax do they pay? What sorts of public services do they get? How well does the government handle financial crises? Do children get a good education? Is the nation protected against its enemies? Part IV of the book is about the policies and performance of governments. A 'policy' is a general set of ideas formulated into a plan that has been officially agreed, and which is used as a basis for making decisions. Although ideas and plans are important, most people care about performance. By 'performance' we mean the results governments get – is inflation low and economic growth good? Is crime under control? Are schools well staffed and equipped? Is hospital care effective? Plans are no good if they do not achieve their goals, and performance is no good if it is based on muddled or dangerous plans in the first place. Citizens want good plans and good performance together, but they care most about performance.

Part IV of the book has chapters on both the policies and performance of democratic states. Since plans and policies are what parties and governments start with, chapter 14 examines the 'isms' of politics – competing ideas about what governments should do, and how they should do it. These are known as 'ideologies'. There are a great many of these, but the four main ones in Western politics are socialism, liberalism, Christian democracy and conservatism. Each is built on different basic values, assumptions and concepts such as individualism and collectivism, liberalism and the role of the state, equality and freedom. Different attitudes towards these basic concepts and values are what define the 'isms' of politics and the fundamental difference between parties.

Chapter 15 then focuses not on the theory but on the practice of making government decisions and implementing them. This can be seen as an endless cycle, starting with a general plan of action and ending with an evaluation of the results achieved by implementing it. We will see that for all the variation in the details of their policy-making processes, states tend to follow one of two general logics. Some incorporate their main social and economic interests into a formal structure of cooperative decision making. Others lean towards conflict and competition between different groups.

Chapter 16 deals with the ways states have dealt with costs of public policies and especially how governments provide its citizens with social security. Of course, government is involved with a far wider range of public services than taxes, subsidies, regulation, social security and welfare. In this chapter we have chosen to cover the broad area of state finances, budgeting and social security because they are among the oldest and most important functions of the state. Chapter 17 draws some brief conclusions about the future of the democratic state.

The chapters in part IV, therefore, examine the key aspects of government policies and performance:

- Political ideologies
- Decision making
- State intervention.

14 Political ideologies: conservatism, liberalism, Christian democracy and socialism

Politics is confusing. A casual look at the daily news shows a profusion of fast-moving events, with many conflicting and incompatible interpretations of them. How can we ever make sense of such a bewildering business? The answer lies partly in our ideas, preconceptions and assumptions about politics. This mental framework of ideas, known as an ideology, helps us to understand and interpret politics and to make judgements about them.

Some analysts reserve the term '**ideology**' to a highly abstract, internally logical, and comprehensive set of values, beliefs and ideas. In this case, relatively few individuals have an ideology, mainly those with a strong commitment to one particular approach to politics. Such people are called '**ideologues**' (see chapter 9). Other analysts use the term more generally to cover more loose-knit, but still relatively coherent systems of ideas and values. If it is used in this way,

Ideology: A more or less systematic, well-developed and comprehensive set of ideas and beliefs about politics consisting of both (empirical) statements about what is, and (prescriptive) statements about what ought to be.

Ideologues: Those with an informed, broad, sophisticated and more or less consistent (systematic) view of the political world.

many citizens have an ideology. In this chapter we use the term in its more restricted sense to refer to a more or less conscious and interconnected set of ideas and theories about politics.

Ideologies are about more than understanding, however. If politics is a struggle for power, then ideologies are part of that struggle. Politicians in democracies know that they must win the tacit support, if not the 'hearts and minds', of most of their citizens if they are to continue in power. Ideologies are the tools – perhaps one of the most important tools – by which they do this because ideologies are built around the basic interests of the most important groups in society.

Because people have contrasting interests and ideas and live in different circumstances, they see politics in radically different ways. Consequently they have different ideological world views. These include liberalism, neo-liberalism, libertarianism, conservatism, anarchism, Marxism, Maoism, socialism, democratic socialism, Christian democracy, jihadism, fascism, Nazism and libertarianism, among others. Fortunately, there are only four main ideologies to be found in democracies, which helps to simplify the life of comparative political scientists to a great extent. These are conservatism, liberalism, Christian democracy and socialism/social democracy. There are also three other systems of thought – nationalism, Green political thought and populism – but their status as ideologies is disputed, so we will discuss them after the main four.

In this chapter, we present an account of the main party ideologies in democracies. The chapter analyses the nature of ideology itself and discusses the future for ideological thinking in a world where ideology is said by some to have come to an end. The main topics in this chapter, therefore, are:

- The nature of ideology
- Four main democratic ideologies
- Three other types of political thought
- Theories of ideology
- The end of ideology and of history.

■ The nature of ideology

Ideology is a confusing concept that has been given different meanings in its history, but for the social scientist it has four main characteristics:

1. *Complexity and abstraction* Ideologies are relatively complex, abstract, comprehensive and integrated systems of beliefs about politics. They are based on fundamental ideas and assumptions about human nature, society and politics, and on a set of basic values relating to the central concepts of political life including justice, liberty, equality, freedom and democracy. Ideologies are, therefore, far more than a loose bundle of beliefs about politics; they offer a systematic and well-articulated view of the political world and a consistent and general interpretation of it. This means that

an ideology must be specific enough to fit particular circumstances, but abstract enough to be able to endure and travel widely across the globe.

2. *Empirical explanation* Ideologies claim to explain the political world. They pick out what they think is important from the mass of political details and events and offer explanations of what is happening and why. This does not mean that they are right or wrong, only that they try to explain the facts of the political world as they see them.

3. *Normative prescription* Ideologies offer a vision of how political life could be and ought to be. They present a vision of good government. In this sense ideologies are **normative statements** and prescriptive. They are therefore subjective statements that are neither scientific nor unscientific but non-scientific.

> **Normative statements:** Statements based on faith, values or evaluations. Sometimes referred to as prescriptive or evaluative statements, they are neither scientific nor unscientific, but non-scientific.

4. *A plan for action* Ideologies spell out a set of beliefs about how political goals should be achieved. They claim to answer Lenin's (1870–1924) question: 'What is to be done?' Since there is often agreement in democracies about political goals – who is against liberty, justice, democracy and progress for all? – ideological differences are commonly about political means, rather than goals. Should we form political alliances with this or that group, or remain 'pure' and separate? Should we support this policy or a slightly different one? Should we vote for this democratic party or another?

Some writers are suspicious of ideologies, claiming that they are closed systems of thought that are not amenable to reason or disproof by empirical evidence. In the hands of ideologues who use their ideology in this way, any argument and evidence against their beliefs is explained away or even turned around to confirm what they believe. According to Karl Popper (1902–94), ideologies are to be distinguished clearly from scientific theories that can, in principle, be tested and falsified against evidence. In his book *The Open Society and Its Enemies*, Popper argues that some ideologies (not all, by any means) can be turned into closed and totalitarian systems of thought that can always justify themselves on their own terms. Those with a dogmatic and rigid way of thinking may manipulate their ideology to explain anything and to fit the facts whatever these may be, even those things that seem to contradict the ideology. However, ideologies do not necessarily turn into closed and totalitarian belief systems. John Stuart Mill (see below) proposed an open and self-critical set of liberal political beliefs and lived up to these standards in his own life.

Ideologies are not the same as political cultures. Ideologies are more or less explicit, whereas much of political culture is implicit and built on assumptions and deep-seated values that are taken for granted (see chapter 9). The language of ideologies consists of abstract concepts – liberty, equality, fraternity, rights, justice and freedom, for example. Political cultures are built on assumptions about trust, happiness, national pride and political competence. To oversimplify, individuals are socialised into a culture in the family, at school and in the community, but they learn an ideology by thinking, arguing and reading in a more self-conscious way.

Before we start our exploration of the main democratic ideologies, two last general points should be made:

Essentially contestable concept: A concept that is inevitably the subject of endless dispute about its proper use (e.g. art, democracy, justice, beauty, goodness).

1. Ideologies are **essentially contestable concepts**, which is a shorthand way of saying that there is often little agreement about what they mean. This is why even members of the same political party sharing the same ideology will often argue interminably with each other.

2. Closely related to this point is the fact that each major ideology has many variations within itself, and each different ideology has points in common with rival ideologies. It is difficult to draw a clear line around any ideology, or its variants, and difficult to summarise them in a clear and simple way.

■ Four democratic ideologies

In chapter 13, we organised party families along a left–right continuum according to their general views about the central issue of state intervention in society and the economy. We can do the same with ideologies, from conservatism on the right to liberalism and Christian democracy in the centre and socialism and social democracy on the left. The three other schemes of thought (nationalism, Green political thought and populism) do not fit neatly on the left–right continuum, and so they will be discussed separately.

Conservatism

Because conservatism is pragmatic and flexible, some argue that it is not an ideology so much as a loose collection of ideas defending the status quo. However, conservative thought can be based on a systematic set of fundamental ideas. Two are particularly important. The first concerns social and political life, the second economic matters.

Social and political affairs

• *Organic society* Conservatism places great value on the preservation of the status quo and its traditional institutions. It is a pragmatic ideology that argues that old institutions survive and work well because they are the accumulated wisdom and experience of the past. Society is like a natural organism that has changed slowly but surely over a long period. Moreover, it is composed of a complex set of interdependent parts, and reform that moves too fast will almost certainly destabilise the system and do more harm than good. Reform should be piecemeal, slow and cautious.

- *Pessimistic view of human nature* Conservatives tend to be pessimistic about human nature, arguing that dissatisfaction, selfishness and irrationality, perhaps civil disturbance, are possible if there is no clear social hierarchy to locate citizens in the social order and a strong state to maintain it. Consequently, conservatism generally rejects the ideas about the natural goodness or 'perfectibility of man'. Instead it argues for a strong police and legal system to maintain the social order, and a strong army to protect the state from its enemies.

- *Representative democracy* Conservatives tend to believe that democracy is best preserved in the hands of a relatively small and well educated elite. The masses are not naturally democratic and it is dangerous to give them too much power. Hence conservatives often prefer indirect and representative democracy to direct, participatory forms.

- *Inequality* Conservatives tend to believe that people are inherently unequal in their intelligence and abilities, and that some economic and social inequality is natural and inevitable. Some conservative thought goes on to emphasise the social responsibilities of the rich and powerful for the poor and weak. Since this style of conservatism fits well with a religious emphasis on the importance of the family and traditional social values, it is often aligned with traditional Christian beliefs. Other conservatives, however, do not emphasise the importance of social conscience but argue, instead, that wealth produced by a small minority of energetic and able entrepreneurs will 'trickle down' to the poor.

Economics

- *The invisible hand of the market* The second fundamental tenet of conservatism is a belief in the market, and the claim that economic competition will result in efficiency and the achievement of the public interest. The 'invisible hand of the market' (see briefing 14.1) means that the best way of optimising the general interest is to allow each individual to act in her own economic interests. Economic competition will force businesses to produce the best goods and services at the lowest price in order to keep their customers happy. If they do not, then customers will shop around for a better deal. Market competition and individual self-interest will thus, paradoxically, result in efficiency, innovation and the public good. Attempts to improve or modify the workings of the market will result only in inefficiency and poor performance. Therefore a main plank of conservatism is the belief that the state should intervene as little as possible in the economy, although the left and right wings of conservative thought argue about how much or how little this should be.

Liberalism

Liberalism is an ambiguous term. In classical political theory its essence is the belief that individual liberty is the highest political value and can be preserved only by limiting the powers of the state. In modern politics, especially

Briefing 14.1

Conservative thinkers

■ Edmund Burke (1729–97)

An Irish philosopher and MP, he formulated many of the social and political principles of modern conservatism. He argued that society was like a complex organism that was easily ruined by attempts to reform it too quickly, and pointed to the disastrous experience of the French Revolution to support his claim. He believed in a 'natural aristocracy' in society, and that the mass of ordinary people could sustain a democracy only with the guidance of a political elite. Above all, he claimed that practical experience and wisdom are always to be preferred to abstract rationalism.

■ Adam Smith (1723–90)

The Scottish philosopher and economist Adam Smith laid the foundations of classical economics in his book *The Wealth of Nations* (1776). He claimed that individual self-interest on the part of 'the butcher, brewer, and baker' led, by way of the 'invisible hand' of the market, to the satisfaction of the general good. The butcher and the baker do not provide a good service because of their concern for others, but because the workings of the market economy make it in their own interest to do so. The state should leave this invisible hand to play its part by setting up the right conditions for laissez-faire economics and a free market.

■ Joseph Schumpeter (1883–1950)

An Austrian economist and political scientist, Schumpeter is best remembered for his book *Capitalism, Socialism and Democracy* (1942), in which, contrary to Marxist theory and other theories that place faith in the 'will of the people', he claims that the masses are capable of little, other than stampeding. Democracy should be limited to elites and representative forms of government in which the masses have the power only to vote at regular intervals for representatives who compete for popular support.

■ Friedrich von Hayek (1899–1992)

Another Austrian economist, von Hayek is best known for his book *The Road to Serfdom* (1944), which argues that state regulation and collective action of all kinds tends to limit the freedom of the individual, even if it is moderate and well intended.

in the USA, a 'liberal' is, on the contrary, someone who believes in more rather than less state intervention. This is because the term 'socialist' is not politically acceptable in the USA, so those who advocate even modest government action refer to themselves as 'liberals' to distinguish themselves from conservatives. In what follows the terms 'liberal' and 'liberalism' are used in their classical sense.

Early liberalism emerged in the seventeenth century in opposition to traditional government by kings, aristocracies and elites. Liberals rejected government by monarchs and aristocrats, emphasising instead the importance of individual freedom (see briefing 14.2). This idea continues to lie at the heart of modern liberalism and distinguishes it fundamentally from conservative ideas. It has five main characteristics.

Limited state power

Classical liberalism was built around the principle that the state should be limited to the 'nightwatchman' function of protecting individual rights and property, and should not pretend to any other function. The modern version of this belief claims that 'government is best that governs least'.

Parliamentary government and the division of powers

Because of their concern with individual rights and duties liberals have traditionally placed great importance on parliament, and on the checks and

---

Briefing 14.2

Two concepts of liberty

Freedom (or liberty – the two terms are used interchangeably here) may be defined as the absence of restraint. According to this simple definition, we are free when we are not prevented from doing what we wish. In political matters, however, this definition does not get us very far. I may be free under the law to set up my own political party or pressure group, or free to start my own newspaper, but these formal freedoms are no good to me if I am living in poverty, hunger, fear, disease and ignorance. Formal freedom under the law, and substantive freedom – freedoms that people can actually use – are quite different.

Along these lines, Isaiah Berlin (1909–97) distinguished between two concepts of liberty, 'liberty from' and 'liberty to'. Liberty from, or negative liberty, is the absence of restraint. Those who believe in it will argue for a minimal state as a matter of principle. Liberty to, or positive liberty, is concerned with the actual capacity to do things. For example, to play their role as citizens people need to be educated and informed enough to make sensible judgements about political issues. Since the economic market typically makes a good education available only to the small number whose parents are able and willing to pay for it, the state must provide free public education for all. The implication of the positive notion of freedom is that the state must ensure that citizens are able to make use of their formal freedoms. This means that the state must tax to provide education for all, which means restricting the liberty of people to control their own money.

The two main schools of liberal political thought take different views of liberty. Classical liberals, neo-liberals and libertarians favour freedom from state regulation to maximise individual freedom. Radical or progressive liberals and liberal democrats argue for enough state regulation to overcome the main social and economic obstacles to substantive freedom. According to them the state can intervene as a liberator, not as an oppressor.

balances of divided government that protect citizens from arbitrary power. But though early liberals believed in parliamentary government, they did not necessarily believe in democracy, because they feared that giving power to the mass of uneducated and unsophisticated citizens would threaten democratic practice and values. They feared that the 'tyranny of the majority' would replace the tyranny of monarchs and aristocracies. In the twentieth century, however, liberals came to accept mass democracy, hence the term '**liberal democracy**'.

> **Liberal democracy:** The form of democracy that tries to combine the powers of democratic government with liberal values about the freedom of the individual.

Optimistic view of human nature

Unlike conservatism, liberalism takes an optimistic view of human nature, assuming that mankind is rational and reasonable when left to its own devices. Liberals also assume that individuals should be formally equal before the law – not that they are equal in capacities, abilities or intelligence but that they have equal rights and duties.

Slow reform by individual action

Because classical liberalism assumes that most citizens are rational and responsible, they also tend to argue for slow reform brought about by the individual action of free people, rather than the radical collective action favoured by socialists or conservative reaction.

Free trade

Like one school of conservative theory, classical liberalism believes strongly in laissez-faire economics and free trade. Its defence of market economics is logically consistent with its strong belief in a limited state, and of the rights of individuals to make their own economic decisions.

As liberal thought developed in the eighteenth and nineteenth centuries, it divided into two schools. One continued to hold to the classical position of individual rights and a minimal state, especially in economic matters, but a second took the view that some freedoms require a degree of state action to eliminate the obstacles to real or substantive freedom (see briefing 14.2). According to this view, the state should intervene to create the conditions necessary for individuals to develop their full potential. For example, early social liberals argued for the state to raise taxes to pay for education, public health and housing for the poor, on the grounds that poverty, disease and ignorance were incompatible with human freedom.

The ideas of classical liberalism were revived in the late twentieth century by neo-liberals who believe that the powers of the state should be drastically reduced and the economy deregulated and privatised. At the same time, the state should be strong enough to protect itself from all internal and external enemies, which requires a strong army and firm rule of law at home. Neo-liberalism of this kind exercised a strong influence over some conservative politicians, notably Margaret Thatcher in Britain and Ronald Reagan and

George W. Bush in the USA. Many other countries, as diverse as Bolivia, Chile, India, Mexico, New Zealand, South Korea and Taiwan have implemented varying degrees of neo-liberal economic policies.

Some ideologists take neo-liberal ideas even further. Known as libertarians, they argue for the abolition of almost all state regulation, even of such things as pornography, drugs and prostitution, on the grounds that all regulation infringes liberty, and that responsible adult citizens should be free to make up their own minds about such matters (briefing 14.3).

Briefing 14.3

Liberal thinkers

■ John Locke (1632–1704)

Locke wrote that natural law guarantees to every individual the right to 'life, liberty, and estate' (private property). Citizens enter into a 'social contract' with their government to protect themselves against those who would try to infringe their rights. The proper role of government is limited to upholding natural rights. It has no other function.

■ John Stuart Mill (1806–73)

J. S. Mill drew a distinction between self-regarding and other-regarding actions. Self-regarding actions have no impact on others, and should not be subject to any restraint by government or any other power. According to Mill 'the only purpose for which power can be rightfully exercised over any member of a civilised community, against his will, is to prevent harm to others. His own good, either physical or moral, is not a sufficient warrant.' Other-regarding actions that have an effect on others are a different matter and may be constrained by the force of the law. Some argue that since there are few purely self-regarding actions, many of them trivial, Mill's distinction allows for many forms of state intervention that restrain the freedom of some individuals to act as they wish. Consequently, Mill's ideas can be interpreted as clearing a way towards socialism.

■ John Rawls (1921–2002)

John Rawls is among the most influential liberal thinkers of the last decades. In *A Theory of Justice* (1971), he introduced the idea of 'justice as fairness' and strongly defended the idea that equality and liberty should be closely related. In his view the unequal treatment of individuals is acceptable only if it improves the situation of those who are in the worst social position. He is not, however, willing to accept limitations on basic liberties: each person is to have an equal right to the most extensive liberties, a principle that precedes all others. Even so, libertarian philosophers such as Robert Nozick (1938–2002) have criticised Rawls for his willingness to consider restrictions on individual freedom. Nozick strongly defended the idea of a 'minimal state'.

Christian democracy

Pope Leo XIII (1810–1903) laid out the basics of Christian democracy in the encyclical *Rerum Novarum* (1891). This was partly in reaction to classical liberalism which tended to be secular or anti-clerical, and to anti-religious socialism. But it was also an attempt to incorporate Catholic thought into a practical ideology. Christian democracy is neither liberal, nor socialist, nor conservative, but somewhere in between. It has five main characteristics.

Natural law

Christian democracy starts from the premise that natural law is the basis of society and its rules of conduct. Natural law is not given by the state (kings, courts or parliaments), but by God and is revealed to human beings by their capacity to reason.

Family, church, community

Christian democracy rejects the conservatism of traditional social orders, the atomistic individualism of classical liberalism and the 'tyranny of the masses' advocated by the political left. In place of these, it stresses the importance of 'natural' groups in society, above all, the family, the church and the community.

Subsidiarity

Natural groups should be allowed to run their own affairs in their own way, which means subsidiarity (chapter 6). Christian democrats assert the importance of the autonomy of 'natural groups' in society to run their own affairs, without interference or regulation by the state. Private and semi-private agencies are morally superior to public ones, because they give individuals the opportunity to exercise their Christian conscience. They are also more effective in meeting human needs. The state should, therefore, intervene only when it has to, and only in order to restore the natural community to its proper functioning. In this way, it argues, solidarity and harmony in society will be preserved.

Protection of the weak and poor

Christian morality requires that the state protects the weakest and poorest members of society. In turn, this means a moderate welfare state with special support for the family (family allowances), education (financial support for schools, many of them church schools) and the community (to alleviate poverty and protect people against illness and unemployment).

Harmony, integration, consultation

Christian democracy emphasises social harmony and integration. This means the reconciliation of class, religious and other differences by means of formal social institutions that enable social groups to consult and discuss with one another, something known as the 'concertation of interests'. This involves an elaborate consultative machinery in which government, business, trade unions and other interests participate.

Christian democracy is a middle way between conservatism and unbridled capitalism, secular liberal individualism and atheistic socialism. It is neither for nor against state intervention in principle, but argues for enough of it to protect human dignity in accordance with natural law. Some forms of it are close to socialism, others to conservatism.

Socialism and social democracy

It is important, first of all, to distinguish between the communism found in China and the former Soviet Union, and the socialism and social democracy found in the democratic world. Communist countries have undemocratic regimes controlled by Communist parties, and their dominant ideologies are better known as 'Marxism' or 'communism'. Socialist and social-democratic ideologies are strong in democracies. To distinguish themselves clearly from Marxism and communism, some socialist parties prefer to call themselves social democratic (see briefing 14.4). Social democracy has five distinguishing features.

Optimistic view of human nature
Human nature is naturally reasonable, rational and sociable. It is capitalism and its allies (religion, capitalist education, capitalist media) that makes people greedy and ignorant.

Equality of opportunity
Inequalities between individuals are a product of their social environment rather than their inborn talents. The function of the state is therefore to eliminate inequalities of opportunity and release natural abilities.

Participatory democracy
Democracy is built on the free and equal participation of all, and on participatory rather than representative democracy.

Mixed economy
At the heart of socialist ideologies is the belief that some of the most important parts of the economy should be owned or regulated by the state in order to eliminate the worst forms of inequality, exploitation and social injustice. Capitalism produces unacceptable and inefficient inequalities of wealth and opportunity, and market failure means that capitalism is unable even to support itself as an efficient form of production. Economic inequality means injustice, poverty and economic inefficiency. Market failure is a capitalist inevitability and it means periods of economic depression, monopolies and oligopolies, and underinvestment in collective goods, including health, housing, education, welfare, research and communications.

Briefing 14.4

Socialist thinkers

■ Karl Marx (1818–83)

Karl Marx and his collaborator Friedrich Engels (1820–95) had an immense impact on Western politics, and discussions, amendments and attacks on his work form a whole library of books in themselves. Marx argued that capitalism would inevitably produce an extremely polarised society consisting of a few immensely rich and powerful capitalists, on the one hand, and a mass of poor wage-slaves, on the other. The result was that the workers, encouraged by their overwhelming weight of numbers, and with 'nothing to lose but their chains', would organise themselves, rise up in revolution to capture power and overthrow the capitalist state and economic system. In power they would set up a socialist state in which the means of production would be collectively owned, allowing wealth to be equally distributed. The state would then wither away and a stateless communist society would replace it. The Russian Revolution of 1917 was initially driven by Marxist principles, but these did not last long, and the communist systems of the Soviet Union and its central and eastern European dependencies soon ceased to be Marxist. Outside the Soviet Union and its dependencies in eastern Europe, Marx's main impact has been through socialist and social democratic movements, and the revisionist thinkers who guided them.

■ Karl Kautsky (1854–1938) and Eduard Bernstein (1850–1930)

Both leading members of the German Social Democratic Party (SPD), Kautsky and Bernstein were influential revisionist leaders who argued for evolutionary rather than revolutionary socialism, on the grounds that the working-class movement could and should gain power through peaceful, parliamentary means.

■ John Maynard (Lord) Keynes (1883–1946)

The English economist John Maynard Keynes was perhaps the biggest influence on social democratic economic thinking after Marx. He argued, against the conventional wisdom of the time, that governments should reduce taxes and public expenditure in times of economic recession in order to balance their budgets. Keynesian policies of economic demand management appealed to many governments because they offered a way of controlling the business cycle of 'boom and bust' without centralised socialist planning and without total state control of the economy. Keynesian theory was the economic orthodoxy in many Western states from 1945 until the 1970s. It was replaced by neo-liberal, free-market ideologies at least until the economic crisis and collapse of 2008, when variants of Keynesian thought reappeared.

Socialism, however, differs from communism in that it rejects total state control (the command economy) in favour of a mixture of public, private and joint enterprise (the **mixed economy**).

> **Mixed economy:** An economy that is neither wholly privately owned (a capitalist market economy), nor wholly publicly owned (a communist command economy), but a mixture of both.

Peaceful reform

By gaining power through the ballot box, socialist and social democratic governments can change the capitalist system to produce a more just mixed economy.

Socialism, like most other 'isms', takes many forms. Most are to be distinguished not by their political goals, for most socialists agree on the aim of achieving justice, liberty and equality of opportunity – as do most democratic politicians. Socialists argue mainly about how best to achieve these sorts of goal: the far left argues for revolution, the moderate left for evolution. Moderate and evolutionary forms of democratic socialism have had most influence in democratic states, where socialist parties have been elected to power, sometimes with the support of sections of the middle class, and centre and centre-right parties.

■ Three other schools of thought

Three other ways of thinking about democratic politics are looser and less specific than the four discussed above – nationalism, Green political thought and populism. Some writers reject their claim to be ideologies, but they do have things in common with ideologies.

Nationalism

Nationalism has been an extraordinarily potent force in politics. Its enduring strength can be seen in the fact that the French Revolution of 1789 set off a train of nationalist movements in the name of freedom. The twentieth century was also the age of nationalism because even more states were born then (see chapter 1). Yet it is hard to capture the ideas of nationalist ideologies in a few paragraphs because they vary greatly from one place to another and have been advocated by communists and conservatives, fascists and democrats, imperialists and anti-imperialists alike. Because nations differ tremendously, so also do nationalist ideologies. For this reason, some analysts reject the idea that nationalism is an ideology, claiming that it is an empty bottle into which can be poured any doctrine. At the same time, nationalist thought has features in common with ideologies based on the three main features of modern states: territory, people and sovereignty.

Ethno-nationalism and territory

All nationalist ideologies believe that a common national identity is more important than any differences of class, race or religion that might exist within the area. Usually, this common identity is formed by the ethnic, linguistic, religious, cultural or historical characteristics that distinguish the population of a given territory. Nationalism, territory and ethnicity are thus often linked under the concept of ethno-nationalism – in Belgium, Canada, Northern Ireland and Spain, among many other countries.

National independence

Nationalists believe that common identity should be turned by separatist movements campaigning for national self-determination. Sometimes this takes the form of full-blooded independence and sovereignty, sometimes the devolution of power from the centre. In this sense, there is a difference between political nationalism demanding full independence and sovereignty, and cultural nationalism that is satisfied with greater autonomy for a region within a state to preserve its own language, run its own television stations and teach its own history and culture. Nationalism was given great impetus by the dissolution of empires after 1918 and 1945, and then by the collapse of the Soviet empire in 1989, events caused, in part, by the strength of nationalist movements in the first place. Having gained independence, the new nations then added to the nationalist culture of the world with their own flags, national anthems, leaders, full UN membership, national airlines and football teams. Nationalism does not manifest itself only in the new states of the world, however. On the contrary, it is so much a part of everyday politics in 'old' states that it is often taken for granted. Nationalism is all around us, not just when our country happens to be playing in the World Cup or participating in the Olympics. Most people simply presume that the territory of the globe should be divided between states and that the borders of our own state are natural and inevitable. As a result much nationalist ideology is taken for granted. A much more visible form of nationalism followed the increase of migration in many countries in the last decades. By stressing the specific character of their own society, nationalist parties, such as the Front National in France or the Party for Freedom in the Netherlands, combine a nationalist programme with clear anti-immigration stands and especially a rejection of the Islamist activities in their countries. In a similar way the Republican Party in the USA opposes the legalisation of Mexican immigrants in their country.

In spite of the recent clear revival of nationalism in many countries some people claim that the long era of nationalism is coming to an end. Their theory is that modern society will bury the state and nationalism in the 'borderless world' of the 'global village'. The nation-state is bound to become less and less relevant the more McDonalds and global television expand, the larger transnational corporations (TNCs) become, the more powerful transnational authorities grow (the UN, IMF), the greater the penetration of Hollywood films and the Internet, and the more urgent the need to solve problems of natural disaster, terrorism and global warming. The argument may be plausible but, as we have seen in chapter 2, nation-states are still powerful and still popular, and their number is still growing. Nationalism seems to have a lot of life in it yet.

Green political thought

Green political thought, also known as the environmental or the ecological movement, emerged as a political force in the late 1960s as part of what has been termed the 'post-materialist' ethos. As we saw in chapters 9 and 12, this stresses the importance of the quality of life, self-fulfilment and the protection of the environment, rather than money, obedience and material possessions. Greens often stress their opposition to all the 'isms' of conventional politics, and argue that they are trying to create entirely new kinds of political organisation with entirely new political aims.

There are many forms of green political thought, including green socialism, green Marxism, green anarchism, green feminism, green libertarianism and even green capitalism, which favours the use of state power and financial inducements to push production and consumption in a 'green' direction. The environmental movement includes those who want to use the traditional means of influencing government policy, and radicals who advocate direct and revolutionary action. There is a tendency for Green parties and movements to fragment into smaller splinter groups because of disagreements about means and ends. Like nationalism, some argue that Green thought is so diverse that it cannot count as an ideology, but, like nationalism, it has common themes that are of an ideological nature, namely, sustainable development, decentralisation and direct participation.

Sustainable development

The idea of sustainable development reached a wide audience in 1987, when the *Report of the World Commission on Environment and Development: Our Common Future* (also known as the Brundtland Report) laid out the case for environmental action and the means of achieving it. The affluent parts of the world, it was argued, would have to adapt their way of life to ecological demands by reducing energy consumption and by producing energy by wind and water power, for example. In addition, the existing institutions of government and international relations that are based on nation-states would have to give way to a broad, integrated and comprehensive approach involving popular participation and international cooperation.

Decentralisation

Localism and decentralisation mean the local production of goods and services for local consumption. This reduces the power of large MNCs and the need for long lines of transportation and communication which degrade the environment and the local **ecology**. It is also argued that local production improves the satisfaction of people, who can see the fruits of their labours. Local markets are said to be more responsive to local demands, and deliver fresher produce. Politically, localism means community participation and self-regulation, hence the slogan 'Small is beautiful'.

> **Ecology:** The relationships (or the study of the relationships) between organisms and their environment.

Direct participation and democracy

Greens favour direct democracy and participation and the rotation of elites, rather than representative democracy and its hierarchies. Some Green parties have tried (not always successfully) to ensure that no one stays in a leadership position for long, and that no one is paid more than the average wage or much more than the average. Some critics argue that Green thought is inherently anti-democratic if it puts the utmost importance on taking action to protect the environment now, before it is too late, irrespective of public opinion and the slow processes of democracy. Others claim that the decentralist and participatory thrust of Green thought guarantees its democratic credentials.

Green parties have rarely been as successful as some nationalist movements, but it seems that more people support green objectives than join Green movements or vote for them. Moreover, some of the older parties have taken Green ideas, and built them into their own programmes.

Populism

There is some doubt about whether **populism** is an ideology at all, and if it is, about its democratic credentials. It is mentioned briefly here because it can have democratic tendencies and has appeared, strongly at times, in some democracies, especially in Latin America and in many European countries. Like nationalism, populism is a loose and varied approach to politics with many different contents. It is characterised by political **demagogues** who appeal to the prejudices and emotions, particularly of citizens who believe that the elites of society are misleading, oppressing or exploiting them. Populism can take a left-wing Marxist form and a right-wing fascist one. In some places it is mixed with extreme nationalism, religion and racism, while in others it is based on attempts to improve living standards and education in poor areas. Populism in one form or another is often found in the catch-all parties of Latin America, and in countries with large, poor and rural populations. It has appeared as a strong political force mainly in defective democracies, including Mexico, Peru, Dominican Republic and Argentina, but also in France, Denmark and the Netherlands. In these last countries populism is mixed with nationalism.

> **Populism:** A style of politics that appeals to political prejudices and emotions, particularly of those who feel exploited and oppressed by the rich and powerful.

> **Demagogues:** Political leaders who use impassioned appeals to the emotions and prejudices of citizens to try to gain political power.

■ Theories of ideology

We have seen that ideologies mix empirical and normative statements. **Empirical statements** are 'is' or factual statements about the world, and normative statements are value judgements

> **Empirical statement:** Factual statement about or explanation of the world that is not necessarily true or false, but amenable to falsification.

about how it ought to be. When discussing ideologies, however, political scientists try to avoid value judgements about whether they are 'true' or 'false', 'good' or 'bad'. They try to be objective and neutral, limiting themselves to fair, accurate and impartial accounts of what they are. Similarly, they try to give a full and fair account of the various theories of ideology. With this in mind the last section of the chapter turns to theories of ideology.

Marxist and neo-Marxist theories

Marxist theory

Marxist theory is a materialist theory of history and politics (**materialism**). It distinguishes between the sub-structure and the super-structure of society. The sub-structure consists of the material conditions of society, especially its economic conditions, and the super-structure includes ideas and ideology, art, philosophy and culture. Marxists argue that the material sub-structure fundamentally determines the super-structural world of ideas. Accordingly Marx wrote: 'It is not the consciousness of men that determines their being, but, on the contrary, their social being that determines their consciousness.' This is the essence of the Marxist materialist theory of political ideas and ideology.

> **Materialism:** The theory that ideas are rooted in the material or physical conditions of life, as opposed to spiritual ideals and values which are constructs of the mind which can be independent of material and physical conditions (see Idealism).

According to Marxist theory, ideologies are ways of thought that justify the interests of the ruling class. Under capitalism, the bourgeoisie uses its power to delude and manipulate other classes into believing that capitalism is not only natural but in the best interests of everybody. According to Marxists, therefore, an ideology is a false set of beliefs, a mystification of the real world, a myth or a lie. Those who believe it suffer from false consciousness (chapter 9). In contrast, Marxists claim that their own theory is not ideology but scientific and true.

According to Marxist theory, religion is no more than the 'opiate of the masses'. It justifies the social order as God-given. Nationalism is a way in which the ruling class prevents the working class from seeing its common interests with workers in other countries. Wars are a way of fighting for capitalist advantage, markets and profit. Respect for the aristocracy, deference towards economic elites and love of the monarchy and the national football team are means by which the ruling class divides and rules, and conceals the nature of capitalist exploitation. Belief in parliamentary government obscures the fact that real power lies with the owners of property. In this way, Marxist theory tries to explain away other ideologies and religions as false beliefs designed to maintain capitalism.

Neo-Marxist theories

Marxist ideas of ideology were especially developed by the Italian Antonio Gramsci (1891–1937), who spent much of his life as a prisoner of Mussolini's

Fascist government. Gramsci was struck by the fact that the ruling class in Western society managed to maintain its economic and political power, without exercising much overt force. He concluded that it managed this by virtue of its ability to infuse society with its own values. It maintained its hegemony (see chapter 9) not by naked power but by more subtle and indirect control over what people thought. It won 'the hearts and minds' of people, and gained their willing consent by use of religion, education and the mass media.

Gramscian ideas have been developed more recently by the French structuralist theorist Louis Althusser (1918–90), who argued that the ideological state apparatus was important for maintaining the capitalist system. The main institutions of this ideological apparatus were the churches, schools and universities, families, the legal system, the means of mass communications, culture and parties and trade unions.

Marxist and neo-Marxist theories of ideology have been important for introducing realist and materialist theories of ideologies into the social sciences, which focus on the relationship between social and economic conditions and what people think about politics. This aspect of their approach is commonly accepted or assumed in contemporary theories. Nonetheless, critics of Marxism and neo-Marxism pose four questions about them:

- To say that a person suffers from false consciousness and does not know what is in their own best interests opens up the possibility of forcing them to do things against their own will. Do you suffer from false consciousness? If not, what reason is there for claiming that others do?
- Is it plausible to argue that most of the major institutions of modern society are instruments of a hegemonic ruling class? Is this true of schools and universities, political parties, trade unions, families, the legal system and television and newspapers?
- Are all ideologies a matter of false consciousness and Marxism alone a scientific theory?
- Is it possible to distinguish between the material sub-structure and the ideological superstructure? Do ideas help to shape the social and economic structure, as well as the other way round?

Beyond these criticisms there also lies a deeper argument about the role of ideas in politics and history that involves a confrontation between materialist theories on the one hand and idealist theories on the other. A third school of thought claims that both material and ideal interests play their own role in history.

Material and non-material interests

Born in the year that Karl Marx finished the first volume of *Capital*, Max Weber (chapter 1) was a German professor who managed for most of his life, as he said, to avoid the 'drudgery' of university life. Weber much admired the work of Marx and declared it to be profoundly true, but he also tried to show that Marx's materialist interpretation of history was insufficient. Weber argues that modern capitalism could not have developed without the ideas of the *Protestant ethic*. Capitalism is the ever-renewed pursuit of profit, and the Protestant ethic entails a commitment to the sort of hard and systematic work that is capable of producing renewed profit. Moreover, capitalism and Protestantism are linked, because some Protestants came to believe that economic success was a sign of God's favour.

The link between capitalism and Protestantism was entirely unrecognised and unintended by the leaders of the Protestant Reformation, Luther and Calvin. They were interested in religious matters, not economic ones. Nevertheless, their ideas, Weber argues, were necessary to start capitalism on its successful world-wide career. Once in the saddle the capitalist system would ride forever because its own logic and imperative would force others to copy it, or perish economically, but it took the ideas of the Protestant ethic to launch it in the first place.

Weber did not try to replace Marxist materialism with the opposite theory, known as **idealism**. Rather his work has been described as a 'debate with the ghost of Marx', in which he argues that it is not material conditions but material and ideal interests that drive the behaviour of individuals. Ideal interests – related to ideological beliefs – are no less important than material ones. In this case, if politics is a struggle between competing forces, ideas and ideologies play an important role in the struggle.

> **Idealism:** The theory that ideas have a life of their own as the products of consciousness or spiritual ideals and values that are independent of material conditions. In international relations, idealism emphasises the role of ideas and morality as a determinant of the relations between states.

The end of ideology and the end of history

In the 1960s, the end of ideology was widely proclaimed by social scientists such as Daniel Bell (1919–2011) in *The End of Ideology* and Seymour Martin Lipset (1922–2006) in *Political Man* (both published in 1960). They argued that the appeal of ideologies, especially communism, fascism and other utopian theories, were exhausted. The main problems of the Industrial Revolution had been solved and the main issues of the class struggle resolved. As a result, there was a non-ideological consensus about the virtues of liberalism, democracy, the welfare state, decentralised power, pluralism and the mixed economy. This, it was claimed, amounted to the exhaustion of political ideas during this period.

The 'end of ideology' thesis depended on the idea that only extreme and utopian systems of thought counted as ideologies. In this sense there may well have been some truth in the thesis, but if the term 'ideology' also applies to any well-worked-out system of ideas about politics, including liberal and democratic ones, then there was no end of ideology. Besides, new ideologies and ideological disputes arose in the late twentieth century, including neo-conservative ideas about free markets and minimal government, the emergence of post-materialist and green thought, feminist theory and political ideas based on fundamentalist Christianity in the USA. In addition, a deep divide emerged between the Western world and some parts of the Muslim world. As a result theories about 'the end of history', based on the universal acceptance of democracy were challenged by theories about 'the clash of civilisations', based on fundamentalist religious beliefs in both the Eastern and the Western world.

■ What have we learned?

This chapter deals with frameworks of ideas known as ideologies, which help people to understand and interpret politics.

- The term 'ideology' is used here to mean a broad and systematic set of ideas that mix empirical and normative statements about politics with a programme for political action.
- Once again we find that the political world is simpler than it might seem at first glance. Although every ideology is different in thousands of particular ways, we can see that there are four general democratic ideologies – conservatism, liberalism, Christian democracy and socialism/social democracy – and three more minor ones – nationalism, green thought and populism.
- Conservatism is distinguished by its core beliefs that society is an organic entity that has evolved slowly and should be reformed slowly; that the natural failings of human beings are best restrained by a strong state that maintains social order and the social hierarchy; that some inequality in society is inevitable; in representative democracy; and that the market is the best way to achieve the public economic good.
- Classical liberalism is distinguished by its core belief that individual rights and freedoms can be maximised only by limiting the powers of the state. Neo-liberals hold to the negative definition of freedom and argue for limited state intervention, but social or progressive liberals argue for some state intervention to secure positive freedom.
- Christian democracy incorporates Catholic thought into a practical ideology that emphasises community, family and church; the devolution of power; institutions to bring different interests in society together to achieve social integration and reconciliation; and state services to protect the weak and the poor and to prevent the failure of key private institutions.
- The distinguishing features of socialism and social democracy are: an optimistic view of human nature; a participatory form of democracy; the legal and peaceful attainment of parliamentary power through popular election; a mixed economy, with state power to control or regulate key elements of the economy: a guaranteed minimum standard of living for all; and equality of opportunity.

■ Lessons of comparison

- Families of ideologies correspond in general terms to families of political parties (chapter 13) and hence examples of the four main ideologies and the three others can be found in most democratic countries, and often play a major role in their politics.
- Political ideas are related to social and economic life and are closely associated with the history, culture and social and economic circumstances of countries and the social groups in their populations.
- Materialist theories, notably Marxism and neo-Marxism, argue that ideologies are the products of social conditions, but other theorists claim that both material and ideal interests are crucial for understanding ideologies.
- Comparison of different places and different historical periods shows that neither ideology nor history seem to have come to an end. The world is divided by ideological clashes as much as ever it was, and probably always will be.

Projects

1. Examine the political programmes of three main parties in your country, and summarise the main normative and empirical features that distinguish them.
2. What are the ideological differences that distinguish each of the following:
   (i) classical liberalism (of the John Stuart Mill kind), liberal democrats (of the modern centre party kind), liberalism (of the kind often used to describe Democratic voters in the USA) and libertarianism?
   (ii) conservatives and neo-conservatives?
   (iii) Marxism and democratic socialism.
3. Do you think that there can be a 'scientific' ideology?
4. Do you have an ideology? What are the main normative and empirical features of your political ideas?

Further reading

A. Heywood, *Political Ideologies*, 5th edn. Basingstoke: Palgrave Macmillan, 2012. Covers the main beliefs and ideologies of the world, including liberalism, conservatism, socialism, feminism, ecology and political Islam.

M. Festenstein and M. Kenny (eds.), *Political Ideologies: A Reader and Guide*. Oxford University Press, 2005. A collection of extracts from the writings of major political theorists and politicians, with commentaries on them.

B. Goodwin, *Using Political Ideas*. Chichester: John Wiley & Sons, 2007. Combines political philosophy, theory and history of political thought to analyse the main ideologies of the modern world.

A. Vincent, *Modern Political Ideologies*, 3rd edn. Chichester: John Wiley & Sons, 2009. Covers liberalism, conservatism, socialism, anarchism, fascism, feminism, environmentalism, and nationalism, fundamentalism and the global impact of ideologies.

Websites

Virtually all political philosophers and political ideology have websites dedicated to them. Simply submit a name (for instance 'Edmund Burke') to any major search engine and you will easily find these sites.

www.psa.ac.uk/sites/default/files/Suggested%20Reading%20List%20-%20Political%20Ideologies.pdf.

A useful list of work on most major 'isms'.

www.encyclopedia.com/searchresults.aspx?q=ideology.

Contains extensive entries on almost every modern and classical ideology and their associated thinkers and systems of political thought.

www.britannica.com/EBchecked/topic/281943/ideology.

Has entries on the origins and characteristics of ideology in general and on a long list of specific ones.

15   Decision making

Government exists to solve problems. To do this it must take decisions. In one sense, the whole process of government is little else than a ceaseless process of decision making: how to respond to the latest international crisis; whether to increase taxes or cut services; how to balance economic development against environmental needs; how to handle an economic crisis; what to do about traffic congestion. Politics never sleeps, and governments can never pause for rest. They are assailed from all sides by endless cycles of demands and events, and they must constantly make decisions about options, priorities, policies and courses of action.

This chapter deals with public policies and decision making. A policy is a general set of ideas or plans that has been agreed and which is used as a basis for making decisions. *Public policy* refers to the activities, decisions and actions carried out by officials of government in their attempts to solve problems that are thought to lie in the public or collective arena. In that sense, we speak of 'environmental policies' if government shifts from coal and nuclear power to oil and wind-powered generators, and of 'educational policies' if the school leaving age is raised or money is redirected from primary to secondary education. This chapter deals not with the content of public policy but with its process – how decisions are taken rather than what decisions are taken, and how governments differ in the ways that they make these decisions. How do governments respond to public demands and what interests do they take into account or exclude? After all, one of the most important decisions for any political system is what is to be treated as a public matter for government attention, and what is regarded as a private matter of no concern to public bodies. The borderline between the public and private changes as governments take on new tasks and discard old ones.

The four main topics of this chapter are:

- Public policies: their nature and importance
- The public-policy cycle
- Public-policy structures
- Theories of decision making.

■ Public policies: their nature and importance

Goals and results

Public policy is designed to achieve goals that produce particular results. Public policies are supposed to solve public problems, or at least reduce them. In this sense, public policies are the main **outputs** of the political system – the actions it takes in response to the demands made on it and the problems it faces. Two points follow from the idea that public policy and decision making aim to improve the world:

> **Outputs:** Policy decisions as they are actually implemented.

- *Public policy is important* Almost everything we do is affected by public policies, sometimes in many trivial ways, but also in many crucial ones. They determine which side of the road we drive on and whether we carry identity cards. They decide whether we receive a free university education, have to pay for health care, pay a lot or a little tax and, in the extreme, whether we are sentenced to death if we are found guilty of murder.
- *Public policy is conflict-ridden* Because public policies are so important, they are the focus of fierce and constant political battles. Which policy is adopted depends on the competing and conflicting political forces that operate on the state from both within and without – the executive, legislative and judiciary, the state bureaucracy, other states and international organisations, sub-central governments, parties and pressure groups, public opinion and the mass media. A public policy is the 'end product' of the battle between these political forces. Consequently, public policies and political decision making tell us a lot about how political systems actually work, and about who is powerful. If politics is to be about who gets what, when and how, then the study of public policy making can tell us a lot about who gets what and how they obtained it.

The nature of policy-making processes

Discussions about public policies usually start with the clich that public policy making is extremely complex and difficult to analyse. This is certainly true. Yet, paradoxically, we all know about decision making because we do it all the time. Take a simple decision: at this minute you are reading chapter 15 of this book, but you might have made the decision to go to the cinema, drink with friends, update your Facebook account or catch up on sleep instead. If you analyse your decision to read the textbook, you know well enough that you are not completely free to do what you want. Perhaps you have an essay deadline tomorrow, or not enough money to go to the cinema. So the first thing to notice is that your decision is subject to constraints. Second, your decision is also partly in response to the decisions of others. You made your own decision to go to college and study this course, but your teachers put on the course and set essays, and your friends may have decided to work today and go to the cinema tomorrow. In other words, your decision is closely tied up with the decisions of others. And, third, you know that today's decision has implications for future decisions you might make – what you do tomorrow, and if you write a good essay, what courses you study in the future, even what kind of job you get. In other words, today's decisions are influenced by a long chain of decisions that reaches back into the past, and has implications for decisions in the future.

These simple aspects of decision-making processes can be used to characterise features of public policy making as follows.

Constraints

Policy making is beset on every side by constraints. No government can do what it likes. It is always faced with shortages of time and resources, or by pressure from foreign governments and economic forces. It is subject to the conflicting demands of public opinion, the mass media, pressure groups and opposition parties. It must meet the requirements of the law and the courts. The permanent officials of the state bureaucracies may have views and powers of their own, and so have many sub-central units of government and other public agencies. Indeed, governments themselves are invariably composed of factions that push and pull in different directions. Politics is the art of the possible, and what might appear to be the most obvious or most sensible course of action is often ruled out by circumstances.

Policy processes

The repeated use of the term 'policy processes', in the plural, is deliberate because there is no single 'policy process' – there are many of them. Governments, like any large organisation, are not integrated, coordinated and centralised machines: they are fragmented and disjointed, with different departments and units that compete, overlap and frequently work unknown to each other. The agricultural ministry may want to preserve farmland, the transport department may want to cover it with a road and the military may want it as a training ground. One of the big problems for the huge and sprawling apparatus of the modern state is how to produce 'joined-up' government, where public policies are more or less coherent and point in roughly the same direction. This may be an impossible ideal. Even within the same ministry, there are likely to be different views on any given matter, and each matter may well involve parties, pressure groups, international government agencies, the mass media and public opinion – each with its own set of goals.

Unending policy cycles

Policy processes consist not of discrete decisions, distinct from one another, but of a continuous and unending cycle of decisions and policies which merge into one another without a break:

- In the first place, no policy decision is independent of the decisions that have gone before. A government that has invested heavily in nuclear power will frame its current power policies with this in mind.
- In the second place, every policy has knock-on effects that require a further round of decisions. Bigger and better roads have been built in an attempt to solve traffic problems and reduce accident rates, only to discover that this has increased car sales, which feeds back to cause traffic problems. Successful promotion of economic growth in the post-war years has resulted in a much higher standard of living, which has led to all sorts of environmental problems. Higher standards of living and improvements in public health have also produced an aging population, which has generated severe problems for state pensions and the costs of health care for the elderly.

Almost every public policy has its unintended and unanticipated side effects, which then become another problem for public policy. The result is an endless cycle of policy and decision making that tries to solve both the new problems of the world and also the side effects of old policies.

■ The public-policy cycle

It is helpful to imagine policy processes as consisting of six stages. Analytically, each policy process starts with selecting the most urgent problems to be dealt with (agenda setting). Then decisions have to be taken about the course of action (decision making) and appropriate means to be used (choice of means). The next stage consists of putting the plan into action (implementation), which results in specific consequences (outputs and **outcomes**).

Outcomes: The impacts, or effects, of outputs.

Finally, the effects and costs of the policy are assessed and conclusions are drawn for future actions (evaluation and feedback). This last stage leads directly back into the first stage, so it is helpful to think of the process as a continuous and unending cycle, not as a one-way flow with a clear beginning and end (see figure 15.1). In real life the different stages of the cycle are not separate and distinct. On the contrary, they merge and overlap with one another, and sometimes the stages get mixed up, but nevertheless they are helpful analytical categories.

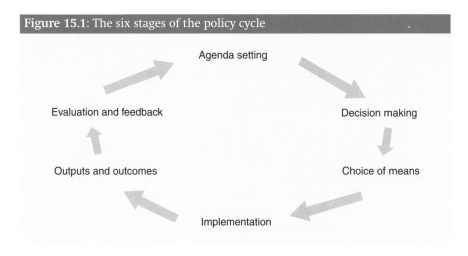

Figure 15.1: The six stages of the policy cycle

Agenda setting

The world is full of political problems and it is impossible to give much attention to more than a small number of them at any given time. Consequently, an important part of the political struggle is the attempt by different groups and interests to put their issues at the top of the agenda, or at least to push them up the agenda, so that they have a better chance of being considered. This struggle is called 'agenda setting' (chapter 11). Being able to control or influence the agenda is an important source of political power. The struggle is endless because as the world changes so priorities and agendas also change. For example, according to post-materialist theory (see chapter 9) the public agenda is shifting from safety and security, money and material advantages, to the quality of life, self-fulfilment and environmental protection. Although new political parties, such as the Greens, have rarely played a direct role in government, they have had a political influence to the extent that they have changed the political agenda.

One important aspect of the public agenda is the divide between what is thought to be the proper concern of the state, and what is outside its sphere of action, and therefore off the public agenda. What is thought to be a public matter varies considerably from one country to another, and from one historical period to another (see briefing 15.1). In fact, political conflicts frequently concentrate on the question of whether government should deal with specific problems such as passing equal opportunities legislation, banning genetically modified (GM) food or regulating tobacco and alcohol sales. The shifting divide between the public and the private reminds us that the scope of politics is itself constantly contested.

As we have seen in chapter 11, the mass media play an important role in public debates and therefore also in agenda setting. The argument is that although the mass media cannot do much to influence what people think,

Briefing 15.1

The public–private divide
The boundaries between the public and the private vary from one country to another, and from one historical period to another.

■ Historical changes

As we saw in chapter 14, the distinction between the public and private sphere is at the heart of the battle of political ideas between liberals, conservatives and socialists. These ideologies have waxed and waned over three historical periods.

The dominant liberal ideology of the nineteenth century argued for a minimal, 'night watchman' state.

As the welfare state grew in the late nineteenth and twentieth centuries, so the public sphere expanded, taxes increased, more public services were delivered.

In recent decades the neo-liberals have been successful to some degree in rolling back the frontiers of the state, by privatisation, deregulation and tax and service cuts.

■ Country differences

- In some countries there is a state-recognised list of saints' names for children. In other countries naming children is a private matter.
- In north European countries the sale of alcohol is often closely controlled by the government, sometimes through state monopoly shops.
- Until recently, Norwegian municipalities owned cinemas and spent the profits on public services. In most countries cinemas are in the private sector.
- In some countries shops can open when they like. In others, their opening hours are restricted.
- In some countries all citizens must carry ID cards. Others have no such requirement.
- A good indicator of the breadth of the public sector is the proportion of total national production spent by all public authorities. Countries vary substantially in this respect, as figure 15.2 shows.

■ The public–private mix

There is no clear line to be drawn between the public and private. They overlap a good deal in some policy areas where private or semi-private groups and organisations cooperate closely with government to provide services with financial and other help from the state. In Germany the state collects taxes for the Catholic and Protestant churches, which provide social and other services with the money. Scandinavian housing associations are neither public nor private organisations, but **public–private partnerships (PPPs)**. Many politicians have turned to PPPs since the 1980s as the best solution to a wide range of problems.

Public–private partnerships:
Formal cooperation between government and private groups to achieve specific goals.

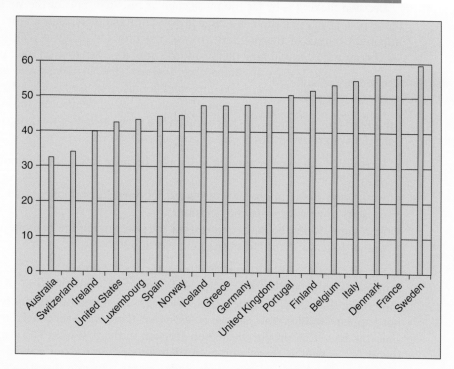

Figure 15.2: General government expenditure as a percentage of GDP, OECD countries, 2012

Source: OECD, *National* Accounts Statistics (http://stats.oecd.org/BrandedView.aspx?oecd_bv_id=na-data-en&doi=data-00001-en)

they can exercise a good deal of influence over what people think about. The news media have an unquenchable thirst for new issues and stories and from time to time they engage in 'feeding frenzies' about road rage, football hooligans, new diseases, crime, drug crazes, political corruption and terrorism. Known as 'moral panics', these matters hit the headlines for a time and focus public attention on them, but then disappear in favour of another issue, perhaps before anything has been done about the matter, or perhaps prompting hasty and ill-considered action from policymakers.

Decision making

Having decided on the issues to be put at the top of the political agenda, decisions must then be taken about them. In democracies, major policy decisions should be taken by publicly accountable bodies, normally the elected executive or the legislature, or both. Nonetheless, many other public and private organisations and officials may have an impact on the circumstances that precede particular decisions and the constraints on them. These include public opinion, the media, political parties, pressure groups and public-sector bureaucrats and officials.

Decision making is by far the most popular research topic of the six stages of the policy cycle and there is a huge literature on the topic. They are the most important output of the political process, not only for practical politics, but also because they reveal how political forces mix together to produce a policy. Remember, however, that *not* making a decision is also important because that itself is also a decision. A **non-decision** has its consequences and reveals the interplay of political forces just as much as a decision to do something. In fact politicians often favour this course of non-action because:

> **Non-decision:** The decision not to deal with an issue, perhaps not even to consider it.

- Sometimes the issue is 'too hot to handle' because it is a highly emotional one.
- Sometimes government may be faced by powerful opponents with the capacity to veto its preferred decision.
- Sometimes it may be in the interests of the government not to make a decision or to leave it until after the next election.

For all their possible importance, non-decisions frequently escape attention in academic study for the simple reason that a non-decision involves something that did not happen, and how does one study something that did not happen? Besides, how can we be sure that there was ever a need to consider the issue that produced the non-decision in the first place? 'Conspiracy theorists', as well as those who hold minority opinions about a wide range of matters are always claiming that governments refuse to investigate their favourite theory. Is this a case of non-decision making or a case of governments refusing to take some theories seriously? The methodological problems of non-decision making have been heatedly discussed by community politics studies, and no firm conclusions have been reached, although non-decisions have been clearly documented in several carefully developed case studies.

Choice of means

Choosing the best means for a policy, once it is decided, is the next step confronting policy makers. This may seem a straightforward job after priorities have been set, but it is not simple at all. There is usually a wide variety of possible policy instruments available to achieve a given end, and deciding which to use is no easy task. The options include:

- *Taxing specific products or services* to change the costs of action – excise duties on cigarettes and alcohol, for example, or lower duties on lead-free petrol or diesel oil to encourage more environmental motoring.
- *Imposing regulations* – shop opening hours can be restricted, dogs required to have a licence, toxic products banned, industrial plants regulated and minimum wages imposed.

- *Encouraging citizens* to do certain things – some governments carry out intensive and expensive publicity campaigns to persuade people not to smoke, to use condoms, to eat healthily, to recycle their garbage in the required way, or to take exercise.
- *Offering subsidies or grants* – many countries subsidise food production and some offer tax reductions to home owners or child benefits.
- *Direct provision* of services by the state itself – education, health services, transport and so on, especially if the private provision of these services is problematic.
- *Encouraging private organisations to regulate themselves* – governments are often reluctant to intervene directly in, for example, the conduct of the mass media where the principle of the freedom of the press is involved.
- *Passing new laws* – not only to make things legal or illegal but to introduce one of the measures mentioned in the list above. Changing the law may appear to be the obvious method, but it can be cumbersome and ineffective because it usually takes a long time, and the effects are uncertain.

In many cases, decision makers choose a combination of these, since it is unlikely that any single one will work well.

Implementation

As we saw in chapter 7, policy making is supposed to be the responsibility of elected and accountable politicians, whereas implementation (chapter 8) is mainly a matter for state bureaucracies. In practice, the distinction between policy making and implementation is not clear, because policy goals cannot be separated from the means of implementing them, and vice versa. Besides, in political life policies often get changed in the process of implementation:

- Sometimes, this is for very good practical reasons (economic pressures, bureaucratic procedures, avoidance of unforeseen side effects) that may not have been recognised when the policy was formulated.
- Sometimes it is because implementing agencies have their own interests, and bend the policy to their own wishes as much as they can.
- And sometimes it is because legislation deliberately gives agencies discretion over how to implement a policy because of difficulties in deciding in advance.

Private organisations and pressure groups may also try to influence implementation in their own interests. One way or the other, therefore, there may well be slippage between what policy makers intend and what is actually implemented.

The book *Implementation* (1973) by Jeffrey L. Pressman and Aaron Wildavsky is a classic study of policy in practice. It reveals its main message in its subtitle: 'How Great Expectations in Washington are Dashed in Oakland: Or,

Why It Is Amazing that Federal Programs Work at All'. They found that federal policies in the USA were changed as they passed down through a long chain of 'clearance points' between the policymakers in Washington and local street-level bureaucrats who made decisions on the ground 4,000 km away.

Outputs and outcomes

After a policy has been applied, its results or consequences may become clear. Political scientists find it useful, therefore, to distinguish between outputs and outcomes. These terms reflect the often unintended and unrecognised nature of policy effects, and the differences between policy decisions and what is actually achieved. Since society is exceedingly complex, and since decision making is no less difficult, governments quite often fail to achieve their intended goals, and sometimes policies have an opposite effect. In practice it can be exceedingly difficult to establish outcomes because causes and effects may be tangled. Besides, monitoring policy effects can be expensive and time-consuming, and sometimes they are embarrassing for the public agency that took the decision and implemented it.

Evaluation and feedback

Policy evaluation provides a feedback loop, enabling decision-makers to learn from their experiences. Policies should be evaluated for their efficiency (using the least resources to the maximum effect) and effectiveness (achieved what was intended). Since all but the most trivial public policy decisions are likely to have unintended and unexpected side effects, there is almost always something to be learned from evaluation, and it can be a nasty lesson. It is this feedback loop that creates an endless policy cycle. At any rate, one policy decision may simply lead to another, or serve as a background context for new decisions. In this sense, there is no such thing as a decision, but only a ceaseless and unbroken flow of them.

In practice, evaluation and feedback are the 'Cinderella elements' of policy processes, for several reasons:

- Policies should be evaluated in terms of their objectives, but policymakers may deliberately leave their objectives vague in order to avoid political controversy, or in order to avoid responsibility for failing to meet them.
- Policymakers and implementers rarely want their failures evaluated.
- Policymakers may pay little attention to the evaluation, no matter how well it was carried out, because the public agenda has already changed.
- Monitoring policy effects can be expensive and time-consuming.
- It is not unknown for governments to insist that other organisations should carefully monitor their policies and report back, but exempt themselves from this requirement.

- Efficiency in the public sector is difficult to measure. Some services are taken into the public sector precisely because they are not amenable to the usual market measures of efficiency.

And, last, it should be noted that even properly executed evaluations may not have their appropriate effects. Their conclusions may be ignored or even suppressed because the agency responsible does not like them. Citizens or governments may misunderstand their conclusions or focus on a minor point, not a central one. Some may argue that the evaluation is a 'whitewash' and a cover-up of government failure and, since such things have happened in the past, they may be right. In other words, policy evaluations, like policies themselves, can have unexpected and unanticipated results.

In this brief overview we have emphasised the complexity of the policy cycle and the difficulties of making decisions, implementing them and evaluating them. We have frequently used the phrase 'unrecognised and unintended effects'. However, in spite of all this, public policies are often drawn up and implemented more or less effectively. That is to say, children are educated, health systems operate, transport is available, welfare benefits paid, pension schemes funded and so on. No doubt no policy works quite as well as it is supposed to, but many of them work nonetheless and, for the most part, they manage to avoid the worst disasters. As Pressman and Wildavsky observe, it is 'amazing' that (government) programmes 'work at all', but then the same might be said of large-scale private organisations and bureaucracies as well.

■ Public-policy structures

Policy and decision making is full of conflict between groups and organisations with different and often incompatible interests. Sometimes this conflict is protracted and bitter, because the stakes are high or the moral issues of great importance. At the same time, the public policy process is rarely a free-for-all battle between warring interests because there are structures and rules to organise them. Even the freest of all free-market competition is constrained by government controls, regulations, international trade agreements or by economic interests themselves which try to limit unrestricted competition. Public policy and political decision making are no different. They occur within 'structures and rules of the game' that try to ensure that public policy making is relatively smooth, ordered, regulated and predictable (see chapter 4).

The public policy making structures in democracies usually fall into two main types: **corporatism** and **pluralism**. Corporatism is the more top-down, state-centred and structured

> **Corporatism:** A way of organising public policy making involving the close cooperation of major economic interests within a formal government apparatus that is capable of concerting the main economic groups so that they can jointly formulate and implement binding policies.

> **Pluralism:** A situation where power is dispersed among many different groups and organisations that openly compete with one another in different political arenas.

arrangement, whereas pluralism is more 'bottom-up', decentralised and loosely organised.

Corporatism

Corporatism or neo-corporatism, as it is often known, is discussed fully in chapter 10, but the main outlines of the concept will be summarised here. In order to minimise conflict, maximise consensus and ensure smoothly executed policies, corporatist structures consist of:

- A small number of hierarchically organised peak associations or federations that speak authoritatively for all their members, usually trade unions, and business and farming organisations.
- An elaborate structure of government decision making, consultation and negotiation in the form of consultative committees, advisory bodies and social and economic councils. The peak organisations are co-opted members of these bodies.
- An ability to make policies that are passed down and implemented by government bodies and the peak associations.
- Participants in corporatist arrangements must compromise. They cannot get everything they want, but they can get some of it, by 'playing by the rules'. It may be much better to stay within the system, where they can be heard, than to be on the outside.

To avoid confusion with the fascist theory of 'state corporatism', corporatism in democratic states is also referred to as 'neo-corporatism', 'liberal corporatism', or 'social corporatism'. In this chapter, however, we will use the simple term 'corporatism', on the understanding that this is a form of political decision making in some democracies.

Modern corporatist theory evolved in the late nineteenth century as a reaction to both socialism and laissez-faire capitalism. In this sense, it owes a lot to Christian democracy (see chapter 14). To create social harmony and a common purpose it is necessary to create collective institutions in which major social and economic interests can participate in the formulation and implementation of mutually acceptable policies.

In modern societies, corporatism has generally worked best in economic policy making where hierarchically organised business interests, trade unions and government have been brought together to consult, and negotiate and reach policy agreement. Countries vary in their degree of corporatism, with Denmark, the Netherlands, Norway, Sweden and Austria among the most corporatist, and the Anglo-Saxon democracies of Australia, Britain, Canada, New Zealand and the USA have very little in common with them (see table 15.1).

Corporatism developed in the 1970s and 1980s, especially in western Europe, as a method of promoting and managing economic growth. According to the research of Markus Crepaz (see 'Further reading' below), corporatist countries had lower rates of unemployment, lower inflation,

Table 15.1 Corporatism in eighteen democracies, 1950s–1970s

Country	Corporatism rating
Austria (highest)	2.9
Norway	2.8
Sweden	2.7
Netherlands	2.4
Denmark	1.9
Switzerland	1.9
Germany	1.9
Finland	1.8
Belgium	1.6
Japan	1.4
Ireland	0.8
France	0.7
Italy	0.6
Great Britain	0.5
Australia	0.3
New Zealand	0.2
Canada	0.0
USA (lowest)	0.0

Source: Derived from Arend Lijphart and Markus Crepaz, 'Corporatism and consensus democracy in eighteen countries', *British Journal of Political Science*, 21, 1990: 235–56.

less working time lost from strikes, but no better rates of economic growth. Although its main goal – promoting exceptional economic growth – was not reached, the successes of corporatism were widely recognised.

In spite of these successes, however, corporatism began to weaken its hold in the 1980s:

- Corporatism is easier to work in periods of economic growth (the 1960s and 1970s), when there are additional resources to distribute, than in harder economic times (the 1980s), when some groups lose.
- Corporatism works best with issues that are amenable to bargaining, compromise and incremental change, such as those between management and workers over pay, hours and conditions of work. The issues raised by new pressure groups and new social movements – peace, minority rights, equal opportunities and the environment in the 1970s and 1980s are moral issues that are less easily handled by corporatist negotiation and incremental bargaining.
- The shift from heavy industry and manufacturing to service industry has fragmented business organisations and trade unions, making them less centralised and hierarchical and hence less able to formulate and implement policies. Trade union membership has fallen in many countries, making it difficult for peak organisations to speak authoritatively for workers.

- Globalisation has made it more difficult to control national economies, and to impose regulation on them.
- Keynesian policies have tended to give way to a neo-conservative belief in market competition (see chapter 14).
- Demands to extend political participation have tended to erode the closed circles of corporatist policy making. Excluded groups (students, immigrants, peace and anti-nuclear campaigners, the Greens and minority groups) have muscled into the political arena, and other groups have used direct forms of participation, often of a protest kind, to make their voices heard.

Pluralism

The Anglo-Saxon democracies in table 15.1, and others like them that rank low on the corporatism scale, make policy in a more fragmented and less centralised/hierarchical manner. In these countries, power is dispersed among many different groups and organisations that openly compete with one another in different political arenas. Because there are supposed to be many competing interests and organisations, and many centres of power, this sort of policy process has been labelled 'pluralism' (see chapter 10). There may be consultation and consensus seeking in pluralist systems, but the absence of fully-fledged corporatist structures makes it difficult to reach binding agreements. Even if such agreements could be hammered out, the absence of centralised and hierarchical interest groups means that compliance with decisions could be hard to obtain.

A lack of corporatist structures does not mean that policy and decision making is an unorganised free-for-all struggle for power. There are two main ways of organising and integrating policy making to make the power struggle more predictable and manageable: tripartite arrangements and policy communities (chapter 10).

Tripartite arrangements

Pluralist systems sometimes use what are known as tripartite arrangements in which the three 'corners' of the economic 'triangle' (business, unions and government) cooperate formally and informally to make economic policy. The formal channels include a variety of official committees and consultative bodies and the informal can include close personal relations between the elites of government, business and even unions. Such arrangements existed in France, Italy, Japan and the UK, especially in the 1960s and 1970s, but less so in the 1980s and 1990s. Tripartism (chapter 10) is most often found in economic policy making, including employment policy, taxation, inflation, industrial and agricultural policy. In the USA a three-cornered working relationship between interest groups, executive agencies and Congressional committees are known as 'iron triangles'.

Policy communities

Outside the economic sphere pluralist policy making can also be organised and given a degree of integration by what are known as policy communities (see also chapter 10). These are small and exclusive groupings of government officials (both elected politicians and appointed bureaucrats) and pressure group elites, who agree on many of the broad issues in a particular policy area. They meet often, sometimes in formally constituted public bodies (committees, councils and consultative bodies) and sometimes informally. These groupings are often influential and sometimes very powerful in their particular policy area, though not necessarily outside it. Policy communities tend to form around food and drink, education, health, the law, defence and technical issues of government policy making. They often involve the most established of the 'insider' groups drawn from the world of professional and business organisations.

Policy communities have some advantages:

- They keep government and those most directly affected by its policies in close contact.
- They exchange information on both policy and technical matters.
- They help to formulate and implement policy in the most effective and efficient manner.

Policy communities also have their disadvantages:

- They are exclusive, keeping 'outsider' groups and interests at a distance from policy making.
- Close and constant contact may also result in government officials and group representatives ending up in each other's pockets. Officials may 'go native' and be unable to represent the public interest properly. Group representatives may be 'captured' by government officials, and be unable to represent the interests of their organisation properly (see chapter 10).

Nevertheless, by containing group conflict, limiting participation in policy-making and establishing close working relations between public officials and private interests, policy communities can contribute to the stability and continuity of decision making. In pluralist systems, this form of policy making is most usually found in Canada, India, New Zealand and the USA – the more decentralised countries among the Anglo-Saxon democracies.

Policy networks

Policy networks (chapter 10) are looser and less exclusive than policy communities. They consist of all the organisations, groups and actors that cluster around a concern in a given policy area and that participate in public discussion about it. Their advantage is that they are more open and less exclusive than communities, so they are less likely to create resentment on the part of groups and interests that are outside the system. At the same time, because they are more open to all sorts of interests they are also likely to be more conflictual, and therefore decision making is likely to be less smooth and predictable.

■ Theories of decision making

Decision-making theories often mix analytic and prescriptive elements; they try to help us understand how decisions are made and how they should be made. Generally speaking, two broad approaches have been developed, one based on economic theory and rational behaviour, another based on more pragmatic considerations of actual policy-making processes.

Rational-comprehensive models

The rational-comprehensive model draws from economic theory how rational individuals make decisions in complex situations. Analytically the four main characteristics of this model are as follows.

- First, rational participants collect all the information relevant to a decision, and carefully analyse it. They rank and define their policy objectives and the means of achieving them, choosing the most efficient and effective.
- They then compare the likely costs and effectiveness of the alternative strategies.
- They implement the most effective and efficient alternative.
- Finally, rational individuals evaluate their policies so that they can learn from the experience and improve them in the future.

Applied to public policy making, such a model assumes a single, centralised and coordinated decision-making body, and a smooth and efficient government machine that implements decisions in the specified way. It should be kept in mind, however, that the rational-comprehensive model of decision making is like the Weberian ideal-type of bureaucracy (see chapter 8). It is not an account of how decisions are actually made but an abstract model for judging reality.

The rational-comprehensive model may approximate to the kind of decision making that is possible, even if rarely found, in relatively small and highly effective decision-making organisations, especially those concerned with technical problem solving. Something like it was used in the USA by the National Aeronautics and Space Administration (NASA) to land a spacecraft on the moon in 1962. But the model is usually far removed from the reality of complex decisions in large governments, as the fate of the centralised command economies in former socialist states clearly demonstrates. In real life, decision makers:

- rarely have even adequate, much less complete, information;
- often handle crises with little time to think or prepare; they have to 'rebuild the ship at sea', sometimes in a force 10 gale;
- are surrounded by powerful political constraints;

- rarely have adequate resources;
- sometimes are pushed by powerful political forces to make policy decisions that are incompatible or contradictory;
- may already have invested heavily in other policies that they feel should not be compromised by a later one, even if the latter would be better;
- have limited control of the bureaucracies that implement central policies, especially if state and local governments with their own democratic legitimacy are involved;
- have to deal with unknown and unintended consequences that blow their policies off course;
- have their own blind spots, prejudices and ideological preferences.

Some techniques have been devised to help rational decision making, most notably **cost–benefit analysis (CBA)**. It assumes that all the important factors to be taken into account can be quantified and that the costs (not just financial, but everything including social, environmental and aesthetic) can somehow be weighed against all the benefits. Advocates of the method argue that it forces decision makers:

> **Cost–benefit analysis:** The attempt, at an early stage of decision making, to calculate all of the costs of a policy and the benefits it will bring.

- to think carefully and systematically
- to take a broad range of factors into account
- to question assumptions
- to make decisions transparent.

Critics have called CBA 'nonsense on stilts' or have argued that it has limited applicability. How would you calculate the costs and benefits of, say, building a motorway through a beautiful and untouched mountain pass? CBA sometimes involves trying to estimate labour costs for a particular project by getting workers on the project to apportion the time they spend on it. This is notoriously difficult and imprecise where, as often happens, office and managerial staff work on different projects at the same time, or where capital costs are shared between different projects. Perhaps this is why the estimates for large projects (public buildings, the Olympic Games, the reorganisation of institutions or reform of health and social welfare projects) are often inaccurate.

Muddling through

If the rational-comprehensive model is an ideal, the **incremental model** is a realistic and pragmatic account of how decisions are actually made. Since political problems are so complex, and since policies have all sorts of unintended

> **Incremental model:** The idea that decisions are not usually based on a comprehensive review of problems, but on small, marginal changes from existing policies.

and unrecognised effects, it is better to minimise risk by proceeding cautiously, a small step at a time (incrementally). The result is piecemeal, gradual, ad hoc decision making, not a fundamental reappraisal of all goals and means. Since public policy is a political matter, it is also characterised by political bargaining, negotiating and compromise. This is especially true in fragmented and decentralised political systems where many different actors and organisations can get in on the act – that is, in pluralist systems. These can make centralised, rational decision making very difficult to achieve.

According to the American political scientist Charles Lindblom (1917–), in real life decision makers respond to problems, rather than anticipating them or creating new goals. Instead of formulating an ideal model of rational behaviour, Lindblom describes the behaviour of decision makers as follows:

- They consider only a few alternatives for dealing with a problem.
- They pick those that differ marginally (incrementally) from existing policies.
- They evaluate only a few of the most important consequences.
- They continually review policies, making many small adjustments.
- They do not search for the best single solution but recognise that there are many alternatives and pick those that are politically expedient and have political support.

This, says Lindblom, is the science of 'muddling through'. Though widely accepted as a rough and ready account of how decisions are made, the model has also been criticised for being:

- too conservative and too reactive: it concentrates on existing problems and solutions, instead of widening the search for new solutions;
- unable to deal with emergencies and crisis situations requiring radical solutions;
- unable to bring about fundamental re-thinking: the accumulation of incremental decisions over a long period of time can result in a 'policy morass', consisting of all sorts of conflicting and incompatible policies. In such a situation, fundamental re-thinking may be absolutely necessary. Sometimes it actually occurs.

Bounded rationality and advocacy coalitions

Nobel laureate Herbert Simon (1916–2001) emphasised the limits of rational decision making caused by the personal values of decision makers, the culture and the structure of the organisations they work in and the complexity and unpredictability of political events. These constraints mean that decision makers 'satisfice' – a word Simon coined to describe policies that are satisfactory and suffice (are sufficient) for the time being. Decision makers will not search exhaustively for the very best policy but accept one that is adequate under the circumstances.

The importance of organisational cultures and structures is emphasised by Graham Allison (1940–) in his book *The Essence of Decision*. He found that

American decision making about the 1962 Cuban missile crisis was the result of bargaining and negotiating between a small group of key decision makers representing departmental interests. Decisions were made not by a single, rational process, but by departments and departmental coalitions engaging in a political power game of 'pulling and hauling', amid a lot of noise, confusion and lack of information.

This idea is developed further by Paul Sabatier (1944–), who argues that policy areas create 'advocacy coalitions' consisting of interest groups, politicians, professionals, journalists, researchers and others, who compete, bargain and compromise with each other. They also learn as circumstances change, so that policies also change.

■ What have we learned?

- Policy making can be seen as a circular process with six main stages: agenda setting, decision making, choice of means, implementation, outputs and outcomes, and evaluation and feedback into agenda setting.
- Non-decision making is just one form of decision making (the decision not to make a decision) that is favoured by politicians who do not want to face an issue. Non-decision making may be frequent but it is difficult to study empirically.
- Policy making is a ceaseless process because many policies have unintended and unanticipated consequences, some of which are thought to be bad, and have to be 'cured' by a further round of policy making.
- Policy-making structures range from centralised, hierarchical and consensus seeking neo-corporatism to open, competitive pluralism.
- A feature of many decision making systems – whether neo-corporatist, iron triangles or the policy communities – is a tendency to form a closed circle of decision makers who are formally or informally organised around common interests, have common understandings and follow the same rules of discussion, negotiation and bargaining.

■ Lessons of comparison

- The scope of government varies across countries and time. The 'night-watchman' states of the early nineteenth century broadened into the welfare states of the twentieth century and then narrowed somewhat in the recent neo-conservative era. The scope of government is generally broader in north and central areas of western Europe, narrower in North America and Asia-Pacific regions.
- Policy-making processes are structured in various ways in different countries. Formal neo-corporatist institutions are mainly found in northern Europe, and more informal and loose-knit pluralist systems are more usual in Anglo-Saxon democracies.

- Approaches to policy making can be broadly divided into models emphasising rational behaviour (systematically selecting alternatives and strategies, optimising costs and benefits) and those stressing the limitations of the process ('satisficing' instead of 'optimising') and the relevance of cultural and political factors.
- Comparison of decisions made in different countries demonstrates the constraints on decision making, whether lack of information, lack of time and resources, political pressures or international circumstances.

Projects

1. Imagine that you have spent a year abroad studying at a university. Present a clear account of how you would make this decision and the university you chose using the six stages of the policy cycle in figure 15.1.
2. You have chosen to study comparative politics. What were the constraints on your decision to do so? Did you optimise your preferences or did you satisfice and why? Did you follow something like the rational-comprehensive process or did you muddle through, or neither? Are there any unintended and unexpected results?
3. Compare neo-corporatist and pluralist policy making of the iron triangles and policy community type. What are the differences between them?

Further reading

J. E. Anderson, *Public Policymaking*, 8th edn. Boston: HoughtonMifflin, 2014. A basic policy-making textbook that follows the policy cycle through its stages with American case studies.

P. Cairney, *Understanding Public Policy: Theories and Issues*. Basingstoke: Palgrave Macmillan, 2011. A text that concentrates on theories of policy making rather than descriptions of policies.

M. Crepaz, 'Corporatism in decline? An empirical analysis of the impact of corporatism on macroeconomic performance and industrial disputes in 18 industrialized democracies', *Comparative Political Studies*, 25, 1992: 139–68. A good analysis of the impact of corporatism on public policy.

C. Knill and J. Tosun, *Public Policy: A New Introduction*. Basingtoke: Palgrave Macmillan, 2012. A comparative study of policy making in different countries.

H. Lelieveldt and S. Princen, *The Politics of the European Union*, 2nd edn. Cambridge University Press, 2015. Chapter 8 contains a good account of policy making in the EU.

M. Moran, M. Rein and R. E. Goodin (eds.), *The Oxford Handbook of Public Policy*. Oxford University Press, 2008. A comprehensive and authoritative set of chapters on all aspects of public policy.

Websites

http://publicadministrationtheone.blogspot.co.uk/ 192012/08/public-policy-models-of-policy-making 27.html.
A useful article on types, models and theories of public policy making with a typology of states and policy making.
http://pages.uoregon.edu/vburris/whorules/policy.htm.
Extensive website on policy research with a number of links to different organisations and projects.

16   Public spending and public policies

Life can be very pleasant in democratic countries. The state provides schools and hospitals, roads and bridges, and parks and libraries, and sometimes it even subsidises opera and sport. But not all states do all these things and certainly not at the same cost to taxpayers, or to the same quality or with the same effects. Consider the following:

- Will the state help you if you are ill, poor, disabled or unemployed?
- Should the state tax you to help others less fortunate?
- Should everybody contribute to public goods and services or only those who use them?
- What is the right balance between taxing its citizens and providing them with public goods and services?

Some states provide a very large number and wide range of public services; others do not, but even in minimal states a full list of public functions would be long and their administration too complex to be described briefly. The politics of taxing and spending are also highly controversial and the source of fierce political debate. Consequently, we cannot cover all aspects of government activity in one chapter, so this one focuses on social protection to illustrate the ways in which democratic states are similar and different in the services they provide, how much they tax and spend, and how they use different means to achieve their goals.

When comparing countries we might choose to examine the quantity of public services, or their quality, or their effects on people's lives, but these are difficult and complex matters to define and quantify. How would you define and measure the quality of education you receive and would others agree with you? The easiest yardstick for comparison is public expenditure (see chapter 15; Figure 15.2). This is by no means the only way of studying public policy but it is an important and useful entry into the subject. It is important because taxes and public services have an impact on every resident and citizen in hundreds of different ways from birth to death. It is useful because state finances are a shorthand and concise way of capturing some of the most significant differences and similarities of democratic governments, even though the figures themselves are often difficult to pin down and must be treated with caution.

The major topics in this chapter are:

- The ends and means of government
- General government expenditure
- Social protection
- Theories of state activity.

■ The ends and means of government

We saw in chapter 14 that state activities are a major point of conflict between the left and right wing in politics. Conservatives and classical liberals place a high priority on individual freedom and responsibility and on the negative concept of 'freedom from' state regulations and taxation. Therefore they want a small state with minimal 'nightwatchman' functions and low taxes. Socialists and Christian Democrats emphasise the positive kind of 'freedom to' in which poverty, ignorance and disadvantage are reduced so that all individuals have a chance of achieving their potential. They also point out that individuals and the market economy are unable or unwilling to provide many of the services and facilities demanded of modern life – roads, street lighting, water, education, public health, fire services and some forms of research, among others. These things require a broad and diverse array of public services and taxes to pay for them.

As we saw in chapter 15, historical developments in various states resulted in very different 'mixtures' of private and public government spending in different countries. Nowadays the broader conception of state activity is widely shared in many countries, although controversy and conflict arise when specific policies are under discussion. This is usually because public services – judged by many to be desirable from the social, ethical and economic point of view – have to be paid for. Some citizens feel, often wrongly, that they pay for more than they get while others get more than they pay for, even when they neither need nor deserve what they receive. Public services are often in great demand but willingness to pay for them is in short supply. For this reason high taxes are a common complaint, and yet it is difficult to cut services. This is one of the central dilemmas of modern states and a source of conflict that runs throughout their daily politics.

Governments not only have a wide variety of services they can choose to deliver, but they also have a wide array of ways of paying for them. Indeed, an important part of the history of modern states is how they have invented ever more tools of government to do different things – and invented means to cover the costs. Among the most important ways of raising money are the following.

- Governments can raise money by direct and indirect taxes on a wide variety of things and economic activities – income, wealth, sales, property, businesses, profits, death duties, alcohol, petrol, tobacco.
- They can sell public services (car parking, water, power, education, tolls on roads and bridges). More recently, they have sold off public enterprises as a one-off way of raising income.
- Governments impose fines on unlawful behaviour (from car parking offences to financial fraud).
- Governments borrow huge amounts of money through loans and bonds, much favoured because they avoid tax increases and shift costs on to future generations and governments.
- Governments can also simply print money, although if their currencies are not strong this runs the risk of inflation.
- Some public activities are performed by international organisations (Interpol, the EU, the IMF) and some sources of money are also international organisations (the World Bank, the IMF, the EU). As a result a lot of money flows between these organisations and distinct levels of government.

The growth of the state can be seen clearly enough in the growth of income raised by governments. The average level of total tax revenue was about 27 per cent of GDP in democratic states in 1970; by 1988, it had grown to 33 per cent. After a clear drop with the economic and financial crises starting in 2008, the indicator reached 34 per cent in 2013. These figures are drawn up by the Organisation for Economic Cooperation and Development (OECD) which has a membership of twenty-eight countries, mainly economically developed and established democracies. High levels of tax revenues do not, of course, imply that citizens happily bear their share of the costs of government activities, and taxation is often an issue of serious political conflict. And yet the considerable burden of taxes and contributions was accepted with surprisingly little complaint and protest in many countries for a long time. In fact, the rapid expansion of social security programmes in the 1960s and 1970s was widely accepted and fundamental disagreement did not figure very largely in legislative debate. The reasons for broad support are easy to understand if we look at the many accomplishments that governments have achieved:

- *Political* Government activities do a great deal to ease political conflict between groups, not least by including all of them as citizens of the state with their own rights and duties.

- *Economic* Government interventions reduce the negative aspects of fierce competition (market failures) and social programmes improve the quality of the labour force and its productivity by maintaining a healthy and educated population.
- *Social* Government activities stabilise society by protecting the family and communities on which society itself depends. Conservative forces opposed to socialism in most of its forms place great importance on family and community.
- *Cultural* Government interventions help to create a fair and just society, which serves to enhance the legitimacy of the state and its social arrangements. Welfare helps to create a culture of support for society and the state.

Government activities are in the interest of many diverse groups in society, ranging from big business in search of efficient workers or early retirement schemes and banks to be bailed out after the crises in 2008 to students requesting adequate education or local charities supporting disabled children. Put somewhat strongly, extensive government activities are widely accepted because they meet the diverse needs of many different social and economic groups in society, while their costs are spread collectively. It does not follow that each and every activity is universally welcomed, only that the basic principles are often widely recognised.

■ General government expenditure

Given the variegated array of ends and means, it comes as no surprise that democracies also vary in the amount of public money they spend, what they spend it on and how they spend it. The point was already illustrated at the most general level in chapter 15 (figure 15.2), which shows the proportion of the gross domestic product (GDP) spent by general government (central, state and local). One of the lowest spenders is Switzerland; one of the highest is Denmark. They are similar in many ways, but public expenditure in Switzerland is barely more than a third of GDP (33.9%), while it is well over half in Denmark (57.7%). Switzerland is a wealthy country where taxes are generally low and citizens are mainly expected to finance their own needs for welfare, pensions, health and education. Denmark is also a wealthy country, but taxes and public spending are high. The neighbouring and relatively similar countries of Switzerland (34%) and Austria (51%) are also at different ends of the scale, while Poland (43%) and Norway (44%) are virtually identical, as are Italy and Hungary, and Slovenia and Austria. In other words, similar countries can spend very differently while dissimilar ones can match each other's spending levels.

What determines these similarities and differences? Levels of government spending are influenced by many considerations including, among others, national wealth, age of democracy, absence of corruption, a sense of common citizenship, national integration, demographic characteristics, and confidence in government and public agencies to do their job effectively and efficiently. Cultural and ideological differences also play their part, as the contrast between Switzerland and Denmark suggests.

There are also some common patterns in expenditures, as shown in table 16.1. Average public expenditure across OECD countries falls into three groups. Accounting for less than 1 per cent of GDP are housing, environment, culture, defence and internal security. Economic affairs, education, general services and health consume between 2 and 4 per cent. The broad category of social protection alone accounts for almost 10 per cent (9.6%). However, these averages conceal variations between countries that are often substantial and sometimes huge, as table 16.2 shows. Perhaps the largest of all is the figure for debt, which is minimal in Luxembourg and Norway, and vast in Japan, Greece and Italy. Debt has risen sharply in some countries because of the economic crisis, which led to governments bailing out banks and financial institutions at the cost of many trillions of dollars – tens of trillions in the USA alone.

As the figures for 'range' in the right-hand column of table 16.1 show, the broad categories and averages conceal even larger variations between countries, especially for the most expensive functions of social protection, health, education and general services. As table 16.2 shows, government spending on health as a percentage of GDP in the Netherlands is four times as much as it is in Switzerland. Iceland spends twice as much on education as Japan. Denmark spends more than six times as much as South Korea on social protection. Japan's national debt is eighteen times larger than Estonia's, and in Belgium central government expenditure accounts for two thirds of the total, compared with 13 per cent in the Czech Republic. The more one disaggregates (refines and sub-divides) into ever smaller categories, the greater the variation between countries.

Table 16.1 Average and range of general government expenditure in OECD countries, by main functions, as a percentage of GDP, 2011

	Average	Range
Social protection	9.6	4–25
Health	3.8	2–9
General public services	3.5	3–13
Education	2.7	2–13
Economic affairs	2.3	3–8
Public order and safety	1	1–3
Defence	1	0–7
Recreation, culture and religion	1	0–3
Environment	0	0–2
Housing	0	0–2

Source: https://data.oecd.org/gga/general-government-spending.htm#indicator-chart.

Table 16.2 General government spending as a percentage of GDP by main functions of OECD member states, 2011

	Lowest	Percentage	Highest	Percentage
Total	South Korea	30	Denmark	58
	Switzerland	34	France	56
	Turkey	37	Finland	55
Debt	Estonia	13	Japan	235
	Luxembourg	5	Greece	164
	Norway	6	Italy	136
Central government	Czech Republic	13	Belgium	67
	UK	14	Greece	62
	Estonia	15	Spain	56
Defence	Iceland	0.0	UK	1.5
	Ireland	0.4	South Korea	2.6
	Luxembourg	0.4	Israel	6.6
Health	Switzerland	2.2	Netherlands	8.5
	Turkey	2.1	Denmark	8.3
	South Korea	4.6	France	8.2
Education	Japan	3.6	Iceland	8.1
	Slovak Republic	4.0	Denmark	
	Greece	4.1	Israel	7.4
Social Protection	South Korea	3.9	Denmark	25.2
	Israel	11.5	Finland	23.8
	Iceland	11.6	France	23.8
Destination: Social/ Collective	Germany	6.8	Greece	10.9
	Norway	7.0	Hungary	10.1
	UK	7.2	Czech republic	9.5
Destination: Individual	Greece	8.9	Sweden	19.0
	Slovakia	9.2	Denmark	18.8
	Portugal	9.8	Netherlands	17.3

Source: https://data.oecd.org/gga/general-government-spending.htm#indicator-chart.

Note: The numbers are for illustrative purposes and have been rounded to the nearest whole number. Even so, 1 per cent of GDP may amount to millions or billions of dollars.

Available statistics distinguish between social expenditure on public goods and services for collective consumption (e.g. defence, justice) and expenditures for individual and household consumption (e.g. health, housing, education). These differences are shown in the bottom part of table 16.2. Expenditures with a social/collective destination do not vary across countries as much as the individual and household ones, but there is a tendency for the

Figure 16.1: Highest and lowest spenders on social and individual public expenditure items, OECD member states, 2011

Individual and household expenditure items	Social/collective expenditure items	
	High	Low
High	Netherlands, Iceland, France	Sweden, Denmark, Norway, UK
Low	Greece, Hungary, Czech Republic, Slovakia, Estonia	..

poorer Mediterranean and central European countries to be high on social/ collective and low on individual items. The reverse pattern holds for the richer countries of northern Europe. In a few cases (the Netherlands, Iceland and France) the figures are comparatively high on both counts, but no country is low on both (see figure 16.1).

We would find the same great variation if we had examined how states raise their incomes or which tools of government they use to deliver their services. In government, as in many other things there are, to quote the old saying, many ways to bake a cake. What is strange is not this diversity but how often it is claimed by politicians, commentators and administrators that their own way is the best or only way to do things. Comparing countries shows how wrong this sort of 'we have no alternative' claim is.

■ Welfare states and redistribution

Over the past two centuries the democracies of the Western world have gradually accepted the idea that government intervention is sometimes necessary to correct market failure and to rectify the morally unacceptable and economically inefficient consequences of a free and unrestrained economy. In particular they developed their welfare states, with the general goals of:

- reducing poverty
- promoting equality of opportunity
- promoting individual autonomy and maximising individual potential
- promoting social stability
- promoting social integration.

Closely related to these is the issue of how to define and measure poverty. The 'poverty line' shifts from one generation to the next: poverty now is not the same as poverty in 1960, even less that in 1900. Similarly, poverty in Ghana, Mali or Senegal is not the same as that in Austria or Australia.

Comparing social security systems

Since social and welfare services can be delivered by both public and private organisations, the OECD defines **social expenditures** as the provision by public and private institutions of benefits to households and individuals in order to provide support during circumstances which adversely affect their welfare. In some states, private spending (mainly pensions and health) is comparatively high and this group of countries consisting of the USA, Denmark, the Netherlands, Iceland and the UK are a mixed bag. It is lower in others and this is also a mixed group – Spain, the Czech Republic, New Zealand, Poland and Ireland. Across the OECD as a whole, in 2014 private social spending constituted 2.6 per cent of GDP, compared with public social spending of 22 per cent. Moreover, social protection is easily the largest item in the public budget. Therefore the rest of this chapter will deal with public spending for social protection, a term that is broader than welfare.

> **Social expenditures:** The provision by public (and private) institutions of benefits to households and individuals in order to provide support during circumstances which adversely affect their welfare.

As can be seen in figure 16.2 some countries spend about half as much of their GDP on social protection as others. Israel, Iceland, Estonia and Switzerland are low spenders; Denmark, Finland, France, Austria and Sweden are high. And while some similar countries have very different levels of expenditure, some dissimilar ones spend much the same – compare Switzerland with Austria and the Slovak Republic with Slovenia. In general, however, the continental European countries spend much more than the

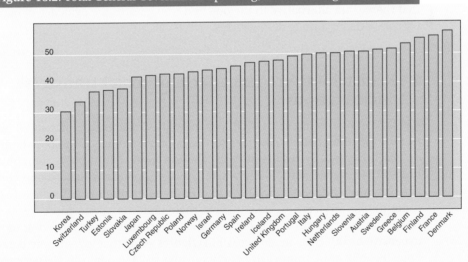

Figure 16.2: Total General Government Spending, as a Percentage of GDP, 2011

Source: https://data.oecd.org/gga/general-government-spending.htm.

others. Japan is the highest of the non-European countries and its figure is usually close to the OECD average.

Some of these differences are explained by demographic variations. For example, wealthier countries often have ageing populations, which require special social services that are sometimes expensive. Equally the poorer nations often have a large child population, which also has its special needs. But population characteristics do not necessarily explain country differences in spending. For example, Denmark spends almost five times as much on unemployment than the UK, but does not have five times as many unemployed people. On the contrary, their (official) unemployment rates are roughly the same.

Nor do countries spend money in the same way on any given service. The OECD distinguishes between cash benefits and goods and services. Cash benefits comprise money transferred to individuals or families, and goods and services are supplied free or at low cost. Cash benefits generally account for the largest proportion – heavily so in continental Europe – though there are exceptions. However, the two types of spending usually balance each other in the sense that when one is comparatively low the other is high, and vice versa.

What we learn from these comparisons is that similar countries can vary considerably in their expenditure patterns, just as dissimilar countries can converge on similar patterns of spending. In previous chapters we have seen that there are many constitutional forms of democracy, different ways of dividing and balancing government powers, various options for organising democratic elections, different methods of holding the public bureaucracy accountable, and so on. So also there are many different ways of raising and spending public money in democracies, different ways of achieving the same ends, and different ends to be achieved in similar ways. Here, too, the claim that there is no alternative to the one best way ignores the evidence of country comparisons among democracies.

■ Redistribution? The effects of social transfers and taxation

It should not be assumed, as it often is in political discussion, that social protection spending necessarily goes to the poorer sections of the population, or that it necessarily results in redistribution from rich to poor. Sometimes it does the reverse, particularly when it involves pensions, health and child benefits. More affluent individuals and households often benefit most from some public services, especially since their children spend more years in free, full-time education and because they live longer, thus incurring more expensive health costs in old age. OECD figures show that low-income households benefit most from cash benefits in the UK, Canada, the Netherlands, and especially in Norway and Australia. But in Greece, Italy, Spain and Portugal a larger proportion of social transfers go to wealthier sections of the population. In Austria, France and Luxembourg the wealthier also tend to benefit from substantial insurance payments of various kinds.

The redistributive effects of social expenditures are also affected by tax systems. Some countries tax social benefits – they use direct and indirect forms of taxation to 'claw back' with the left hand a proportion of what is given with the right. This can reduce the redistributive effects of social spending. In contrast, other countries give tax breaks in the form of tax allowances or credits with the aim of increasing social support. In the USA, such tax breaks for private medical schemes amount to billions of dollars, which means heavy loss of income for the government and a net benefit to individuals, usually self-employed and middle-income groups.

Social transfers and tax systems, together with private social spending, have the effect of narrowing the government spending differences between countries shown in figure 16.2. Tax claw-backs reduce the spending on social protection in Austria, Luxembourg and Scandinavia, while private expenditure more than compensates for them in the UK, the Netherlands and Iceland and increases their net spending. Australia, Canada and Japan have small tax effects but large private expenditures, which increases their overall spending substantially, and the same combination has a startlingly large impact in the USA. When allowances are made for small tax effects and large private spending the USA moves from twenty-third to second in the OECD league table for social spending (see controversy 16.1). This underlines the fact that when looking at the distribution of costs and benefits of public services it is necessary to take into account both public and private expenditure.

CONTROVERSY 16.1

The American welfare state: unusually small?

Comparing social security programmes is a complicated matter requiring us to take into account different tax systems, exchange rates, costs of living and the value of benefits in cash and in kind. Most analysis is based on gross payments (total payments to fund welfare service) or an estimation of income deductions made by the state. A careful estimate of these deductions, however, may change our conclusions about the differences between welfare states:

I challenge the most commonly made claim about the exceptional nature of the American welfare state – that it is unusually small. This judgement, in my view, is misleading. It is based on an overstatement of the social benefits received in other nations and an underestimate of the social benefits distributed by the United States. The latter results from a narrow focus on just two tools of government action, social insurance and grants, and from a misleading measure of welfare state effort ...

In short, the American welfare state may be unusual less for its small size than for its reliance on a wide variety of policy tools to achieve what many European welfare states do primarily through social insurance. While it is hard to be 100 per cent sure of this conclusion, given the difficulties of comparing direct spending, tax expenditures, regulation, loan guarantees, and the like, the evidence certainly suggests that we should be highly suspicious of anyone who declares that the United States has a small welfare state.

(Christopher Howard, 'Is the American welfare state unusually small?', Political Science & Politics, 34(3), 2003: 411–16)

Although taxes, transfers and private spending have the effect of reducing country variations in government spending, the final figures for net spending are still substantially different, with a range of 8 to 32 per cent of GDP. France, the USA, Belgium, Denmark and the UK are at the top of the league table with net total social expenditure of more than 25 per cent of GDP. South Korea, Estonia, Israel, Poland and the Slovak Republic are at the bottom with 17 per cent or less. The gap between the west European average and other democracies remains, but is smaller than figure 16.2 suggests. The final net expenditure figures show how tricky it can be to deal with public expenditure data and how easy it is to present misleading information.

Trends in social expenditure

Modern states have passed through several phases in their development. For a long time after consolidating their territory and sovereignty, liberal theory held that they should limit themselves to the minimal 'nightwatchman' role of protection against physical attack, theft, fraud, and invasion. Consequently the main state institutions were the police, courts and military, but also tax collectors and spies, both of which are ancient professions. As states gradually granted civil and political rights to citizens, so they started to provide them with services to protect the poorest and most vulnerable (see chapters 1 and 2). Initially, the intention was to provide no more than a minimal safety net for those in the greatest danger, but gradually public services were extended to include larger sections of the population, and then to work towards equality of opportunity for all. Attempts to equalise opportunity and redistribute resources usually involved political conflict, sometimes severe.

At the same time, technological developments and the growth of large-scale urban–industrial society made it possible and necessary to provide collective services and facilities such as street lighting, water, sewerage, public health, fire services, police and public buildings. Individuals and business either could not or would not provide such things, making it necessary for the state to step in. There was also growing recognition of the need for state regulation of such things as child labour, public health and trading practices. The growing demands of an industrial and bureaucratic society also required a more educated and highly trained population, hence the expansion of public education.

The traumatic experiences of the Great Depression of the 1930s and the post-war economic chaos of the late 1940s hastened the growth of state activities. Democratic states gradually accepted the idea that markets did not always function well and that government intervention was necessary to correct market failures. The traditional **laissez-faire doctrines** associated with emerging capitalism in many countries was replaced by the modern state with a broad scope of government.

Laissez-faire doctrines: The literal translation from the French is 'allow to do': maximum freedom for the economic forces of the market, and minimum intervention from the state.

Social security programmes began in Germany and Austria in the 1880s. A second phase of development followed the First World War, when other countries took up the idea, and a third phase followed the Second World War, when there was a very rapid expansion of a wide variety of programmes in many Western countries. These were generally well established by the mid-1970s, but from then onwards until the 1990s there was a fourth phase of stability or reform. We have already seen how the level and composition of spending varies from one country to another, but to talk about 'phases of development' in a collection of countries suggests that their trends over time may be rather similar. In fact we have already seen this in chapter 2, which showed how redistribution of resources was a characteristic of developing democracies in the nineteenth century. We can make two points:

- It may be that since most industrial democracies are confronted with similar problems as they develop, so they also follow similar trends in their social security spending?
- In which case perhaps democratic countries have become more alike (converging) in this respect?

Social security expanded rapidly in many European countries in the 1960s and 1970s, when the worst damage of the Second World War had been repaired and economic growth provided the necessary finance. In the period between 1960 and 1980 social expenditure rose in Denmark, for instance, from 11 per cent to almost 30 per cent of GDP. On average, the OECD countries doubled their social spending between 1960 and 1980. This was primarily because social security was extended to larger sections of the population and because higher-quality services were provided at higher cost.

Trends in the level of spending as a percentage of GDP in selected countries are presented in figure 16.3. At first glance they confirm our conclusion about the large differences between countries. Although the trend lines show more or less similar developments, differences between countries have narrowed in the last few years. The trend lines show that:

- Expansion reached a ceiling in the 1980s, when few new commitments were added, and spending started to flatten out or even declined slightly. The economic recession of the 1970s made it clear that economic growth could not be taken for granted, and several governments tried to curtail social expenditures.
- However, severe economic problems and rising unemployment at the end of the 1980s and the early 1990s forced some countries to spend more on social security. Increases were evident in Sweden, but also in Austria, Denmark, Finland, France, Germany, Portugal.
- Social spending again declined in many countries in the 1990s, once more for economic and financial reasons – benefits were cut, the people eligible for them restricted and private provision was encouraged, especially for pensions, and health and personal insurance. In other words, neo-liberal policies may have prevented social spending from rising, but it did not

Figure 16.3: Trends in public social spending, selected countries as a percentage of GDP, 1980–2014

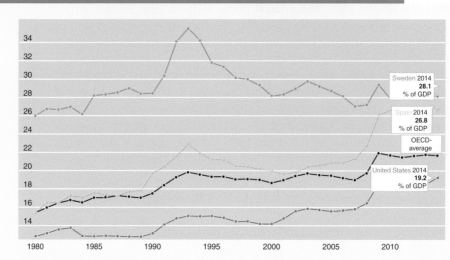

Source: OECD Social Expenditure Database (www.oecd.org/social/expenditure.htm)

succeed in cutting it. The irony is that neo-liberal policies of deregulation and privatisation of financial institutions were, in large part, responsible for the financial crash of 2008, which then caused a significant rise in spending in the next two years.

- The financial and economic crisis of 2008 initially led to a rise in social spending in many countries. Yet widespread support for austerity policies halted this rise and resulted in a stabilisation of social spending levels since 2009. From its peak level in 2009, social protection spending fell as a percentage of GDP by 1.5–2.5 per cent in Canada, Germany, Iceland, Ireland and the UK and especially in Estonia and Greece. Nevertheless, in seven countries it was 4 per cent higher than its highest level before the 2008 crisis, and in only one (Hungary) is it actually lower.

The expectation that states converge and become more alike in their social expenditures as their economies develop is only partly supported by the data, which show that each country has its own combination of social security programmes and its own approach to reform. What we observe, however, are similar patterns in the time trends, with rising expenditures and attempts to reform social security in economically difficult periods. In the period between 1980 and 2014 the differences in social spending between the top spenders and the countries with much more modest programmes are reduced, mainly due to a general rise in social spending in countries which previously spent less on the social protection of their citizens.

Chapter 14 discussed the revival of classical liberalism – now known as **neo-liberalism** or neo-conservatism – among people who believe that the powers of the state should be drastically reduced, the economy privatised and deregulated and state spending drastically cut. Neo-liberal politicians set out their programmes for cutting back the power and functions of government, especially their spending on social services and welfare. These, it was argued, interfered with the efficiency of the market, and cre-

> **Neo-liberalism:** An economic and philosophical outlook which advocates a reduced role for the state in economic affairs, and a strong belief in the functioning of markets and free trade policies.

ated a culture of dependency on the state and a poverty cycle in which the children of welfare funded parents became dependent on welfare when they became adults.

However, the neo-liberal movement was interrupted by the financial crash of 2008, the worst in seventy-five years, which caused severe economic problems for almost all Western governments. On the one hand GDP fell and a period of economic austerity set in, triggering a need for greater government social spending. On the other hand, the tax base also fell as incomes declined and unemployment rose, but governments also had to find huge amounts of extra money to save the financial institutions that caused the crash and to avoid a further deflationary spiral. To do this they had to borrow not millions, or billions or trillions of dollars but tens of trillions of dollars.

The combination of neo-liberal politics and severe economic crisis raises the question of what has actually happened to social spending in democracies. Has it fallen, in line with 'Thatcherite' and 'Reagonomics' thinking? As already observed in this chapter, many people want taxes and services cut, but most resist strongly any attempt to cut services that benefit them. The fierce political battle between spenders and cutters has been revived and will continue in the foreseeable future.

■ Theories of the welfare state

The question of how and why democratic states gradually came to accept responsibility for their young and old, sick and disabled, unemployed and poor has fascinated scholars. Their interest is related to the fact that welfare systems vary hugely between states, and that social security expenditures, as a form of redistribution between citizens, are most usually the source of serious social, political and economic conflict. The welfare state involves some fundamental moral issues about social justice, the nature of the modern state and its relationship with its citizens. As a result, theories about it typically mix normative and ideological approaches (see chapter 14) with empirical research. There are two fundamentally opposed views of the matter:

- *Liberal approaches* regard the welfare state as a left-wing institution that taxes the rich, constrains their liberty and encourages laziness and dependency on the part of the workers.
- *Socialist approaches* see the welfare state as a right-wing device that enables the capitalist system to function (that is, to maintain an educated and healthy working population) without having to rely on force while avoiding the costs.

We do not wish to cover the ground of chapter 14 again, but will concentrate instead on empirical theories that explain why very different types of social security programmes arose in various countries and why these expenditures occupy an ever-larger share of GDP. Empirical theories come in four major forms.

Conflict-oriented approaches

These explain the very different paths taken by countries on the basis of power conflicts between groups in society. A well-known example of this approach is the work of the Danish political scientist Esping-Andersen (1947–). In his view, the historical role and position of the labour movement was decisive, especially its resources and its ability to mobilise workers. Opposing social elites – capitalists, some churches, and politicians – were forced to compromise on redistribution policies if they were faced by a strong labour movement. Since the division of power varies in different countries according to their historical circumstances, different social security programmes are likely to arise (see briefing 16.1). Other scholars believe that conflicts between political parties are decisive, particularly given the important role that Christian democratic parties have played.

Briefing 16.1

A typology of welfare states

One of the most comprehensive treatments of welfare state policies and the various ways of organising them is presented by the Danish political scientist Esping-Andersen in his *The Three Worlds of Welfare Capitalism* (1990). He distinguishes between different types of welfare state according to entitlements to benefits, levels of support, degree of redistribution and success in reducing or reinforcing inequalities. The three major types are as follows.

■ Liberal welfare capitalism

A liberal type of welfare capitalism is found in Anglo-Saxon countries, particularly Australia, Canada and the USA. Benefits are modest and available mainly for low-income groups. Conventional work-ethic norms play an important role and entitlement rules are strict. The state encourages private initiatives to provide social security.

■ Conservative welfare capitalism

A conservative type of welfare capitalism is found in continental Europe, including Austria, France, Germany and Italy. This type is characterised by corporatism – that is, unions, employers' associations and governments collaborate closely to arrange social security programmes (see chapter 15). Because the government relies heavily on the collaboration of both union and business, redistribution is usually limited: entitlements are linked to status and class. Because the church plays a major role in corporatist regimes, social security programmes emphasise traditional family values.

■ Social-democratic welfare capitalism

A social-democratic type of welfare capitalism is found in Scandinavian countries. The goal of social security is not 'equality of minimal needs', but equality based on the highest standards. This means, first, that cash benefits are generous and services of high quality and, second, that every citizen participates equally in the system (the principle of universal entitlement). The ideal is to maximise individual independence, rather than emphasise either the family or the market.

Esping-Andersen's typology was at the core of debates about the welfare state in the 1990s. Although critics point to limitations – such as the neglect of gender issues, the special features found in southern Europe and the interdependence of 'welfare capitalism' and negotiations between unions and employers' associations about benefits – his typology is indispensable. As with every good typology, its main advantage is the way it groups a large number of disparate systems into a few categories that make sense and are helpful.

See *Gøsta Esping-Andersen, The Three Worlds of Welfare Capitalism.*

Princeton University Press, 1990.

A special version of these theories tries to explain the absence of political conflict between workers and capitalists in Britain in the late nineteenth century. At the time, Britain was the most advanced capitalist economy in the world and precisely the place where Marxist theory predicted a revolutionary working-class movement. British workers, however, were anything but revolutionary. On the contrary, most were comparatively conservative and strongly supported what the Marxists regarded as the 'capitalist' Empire and the First World War, which they claim was fought for capitalist reasons. According to the Russian revolutionary Marxist Vladimir Lenin (1870–1924), this was because late nineteenth-century and early twentieth-century Britain could afford to pay higher wages and finance some rudimentary welfare services out of the huge profits it made by exploiting its colonies. These kept the British workers not just happy and docile but turned many of them into counter-revolutionary supporters of the Empire and of the First World War.

Functionalist explanations

The oldest accounts of diversity in social security systems focus on functionalist explanations. Emerging capitalism requires state intervention to support workers and stabilise families. According to this view, social security differences between countries are mainly the result of different levels of socioeconomic development. A recent revival of functionalism argues that welfare policies enable modern societies to shift from industrial to post-industrial economies – for example, to enable coal mines and textile factories to be closed down by pensioning off miners and textile workers, or retraining them for different jobs.

Institutional approaches

These are a rather mixed set of explanations, but they all focus on the importance of institutional structures. Broadly speaking, the idea is that the more institutions are involved in policy making, the more difficult it is to create extensive social security arrangements. States with complex federal structures, and those making most use of referenda, are less developed than unitary states where decision-making power is unified and centralised. Institutional inertia may also explain the persistence of welfare states once they are established, because they are surrounded by bureaucracies and institutionalised interests that protect them against reform (see chapters 8 and 10). This does not explain how and why they arose in the first place.

Two versions of the institutional approach can be applied to different countries according to their decision-making institutions in the welfare field. The first involves the idea of policy networks. We discussed policy communities in chapter 15. Policy networks are looser and more open than communities, generally involving a wider range of interests and, therefore, more disagreement and conflict. Welfare policy networks involve government leaders and top administrators in welfare departments, a wide range of welfare professionals and employees and a wide range of pressure groups representing welfare service consumers. These come together in the network of committees, working groups and consultative bodies set up within government institutions and private bodies such as think tanks. Policy networks in the welfare field are found in the UK, France and Italy, and in a weaker form in the USA.

In other countries welfare policy making is more highly formalised within corporatist institutions (see chapters 10 and 15). Under these arrangements government and a few private interests work closely together within official structures that formulate and implement public policies. Each set of private interests (welfare professionals, for example) is organised into a single peak association that acts authoritatively for all its members and takes decisions on their behalf. This means that all the actors involved at the highest levels of the corporatist structure can bargain and negotiate in the knowledge that the policy outcome will be accepted and implemented by those lower in the system. The advantage is that binding decisions can be made, and stable and predictable policies can be followed. The disadvantage is that the system is more closed and exclusive than policy networks, so that groups outside the corporatist system are excluded from decision making. Corporatism in its most developed form was found in Austria, Luxembourg, the Netherlands, Norway and Sweden between the 1960s and 1980s. Less pure forms were found in Belgium, Denmark, Finland, West Germany, Ireland and Switzerland in the same period.

International and transnational dependencies

Finally, there are approaches focusing on international and transnational dependencies which explain social security systems in terms of relations between states. A heated debate has more recently broken out. One school argues that globalisation forces states to cut their welfare programmes in order to make their economies more competitive in the world market. Another argues that some industries require a highly educated workforce with a full array of services to support it (health, pensions, pre-school and nursery provisions). New Zealand is sometimes presented as a country with a protected economy and a strong welfare state that transformed itself into a market economy with a modest welfare state. Small or vulnerable economies are said to be under pressure to reform welfare policies. In order to protect themselves from the consequences of global capitalism they have to reduce costs, which means cutting their welfare costs or being priced out of the international market. It is not clear why welfare costs have to be cut rather than other public expenditure items, or why cutting welfare might not be counterproductive. To this set of explanations also belong theories focusing on the impact of the European Union on the social policies of its member states: in an open market countries with expensive welfare systems are under pressure to reform these systems in order to reduce costs.

At first sight these various approaches seem to be rival explanations. Yet none seems to be satisfactory on its own. A better explanation involves all of them, because each explains only a part of the puzzle. For instance, the rise of the welfare state has invariably involved acute conflict between workers and employers with different resources and different capacities to mobilise support. At the same time, this conflict has been played out in different institutional contexts, in different legal frameworks and according to different rules. The outcomes are certainly influenced by international circumstances, in which developed economies – especially colonial powers – had greater surpluses to devote to welfare. And none of these explanations prevents the welfare system supporting the family, which may, in turn, fulfil an important function in capitalist society.

It is worth pointing out finally that just as there are different and equally effective ways of setting up a democratic political system, so there are also many different ways of setting up a welfare state. Cash transfers may be better suited to some circumstances or some purposes than others, but cash transfers are not necessarily better or worse than the direct delivery of services. If this is correct, then a variety of welfare state provisions is no more strange than a variety of democratic states: they are simply different ways of getting to the same place.

■ What have we learned?

- Almost without exception the democracies of the world have increased their supply of public services and provisions to a point that could not have been envisaged by the advocates of the 'nightwatchman state' of the nineteenth century. General government spending in these states now accounts for 30 to 55 per cent of GDP.
- The goals of the modern state are many and various, as are the means they use to attain them. Although there are some similarities, they vary enormously in what they spend public funds on and which financial means they use to provide their services.
- The largest expenditure items are social protection, health and education, the smallest housing, the environment, and recreation, culture and religion.
- When calculating total national expenditure on services it is important to take taxes, tax benefits and private spending into account, not just public spending. When this is done the service expenditure patterns of some countries can change substantially.
- It cannot be assumed that public spending is necessarily redistributive or reaches either the poorer or needier sections of the population. Some benefits go to wealthier individuals and households.
- Although the appetite for public services is great, willingness to pay for them is not. This makes them a matter for persistent conflict in politics.

■ Lessons of comparison

- Most democratic states show similar patterns of growth in public expenditure, particularly in the latter part of the twentieth century.
- Despite the common growth, states differ widely in the way in which they organise and provide support for their citizens. Even similar countries vary greatly in how much they spend and how they spend it.
- Democracies are not converging on a common pattern. They often show the same time trends and move in parallel in response to social, economic and political pressures, but they also preserve their differences in what they spend their money on.
- Neo-liberal attempts to cut public spending in the last twenty years or so have not generally been successful. Spending increased in response to the financial crisis of 2008 and some countries have maintained or increased their spending levels compared with the years before the crisis.

Projects

1. What would happen to you if you could not earn an adequate income? Could you apply for public support? What are the requirements and conditions of support in your case, and how much would you receive and for how long?
2. Many states have tried to reform their social protection policies. Present a systematic comparison of these attempts since 1995 in two different democracies. What was the main aim of these reforms? How successful were they?
3. Why do expenditure patterns differ between countries in similar circumstances and why do dissimilar countries have similar patterns?
4. Is the welfare state a capitalist or socialist institution?

Further reading

F. G. Castles, S. Leibfried, J. Lewis, H. Obinger and C. Pierson (eds.), *The Oxford Handbook of the Welfare State*. Oxford University Press, 2010. Contains 900 pages and 48 chapters on every aspect of the welfare state.

G. Esping-Andersen, *The Three Worlds of Welfare Capitalism*. Princeton University Press, 1990. The classic work on European social welfare systems and their origins.

G. M. Guess and L. T. LeLoup, *Comparative Public Budgeting: Global Perspectives on Taxing and Spending*. Albany: Suny Press, 2010. A global comparative analysis of how cultural, institutional, and political forces determine how governments tax and spend.

B. Jordan, *Social Policy for the Twenty-First Century*. New York: Polity Press, 2006. A general discussion of the problems and prospects of public expenditure and policy.

P. Pierson, *The New Politics of the Welfare State*, 3rd edn. Cambridge: Polity Press, 2006. A comparative analysis of the pressures (globalisation, demographic change, immigration and post-industrialisation) for the reform of welfare states in North America and Europe.

Websites

https://data.oecd.org/gga/general-government-spending.htm#indicator-chart. Provides government expenditure figures as a percentage of GDP for OECD, G7, G20, and EU28 countries, broken down into nineteen categories, 1970–2011.

www.oecd.org/els/soc/OECD2014-Social-Expenditure-Update-Nov2014-8pages .pdfis. A recent and comprehensive review of social protection expenditure in OECD countries.

17   The future of the democratic state

At the start of the third millennium, states and democracy seem to be the big winners in the fierce conflicts and wars that scarred the twentieth century. With only a few special exceptions, every place on earth falls within the territory of a state. The number of states has increased rapidly, from about fifty to almost two hundred, since the 1950s. States still claim absolute authority and control over their own territory and residents, and conflicts between states are still one of the most serious of all problems in modern times. Moreover, modern states are not the puny 'nightwatchmen' of the liberal era at the start of the twentieth century: they now provide an enormously wide variety of services, extract vast amounts in taxes and pervade almost every aspect of daily life.

Democracy also seems to have triumphed in the twentieth century. Three successive waves of democratisation – driven mainly by post-war decolonisation after 1945 and the collapse of the Soviet empire in 1989 – have expanded the number of democracies. Depending on how they are measured, there are now around fifty of them. Democracy has grown in depth and strength to cover far more than the most basic rights and duties, and now includes universal adult suffrage, referendums, a wide range of legal, social and economic rights, direct participation, greater control over government and fewer privileges for elites.

If the forces of statehood and democracy seem to be taking over the world, it may be because they are inseparable twins: states are essential for the democratic organisation of political life and democracy is essential for the legitimation of the state. Only a few utopians and anarchists can imagine democracy without the power of the state to create and enforce democratic rules and structures. In the twentieth century, and especially in the last half of that century, states and democracy developed together so that they seemed to be different sides of the same coin.

It is ironic, therefore, that the present time – the very heyday of the democratic state – produces widespread predictions of the imminent decline of the state and a crisis of democracy.

- Could it be that widespread and confident announcements about the end of the state and the crisis of democracy show that they are both past their best?
- Should we now start searching for a new understanding of state and democracy in the twenty-first century, with different theories, fresh concepts and original approaches adapted to the 'post-state' and a 'post-democratic' twenty-first century?

'The Owl of Minerva spreads its wings only at dusk', wrote the German philosopher Hegel (1770–1831), by which he meant that we understand reality only after events have taken place. In which case it may be that the democratic state is so popular today precisely because it is an outdated model!

Those who followed Hegel's approach to the state in the nineteenth century focused on the French Revolution, with its emphasis on citizenship and human rights. They substituted the early morning crowing of the French rooster for the hooting of Minerva's owl. Nevertheless, the great revolutions of France and America that have shaped the development of our contemporary democracies are more than two centuries old. Do we need a new approach and new theories for a new world?

In this concluding chapter, we return to questions about the contemporary relevance of states and the future of democracy:

- Is the state and its sovereignty 'withering away' and, if so, what will succeed it?
- Can democracy survive?
- What reforms might help to preserve both the state and democracy?

The terms on everybody's lips, of course, are globalisation, internationalisation and the crisis of democracy. The major topics in this chapter are:

- States and sovereignty
- The retreat of the state?
- Democracy without borders
- The future.

■ States and sovereignty

The usefulness of the term 'state' may be limited by two difficulties. First, the concept has to cover a huge variety of different forms of democratic (and undemocratic) political organisations: from the comparatively tiny states of

Tuvalu and Nauru to the huge land masses of Brazil, Canada and Australia; from the old-established democracies of Denmark and New Zealand to the new ones of the Czech Republic and Serbia; and from ethnically homogeneous Norway to multi-cultural India. Is it helpful to apply the same term to such a wide variety of political systems? Second, the traditional supremacy of the state is now challenged by globalisation and the 'borderless world', which can no longer be understood in terms of national independence and sovereignty. It was one thing to defend your country against soldiers massing on the border, but quite a different thing to defend it against the power of MNCs, hacker attacks on your computer systems and terrorism. We shall argue that, in spite of all this, states are still the main building blocks of modern government and politics.

Conventional states, proto-states and supra-national states

States are characterised by their territory, people and sovereignty, and if we are to analyse their development or their decline, it is helpful to do so in terms of these three elements. In fact, we can distinguish three broad types of state, according to how they combine their three defining characteristics:

- conventional states
- proto-states
- supra-national states.

Conventional states

Conventional states have a well-defined territory, a developed sense of nationhood (a 'people') and all the institutions of sovereignty. They are found all over the globe and the fact that they are usually associated with peace and stability seems to have a lot to do with democracy and relationships and the balance of power between democratic states. Conventional states remain sovereign within their own borders. In some cases, outside influences are crucial for their creation and persistence (the USA playing a defining role in this respect), but in the majority of cases, the territory, people and sovereignty of conventional states are not disputed, and they conduct relations between each other on this basis.

Proto-states

States in some parts of the world do not have secure boundaries, or a body of citizens who form a 'people', or a single sovereign power with a monopoly of the legitimate use of physical force. They are threatened by putsches, insurrections, separatist movements, foreign intervention, ethnic clashes or civil wars. Sometimes a conventional state divides itself, to be replaced by two or more new ones (Czechoslovakia became the Czech Republic and Slovakia, and Yugoslavia has become seven states: Bosnia and Herzegovina, Croatia, Kosovo, Macedonia, Montenegro, Serbia and Slovenia), but the successors are not guaranteed to turn themselves into conventional states. They may be torn apart by chaos and anarchy, with competing factions and warlords replacing sovereign power. In some instances, no ultimate authority, no sovereign power, no state exists (Libya and Somalia). The label 'proto-state' suggests that conventional states may emerge in these places. This often occurs with the help of foreign assistance, as happened in the Balkans in the 1990s when the republic of Bosnia-Herzegovina was successfully created on the basis of an international agreement in order to end war and genocide. The independence of Kosovo, now upheld with a small military peace-keeping presence, can be seen as a further step towards creating states in this area that come closer to the ideal-type of the conventional state.

Supra-national states

Serious conflicts between states do not necessarily result in state disintegration, separation or chaos. In Europe, the conventional state is in the process of being transformed by cooperation, negotiation and agreement. The member states of the EU are still characterised by their territories and populations, but national borders are becoming increasingly porous and even irrelevant, and the claim of absolute national sovereignty has been given up. Power has not been shifted to other states, however, but to a new supra-national organisation that coordinates its member states and lays down binding rules for them. The EU is the only clear example of a supra-national organisation of this kind and to this extent it still remains a risky adventure that is as ambitious as it is experimental. It is a striking fact that the prototype of the post-conventional state is being created in western Europe, the cradle of the conventional state. Nonetheless, we should not forget that many important policy areas – such as foreign politics and defence, taxation and social security – remain firmly in the hands of national governments, despite continuous attempts by the EU to coordinate and standardise them. Furthermore, recent enlargement of the EU and the rise of anti-EU parties in several countries will make it more difficult to deepen integration. Indeed, attempts to produce a European constitution failed because of divisions among the member states and the rejection of the proposal in Dutch and French referendums. For all this, the EU is a post-conventional state.

Conventional states remain the most common form of organising political power, a situation that will not change overnight or in the near future. It does not follow that every part of the earth, the sea and the sky is subject to the sovereign power of a given state, any more than it means that all political power is state power, but the modern state remains the anchor point for our understanding of modern comparative politics. Apart from anything else, the strongest political power in the world and the only global power of our time is the USA – a conventional state *par excellence*. To the extent that its power is rivalled, it is by the supra-national European Union and by the other conventional states of Japan, China and Russia, and in some ways it is challenged by smaller powers such as Iran and North Korea.

Challenges to the state

Although conventional states rule the world, their position as sovereign bodies is challenged by five developments:

- concentration of commercial power
- rise of international NGOs
- globalisation
- changing nature of conflicts
- importance of international organisations.

Concentration of commercial power

Some commercial organisations are wealthier than states, and are able to challenge their power. The GDP of Eritrea – one of the poorest countries of the world – was only US$3.4 billion in 2014. Even in wealthy Europe, Portugal and Slovenia had GDPs of US$227 billion and US$48 billion respectively. These figures are far below the worth of the largest business companies in the world, some of which have annual revenues of more than US$400 billion (see table 17.1). Although economic indicators are difficult to compare directly, not even the total wealth of Portugal puts it within reach of the dozen largest companies. For that matter, an increasing number of individuals – the top dozen are each worth $40–80 billion – have more money than many whole countries. If power follows wealth, and if wealth generates power, then it is no surprise that the big MNCs can influence economic development and set their own terms when dealing with national governments, not least because the mobility of their capital gives them great locational flexibility.

Table 17.1 The ten largest corporations in the world, 2014

Corporation	Origin	Main business	Employees	Revenues (US$ million)
Wal-Mart Stores	USA	Retailing	2,200,000	476,294
Royal Dutch/Shell Group	UK/Netherlands	Oil	87,000	459,599
Sinopec Group/China National Petroleum and Chemical Petroleum	China	Oil	1,015,039	457,201
PetroChina/China National Petroleum	China	Oil	1,656,465	457,201
Exxon Mobil	USA	Oil	88,000	407,666
BP	UK	Oil	85,700	396,217
StateGrid	China	Electric utilities	849,594	333,386
Volkswagen	Germany	Automobiles	549,763	261,539
Toyota Motor	Japan	Automobiles	333,498	256,454
Glencore	Switzerland/UK	Trading and mining	61,000	232,694

Source: http://fortune.com/global500/.

Rise of international NGOs

International NGOs (see chapter 10) are neither branches nor agencies of the state, nor are most of them created by states. They include, for instance, Amnesty International, Greenpeace, Médecins Sans Frontières, the Scottish Catholic International Aid Fund and Volontari nel Mondo and their main characteristics are that they:

- are founded and run by citizens independently of governments and states,
- are non-profit or charitable organisations,
- reject the use of violence.

In their modern form, international NGOs were founded in the nineteenth century, but their numbers and importance increased after the Second World War. It is difficult to estimate their numbers, but according to the UN there were 1,083 international NGOs in 1914, which increased to more than 40,000 in 2000. Nearly one-fifth of them were formed in the 1990s. Most developing countries have seen an even sharper increase in the number of domestic NGOs: Brazil has an estimated 220,000, India an estimated 1.2 million.

NGOs are non-state organisations and for the most part they are privately financed, but some of them receive financial and other support from states or international organisations such as the European Union and the UN. When they are heavily dependent on public money, and when NGO and government activities are closely interwoven, the sharp distinction between 'private' and 'public' vanishes. Governments also find it useful to create organisations that are independent of them, but which provide public services with the help of public funding. Such organisations are known as QUANGOs (see chapter 11), and are useful in politically sensitive areas which fall within the public sector, but which governments do not wish to control directly (see chapter 10). Public broadcasting is the classic case where QUANGOs operate in the public sector at arm's length from government. As with NGOs, it is exceedingly difficult to estimate QUANGO numbers, but they are also rising steeply.

NGOs (and QUANGOs to a lesser extent) are widely believed to be increasingly powerful actors in national and international government. This is not so much because they are wealthy, like the MNCs, but because NGOs often have a powerful emotional and moral appeal. Organisations such as Christian Aid, Greenpeace, Oxfam and the Red Cross use their popular appeal to gain widespread publicity for their activities, and they can use this to 'leverage' political influence. They represent another force that challenges the power of the state.

Globalisation

The 'interdependence' and 'connectedness' of the world today is evident when we look at the environment and the use of natural resources, or at terrorism and the global drug and armaments trade. It is most evident in the economic and financial sectors, where capital and production is free to move around the world in pursuit of the highest profits and lowest taxes. Since welfare states are tax states with high labour costs, they are under pressure by businesses threatening to relocate investments and jobs. A whole range of mini-states – the Bahamas, Singapore – serve as international tax shelters and places where companies can be legally registered. There are also banking centres where it is easier to launder money. Not only do these have implications for the ability of states to control international business and illegal trade, but they reduce government revenues that are used to pay for public services. Some countries (Brazil, for example) encounter serious problems if large amounts of money are transferred to foreign bank accounts.

Globalisation is also evident in the rapid spread of the World Wide Web and of satellite communications. States find them difficult, sometimes impossible, to control. Similarly, population movements from one side of the globe to another, and especially from poor countries to rich ones, have created huge problems. It is estimated that the total number of people living outside their home country rose 40 per cent between 2004 and 2014, to reach 200 million. No one knows what proportion of these are illegal immigrants but the International Organization for Migration in Geneva estimates it at between 30 and 40 million.

Changing nature of conflicts

Violent inter-state conflict has not increased in recent decades, in spite of an increase in the number of states. Indeed, national borders are no longer disputed in most established democracies, and in some of them there is no longer a need for passports to cross borders. To this extent, the age-old argument that a state is needed to provide border controls and military protection is reduced. At the same time, new threats to the state have appeared:

- First, violent conflict within states has increased and the role of the armed forces is certainly not reduced in many pre-conventional states (the Caucasus and many parts of Africa and Latin America), and in some conventional ones as well (Cyprus, Democratic Republic of Congo). This creates a need for highly trained and specially equipped peacekeeping forces, which are provided mainly by the conventional states.
- Second, the threat of terrorism took a dramatic form with the attack on the World Trade Center in New York in September 2001. States that are no longer endangered by foreign armies have to deal with a completely different problem that cannot be handled by the conventional armed forces. Instead conflicts increasingly involve combatants who do not belong to regular forces, operate in- or outside their own country and usually rely on subversive actions or terrorist attacks.

Importance of international governmental organisations

States have created a large number of international organisations to deal with relations between them and to try to settle conflicts in an orderly and peaceful manner. These organisations are institutionalised forms of cooperation and collaboration, and although they work at the international level they are still the product of state cooperation, and states take their own decisions about whether to join or leave, and to comply with their decisions or to reject them. The main example is the UN and its many subsidiary organisations, but the list includes thousands more, such as the OECD and the Organization of the Petroleum Exporting Countries (OPEC). International organisations such as these are clearly different from states, in that each has a clear and limited task:

- The OECD is concerned with economic matters and collecting statistical information for a comparatively small number of wealthy nations.
- The WHO deals with medical matters.
- The IMF fosters global monetary cooperation, stability, trade and employment.

A very few international organisations (the EU and the Security Council of the UN) can give orders to states and the UN can even use military force to back them up, but most do not have this sort of power.

As the intensity and scope of relations between states has increased, so has the number of international organisations. As a result, states are increasingly caught up in a web of directions, advice and instructions. Globalisation and rising numbers of NGOs will further stimulate this process. Even if most of the decisions taken by international organisations are voluntarily accepted by states, their scope for action is still restricted.

■ The retreat of the state?

The combination of MNCs, NGOs, globalisation, the changing nature of conflict and the importance of international organisations casts doubt on the continuing relevance of the state. It seems to be only one actor among many, and one that is rapidly declining in power and importance at that (see controversy 2.1). Should we even drop the concept of the state, and concentrate on the 'real' and important actors in the world today? This suggestion, however, fails to notice that states are still the most important actors on the world stage, and that sovereignty and the legitimate use of physical force within their given territories are still the main form of organised political power. States continue:

- to be the main actors in modern warfare (Afghanistan, Iraq, Syria);
- to create international and supra-national agencies of government such as the EU and the UN, and control them;
- to be responsible for the vast majority of public services delivered to citizens;
- to raise vast amounts of money in taxes;
- to be mainly responsible for the defence of their territory and their citizens and for the maintenance of internal law and order;
- to define the rights and duties of citizens in most democracies (with certain EU exceptions);

- to decide who will live and work within their borders (though admittedly with the increasing exception of illegal immigrants);
- to issue passports, travel and identity documents to their citizens;
- to control and influence a great many aspects of the daily life of their citizens with an accumulation of laws and millions of ordinances, rules, orders, commands, regulations, precepts, decrees, directives, instructions, edicts, dictates, injunctions, promulgations, guidelines, advisory documents, circulars, specifications and requirements;
- to be attacked: even international terrorism is mainly directed towards states or their representatives, even when it attacks ordinary citizens.

Arguments about the decline of the state also seriously underestimate the force of another characteristic of our times: the rising strength of nationalism (see chapter 14). While it is true that technology promotes global integration and weakens national boundaries in some respects, in others it makes it easier to sustain nationalism. Communications technology helps to preserve minority languages and culture with local radio and television stations and desk-top publishing. Moreover, as each ethnic minority creates its own independent state, so it is likely to create another minority within its own borders. Nationalism seems to have a lot of life in it yet – and, by definition, it implies a strengthening of the state. Summarising the confusing and contradictory trends and arguments about the state, the political scientist Susan Strange (1923–98) presents three hypotheses in her book *The Retreat of the State* (1996):

1. Political power has shifted upwards from weak states to stronger states. Strong states are able to influence, even determine, developments far outside their territory. The best example is, of course, the USA, but one can also think of the influence of France in north and west Africa, and of Russia in central Asia and eastern Europe.
2. Political power has shifted sideways from states to markets, strengthening the position of giant MNCs and of international organisations such as the G9, the IMF and OPEC. Some writers now prefer to use the term 'governance' rather than government (see chapter 4), because the term implies the coordination of many actors in the political system rather than the old 'top-down' system whereby government controlled everything else.
3. Some political power has 'evaporated', in the sense that state power is exercised weakly or not at all. Examples include some areas of the former Soviet Union, and some parts of Africa and Asia (Afghanistan, Democratic Republic of Congo, Ethiopia, Libya, Syria), where legitimate authorities have been replaced by local potentates, warlords and gang leaders.

Although some organisations have successfully challenged the claims of the state to be the sole source of legitimate political power, and although political power has shifted, or even 'evaporated' in some parts of the world, states remain the point of departure and main focus of organised political power. The state is not 'withering away': on the contrary, it seems to be changing and expanding its power to deal with new circumstances and forms of organised power. So the answer to a key question of this chapter – are states disappearing? – is an unambiguous 'no'. Circumstances are changing, and states with them, but the result is that states are both stronger and weaker in some respects, just as some states have become stronger and others weaker.

■ Democracy without borders

We know that states can do very well without being democratic, but so far it has taken the organised and limited forms of political power of the conventional state to promote democracy (see chapter 2). To put it in a nutshell: no state, no democracy. To this extent, our conclusion that the state is likely to survive – and even grow stronger in some respects – is a comfort for the foreseeable future. But it does not necessarily follow that future developments of the state will continue to promote democracy, even less improve the quality of democratic government. A second key question of the chapter, therefore, is: What is the future for democracy?

The quality of democracy

Neither states nor democracies are created overnight. The first democracies developed over a period of two hundred years or more, and suffered war, civil disturbance and national trauma in the process. In many cases, the most important democratic milestones have been relatively recent ones: the French Revolution secured basic rights for every citizen in the late eighteenth century, but French women had to wait until the 1940s for the right to vote; violations of human rights occur in such countries as the Netherlands and Sweden even now. It is no surprise, then, that democracy has a fragile presence in many of the states that have recently joined the list of free nations in the world. Besides, democracy itself is not a fixed or given entity. It is constantly changing and developing as citizens make new and greater demands on it.

The end of the Cold War resulted in a great deal of optimism about the spread of democracy. The 'triumph of liberalism', 'the end of history' and the 'victory of democracy' were announced (see chapter 14). But, in 2002, the UN concluded that although a majority of the people in the world lived in nominal democracies, political freedoms and civil rights were limited in more than a hundred countries. Worse still, the spread of democracy had not done much for many people in the world: civil wars claimed 3.6 million lives in the 1990s, and about 1.2 billion of the world's 7 billion people live on less than US$1.25 a day (UN *Human Development Report 2014*). Democracy, it seems, takes more than organising free, multi-party competitive elections at regular intervals.

After a hopeful start, the third wave of democracy seems to have lost its momentum in some countries, because it turns out that it is fairly easy to mix formal democratic processes with political corruption, civil rights abuses and autocratic rule (see chapter 3). While only a few countries have slid backwards into military rule (Pakistan 1999, Egypt 2014), many more seem to have reached a 'stand-off' or 'ceasefire' between democratic and non-democratic forces where elected government has failed to regulate or take control of the most powerful social and economic groups in society. It was easier to introduce free multi-party elections and the semblance of democracy than to guarantee civil and social rights for all. In such cases, it is not too much to claim that elections do less to guarantee political freedom than to legitimise illiberal democracy. In many of the new democracies, violations of freedom and human rights are hard to prevent because these countries lack adequate institutional safeguards for minority, or even majority rights. As a result, simple electoral democracy has swept countries such as Russia and Venezuela towards authoritarian rule that has little in common with the broader principles of democracy. Nonetheless, Freedom House studies continue to record the faltering spread of democracy around the world (see chapters 2 and 3). Happily, these surveys clearly reveal that freedom and liberty are not restricted to wealthy countries, since many poor and developing states have a record of respecting political rights and civil liberties.

Reform of state and government

Democracy, it is worth saying again, involves a never-ending search for improvement. Even the world's most advanced democracies such as Denmark, Finland, New Zealand, the Netherlands, Norway and Sweden debate and implement reforms. In fact, they do as much, if not more than other democracies, to improve their political systems, though discussion about how political life should be conducted is in many countries as important as the actual substance of politics in the form of taxation, services and support for or opposition to the Iraq war or the EU (see controversy 17.1).

CONTROVERSY 17.1

Complaints about democracy?
Complaints about states that have emerged from dictatorship but have not effectively democratised lack perspective. It took American democracy 86 years to abolish slavery, 144 years to enfranchise women and 189 to assure black people the vote. After a century and a half, American democracy produced the Great Depression. Democracy is not a rose garden. It is as fallible as human beings.

(Joshua Muravchik, 'Democracy is quietly winning',
International Herald Tribune, 21 August 2002).

Virtually every institution of democracy discussed in this book is currently the object of disputes about reform and improvement. The most important items on the agenda for democratic reform are as follows.

- *Constitutional reform* Since constitutions define the major political institutions and their relationships (see chapter 4), proposals for reform are often basic and far-reaching. Some countries have recently added social rights and a ban on discrimination in order to guarantee equal opportunities for all citizens. Because constitutional matters are so basic and controversial, it is sometimes difficult to reach agreement about them. The European Union failed to get agreement on its new constitution in 2003 and its 'democratic deficit' is likely to rise back up the political agenda when economic matters are more settled.

- *Strengthening parliaments* Monitoring and controlling the executive is one of the main functions of parliaments in representative democracies (see chapters 5 and 7) and many parliaments have attempted to strengthen their powers in this respect. Some are using parliamentary commissions or committees to investigate specific policy matters, and to hold ministers to account. At the same time, there is concern that parliaments are becoming less and less relevant in the face of the growing power of executives (presidents, prime ministers, cabinets) and the inability of governments to solve problems such as global warming, terrorism, population movements, economic interests and growing inequality both within and between states.

- *Freedom of information and open government* This concerns public access to documents and the use of electronic media to improve communication between citizens and MPs. Some countries have adopted legislation making government information accessible to the public. On the other side of the coin, there is the issue of electronic surveillance of whole populations by their governments, of spying on other governments, whether friends or enemies, and of the collection of massive data files on citizens by business interests.

- *Decentralisation of power* Recent decades have seen a wave of attempts across many democracies to decentralise and de-concentrate power to regional, local and community levels of government (see chapter 6 and briefing 17.1). In some countries, city and urban authorities have been strengthened and budgetary powers have been decentralised. Within cities, neighbourhood and community councils have been created or strengthened in order to reduce the 'distance' between citizens and government. However, while some believe that central governments are trying to decentralise power in the interests of democracy, others claim that this is simply a way of 'exporting financial problems' to lower levels of government. That is, central government simply hands the hot potato to lower levels of government.

- *Making bureaucracies more responsive and efficient* Bureaucratic reforms (see chapter 8) include proposals to improve efficiency by adopting cost-benefit management and book-keeping practices. Other reforms have tried to make public bureaucracies more responsive to citizens by involving them in the early stages of decision making. Most far-reaching of all, many Western governments have privatised a number of public services. One view among the experts is that some of these will have to be taken back under public control, which will be expensive and controversial, or else de-regulation will have to be followed by re-regulation, as market failures are revealed.

- *Improving citizen participation* Citizens have been creative in inventing new forms of political participation and new ways of making their voices heard, including boycotts, demonstrations, sit-ins, civil disobedience and attracting the attention of the mass media (see chapter 9). Governments, for their part, have often responded by reforming laws relating to protest activity and expanding opportunities to vote (neighbourhood councils, referendums, the recall of elected representatives) and to participate in public enquiries and hearings. Many experiments with public opinion and participation are being conducted, including reforms of electoral and registration systems, greater use of referendums, citizen juries and assemblies of various kinds, experiments with co-governance involving the sharing of power and influence between governments and citizens, and the use of new and interactive means of electronic communication.

- *Strengthening the role of associations* Many governments now acknowledge NGOs and are willing to cooperate with them and support their activities, including their participation in decision making, especially at the local and community level (see chapter 10). Some governments are even attempting to 'unlock' policy communities and networks so they include a wider range of interests and organisations. But organised groups may be part of the problem as well as the solution. They all have a right to participate in political life, but huge disparities between them in power and money give some unprecedented influence which they use to promote their financial interests, making it difficult or impossible for the state and governments to operate as the majority of citizens wish.

- *Strengthening the independence of mass media* Many governments are concerned about the concentration of the ownership and control of the mass media (see chapter 11) and are wrestling with ways of dealing with it. Some feel that the answer lies in allowing the 'old' and 'new' communication technologies to develop within an unregulated market, in the belief that they will form a highly diversified and competitive system. Other governments take the opposite view, maintaining or strengthening market and content regulation laws, including anti-cartel and cross-media ownership regulations and a wide variety of laws relating to such things as cigarette advertising and pornography. As with organised groups, the media are part of both the problem and the solution. Democracy without free media is inconceivable but, at the same time, the free media in some countries exploit their 'power without responsibility', exercising influence over politicians who believe the press can make and break political leaders, control public opinion and swing elections.

- *Protecting and strengthening human rights* As we have seen, some defective democracies have elections, but do not protect the rights of their citizens.

To do this, they should guarantee the independence of their courts and the police, but this means giving up power and possibly falling into the hands of the courts themselves. NGOs such as Amnesty International try to mobilise opposition, and a range of institutions has been created to prosecute violations of human rights and empower citizens to take action against governments. These include the European Court of Justice – the highest court of the EU – and the European Court of Human Rights, as well as special courts created by the United Nations to prosecute war criminals and to regulate conflicts between states. There are often powerful interests and forces opposed to the granting of Human Rights in their countries. As controversy 17.1 points out, 'it took American democracy 86 years to abolish slavery, 144 years to enfranchise women and 189 to assure black people the vote'. On top of that, the modern world faces the problem of how to defeat terrorism without spying on its own citizens and on other countries, or denying what are regarded as the inalienable rights to freedom of speech and assembly. Age-old democratic rights are being questioned and threatened in the name of the 'war on terror'.

- *Social security* Social security and welfare continue to be a central issue in democratic countries. Some argue that a healthy, educated and secure population is a precondition of both democracy and economic growth, and that, in any case, the state is morally obliged to create the conditions of civilised life for its citizens. They argue that a developed welfare and social security system is essential. Others, especially in the late twentieth century, argue that the best way of meeting the material and spiritual needs of citizens is to leave as much as possible to the 'invisible hand' of market economics, in the belief that this is the most efficient way of generating and distributing wealth and freedom. They argue that globalisation makes welfare states uncompetitive and that a return to laissez-faire economics is inevitable and efficient. The debate rages on, fuelled by an economic crisis which has left governments and citizens struggling with reduced incomes.
- *The elimination of corruption and patronage* Corruption is not limited to the developing world. It is commonplace in some established democracies and developed economies, where it poses a threat to democracy and good government, to fairness and justice, and to the efficient conduct of both private and public life. It seems to have a pervasive effect on society, the economy and government. It is hard to eradicate corruption. Max Weber pointed out that once in the saddle, capitalism rides for ever because, no matter how well meaning and humanitarian business people are, they are forced to obey the laws of supply and demand and to be ruthless in cutting the costs of labour and taxes so as to maximise profits. The same is true of corruption. In many new democracies, state officials are poorly paid and rely on bribes to maintain a minimum standard of living. Citizens are often desperate enough to pay them. Unfortunately, many international organisations are deeply corrupt, as recent events in sporting organisations show.

Briefing 17.1

The need for good governance

Political reforms, such as decentralising budgets and responsibilities for the delivery of basic services, put decision-making closer to the people and reinforce popular pressure for implementing the goals. Where decentralisation has worked – as in parts of Brazil, Jordan, Mozambique and the Indian states of Kerala, Madya Pradesh and West Bengal – it has brought significant improvements. It can lead to government services that respond faster to people's needs, expose corruption and reduce absenteeism.

But decentralisation is difficult. To succeed, it requires a capable central authority, committed and financially empowered local authorities and engaged citizens in a well-organised civil society. In Mozambique, committed local authorities with financing authority increased vaccination coverage and prenatal consultations by 80 per cent, overcoming capacity constraints by contracting NGOs and private providers at the municipal level.

Recent experiences have also shown how social movements can lead to more participatory decision making, as in the public monitoring of local budgets. In Porto Alegre, Brazil, public monitoring of local budgets has brought huge improvements in services. In 1989, just under half of city residents had access to safe water. Seven years later, nearly all did. Primary school enrolments also doubled during that time, and public transport expanded to outlying areas.

(Human Development Report 2003. New York: UN, 2004: 2;
http://hdr.undp.org/en/media/hdr03_overview.pdf)

Reforming democracies is not easy. Strong interests most generally try to protect their position, and democratic reform is often entangled with a lot of other complicated matters. This is because democracy is not above social and economic life; it is not something set apart from 'real' social existence. On the contrary, government and politics are an integral part of daily existence that is rooted in social and economic circumstances. Often it is not possible to change social and economic patterns without first changing political patterns. The suffragettes in the early-twentieth-century Britain, for example, did not campaign for 'Votes for Women' because they saw the vote only as an end in itself, important though this was. They also knew that they could not change their social, legal and economic status without first gaining power in government. In this respect, improving government – that is, improving democratic government – seems to be the key to numerous other problems (see briefing 17.1).

The fate of democracy in the world is by no means assured. It is as well to recall its recent history. In 1925, there were fewer than twenty full and stable democracies in the world, and, with the spread of fascism and Nazism, this was reduced to no more than ten. After the Second World War, some countries which had taken steps to introduce free elections, party competition and citizen rights were thrown back into dictatorship under communist rule. In response, some Western powers interfered with democratic processes in other countries and continued to do so after the fall of communism and the end of the cold war. Politics can make many strange bedfellows according to the logic of 'the enemy of my enemy is my friend', and, as a result, Western powers sometimes align themselves with undemocratic and anti-democratic regimes. In the last decade, the spread of democracy has halted and more countries have slipped back into their bad old ways than have made progress. Meanwhile, democratic practices have come under pressure, even within the full democracies, sometimes from their own populations, sometimes from their leaders and especially from events caused by external forces.

At the same time, according to the best evidence we have, there are now about two dozen full democracies in the world, and another fifty flawed democracies. That is a great many more than existed in 1925 and it includes many countries that have made a successful transition from fully fledged military dictatorships to full democracies that are more advanced than some of the oldest members of the democratic family of nations. Standards are also much higher in 2015 than they were in the 1920s.

It should be said that democracy has always been in crisis. At least, ever since the 1950s, successions of political analysts have written of an actual or coming crisis. First, there was mass theory, then government overload, followed by new social movements and, a decade or so later, the post-modern revolution, and at the end of the twentieth century there were fears for decreasing levels of social capital, trust, political participation and confidence in democratic institutions. All these theories had more than a grain of truth in them, but democracies survived.

■ The future

Can democracy now spread and survive in a changing world? As always, the prognosis is difficult and uncertain, and conclusions differ. Democratic institutions are dependent on a sovereign body to establish and maintain them. They need the rule of law, minimal corruption, impartial police and courts, genuinely free elections and party competition, and the active support of political leaders and citizens. Anything that undermines the continuity and stability of states seems to threaten democracy, and there seem to be a great many things that threaten both states and democracies at the present time. The number of states and the number of democracies in the world has increased steadily over the past hundred years, but that is no guarantee that they will continue to do so. The more democratic principles try to find a foothold in the poorer, less literate, more traditional and more corrupt societies, with no previous experience of open government, the harder it may be to make progress. We have some way to go before we see 'the end of ideology' and 'the end of history'.

We know that democracy is unstable in many of the newest democracies, and that they can easily slip back into dictatorship and autocracy or simply fail to become fully developed democracies with free and fair elections, individual rights, a free press, low rates of corruption, impartial courts and properly functioning public bureaucracies. It is easier to establish free, multi-party elections in these countries than to guarantee freedom, human rights and government accountability, much less equality of opportunity and a decent quality of life. In the younger democracies, therefore, our studies should not be confined to elections, parties and formal decision-making procedures, but broadened to encompass wider social and economic matters.

Democracy is certainly no paradise. And yet even modest success in replacing authoritarian, corrupt and abusive government with more democratic practices is desirable. As the UN concluded,

> When governments are corrupt, incompetent or unaccountable to their citizens, national economies falter. When income inequality is very high, rich people often control the political system and simply neglect poor people, forestalling broadly based development. Similarly, if governments fail to invest adequately in the health and education of their people, economic growth will eventually peter out because of an insufficient number of healthy, skilled workers. Without sound governance – in terms of economic policies, human rights, well-functioning institutions and democratic political participation – no country with low human development can expect long-term success in its development efforts or expanded support from donor countries. (UN, *The Millennium Development Compact 2003*, New York: UN, 2004: 3)

■ What have we learned?

This chapter deals with scenarios for the future of the state. It argues that:

- The state is not 'withering away'. Conventional nations are still widely spread and new ones are establishing themselves, especially in parts of east Asia and South America, albeit at a slower pace than before. The world's first supra-national state has appeared in Europe in the shape of the EU. 'Proto-states' are found in several regions (Africa, central Asia and eastern Europe), mainly after the collapse of larger states.
- Developments such as the concentration of commercial power, the rise of NGOs, globalisation, the changing nature of conflicts and the growth of international organisations all cast doubts on the state's claim to be the sole (or the most important) source of political power. The state persists, however, as the body with a monopoly of legitimate physical force.
- Democracy is not fixed or static, but a continuous and developing attempt to make government accountable and responsive to the needs of the people it governs. Reforming and developing, therefore, the democratic system is a regular aspect of democratic government.

■ Lessons of comparison

- The power of some states has increased in some respects, but in other cases, it is shared with other organisations, and in 'proto-states' some state power seems to have disappeared.

- In terms of economic capacities the biggest corporations are much stronger than many states, and all states are now confronted with international economic forces that are difficult or impossible to control.
- The numbers of NGOs and QUANGOs have risen rapidly in all countries, but the increase is especially visible in developing countries.
- Democracy differs between states and therefore democratic reforms differ between states, too.
- The number of democracies in the world is still rising, but some of the newest ones have problems protecting freedom and human rights. Organising multi-party elections seems to be less problematic.
- There is nothing natural or inevitable about the spread or the continuity of democracy. Full democracies are faced by many serious problems and the fact that they have survived wars, economic crises, disasters and fundamental changes in social and economic conditions does not mean that they will continue to do so in the future.

Projects

1. Make a list of two or three countries in the world that have improved their democracy since 2000, and another two or three that have slipped back. What are the main reasons for these changes? How likely is a change in democracy in these countries in the next decade?
2. What democratic improvements have been proposed in your country recently, and which of them have been realised? Discuss the arguments for adopting or rejecting these proposals.
3. Why has it been so difficult to adopt a constitution for the EU?

Further reading

T. V. Paul, G. John Ikenberry and J. A. Hall (eds.), *The Nation-State in Question*. Princeton University Press, 2003. A collection of readings on globalisation in the modern state.

M. J. Smith, *Power and the State*. Basingstoke: Palgrave Macmillan, 2009. An analysis of how modern states have responded to the changing circumstances of the twenty-first century.

G. Sørensen, *The Transformation of the State: Beyond the Myth of Retreat*. Basingstoke: Palgrave Macmillan, 2004. Examines the impact of globalisation on the modern state.

S. Strange, *The Retreat of the State: The Diffusion of Power in the World Economy*. Cambridge University Press, 1996. Discusses the various approaches to the changing role of the state.

S, Tormey, *The End of Representative Politics*. Oxford: Polity Press, 2009. A provocative account of the decline of representative democracy and the rise of direct, participatory democracy.

M. van Creveld, *The Rise and Decline of the State*. Cambridge University Press, 1999. A detailed account of the rise and decline of the state.

F. Zakaria, *The Future of Freedom: Illiberal Democracy at Home and Abroad*. New York, Norton, 2003. A thought-provoking analysis of the rise of democracy that is mainly restricted to electoral procedures.

Websites

www.worldaudit.org/publisher.htm.

An audit of the state of democracy in 150 states, with detailed analysis of particular countries, world league tables and a comparison of 2004 and 2014.

www.wmd.org/movedemocracy.

Website of the World Movement for Democracy, a global network of activists, practitioners, scholars, policy makers, and funders who work to advance democracy.

www.worldaffairsjournal.org/article/democracy-four-reasons-be-optimistic-2015.

A short article about the reasons to be optimistic about democracy in 2015.

www.undp.org.

Website of the UN Development Programme that offers extensive information on the relationship between development and democracy.

Postscript: how and what to compare?

Many things are clear without comparisons. You could learn quite a lot about democracy just by studying present-day India without any sort of comparisons. For example, you could establish that India is a democracy and that its democratisation has gone through several phases without comparing it with another country. Similarly you could learn a lot about democratic innovation by comparing India now with India forty or fifty years ago. So why make everything even more complicated by comparing India with other countries? What can be gained from cross-national comparisons?

In the first place, it widens and deepens our knowledge of the political world. A comparison of India and Canada would show not only that both countries are democratic but also that they are large federal systems with mixed ethnic and linguistic populations and that both were parts of the British Empire. Does one of these characteristics account, perhaps, for their democracy? To answer this question we need to compare the two with other countries. We might select Ghana, Nigeria and Pakistan, for example, and they would show that past membership of the British Empire is not a sufficient explanation of democratic development. We might select Denmark and Japan for our comparison and they would show that there is no necessary connection between federalism and democracy. And since Russia and China are both large and with mixed populations they would rule out the connection between large, heterogeneous populations and democracy. From these simple examples it is clear that we can learn a lot from comparisons, not only about a wider range of countries but also about the similarities and differences between countries, and what might play a role in causing democracy. These similarities and differences, in turn, can be used to develop and to test explanations which go beyond specific cases.

When we compare we start to develop ideas about possible explanations and we can then collect the appropriate evidence to test these explanations. So far so good, but we now face the question of what we should compare. Should we compare India with nearby Pakistan, which is similar in some ways, or perhaps with Russia or Denmark, which are very different? In order to explain and generalise our comparisons must be carefully selected. Broadly speaking, comparison can be distinguished in two ways.

- First, we can distinguish comparisons on the basis of the number of countries considered. Do we spread our net widely over a large number of countries in a search for common patterns among them (for instance, to find out whether economically developed countries are also democracies), or do we focus on one or a few countries and try to understand in depth how they work (for instance, whether Hinduism facilitates democracy in India). Both approaches have advantages and disadvantages and so we might also try to devise a strategy using both of them, to get the best of both worlds.
- Second, we can distinguish comparisons, not according to the number of cases on which they are based, but by the strategy they use in their approach to comparison. We could compare similar countries, say India and Pakistan because both are similar in some important respects, but Pakistan is not as democratic as India and we might be able to find out why. Or we could compare India and Denmark, precisely because they are very different in many ways, though both are democratic.

In this Postcript we discuss four kinds of comparison as a way of outlining the most important problems of designing research in comparative politics.

- Comparing many or a few countries
- Selecting comparable countries
- How many countries is enough?
- Comparing apples and oranges.

■ Comparing many or a few countries?

Comparison does not necessarily involve cross-national comparison. We can compare different conditions within a country, say the voting patterns of different social groups, or different conditions over time in that country, say political opinions before and after democratisation in East and West Germany. A well-known example of comparative research in a single country is Robert Putnam's (1941–) widely quoted study of the development of democracy and civil society in Italy in his book *Making Democracy Work* (1994), which examines the differences between the twenty administrative regions of the country.

These examples underline the fact that the logic behind systematic comparisons of states is identical with the logic of comparing other entities, such as different points in time, or different social groups, regions or elections. However, as the term has developed in political science, 'comparative politics' usually refers to a comparison of countries. In this sense comparative politics involves two basic approaches:

- Comparing many country cases
- Comparing a few country cases.

Comparing many cases

Considering many cases ('**large-n comparisons**') has a lot of advantages at first sight, especially if we want to develop or test broad generalisations across a wide variety of different conditions. It

> **Large-n comparison:** Comparison of many countries, usually based on statistical analyses of strictly comparable evidence about them.

also allows us to identify unexpected or deviant cases that are exceptions to the general rule. These can also throw light on the question we want to answer. While it may be true that many of the ex-colonies of the British Empire are now democratic, it is not always so, and a study of Pakistan might help us understand why. Nor do we need to cover the entire globe in our comparative study. Research on the twenty-three countries of the OECD might be enough, provided we recognised that these are the wealthier countries of the world and our results might not apply to less affluent countries.

There is no exact minimum for a large-n study but most research of this type is based on comparisons of more than twenty or thirty countries. Although this is still a relatively small number, dealing with even as few as this has implications for research:

1. Analysing twenty or thirty cases means that information about them must be both quantified and standardised. By quantified we mean numerical measures of such things as population density, per capita income or percentage turnout in elections. By standardised we mean that these measures are collected on the same basis in every country and are therefore directly comparable. If we wanted a measure of education, for example, it would make no sense to use the percentage of primary school pupils in one country and the percentage of university students in another. We have to make sure that the variables we measure are as close to identical as possible, and if this is not possible because countries often collect their data on a different basis, then we have to use measures that suffice as second best, and explain carefully why this has been done.

    Sometimes the measures take the form of a single indicator of a more complex concept. Per capita income is frequently used as an indicator of the multi-dimensional notion of economic development. It serves as a measure of some development characteristics but not all of them. In other cases we might use an index in which many figures are combined to form a single and more reliable measure of a complex idea. The Human Development Index devised by the United Nations Development Programme combines eight measures to produce a composite index of human development. Composite measures of this kind have the advantage that they can cancel out random errors in data, smooth out the odd or peculiar nature of any one measure and capture the same idea or concept in different ways. They are also useful in reducing a large body of complex and confusing figures into one single measure.

2. Large-n comparisons are best analysed by statistical techniques using computers. Patterns and tendencies in quantified information (data) can be very efficiently and effectively explored in this way. Statistical techniques range from a simple calculation of averages and percentages to sophisticated causal modelling of the combined effects of individual and institutional variables. These techniques have been developed rapidly in the last decades and a number of computer packages are available for statistical analysis. SPSS and Stata are currently the most commonly used.

3. Large-n comparisons are best carried out on large, standardised data-sets. Organisations like the OECD and the World Bank offer a wide range of these, covering many countries. Other specialised data archives provide integrated data-sets covering many countries. These include the World Values Studies, Eurobarometer and the European Social Survey. Some data-sets are known as cross-sectional studies (or 'snap-shot' surveys) because they provide the same measures in different countries at a given point in time. They are useful for comparing the levels of variables across nations, but they cannot tell us how they are changing. For this we have to turn to time-series data that cover the same events in a country or countries at different time points. These are useful for showing time trends and changes, and for how things may change before and after a particular event or events. Since cause always precedes effect we may make a lot of progress in causal analysis by examining what comes first and what follows. Cross-sectional and time-series data have their different values, but many questions in the social sciences need both, and since some things change rather slowly they need comparative time-series data over a long period of time.

Quantitative, statistical analyses of standardised data allow us to search for patterns and tendencies in large data sets. The main goal is to study relationships between various factors or variables that theories tell us might be the cause of the effect we want to explain. For that reason, large-n comparisons are also called '**variable-oriented approaches**'.

Variable-oriented approach: Comparison focused on specific themes, patterns and tendencies in a set of countries.

The apparent advantages of large-n comparisons can turn into serious problems. Not everything that is important or theoretically interesting can be easily quantified, as the complications of measuring democracy or voter turnout, or public expenditure already make clear. Sticking to standardised quantitative data runs the risk that the data available dictates our research questions, in which case we end up studying what is possible, not what is important. Nor is every important measure adequately standardised, for many are subject to technical problems in the way they are collected or presented. Since each country tends to have its own way of doing things, the statistics it collects may not be comparable with those of other countries. Furthermore, many statistical techniques are based on correlations. Correlations tell us if two measures vary together and how closely they do so, but they do not tell us whether one variable is causally related to another. Even if economic development and democracy were always to occur together it would not necessarily mean that economic development causes democracy. The impact might be in the other direction if it is democracy that promotes economic growth. Or perhaps economic development and democracy are consequences of a third factor that is common to both of them, such as Protestantism. Finally, the application of statistical techniques requires a degree of statistical and mathematical understanding that can only be acquired with the appropriate training, and students who do not like such courses are at a disadvantage in comparative politics.

Comparing a few cases

Analysing a few cases ('**small-n comparisons**') seems to be an attractive alternative to the limitations of large-n approaches. Instead of looking for patterns and tendencies among a large

> **Small-n comparison:** Comparison of a few countries, usually based on systematic, in-depth analysis and detailed knowledge of them.

number of countries it studies only a few, but in a more detailed manner that allows us to understand the complexity of relations and possibly disentangle them. In this way the historical and cultural particularities of each country can be taken into account. If we want to know, for instance, how exactly colonial legacies influence democratic consolidation, a thorough and in-depth examination of the history, institutions and culture of Africa and the Indian sub-continent might give us an answer.

How small should a small-n comparison be? No clear line can be drawn between large-n and small-n studies. Typically, small-n studies deal with two to six cases because it is difficult to master a full understanding of more countries. Whatever their number, small-n studies have a common set of characteristics:

1. Since small-n studies focus on exact processes and relationships in a few countries they can include qualitative evidence and methods. There is no need, for instance, for a single index of democratic development in Poland and Russia if we have a detailed understanding of their transition processes. In these comparisons we can discuss the unique role of Solidarność in Poland and the tsarist and communist legacies in Russia.

2. Broadly speaking, the small-n approach can be characterised as heuristic; that is, methods used to explore complex processes and relationships based on trial and error and an intuitive understanding of politics and society. For instance, with in-depth and detailed knowledge of the different nature of the Protestant religion in Denmark and the Hindu, Jain, Sikh and Buddhist religions in India, we might come to an understanding of their relationship with democracy in these two countries. We cannot gain such an understanding of religion by examining statistical data, though such information might help.

3. Small-n studies can handle a mass of country-specific information of a qualitative nature without any need to standardise. Any attempt to understand democratic transformation in Poland would certainly pay attention to the rise of Solidarnošć, but there is no possibility of standardising that information.

Case-oriented approach: Comparison focused on specific countries and the themes, patterns and tendencies within these countries.

The main goal of the small-n approach is to understand actual processes in a few countries, and for that reason it is also known as a '**case-oriented approach**'.

The limitations and disadvantages of small-n comparisons are evident. It is important to know why Poland became a democracy and why Pakistan did not, but even a perfect understanding of them might not help us reach general conclusions about democracy across the globe. Other countries might be different. Furthermore, while small-n comparisons can be carried out without the statistical abilities required for large-n comparisons, they require in-depth knowledge and familiarity with the countries considered. Studying Poland or Pakistan will be fruitful only if the researcher is very well informed about these countries and is fluent in their languages. No one can have this depth of knowledge about more than a handful of countries.

The most serious problem of small-n comparisons is that generalisations cannot be tested rigorously. In an attempt to overcome this limitation,

Qualitative comparative analysis (QCA): The systematic comparison of a few cases using specific techniques to develop and test generalisations.

Charles C. Ragin (1953–) proposed an approach called **qualitative comparative analysis (QCA)**. QCA focuses on the presence or absence of factors or variables in the cases available. Based on logical rather than statistical associations, Ragin developed a clear and strict strategy to sort out the causal relationships between various factors. QCA methods have improved considerably and are now often used in comparative politics.

Selecting comparable countries

What one compares in comparative political science is crucial. Comparing India and Canada will suggest one set of conclusions about democracy in large, mixed, federal systems, whereas contrasting India and Russia will suggest a different set. But why should we choose to compare India with only one other country when we can perfectly well compare four or five cases? This sounds sensible, but it immediately presents problems:

1. *Efficiency* It can be difficult to compare even a small number of countries when it might take many years to master the politics and government of just two of them.
2. *Relevance* There is a far greater range of comparisons available to us than those already mentioned. We might, for instance, compare India with Brazil, which is also a large mixed society, with a developing economy but a different colonial background.
3. *Generalisation* Four or five countries is a rather small number on which to base generalisations, and since there are more than fifty members of the British Commonwealth, we have many more possibilities of testing the ex-British colony hypothesis.

These considerations result in conflicting conclusions. Whereas the first point argues for restricting comparisons to as few countries as possible, the last suggests a systematic comparison of fifty cases. How do we choose between a large-n and a small-n comparison then? In principle the answer is simple. If the selection of cases for comparison is likely to determine or influence the conclusions we draw then the crucial logic of comparison involves not the number of cases, but the purpose of the comparison. What we compare should be determined by what we want to know in the first place. If our theory says that size is important for democracy then we should compare large and small countries. If it says that homogenous and heterogeneous populations, religion or wealth is important then we should select our comparison according to variation in these characteristics. The selection of countries is not a constraint of our comparative strategy but a consequence of the research question we ask. Although efficiency and generalisations are important, it is relevance that finally determines which countries should be included in our comparison, and what is relevant depends on what theory we want to test or what generalisation we are interested in developing.

As convincing as these arguments might sound, designing an appropriate comparative strategy is not just a matter of formulating goals and labelling countries as relevant or irrelevant. The English philosopher John Stuart Mill (1806–73) distinguished between two basic types of comparisons (see briefing 1). Both types aim at testing causal explanations, but differ in the strategies they follow:

- *Method of Agreement* If a phenomenon occurs in two or more situations then the explanation for the phenomenon must lie in the common features of those situations. In the **Method of Agreement**, therefore, the presence or absence of a common crucial factor or factors (the 'agreement' between the countries) must account for the phenomenon we wish to explain. For instance, India and Canada share

Method of Agreement: Comparison of cases which share the presence of effects or outcomes as well as presumed causes.

Briefing

John Stuart Mill on comparisons
The simplest and most obvious modes of singling out from among the circumstances which precede or follow a phenomenon, those with which it is really connected by an invariable law, are two in number. One is, by comparing together different instances in which the phenomenon occurs. The other is by comparing instances in which the phenomenon does occur, with instances in other respects similar in which it does not. These two methods may be respectively denominated, the Method of Agreement, and the Method of Difference.

Source: John Stuart Mill, A System of Logic, Volume I. *London: Harrison: 450.*

the impact of some British traditions, which might account for democracy in both countries.

- *Method of Difference* If two or more situations are similar, but the phenomenon exists in only one of them, its cause must be related to the different features of its situation. If we use the **Method of Difference**, the presence or the absence of a crucial factor (the 'difference' between the countries) is presumed to account for the particular phenomenon or outcome in one of them. For instance, India and China are both very large countries, therefore the fact that India is a democracy cannot be attributed to its size because China is large but undemocratic.

Method of Difference: Comparison of cases which share effects or outcomes but differ in the presence of presumed causes.

Mill stressed that both approaches are useful, but that the Method of Difference provides stronger evidence of causal explanations. In comparative research this method is widely used for regional or area studies. If we group countries under labels such as 'Latin American countries', 'central Europe' or 'the Middle East', we clearly suggest that the countries in these regions have a lot in common. If, for instance, some Latin American countries are democracies and others are authoritarian, the cause of democracy must be sought among factors that have nothing to do with their common Spanish and Portuguese background. In a similar way, we can compare 'OECD countries' and exclude economic development as a crucial factor for the explanation of something that occurs in some, but not all, of these countries.

The ideas of Mill are fruitful for developing comparisons in systematic ways. For comparative politics a very influential elaboration of the two strategies has been presented by Adam Przeworski (1940–) and Henry Teune (1936–2011). Whereas Mill applied his methods mainly to the natural sciences, Przeworski and Teune deal with comparative politics. In a little book on *The Logic of Comparative Social Inquiry* published in 1970, they developed two main strategies for comparisons:

Most Different Systems Design (MDSD): Comparison of countries that have little in common but the effect or outcome we want to explain.

- *Most Different Systems Design (MSDS)* This approach follows the logic of Mill's method of agreement. **Most Different Systems Designs** recommend selecting countries that are very different from each other, but which share the characteristic we want to study. Following this approach, comparing India and Denmark is a good choice because both countries have little in common (are most different systems) apart from being consolidated democracies.

- *Most Similar Systems Design (MSSD)* Following Mill's method of difference, **Most Similar Systems Design** suggests looking at countries that have a lot in common (that is, are 'most similar systems'), but do not show the

> **Most Similar Systems Design (MSSD):** Comparison of countries that have a lot in common but the effect or outcome we want to explain.

same phenomenon or outcome we want to explain. In trying to find out whether British colonial legacies are important for democracy, a comparison between India and Pakistan could be useful since these countries have a lot in common, but only India is a consolidated democracy. Something particular to India in this comparison must be the explanation.

Both MDSD and MSSD are widely used in comparative politics as strategies for the selection of countries, but before we actually select the countries for our own comparative study, two further preliminary steps are required:

- First, a lot of information is required about the countries selected for comparison. Are India and Canada different or similar? What do Latin American countries have in common? Which aspects of British colonial rule could be relevant to democracy? Should Brazil be considered? We can only start to compare if these questions are answered and if we have a very good background knowledge of India, Canada, Brazil, Latin America and the history of the British Empire.
- Second, and even more important, before we can start to compare countries we have to be able to pick out factors that are presumed to be crucial to our causal explanation, and to distinguish them from irrelevant ones. Should we compare India and Canada because of their common British legacy and size, ignoring their obvious differences in economic development, population, climate and religious composition?

It is very important to notice that these requirements have to be fulfilled before the merits of deciding between an MDSD or MSSD strategy can be considered. It is easy to compile an endless list of differences and similarities between various countries, but that does not help us. For this we need a theory that specifies what we think are the causal factors to look for and that guide our selection of appropriate countries for our comparison and our research strategies. Although empirical data of either a qualitative or quantitative kind play a prominent part in comparative politics, it is theory that underpins the whole exercise. Theory guides us in what to look for and which comparative strategy to use. Without theory we are lost in a forest of facts with no way of knowing how to get through them.

■ How many countries is enough?

The distinction between MDSD and MSSD strategies helps us to answer the question of which countries should be selected for our comparisons, but it does not answer the question of how many countries are needed. Efficiency dictates the reduction of cases, whereas generalisation suggests covering as many as possible. How many countries is enough?

In searching for an answer to this question, researchers are confronted with one of the nastiest problems of comparative research. This complication cannot be solved by theoretical specification. In fact, the clear specification of crucial factors in our theories brings the problem to the surface in the first place. Suppose we want to find out if Britain's colonial legacy is relevant for democracy. In the simplest case we have two dichotomous properties (British/ non-British and democratic/non-democratic), which produce four possible types. To study each of these combinations in the real world, therefore, we must base our comparisons on at least four countries. If we use fewer than four countries, we would not even have the opportunity to find an example of each of the four possible combinations.

	Democratic	Non-democratic
Ex-British colony	Type 1	Type 2
Ex non-British colony	Type 3	Type 4

It does not follow that our search will necessarily produce examples of each of the four simply because one of the combinations may not exist in the real world. But it does mean that we must search for all four, and if one is missing, that itself is evidence that we should take into account in drawing conclusions. The nasty problem, however, becomes clear if we make our theoretical explanations more realistic by adding more factors or variables. We must surely do this because the world is a complex place with many possible explanations of one phenomenon and probably with many possible contributory factors explaining it. This raises a difficulty for research. With two dichotomous properties the minimum number of cases required is $2 \times 2 = 4$. If we add country size as a third factor to our explanation of democratic consolidation then the minimum number of cases required is $2 \times 2 \times 2 = 8$. If we want to test four explanatory variables we increase the number to $2 \times 2 \times 2 \times 2 = 16$, and adding more variables increases the number exponentially (the rate of increase would itself increase). With fewer than 200 states in the world it is clear that we run out of enough cases even with only eight explanatory factors. This situation is reached even sooner if we do not use dichotomous properties but variables with more categories – for instance, if we use a distinction between democracies, defective democracies and undemocratic political systems. Since either the number of variables (V) is too large or the number of cases available (n) is too small for a comparison, this problem is referred to as the '**small-n/large-V problem**' in comparative politics.

If we want to test explanations statistically, the number of cases must be much larger than the number of variables. Since in cross-national comparative research the number of cases is very limited almost by definition, it becomes logically impossible to test all but the simplest explanations. Three basic strategies are available to deal with this problem:

> **Small-n/large-V problem:** With each additional explanatory variable (V) the number of cases (n) required for comparisons grows exponentially. Therefore only a few explanatory variables are often too many for the relatively small number of cases available, in which case an empirical test is not possible.

- The first one is, of course, to drop the goal of testing general statements. By opting for MSSD strategies we might be able to delete a number of factors from our analyses and concentrate on a more limited number of factors that we think are important. The problem is that we arrive at limited conclusions that are valid only for the group of countries with 'similar systems'. That might be unproblematic if we want, for instance, to analyse democratic consolidation in Latin America, but it does not help if we want to test a more general theory about democracy and economic development in Africa and Asia as well. For variable-oriented approaches this strategy is unattractive.
- A second strategy is to reduce the number of explanatory variables by specifying our theories more rigorously. If we have clear theoretical arguments to link a few phenomena, we can apply an MDSD strategy and compare a relatively small number of very different countries.
- A final strategy is to increase the number of cases. Germany, for instance, has sixteen middle level units of government – the *Länder* – and Italy has twenty regional units of government. Brazil has twenty-six states and a federal district. Why should we not consider these as sixty-three different political systems, especially since some of them are larger and more powerful than the smaller nations of the world? By doing so we might avoid the implications of the exponential growth function of the small-n/large-V problem. This solution has its complications, though. Lower levels of government within the same nation share their respective national institutions, and something of a common history and culture. Therefore there are not sixteen separate cases but sixteen replications of a single German case. Only if we stress the unique aspects of each of these states are we allowed to treat them as different cases in comparative research. Moreover, if our goal is to compare nations it is not very helpful to recommend a comparison of sub-national entities. Simply looking for 'more of the same' does not solve the problem. This is known as Galton's problem in comparative research, named after the British scholar Francis Galton (1822–1911), who pointed out the complications of replicating cases as early as 1889.

For each of these three strategies it is clear that only by carefully specifying our theory can we deal with the small-n/large-V problem. We have to develop a specific theory stating precisely the causal variables involved and their relationship with the effect that we are trying to explain. This is known as a well-specified theory, but it is easier said than done. There is, for example, no satisfactory general theory explaining the development of states and democracies, at least not one that works for a wide variety of different cases. In this situation relying on MSSD strategies seems to be the easiest way out (that is, restrict comparisons to groups of similar countries such as Latin America, federal states or the Indian sub-continent). And yet this strategy risks falling back into ad hoc explanations that do not necessarily apply to the circumstances of other places, precisely because more general approaches to the problem are excluded in the first place.

■ Comparing apples and oranges

The difficult task of selecting countries is not the only challenge for comparative research. Each state has its own historical development, national institutions, customs and traditions, and so on. Suppose, for instance, that we compare the French and Indian presidents because we presume that they both have the most important political position in their countries. It will become clear very soon that, although the French and Indian presidents have the same title, their position and powers are very different and not much can be gained from a comparison of them apart from the conclusion that they have very different jobs. As it happens, the position of the French president is more like that of the Indian prime minister, and it would make much more sense to compare them than the presidents of the two countries.

This raises the problem of what exactly it is that we want to compare, a question that is ever-present in comparative research. For instance, is the collection of financial support by German voluntary associations 'the same' as 'fundraising' in the United States, even though the American term cannot be directly translated into German? Indeed, if we were to use only the national terms for institutions and practices in our research no comparative work would be possible at all. What the French call their 'president' does not exist in India. Therefore a fundamental problem of comparative research is finding concepts that can be used in different countries when each is unique. Two strategies to deal with this problem are available to us:

• looking for more abstract concepts
• looking for equivalent concepts.

Looking for more abstract concepts

In one sense the problem of comparative concepts is simple and one that we solve all the time in everyday life: apples and oranges are different but we put them in the same category when we call them fruit. In the same way we can compare the French president and the Indian prime minister by treating them both as government leaders and putting them into the category of 'political executives'. Canadian Catholics are different from Indian Hindus, but both are religious. In all these cases we simply use a more general term to cover different sets of objects.

The Italian political scientist Giovanni Sartori (1924–) discussed this procedure in a seminal article, 'Concept Misformation in Comparative Politics', published in 1970. As the title suggests, Sartori sees a number of risks attached to the search for general concepts because this inevitably involves losing detail and information. There are, for instance, more than 7,500 different types of apples and each has properties that distinguish it from the others, so that the word 'apple' loses information and covers up differences. When we move to the still more general term, 'fruit', we lose still more information about the differences between apples, oranges and pears, to take only three examples. Using more general and abstract terms for comparisons implies **conceptual stretching**, which inevitably introduces ambiguity into our concepts because it remains unclear what is to be included and excluded. The advantage of using a more abstract concept is that it makes comparisons of different phenomena possible; the danger is that the actual phenomena we want to study disappear behind a cloud of rather nebulous general concepts and that we lose more information than we gain. The main task of comparativists, then, is to develop general concepts for comparisons which are at the same time precise, clearly defined and well grounded, but which lose as little information as possible.

> **Conceptual stretching:** Broadening the meaning, and thereby the range of application, of a concept or term.

Sartori presents a 'ladder of abstraction' to clarify this procedure. In order to make comparisons we climb the ladder to some higher level of abstraction by using more general terms or concepts. We can also descend the ladder and replace our general concepts by more specific ones. Climbing the ladder makes comparisons easier at the price of losing information; descending the ladder makes more information available but endangers comparisons. Sartori summarised the level of abstraction in three categories:

1. *High-level categories* Universal concepts that can be used for comparisons across the world no matter how different the circumstances. In comparative politics 'political system' is a high-level concept that applies to all circumstances.
2. *Medium-level categories* At this level, general concepts are used to compare reasonably similar things. In comparative politics, 'left-wing party' is pitched at this level, to cover everything from communist to centrist democratic socialist parties in established democracies.
3. *Low-level categories* For country-by-country comparisons specific terms can be used, such as the Indian prime minister or the French president.

Developing appropriate concepts is a theoretical task that should precede the selection of countries as well as the collection of information. Once again, we see that finding solutions for problems in comparative politics can only be based on careful theoretical reflection.

Looking for equivalent concepts

A second strategy to handle country-specific information in comparative politics is to focus on specific contexts. Every comparison must start from the idea that even very similar phenomena or objects are not identical. This does not have to bother us all the time. The fact that German and American voluntary associations differ in the way they raise money does not mean that we cannot compare their roles in community politics. Besides, we can also use devices for making different things similar. One example concerns the exchange rate of different currencies. The money used in our country can be readily changed into that of other countries at a given and recognised exchange rate, but this rate may vary according to whether our currency is over-valued or under-valued for some reason. How can we tell whether our currency is over- or under-valued when each country has its own currency with its own purchasing power in another currency? The *Economist* has invented the 'Hamburger Standard' or 'Big Mac Index' to do this. Since Big Macs are made to exactly the same specification in every country, they should, in theory, cost the same amount in every country at the current exchange rates. The difference between the actual price and official exchange rate price tells you how much a foreign currency is over or under-valued (see www.economist.com/content/big-mac-index).

Hence the Big Mac Index is based on the idea that different things (local currencies) can be compared systematically by means of a standard measure (purchasing power) if we can identify what the different countries have in common (a Big Mac). In a similar way, we could analyse decision-making processes among the executive branches in India and France and see that the president in France has a lot in common with the Indian prime minister. Likewise, no matter how voluntary associations are financed or named in the USA and Germany, the fact that they exist in the spaces between the state, commercial and private spheres in both countries is sufficient ground for comparison.

These examples make clear that we can compare apparently very different phenomena in different countries if we know that they have similar positions in those countries or perform similar functions. Instead of identity, comparisons are based on the idea of **equivalence**. Whether or not the phenomena compared have the same or different names is irrelevant. What matters is that they operate in similar ways or perform similar functions in different situations. It is this contextual correspondence that makes it meaningful to compare them. In other words, it is possible to compare different institutions if they perform the same functions in their respective countries, as the French president and Indian prime minister do. In terms of concepts we cover them with the term 'political executive'. By using information about specific situations in specific countries we can identify similar phenomena without running the risk of losing

Equivalence: Two objects or phenomena are equivalent if they have the same value, importance, use, function or result.

information by stretching our concepts unacceptably. In fact, only if we rely on specific information can we answer the question of what phenomena can be considered as equivalent.

By looking for equivalence, comparisons do not have to rely on identical indicators and we do not have to stretch our concepts. Equivalence can be established by careful analyses of the similarities and differences between countries, but this, in turn, requires that we know what we are looking for in the first place. This is a theoretical and conceptual challenge that requires careful consideration at the outset of our comparative exercise. This brings us back, once again, to the vital importance of theory and the need to start with good theory before we start any empirical work in searching for equivalents.

■ What have we learned?

At first sight, making comparisons seems to be unproblematic: Why should we not just get on with the business of comparing India, Canada, Denmark and Pakistan? Yet the question 'how and what to compare?' is not easy to answer. The complications arise mainly because comparativists are not only interested in learning about other countries, important though this may be. They also want to generalise about political life in different countries and explain in causal terms why it happens. This produces a set of difficult problems:

- Comparing a large number of countries is appropriate for testing general conclusions but depends on quantitative, statistical analyses of standardised data. This means that information that cannot be quantified and standardised is lost.
- Comparing a few countries in order to acquire a broad and deep understanding of them depends on qualitative information. This means that testing more general theories is difficult.
- The number of cases available for comparisons is almost always too small for the number of possible explanatory variables used (small-n/large-V problem). So research has to restrict itself to a few variables, which requires good theory.
- Comparative studies can be divided into Most Different Systems Designs and Most Similar Systems Designs. Whereas MDSD search for causes of similar effects in countries that differ greatly in many ways, MSSD focus on similar countries that differ in one respect that is thought to be important.
- Using more general concepts or terms makes it possible to compare, but at the price of losing specific information. Using specific information, however, makes comparisons much more difficult.
- Comparisons can be based on equivalent, but not necessarily identical, terms.
- Although empirical information about countries plays a very important role in comparative politics, it is only its theoretical underpinning that makes it truly comparative and makes comparison meaningful.

Projects

1. Compare the advantages and disadvantages of MSSD and MDSD strategies. Give an example of each strategy to underline your arguments.
2. Compare and contrast the process of democratic consolidation in your own and two other countries. What conclusions can you reach from such a comparison?
3. Give three examples of conceptual stretching and explain the conditions in which it is appropriate to climb the ladder of abstraction in these cases.

Further reading

T. Landman, *Issues and Methods in Comparative Politics: An Introduction*. London: Routledge, 2008. An accessible introduction to comparative methods, with many examples and explanations.

G. L. Munck and R. Snyder (eds.), *Passion, Craft, and Method in Comparative Politics*. Baltimore: Johns Hopkins University Press, 2007. Interviews with the most prominent scholars in comparative politics.

P. Pennings, H. Keman and J. Kleinnijenhuis, *Doing Research in Political Science: An Introduction to Comparative Methods and Statistics*. London: Sage, 2005. Overview of comparative methods and approaches.

B. G. Peters, *Strategies for Comparative Research in Political Science*. Basingstoke: Palgrave Macmillan, 2013. A textbook on the comparative method in political science (also available on Google Books).

Websites

http://polisci.berkeley.edu/sites/default/files/people/u3827/APSA-TheComparativeMethod.pdf.

An excellent overview of the comparative method in political science.

www.hks.harvard.edu/fs/pnorris/DPI415%20Comparative%20Politics/Mahoney%20Qualitative%20Methodology.pdf.

Qualitative methods in comparative politics.

www.nd.edu/~apsacp/index.html.

The official newsletter of the APSA's Organized Section in Comparative Politics. Provides a forum for discussing trends and innovations and sharing news of general interest to comparativists.

www.u.arizona.edu/~cragin/fsQCA/index.shtml.

Information about qualitative comparative analysis (including literature and software).

Glossary of key terms

Administration   (1) A term synonymous with government – e.g. the Obama administration in the USA, the Merkel administration in Germany; or (2) a term synonymous with the management processes of bureaucracies – e.g. the administration of the state through bureaucratic agencies.

Affirmative action (also known as positive discrimination)   Policies designed to redress past discrimination. Affirmative action may require state bureaucracies to increase recruitment from women and minority groups. Also known in some countries as 'positive discrimination'.

Agenda setting   The process by which a multiplicity of political problems and issues are continuously sorted according to the changing priority attached to them. In communication research, the theory claiming that the mass media may not exercise much influence over what we think, but can influence what we think about.

Alford index   A measure of class voting that calculates the difference between the proportion of working-class people voting for a left party, and the proportion of middle-class people doing the same. The higher the index, the greater the class voting.

Aligned groups   Pressure groups that ally themselves with a political party, the best examples being trade unions and left parties, and business organisations and right parties.

Authoritarian attitudes   Attitudes based on obedience to authority, usually accompanied by prejudice, dogmatism, superstition, low tolerance for ambiguity, and hostility to out-groups (anti-semitism and racism).

Authoritarian rule   Obedience and submission to authority; that is, the concentration of power in the hands of a leader or elite that is not responsible to parliament (or, in turn, to a popular vote). No opposition is allowed to compete for power.

Bill   A formal proposal for a law put before a legislature but not yet accepted by it.

'Black economy'   The 'informal economy' in which goods and services are traded for cash, without bills, receipts, or financial records that would enable the authorities to levy taxes on them.

Bureaucracy   A rational, impersonal, rule-bound and hierarchical form of organisational structure set up to perform large-scale administrative tasks.

Case-oriented approach   Comparison focused on specific countries and the themes, patterns and tendencies within these countries.

Cash transfers   A way to provide social security payments to citizens by giving them money. An alternative to cash benefits is the provision of goods and services.

Catch-all parties   Lacking a clear social basis, catch-all parties try to attract a broad range of supporters by advocating rather general policies.

Caucus   A small but loose-knit group of politicians (notables) who come together from time to time to make decisions about political matters.

Cause groups   Sometimes known as 'promotional groups' or 'attitude groups', cause groups are a type of pressure group that do not represent organised occupational interests, but promote causes, ideas or issues.

Centre–periphery cleavage   The political cleavage between the social and political forces responsible for creating centralised and modern nation-states, which usually became dominant, and other interests, usually on the periphery of the state, which resisted this process. Centre–periphery cleavages are often, but not always, geographical.

Charter of the United Nations   Founding treaty of the United Nations (UN) that defines the purposes of the UN and confers certain powers on it.

Checking and balancing power   *See* Separation of powers.

Citizen   A legally recognised member or subject of a state (or commonwealth) with all the individual rights and duties of that state.

Civic culture   The term used by Almond and Verba to signify the balance of subject and participant political cultures that best supports democracy.

Civil service   The body of civilian officials (not members of the armed forces) employed by the state to work in government departments. In some countries, the term applies to all public officials (local government and teachers), but in most it includes only the officials of central government.

Civil society   That arena of social life outside the state, the commercial sector and the family (i.e. mainly voluntary organisations and civic associations) that permits individuals to associate and act freely and independently of state control.

Class   A group of people sharing certain attributes determined by economic factors, notably occupational hierarchy, income and wealth. In classical Marxist theory class is based on the relationship to the means of production and is divided primarily between workers (the proletariat) and capitalists (the owners of the means of production). In this sense it is based on how people make a living and not on status, which is how people spend their money.

Class de-alignment   A process of decline in the class-based strength of attachment and sense of belonging to class-based political parties.

Cleavages   Deep and persistent differences in society where (1) objective social differences (class, religion, race, language, or region) are aligned with (2) subjective awareness of these differences (different cultures, ideologies and orientations) and are (3) organised by political parties, groups, or movements. Cleavages are often the basis of political conflict.

Clientelism   A system of government and politics based on a relationship between patron and clients. Public-sector jobs and contracts are distributed on the basis of personal and political contacts in return for political support.

Coalition   A set of parties that comes together to form a government. Coalition parties are usually represented in the cabinet, but sometimes one party takes all the cabinet posts with the support of a legislative coalition.

Cognitive bias   A way of thinking about a topic that leads to systematic misunderstanding and misperception of it. Sometimes this kind of bias can be used to protect beliefs that run contrary to logic, evidence and argument. The terms 'heuristics', 'motivated reasoning' and 'belief preservation' are often used in place of 'cognitive bias' to convey the same idea.

Cognitive mobilisation   The process by which increasing knowledge and understanding of the world helps to activate people to play a part in it.

Collective responsibility   The principle that decisions and policies of the cabinet or council are binding on all members who must support them in public in order to maintain the government's united front. What cabinet or council members say or believe in private is a different matter, but public disagreement should be followed by resignation from the government.

Compulsory voting   The legal obligation for citizens to appear at polling stations on election day.

Conceptual stretching   Broadening the meaning, and thereby the range of application, of a concept or term.

Conciliation   *See* Mediation.

Confederations   Organisations whose members give some powers to a higher body, while retaining their own autonomy and independence, including the right to leave the confederation.

Conglomerates   Single business organisations consisting of a number of different companies that operate in different economic fields.

Consolidation   Process of maturing and stabilising a new political system by strengthening and formalising its basic arrangements.

Constitution   A constitution is a set of fundamental laws that determines what the central institutions and offices of the state are to be, their powers and duties, and how they relate to one another and to their citizens.

Content regulation   Regulation of the content of the media by public bodies in the public interest – e.g. to limit violence on television, or ban cigarette advertisements. The content regulation of news and current affairs programmes usually aims at accurate, balanced, and impartial political reporting, and fair access for the parties to the mass media.

Conventions   Unwritten rules that impose obligations on constitutional actors that are held to be binding, but not incorporated into law or reinforced by legal sanctions. (The term is also used to refer to meetings of political groups or parties – the Republican Party Convention, for example.)

Corporatism   A way of organising public policy making involving the close cooperation of major economic interests within a formal government apparatus that is capable of concerting the main economic groups so that they can jointly formulate and implement binding policies.

Corruption   The use of illegitimate means such as bribery, blackmail, or threats to influence or control the making of public decisions, or the secret use of public offices or resources for private purposes.

Cost–benefit analysis   The attempt, at an early stage of decision making, to calculate all of the costs of a policy and the benefits it will bring.

Country   Term usually used as a rather imprecise synonym or 'shorthand' for state or nation-state. It stresses the geographical location or territory of a state.

Cross-cutting cleavages   Cleavages that are laid across one another, thereby reducing their capacity to divide.

Cross-media ownership/Multi-media conglomeration   When the same person or company has financial interests in different branches of mass communication –

e.g. when they own a newspaper and a television channel, or a publishing house and television network.

Cultural imperialism The use of cultural products, particularly films, books, music and television, to spread the values and ideologies of foreign cultures. The term was often used to describe the cultural power of the West, especially the USA, over other parts of the world.

Decentralisation Where some functions of the state are carried out by sub-central agencies that have a degree of discretion or autonomy from the central government.

Declaration of the Rights of Man and of the Citizen The seventeen articles, describing the purpose of the state and the rights of individual citizens, proclaimed by the French National Assembly in August 1789. A similar list had been proclaimed in the USA thirteen years earlier, in 1776.

Defective democracies Systems of government that are neither democratic nor undemocratic, but maintain some democratic characteristics as well as some undemocratic ones that damage and disrupt the institutional logic of embedded democracy.

Delegated legislation Law or decrees made by ministers, not by legislatures, though in accordance with powers granted to them by the legislative body.

Demagogues Political leaders who use impassioned appeals to the emotions and prejudices of citizens to try to gain political power.

Democracy A political system whose leaders are elected in competitive multi-party and multi-candidate processes in which opposition parties have a legitimate chance of attaining power or participating in power (Freedom House). Terms such as 'liberal democracy' are often used as synonyms for democracy.

Democratic deficit The idea that the institutions of the European Union are not fully democratic, or as democratic as they should be. The criticism is often used to support suggestions that the power of the European Parliament should be increased at the expense of the Commission and the Council of Ministers.

Democratisation The continual process of transforming a political system towards more democratic arrangements.

Devolution Devolution occurs where higher levels of government grant decision-making powers to lower levels while maintaining their constitutionally subordinate status.

Direct election Election by the electorate at large (popular election) rather than by an electoral college, the legislature, or another body.

Disproportionality *See* Proportionality/Disproportionality.

Dominant one-party system A party system in which one party dominates all the others. Dominant party systems are found in democratic countries with competitive parties. They must be distinguished from undemocratic one-party systems where only one party is allowed to operate freely.

Doorstep response The tendency of those with no opinion or information to respond to polls and surveys with the first thing that comes into their head, often something they think they are expected to say (sometimes known as 'non-opinion').

Dual system System of local government in unitary states in which local authorities have more independence than in fused systems but still operate under the general authority of central government.

Ecological fallacy   Drawing false inferences about individuals from valid evidence about groups. The word 'ecological' used in this has nothing to do with the ecology (green) movement, and refers only to the problem of making claims about particular individuals based on their membership of a social group.

Ecology   The relationships (or the study of the relationships) between organisms and their environment.

Effective number of parties   The number of parties with significant political strength either in terms of votes in elections (effective number of electoral parties) or in terms of parliamentary seats (the effective number of parliamentary parties). The measure is useful because it takes into account not just the number of parties but also their strength, and hence makes adjustments for the number of small parties in fragmented systems.

Electoral threshold   A minimum percentage of the poll required to be elected (to discourage small parties).

Embedded democracy   A consolidated and stable system that is founded on a well-developed civil society, secure civil and political rights, a set of autonomous institutions of government that act within the rule of law, a system of free and fair elections, and a government with effective power to perform its duties.

Empirical political theories   Theories that try to understand, by examining the evidence, how the political world actually works and to explain why it works that way. Empirical theory is ultimately based on evidence and argument that can, in principle, be tested and verified by political science.

Empirical statements   Factual statements about or, explanations of, the world that are not necessarily true or false but are amenable, in principle, to falsification (*see* normative statements).

'Episodic' groups   Groups that are not usually politically active but become so for a time when the need arises.

Equivalence   Two objects or phenomena are equivalent if they have the same value, importance, use, function or result. They may not be called the same thing but they must have things in common that make comparison meaningful.

Essentially contestable concept   A concept that is inevitably the subject of endless dispute about their proper use (e.g. art, democracy, politics and a Christian life).

Etatism   Approaches to the relationships between state and society with a very strong emphasis on state power and an accompanying reduction of social and individual rights.

Executive   The branch of government mainly responsible for initiating government action, making and implementing public policy, and coordinating the activities of the state.

Externality   A cost or benefit that does not fall on those who are responsible for the decision or action that creates the externality, and which they do not take into account when they take the action.

Failed state   A country that has lost control of some of its territory and government authority and is unable to fulfil the basic functions of a sovereign state. Failed states often suffer from corruption, crime, an outflow of refugees, severe economic problems and attempts by internal and external interests to fill the power vacuum.

False consciousness   The state of mind of the working class induced by the ruling class to conceal the real nature of capitalism and the real self-interests of the workers.

Federal states   Federal states combine a central authority (federal government) with a degree of constitutionally defined autonomy for sub-central territorial units of government (states, or regions, or provinces).

'Fire brigade' groups   Groups formed to fight a specific issue, and dissolved when it is over.

Framing   The theory that the way news stories are set up (framed) influences how audiences interpret them – e.g. the use of human interest stories to illustrate a social problem can deflect attention from government policies that help to cause the problem to the personal inadequacies of individuals who are the subjects of human interest.

Free-ride   To extract the benefits of other people's work without making any effort oneself. The free-rider problem is acute in collective action when individuals benefit from a public good (clean air, for example, or public transport) without paying taxes or making any effort of their own.

Fused systems   Systems of local government in unitary states in which officials appointed by central government directly supervise the work of local government and its elected officials.

Gerrymandering   A form of electoral corruption in which electoral boundaries are drawn to favour a particular party or interest.

Globalisation   The growing interdependencies and interconnectedness of the world that are said to reduce the autonomy of individual states and the importance of boundaries between them.

Governance   The act of governing; that is, the total set of government's activities in each phase of the policy-making process.

Government   A government has a monopoly on the legitimate use of physical force within a state. Securing internal and external sovereignty of the state are major tasks of any government.

'Grand' coalitions   Oversized coalitions that include all parties or the largest of them.

Gross domestic product (GDP)   The value of all final goods and services produced within a state in a given year. In order to compare the wealth of states the measure used is normally GDP per capita.

Hegemony   A situation in which a class, political interest or country is so powerful that it does not have to rely on force or power to maintain its rule because its values and attitudes have been accepted or because people dare not oppose it. Often used now to mean all-powerful – since the collapse of the Soviet Union, the USA has become the 'hegemonic' world power, for example.

Heuristics   Mental shortcuts and rules of thumb that enable individuals to make quick judgements about matters, often when there is a lack of time, information and interest that is necessary to reach a considered opinion about a complex matter. See also 'Cognitive bias'.

Hostile media effect   The belief of people with views on a matter that media reports on it are biased against their own position, irrespective of how objective and balanced those reports may be.

Human Development Index (HDI)   A UN index of national development that combines measures of life expectancy, educational attainment and wealth into one measure.

Human rights   The innate, inalienable and inviolable right of humans to free movement and self-determination in relation to the state. Such rights cannot be bestowed, granted, limited, bartered away, or sold away. Inalienable rights can be only secured or violated.

Hyper-pluralism   A state of affairs in which too many powerful groups make too many demands on government, causing overload and ungovernability.

Idealism   In political theory, the term 'idealism' refers to the theory that ideas have a life of their own and must be understood as the products of consciousness or spiritual ideals and values that are independent of material conditions. In international relations idealism refers to the view of politics that emphasises the role of ideas and morality as a determinant of the relations between states (*see also* Materialism).

Ideal-type   An analytical construct that simplifies reality and picks out its most important features, to serve as a model that allows us to understand and compare the complexities of the real world. An ideal-type is neither a standard of perfection (as in 'an ideal husband') nor a statistical average, but a simplified, theoretical abstraction from the real world that helps us compare individual cases.

Ideologues   Those with an informed, broad, sophisticated and more or less consistent (systematic) view of the political world.

Ideology   A more or less systematic, well-developed and comprehensive set of ideas and beliefs about politics consisting of both (empirical) statements about what is, and (prescriptive) statements about what ought to be.

Immobilism   The state of being unable to move (immobilised) or in a political system of being unable to take decisions or implement policies.

Impeachment   To charge a public official, usually an elected politician, with improper or illegal conduct in office before a duly constituted tribunal, usually an elected legislative body. Depending on the country, an official who is impeached may either be removed from office or be formally tried by another legislative body. Not known much outside the USA, and not often used there.

Implementation   The process of applying policies and putting them into practice.

Incremental model   The idea that decisions are not usually based upon a rational or fundamental review of problems and solution, but upon small, marginal changes from existing policies.

Individual forms of participation   Forms of behaviour used by single citizens aimed at expressing political opinions. These activities are usually driven by ethical and moral reasoning rather than by the wish to influence political decisions.

'Insider' groups   Pressure groups with access to senior government officials, often recognised as the only legitimate representatives of particular interests and often formally incorporated into official consultative bodies.

Interest aggregation   Sorting the great variety of political attitudes and opinions on a political issue, to reduce it to a simpler, more clear-cut and agreed 'package' of opinion.

Interest articulation   The expression of political demands in order to influence public policy.

Interest groups   Sometimes known as 'sectional groups', interest groups are a type of pressure group that represents occupational interests. The main types are business associations, professional associations and trade unions.

Interpellation   A parliamentary question addressed to government requiring a formal answer and often followed by discussion, and sometimes by a vote.

'Iron triangles'   The close, three-sided working relationship developed between (1) government departments and ministries, (2) pressure groups and (3) politicians, that make public policy in a given area.

Issue voting   Voters choosing one issue rather than a total party programme (or some other aspect of the party) as the basis of their voting decision.

Judicial activism   Judicial activism involves the courts taking a broad and active view of their role as interpreters of the constitution and reviewers of executive and legislative action.

Judicial review   The binding power of the courts to provide an authoritative interpretation of laws, including constitutional law, and to overturn executive or legislative actions they hold to be illegal or unconstitutional.

Judiciary   The branch of government mainly responsible for the authoritative interpretation of law and applying it to particular cases.

Knowledge gap   The gap between those with a good education and understanding of the world, which enables them to acquire knowledge and understanding at a faster rate than those with less education and understanding.

Labour productivity   The average production per labourer in a specific period (for instance, the average number of ballpoints produced per labourer in a ballpoint pen factory in one year).

Laissez-faire doctrines   The literal translation from the French is 'allow to do'. Laissez-faire is the principle of maximum freedom for the economic forces of the market, and minimum intervention from the state.

Large-n comparison   Comparison of many countries, usually based on statistical analyses of strictly comparable evidence about them.

The left–right continuum   The observation that parties and voting could be located on a single continuum ranging from communist and revolutionary socialist ones on the political left, to conservative and fascist groups on the right.

Legislation   The body of laws that have been passed by the legislature. Legislating is thus the act of initiating, debating and passing such laws.

Legislative oversight   The role of the legislature that involves the scrutiny or supervision of other branches of government, especially the executive and the public bureaucracy.

Legislature   The branch of government mainly responsible for discussing and passing legislation, and keeping watch on the executive.

Legitimacy   The condition of being in accordance with the norms and values of the people. The 'legitimate use of power' refers to the use of power that is accepted because it is in accordance with the norms and values of the people it concerns.

Legitimation   The process of making something morally or ethically acceptable, proper or right in the eyes of the general public according to accepted standards and values.

Liberal democracy   The form of democracy that tries to combine the powers of democratic government with liberal values about the freedom of the individual.

Lobby   A popular term for pressure groups (based on the mistaken belief that pressure group representatives spend a lot of time in the 'lobbies' or ante-rooms of legislative chambers).

Losers' consent   The willingness of parties and party supporters to accept the outcome of democratic elections when they have lost the election, thus contributing to the peaceful transfer of power that is an essential of democratic government.

Low information rationality   Where citizens do not have a great deal of factual political information but have a broad enough grasp of the main issues to make up their mind about them, or else they take their cues about the issues from sources they trust (sometimes known as 'gut rationality').

Market regulation   The regulation of the media market by public bodies, often to avoid cross-media ownership, foreign control of important channels of national communication, or cases of market failure.

Mass society   A society without a plurality of organised social groups and interests, whose mass of isolated and uprooted individuals are not integrated into the community and who are therefore vulnerable to the appeals and manipulations of extremist and anti-democratic elites.

Materialism   The theory that ideas are rooted in the material or physical conditions of life, as opposed to spiritual ideals and values which are constructs of the mind which can be independent of material and physical conditions (*see also* Idealism).

Means testing   In contrast to public benefits that are universally available, means testing involves investigating a person's income and means of support to ensure that they cannot afford to pay for the service themselves. Means testing is often resented by welfare applicants and is politically controversial.

Mediamalaise   The attitudes of political cynicism, despair, apathy, distrust and disillusionment (among others) that some social scientists claim are caused by the mass media, especially television.

Median voter   Median voters have equal numbers of voters to their left and right, and are usually, but not necessarily, typical, middle-of-the-road voters. The support of the median voter is usually necessary to win an election.

Mediation   Attempt by a third party to reach an agreement between disputing parties by suggesting terms of settlement.

Meso-government   A middle level or tier of government between central and local authorities, and often known as state, regional, provincial or county government.

Method of Agreement   Comparison of cases which share the presence of effects or outcomes as well as presumed causes.

Method of Difference   Comparison of cases which share effects or outcomes but differ in the presence of presumed causes.

Military–industrial complex   The close and powerful alliance of government, business and military interests that is said by some to run capitalist societies.

Minimum connected winning coalitions   Minimum winning coalitions of parties that are ideologically close to each other.

Minimum winning coalition (MWC)   The smallest number of parties necessary for a majority of votes in parliament.

Minority government   A government or coalition that is smaller than a MWC.

Mixed economy   An economy that is neither wholly privately owned (a capitalist market economy), nor wholly publicly owned (a communist command economy), but a mixture of both.

Modernisation   The dual processes of technological and economic development and the societal responses to these changes.

Most Different Systems Design (MDSD)   Comparison of countries that have little in common but the effect or outcome we want to explain.

Most Similar Systems Design (MSSD)   Comparison of countries that have a lot in common but the effect or outcome we want to explain.

Multi-media conglomerates   Single business organisations with financial interests in different branches of mass communications – for example when they own or control a newspaper and a TV channel, or a publishing house and a TV network.

Multi-member districts   *See* Single-member/Multi-member districts.

Multi-party system   A party system in which several or many main parties compete, often with the result that no single party has an overall majority.

Nation   *See* nation-state.

Nation-state   A state based on the acceptance of a common culture, a common history and a common fate, irrespective of whatever political, social and economic differences may exist between the members of the nation-state.

New Public Management (NPM)   Reforms of the public sector in the 1980s and 1990s, based mainly on what were thought to be private sector practice and consisting mainly of privatisation, deregulation, business management techniques and 'marketisation'. Known also as 'reinventing government', it is said to have had the effect of 'hollowing out' the state.

New social movements   Loosely knit organisations ('networks of networks') that try to influence government policy on broad issues, including the environment, nuclear energy and nuclear weapons, economic development, peace, women and minorities.

Non-decision   The decision not to deal with an issue, perhaps not even to consider it.

Non-governmental organisation (NGO)   A non-profit making, non-violent private organisation that is independent of government and seeks to influence or control government policy without actually seeking government office.

Normative political theories   Theories about how the world should be or ought to be. Normative theory is based upon philosophical arguments, and ultimately on subjective values and judgements. Sometimes it is known as prescriptive theory, political theory, or political philosophy.

Normative statements   Statements that are based on faith, or contain a value judgement or an evaluation. Sometimes referred to as prescriptive, or evaluative statements, they are neither scientific nor unscientific, but non-scientific (*see also* Empirical statements).

Oligarchy   Government by a few.

Ombudsman   A state official appointed to receive complaints and investigate claims about maladministration (improper or unjust action) and to report their findings, usually to the legislature.

One-party systems   Government systems in which a single party forms the government.

Outcomes   The impacts, or effects, of outputs.

Outputs   The policy decisions as they are actually implemented.

'Outsider' groups   Groups with no access to top government officials.

'Oversized' (surplus majority) coalitions   A coalition that is larger than an MWC.

Parliamentary systems   Parliamentary systems are characterised by (1) a directly elected legislative body, (2) the fusion of executive and legislative institutions, (3) a collective and collegial executive that emerges out of the legislature and is responsible to it and (4) a separation of head of state and head of government.

Participatory democracy   That form of democracy in which citizens actively participate in government and political processes.

Partisan de-alignment   Decline in the strength of attachment to political parties.

Partisan re-alignment   Change of old party identifications in favour of new ones.

Party families   Groups of parties in different countries that have similar ideologies and party programmes.

Party identification (ID)   The stable and deep-rooted feeling of attachment to and support for a particular political party.

Party systems   The pattern of significant parties within a political system, especially their number and the party families represented.

Peak associations   *See* 'Umbrella' organisations.

People   Group of persons living together on the territory of a state whose common consciousness and identity usually form them into a collective entity.

Pluralism   A situation where power is dispersed among many different groups and organisations that openly compete with one another in different political arenas.

Pluralist democracy   A democratic system where political decisions are the outcome of the conflict and competition between many different groups. Some forms of pluralist theory are empirical attempts to describe and explain how the political system actually works, others are normative theories of how a good democracy should work.

Pocketbook voting   Deciding which party to vote for on the basis of economic self-interest. The economic calculation may be based on beliefs about how the economy has performed in the recent past (retrospective voting), or on its anticipated future trends (prospective voting).

Police   The branch of government employed to maintain civil order and to investigate breaches of the law.

Policy communities   Small, stable and consensual groupings of government officials and pressure group representatives that form around particular issue areas.

Policy networks   Compared with policy communities, policy networks are larger, looser, and more conflictual networks that gather around a particular policy area.

Political alienation   A feeling of detachment, estrangement, or critical distance from politics, often because the alienated feel there is something basically wrong with the political system.

Political behaviour   Term used to refer to all political activities of citizens, including sporadic political activity, inactivity and behaviour with indirect political consequences.

Political cleavage   A political division created when political organisations use social cleavages for their own purposes to mobilise support. Social cleavages are often more important politically when two or more are superimposed on top of one another.

Political culture   The pattern of attitudes, values and beliefs about politics, whether they are conscious or unconscious, explicit or implicit.

Political elite   The relatively small number of people at the top of a political system who exercise disproportionate influence or power over political decisions. If it exercises enough power in the system, it is a 'ruling elite'.

Political identity   The way that people label themselves as belonging to a particular group (e.g. nation-state, class or caste, ethnic group, religious or ideological group).

Political marginality   Being on the fringes of politics and therefore having little influence.

Political orientation   A predisposition or propensity to view politics in a certain way.

Political parties   Organisations of politically like-minded people who seek political power and public office in order to realise their policies.

Political socialisation   The process by which individuals acquire their political values, attitudes and habits. Childhood socialisation is most important, but socialisation continues in adulthood as well.

Populism   A style of politics that appeals to political prejudices and emotions, particularly of those who feel exploited and oppressed by the rich and powerful.

Power   The ability to make other people do what they do not want to do. Power is the ability to apply force.

Presidential systems   In presidential systems a directly elected president is the executive, with a limited term of office and a general responsibility for the affairs of state, who governs with a separate and independently elected legislature.

Pressure groups   Private and voluntary organisations that try to influence or control particular government policies but do not want to become the government or control all government policies. They are sometimes referred to as advocacy groups, campaign groups or lobby groups.

Prevention   Attempt to hinder or deter delinquent behaviour.

Priming   The theory that the mass media can prime us to focus on certain things and in certain ways by highlighting some issues rather than others – e.g. focusing on foreign rather than domestic policy favours parties that are thought to be better at foreign policy than domestic policy.

Privatisation   The process of converting public services and amenities to private ones.

Productivity   *See* Labour productivity.

Proportionality/Disproportionality   A measure of the ratio of seats to votes. The more proportional the system, the closer the ratio of seats to votes. In the most proportional voting system a party getting 43 per cent of the votes should get 43 per cent of the seats, or close to this figure, since seats are not divisible.

Protest vote   Voting for a party not so much to support it as to show opposition to another party or parties, usually those in government.

Provision of goods and services   A way to provide social security for citizens by offering them not money but specific facilities such as housing or job training. Cash transfers are an alternative to goods and services.

Psychological fallacy   Drawing false inferences about groups from valid observations about individuals who are members of those groups. *See also* 'Ecological fallacy'.

(Public) policy   Some general set of ideas or plans that has been officially agreed on and which is used as a basis for making decisions. A public policy is the long series of activities, decisions and actions carried out by officials of government in their attempts to solve problems that are thought to lie in the public or collective arena.

Public–private partnerships (PPPs)   Formal cooperation between government and private groups to obtain specific goals.

Public sector   That part of social, economic and political life that is not private but controlled or regulated by the state or its agencies.

Public service model   The system of organising radio and television in which broadcasting licences are granted to public bodies, usually supported by public funds, for use in the public interest rather than for profit.

Qualitative comparative analysis (QCA)   The systematic comparison of a few cases using specific techniques to develop and test generalisations.

QUANGOs (Quasi-autonomous non-governmental organisations)   Organisations that are partially or wholly funded by the government to perform public service functions but not under direct government control.

Realism   In international relations realism refers to the view of politics that emphasises the role of self-interest as a determinant of state policies and hence the importance of power in these relations. In realist theory, states (and other actors such as business organisations) are presumed to act more or less rationally to promote their own interests.

Referendum   The submission of a public matter to direct popular vote. Sometimes known as a plebiscite.

Reinforcement theory (also known as minimal effects theory)   The theory that the mass media can only reflect and reinforce public opinion, not create or mould it.

Reinforcing cleavages   Cleavages that are laid one on top of the other, making them potentially more important.

Representative democracy   That form of democracy in which citizens elect leaders who govern in their name.

Ruling elite   A political elite that is so powerful that it can make all the important decisions in government.

Salient   Something that is relatively important, significant, or prominent in people's minds.

Semi-presidential system   Semi-presidential government consists of a directly elected president who is accountable to the electorate and a prime minister, who is appointed by the president from the elected legislature and accountable to it. The president and prime minister share executive power.

Separation of powers   The doctrine that political power should be divided among several bodies or officers of the state, often between bodies or officers performing different government functions, as a precaution against too much concentration of power.

Single-member/Multi-member districts   Single-member districts have one representative each in parliament, while multi-member districts have two or more to make it easier to attain proportionality.

Slacktivism   The act of showing support for a cause that requires minimal personal effort, and has little effect. Slacktivism is often associated with social websites and twitter, and electronic petitions make it easy to express an opinion or support with little effort, thought or engagement.

Small-n comparison   Comparison of a few countries, usually based on systematic, in-depth analysis and detailed knowledge of them.

Small-n/large-V problem   With each additional explanatory variable (V) the number of cases (n) required for comparisons grows exponentially. Therefore, only a few explanatory variables are often too many for the relatively small number of cases available, in which case an empirical test is not possible.

Social capital   The features of social organisations, such as trust, social norms and social networks, that improve social, economic and government efficiency by encouraging cooperation and collective action.

Social expenditures   Social expenditures are the provision by public (and private) institutions of benefits to households and individuals in order to provide support during circumstances which adversely affect their welfare. This is the definition used by the OECD.

Social stratification   The hierarchical layering of society into socially unequal groups. It includes peasants and landowners, castes, classes and status groups.

Socio-economic status (SES)   A combination of class (how people make their money) and status (how people spend their money) to form a single measure of social stratification. SES allows for a disjunction between class and status, such as the existence of social attitudes towards the *nouveau riche* (rich and vulgar), and 'distressed gentlefolk' (poor and genteel). *See also* 'Class', 'Status'.

Sociotropic voting   Deciding which party to vote for on the basis of general social or economic circumstances. The opposite is 'pocket-book voting' that is based on the private interests of the voter.

Soft power   In contrast to 'hard power', based on military and economic force, soft power uses popular culture and the media to influence the way that people think and feel and behave. It is the way of winning the hearts and minds of people (usually in international relations) rather than using force, threats and sanctions.

Sovereignty   A state is sovereign when it holds the highest power and, in principle, can act with complete freedom and independence. Internal sovereignty means that, on its own territory, the state can act as it wishes and is independent of other institutions. External sovereignty refers to the fact that the state is seen as autonomous by other states.

Spectrum scarcity   The shortage of terrestrial broadcasting frequencies for radio and television, which meant that there could be only a few channels.

Spin-doctors   Public relations specialists employed to put the best possible light on news about their clients. The term often implies people whose job is to manipulate the news.

State   An organisation that issues and enforces rules that are binding for the people living in a given territorially defined area.

Status   A form of social stratification determined by social prestige rather than economic factors or occupation. It is sometimes said that class is determined by how people make their money, status by how they spend it. Sometimes class and status are combined in the single measure of social and economic status.

Street-level bureaucrats   The bureaucrats who regularly come into contact and deal with the public.

Subjective or internal competence/efficacy   The extent to which ordinary citizens feel that they can make their views and actions count in the political system. The opposites of the term are 'powerlessness', 'inefficacy' or 'low competence'.

Sub-central/sub-national government   All levels of government below national/central government. Sub-national government covers everything below central government from community and neighbourhood government, through local government of all kinds, to the middle or meso-level of state, regional and provincial government.

Subsidiarity   The principle that decisions should be taken at the lowest possible level of government – that is, at the level closest to the people affected by the decisions. Usually the term subsidiarity is used in connection with the territorial decentralisation of government, but it is not limited to this form.

Suffrage   The right to vote. Hence 'suffragettes' were women who fought for the right of women to vote.

Supra-national government   Organisations in which countries pool their sovereignty on certain matters to allow joint decision-making.

System or external efficacy   The extent to which ordinary citizens feel that political leaders and institutions are responsive to their wishes.

Territory   Terrain or geographical area.

Terrorism   The use of violence against civilian targets to create fear, for political aims. What some regard as terrorism is seen as 'freedom fighting' by others.

'Third wave' (of democracy)   Democratisation across the world is often divided into 'three waves'. The first, from the mid-nineteenth to the mid-twentieth century, saw between twenty-five and thirty states achieve a degree of democratic stability, depending on how 'democracy' is defined. The second, from about 1950 to 1975, was mainly the result of decolonisation. The third, from about 1975 to 2000, was mainly the result of the disintegration of the Soviet Union and the spread of democracy in Latin America and Asia.

Tripartism   A looser and less centralised system of decision making than corporatism involving close government consultation – often with business and trade union organisations.

Two-party system   A party system in which two large parties dominate all the others.

'Umbrella' organisations   Association-of-associations that coordinate the activity of their member organisations.

Unitary states   In unitary states the central government is the only sovereign body. It does not share *constitutional* authority with any sub-central units of government.

Values   Basic ethical or moral priorities that constrain and give shape to individual attitudes and beliefs.

Variable-oriented approach   Comparison focused on specific themes, patterns and tendencies in a set of countries.

Veto-groups   Groups with the power to prevent other groups or the government implementing a policy, although they do not necessarily have the power to get their own policies implemented.

Virtuous circle   A tendency for those who are politically engaged and trusting to follow the news regularly, which then feeds back to increase their levels of trust and engagement. The term captures the idea that the political media can and do provide those who are politically interested and aware with information and opinion that sustains their democratic attitudes and participation, rather than undermining democracy.

Volatility   The opposite of stability, volatility involves change in voting patterns from one election to another. Some voting studies refer to it as 'churning'.

Vote of confidence   A vote of confidence (or no confidence), to test whether the government of the day continues to have the majority support of members of the assembly. Its importance lies in the normal convention that governments losing a vote of confidence should resign.

Voting system   The arrangements by which votes are converted into seats on representative bodies.

Voter turnout   The number of citizens casting a valid (i.e. not a spoiled ballot) vote expressed either as a percentage of those eligible to vote (adult citizens), or as a percentage of those on the electoral register.

Welfare states   Democracies that accept responsibility for the young and old, the sick and disabled and the unemployed and poor. Welfare states are characterised by resource redistribution policies.

Index